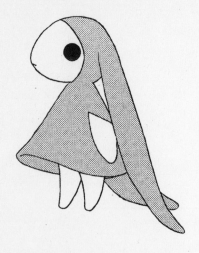

ちょびっツ
Chobits

CLAMP

Satsuki Igarashi
Nanase Ohkawa
Mick Nekoi
Mokona Apapa

ALSO AVAILABLE FROM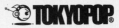

MANGA

ACTION

ANGELIC LAYER*
CLAMP SCHOOL DETECTIVES* (April 2003)
DIGIMON (March 2003)
DUKLYON: CLAMP SCHOOL DEFENDERS* (September 2003)
GATEKEEPERS* (March 2003)
GTO*
HARLEM BEAT
INITIAL D*
ISLAND
JING: KING OF BANDITS* (June 2003)
JULINE
LUPIN III*
MONSTERS, INC.
PRIEST
RAVE*
REAL BOUT HIGH SCHOOL*
REBOUND* (April 2003)
SAMURAI DEEPER KYO* (June 2003)
SCRYED* (March 2003)
SHAOLIN SISTERS* (February 2003)
THE SKULL MAN*

FANTASY

CHRONICLES OF THE CURSED SWORD (July 2003)
DEMON DIARY (May 2003)
DRAGON HUNTER (June 2003)
DRAGON KNIGHTS*
KING OF HELL (June 2003)
PLANET LADDER*
RAGNAROK
REBIRTH (March 2003)
SHIRAHIME:TALES OF THE SNOW PRINCESS* (December 2003)
SORCERER HUNTERS
WISH*

CINE-MANGA™

AKIRA*
CARDCAPTORS
KIM POSSIBLE (March 2003)
LIZZIE McGUIRE (March 2003)
POWER RANGERS (May 2003)
SPY KIDS 2 (March 2003)

ANIME GUIDES

GUNDAM TECHNICAL MANUALS
COWBOY BEBOP
SAILOR MOON SCOUT GUIDES

ROMANCE

HAPPY MANIA* (April 2003)
I.N.V.U. (February 2003)
LOVE HINA*
KARE KANO*
KODOCHA*
MAN OF MANY FACES* (May 2003)
MARMALADE BOY*
MARS*
PARADISE KISS*
PEACH GIRL
UNDER A GLASS MOON (June 2003)

SCIENCE FICTION

CHOBITS*
CLOVER
COWBOY BEBOP*
COWBOY BEBOP: SHOOTING STAR* (June 2003)
G-GUNDAM*
GUNDAM WING
GUNDAM WING: ENDLESS WALTZ*
GUNDAM: THE LAST OUTPOST*
PARASYTE
REALITY CHECK (March 2003)

MAGICAL GIRLS

CARDCAPTOR SAKURA
CARDCAPTOR SAKURA: MASTER OF THE CLOW*
CORRECTOR YUI
MAGIC KNIGHT RAYEARTH* (August 2003)
MIRACLE GIRLS
SAILOR MOON
SAINT TAIL
TOKYO MEW MEW* (April 2003)

NOVELS

SAILOR MOON
SUSHI SQUAD (April 2003)

ART BOOKS

CARDCAPTOR SAKURA*
MAGIC KNIGHT RAYEARTH*

TOKYOPOP KIDS

STRAY SHEEP (September 2003)

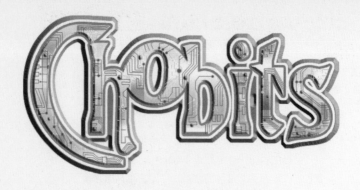

Volume 4 of 8

Story and Art By
CLAMP

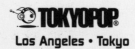
Los Angeles • Tokyo

Translator – Shirley Kubo
English Adaptation – Jake Forbes
Lettering –Tim Law
Retouch – Anna Kernbaum
Copy Editor – Amy Kaemon

Senior Editor – Jake Forbes
Production Manager- Jennifer Miller
Art Director – Matt Alford
VP Production– Ron Klamert
President & C.O.O – John Parker
Publisher- Stuart Levy

Email: editor@TOKYOPOP.com
Come visit us online at www.TOKYOPOP.com

A 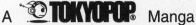 Manga

TOKYOPOP® Manga is an imprint of Mixx Entertainment, Inc.
5900 Wilshire Blvd. Ste 2000, Los Angeles, CA 90036

ISBN: 1-59182-007-3

First TOKYOPOP® printing: February 2003

10 9 8 7 6 5 4 3 2

Manufactured in the USA

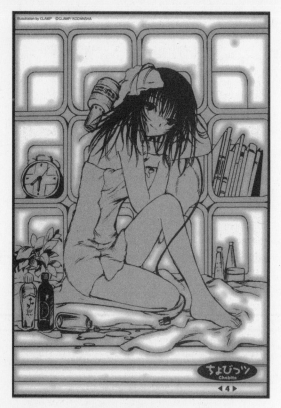

Illustration by CLAMP ©CLAMP KODANSHA

ちょびっツ
Chobits
◀ 4 ▶

www.Contents.com

MUST SEE Persocoms

address:

HOT Chobits

WARNING:
ADULTS ONLY

date: 12/11/26

from: sumomo@clamp-net.com

to: minoruk197@hotmailer.com

subj: RE: The story so far...

Yo Minoru,
Well, I guess the cat's out of the bag. I've eloped with Takako, Hideki and my teacher. She's gonna need some time, so I'm going to stay by her side and giver her the support she needs. I just hope it wasn't a big mistake to leave Plum with Hideki. Speaking of that guy, I hear he got a job for his persocom. That's great, man. I just hope she'll be safe, what with those freaky e-mails you've been getting with pictures of Chi. I'd offer to help you track down their source, but this resort charges an arm and a leg to go online, and I'm blowing through my savings fast enough as is. They've got this great bakery so I'll bring you some muffins when I come back, 'kay?

Peace out,
Shimbo

PS- I don't know if you're familiar with them, but there's this picture book series called "A City With No People" that if I didn't know any better, I'd say was about Hideki and Chi. Check them out if you get the chance. Here's a link to some pirated scans online (which I don't condone!)-
http://www.omochabooks.jp.co/nopeople/pg.1.html

HOT XXX ACTION!

Real girls and persocoms NUDE, READY, and in your bedroom! FREE TRIAL!

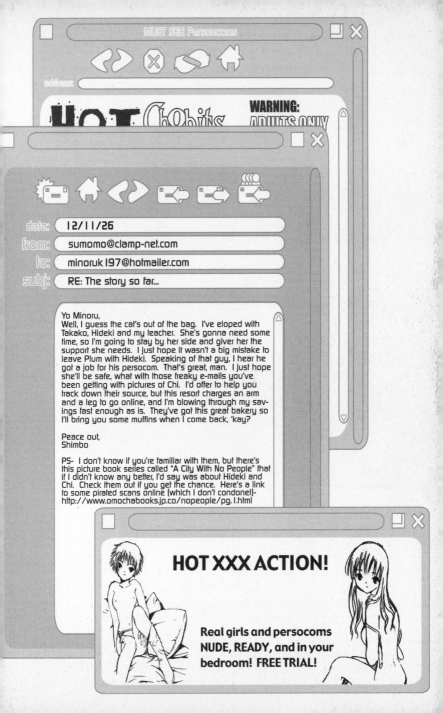

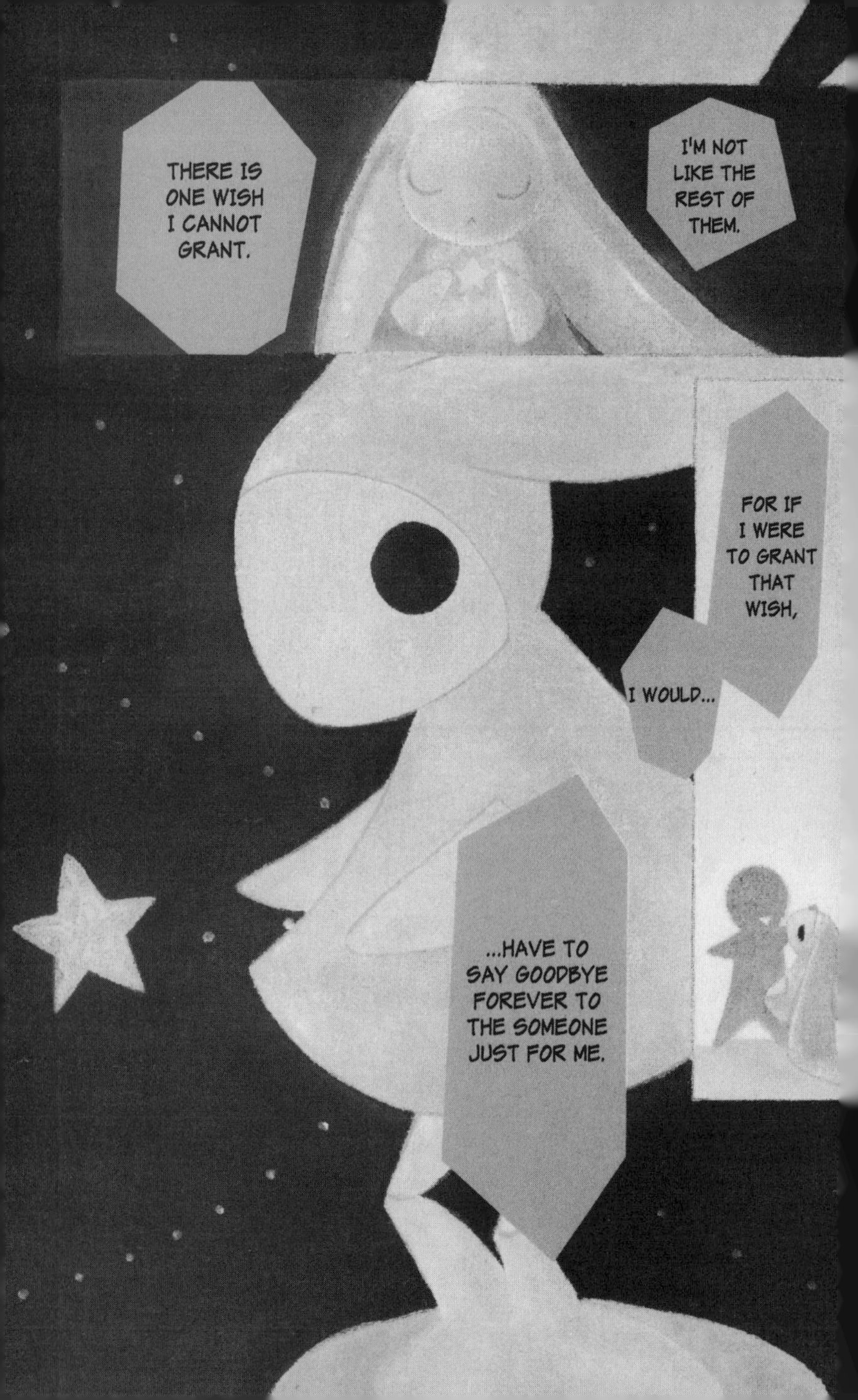
I'M NOT LIKE THE REST OF THEM.
THERE IS ONE WISH I CANNOT GRANT.
FOR IF I WERE TO GRANT THAT WISH,
I WOULD...
...HAVE TO SAY GOODBYE FOREVER TO THE SOMEONE JUST FOR ME.

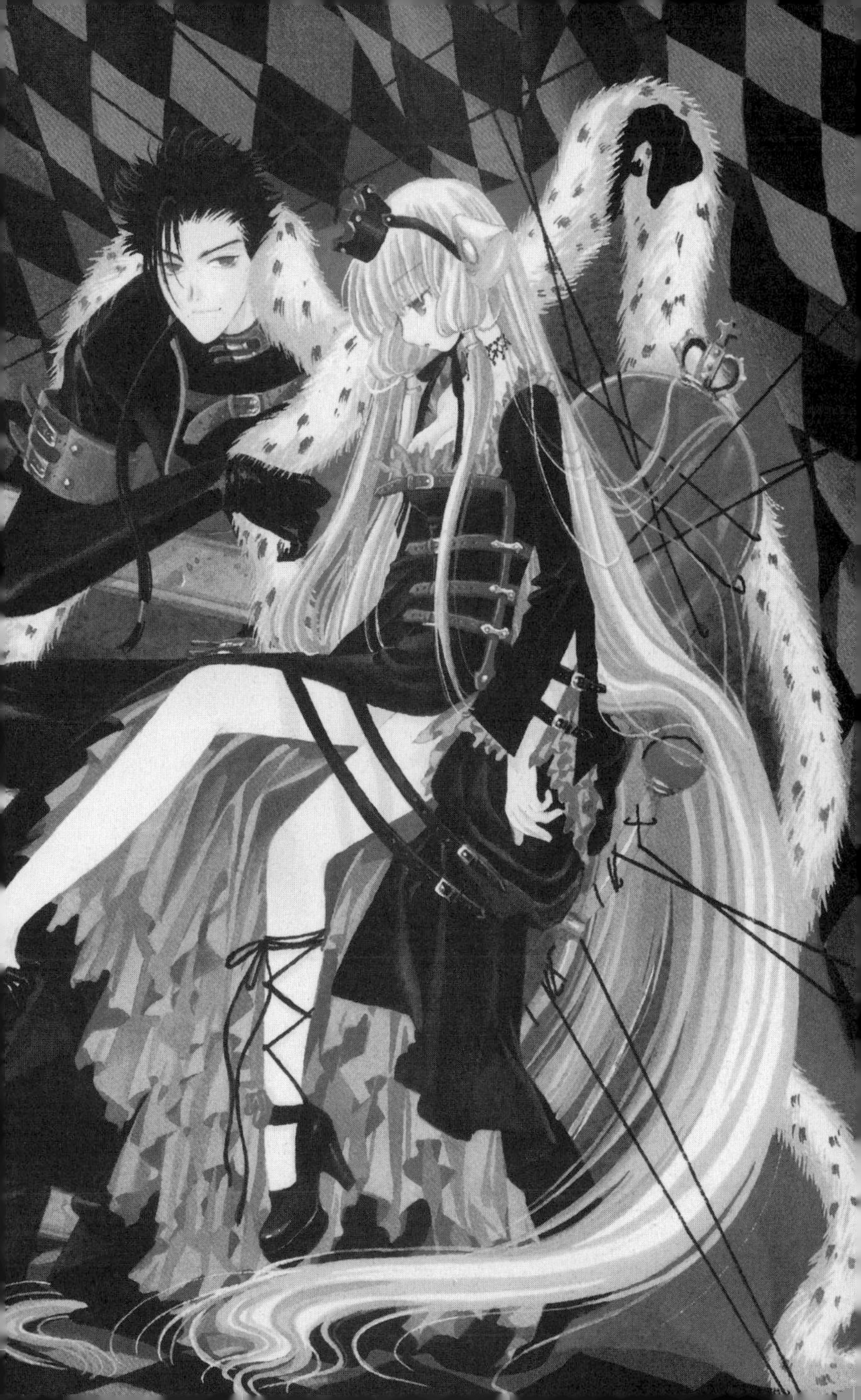

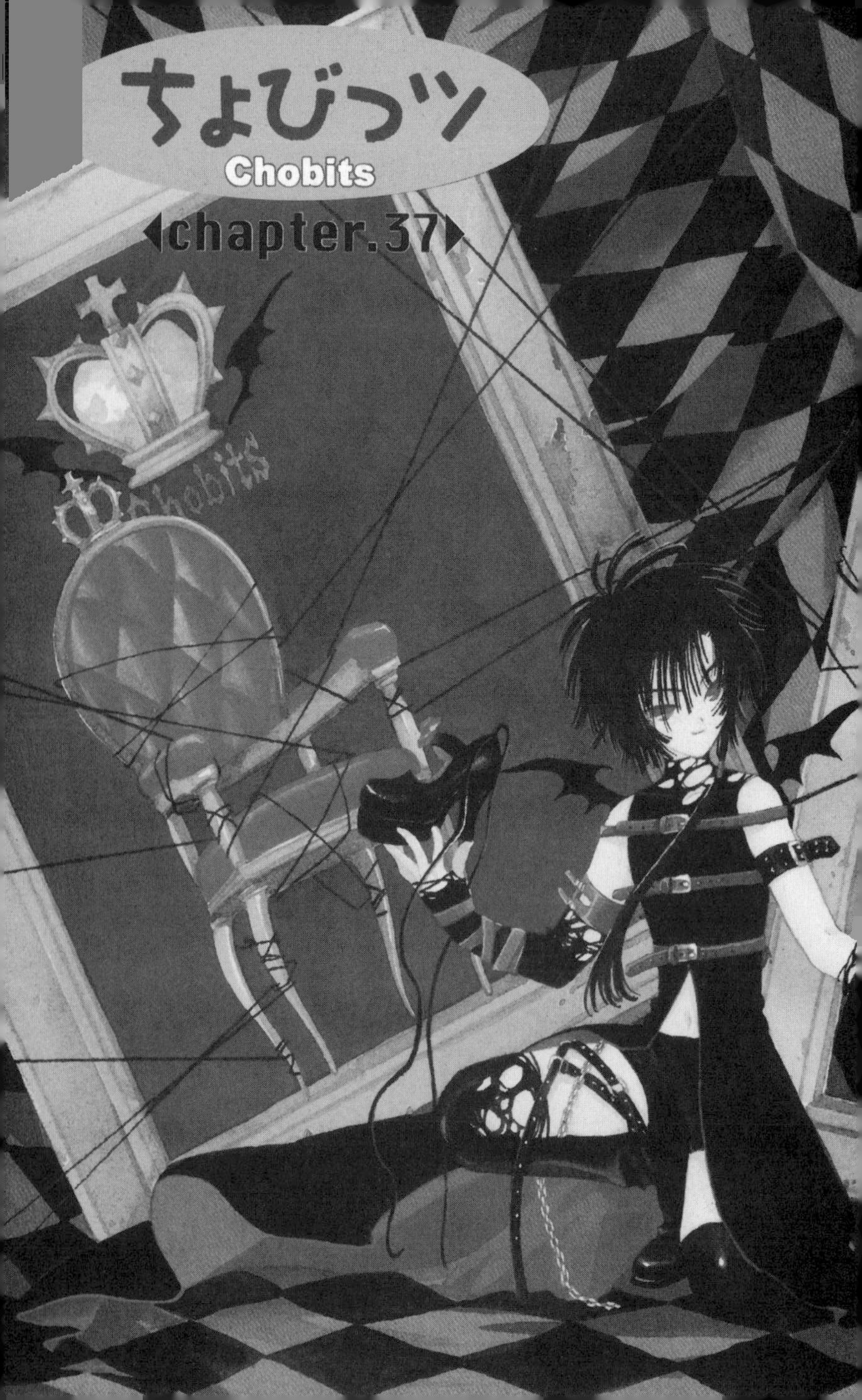
ちょびっツ
Chobits
chapter.37

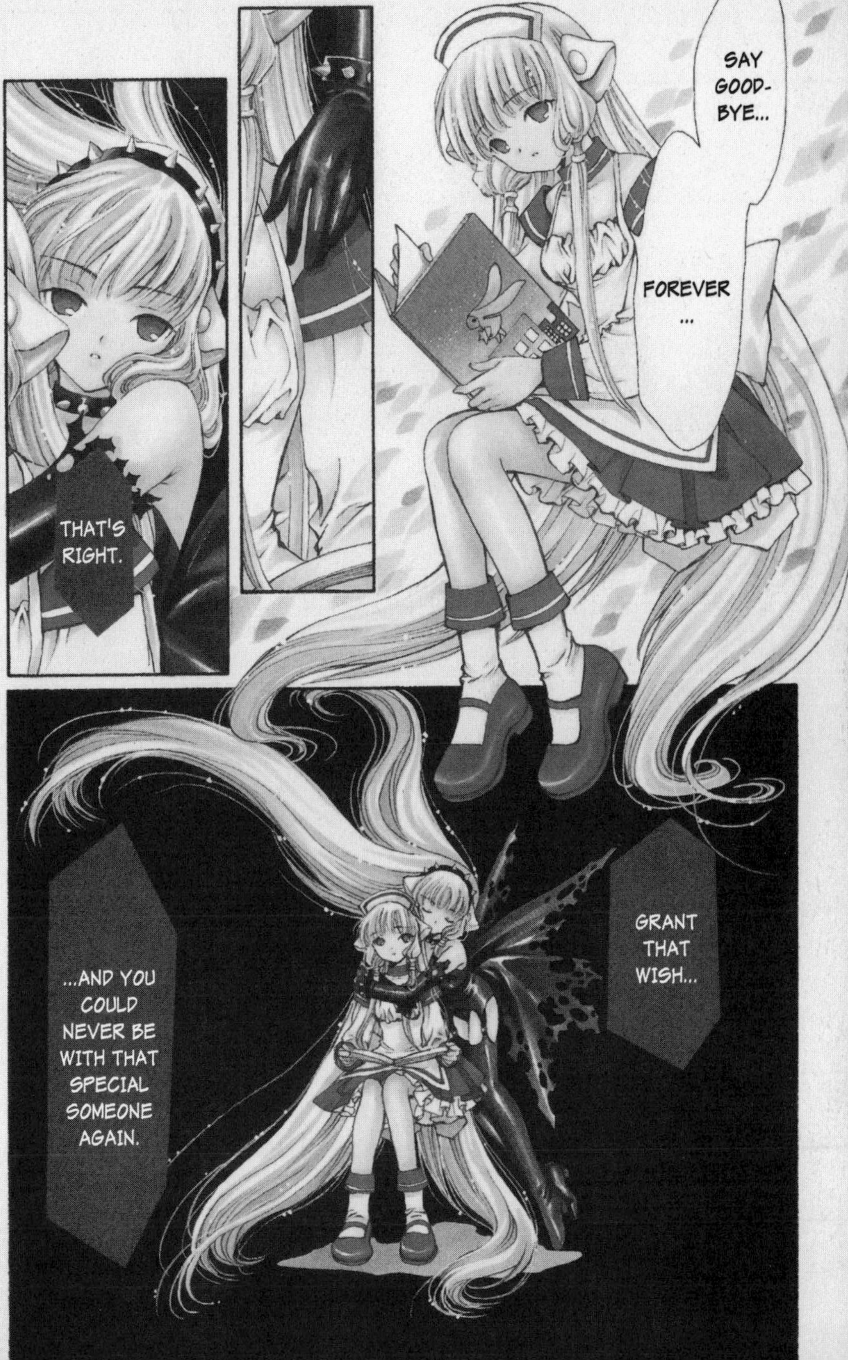
SAY GOOD-BYE...
FOREVER ...
THAT'S RIGHT.
GRANT THAT WISH...
...AND YOU COULD NEVER BE WITH THAT SPECIAL SOMEONE AGAIN.

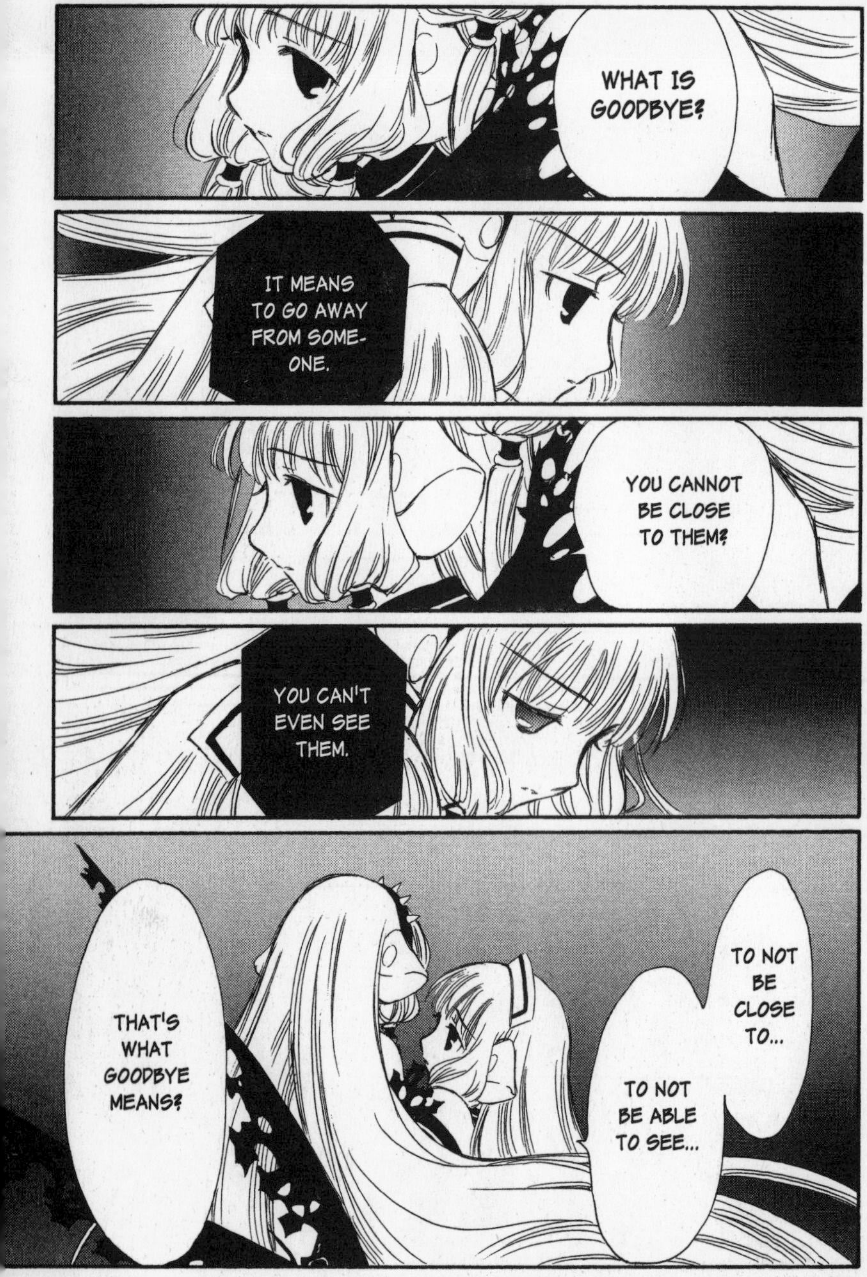
WHAT IS GOODBYE?
IT MEANS TO GO AWAY FROM SOME-ONE.
YOU CANNOT BE CLOSE TO THEM?
YOU CAN'T EVEN SEE THEM.
TO NOT BE CLOSE TO...
TO NOT BE ABLE TO SEE...
THAT'S WHAT GOODBYE MEANS?

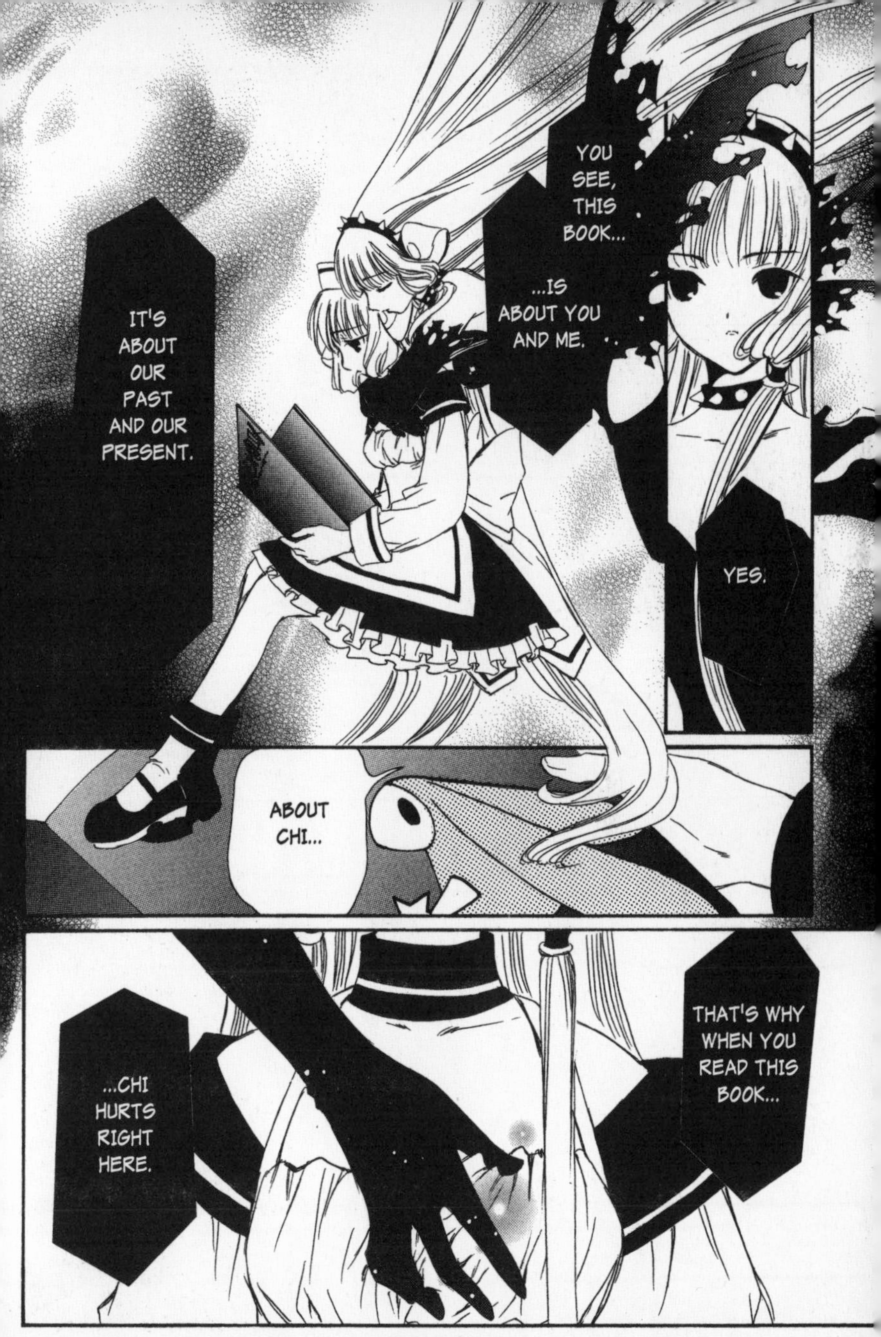
YOU SEE, THIS BOOK...
...IS ABOUT YOU AND ME.
YES.
IT'S ABOUT OUR PAST AND OUR PRESENT.
ABOUT CHI...
THAT'S WHY WHEN YOU READ THIS BOOK...
...CHI HURTS RIGHT HERE.

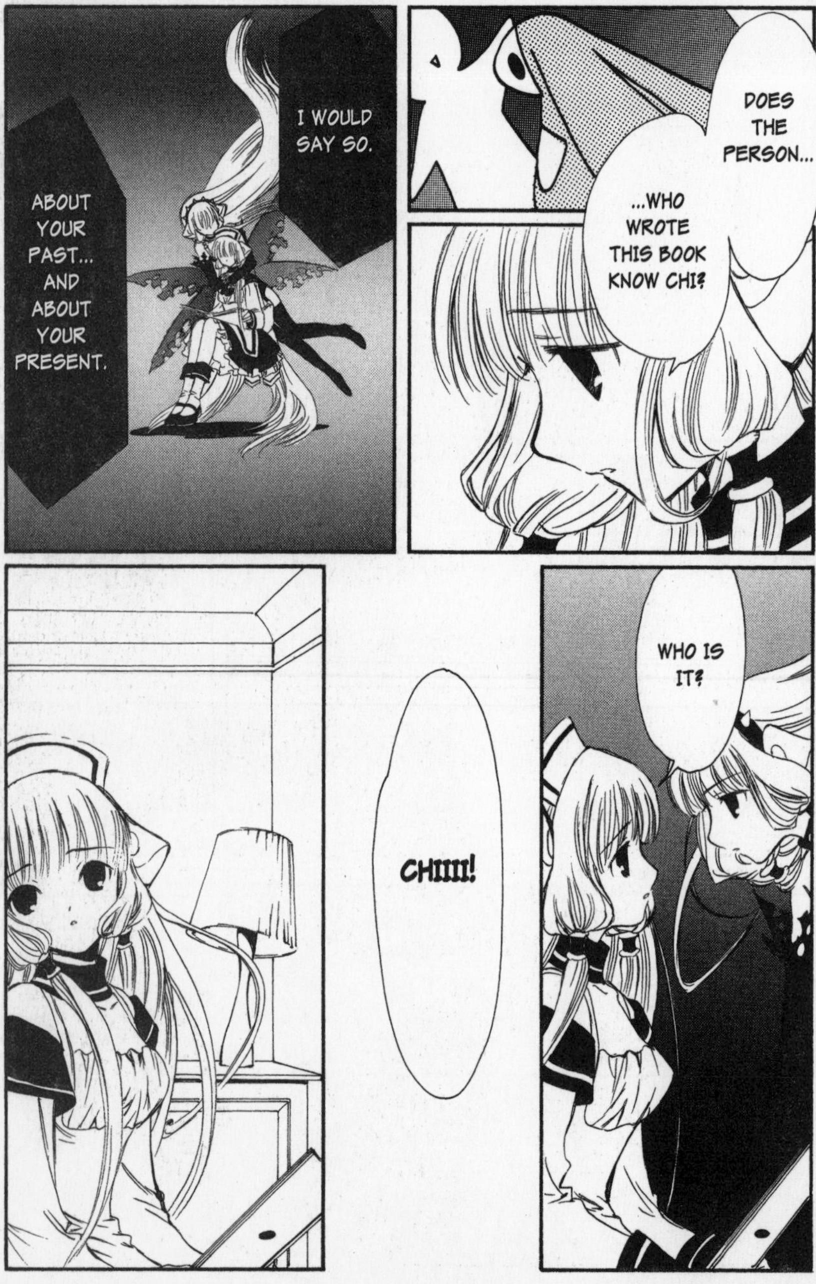
DOES THE PERSON...
...WHO WROTE THIS BOOK KNOW CHI?
I WOULD SAY SO.
ABOUT YOUR PAST... AND ABOUT YOUR PRESENT.
WHO IS IT?
CHIIII!

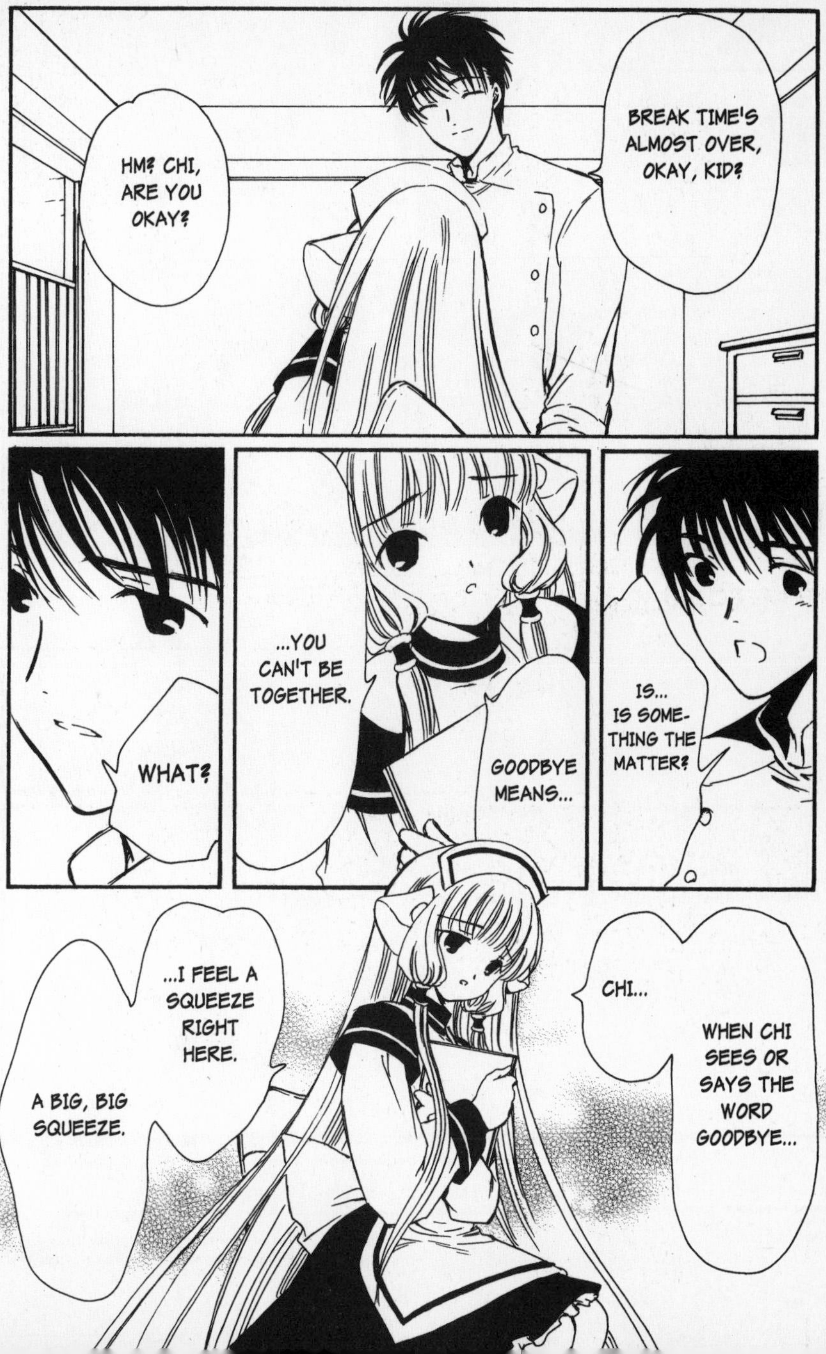
BREAK TIME'S ALMOST OVER, OKAY, KID?
HM? CHI, ARE YOU OKAY?
IS... IS SOME-THING THE MATTER?
GOODBYE MEANS...
...YOU CAN'T BE TOGETHER.
WHAT?
CHI...
WHEN CHI SEES OR SAYS THE WORD GOODBYE...
...I FEEL A SQUEEZE RIGHT HERE.
A BIG, BIG SQUEEZE.

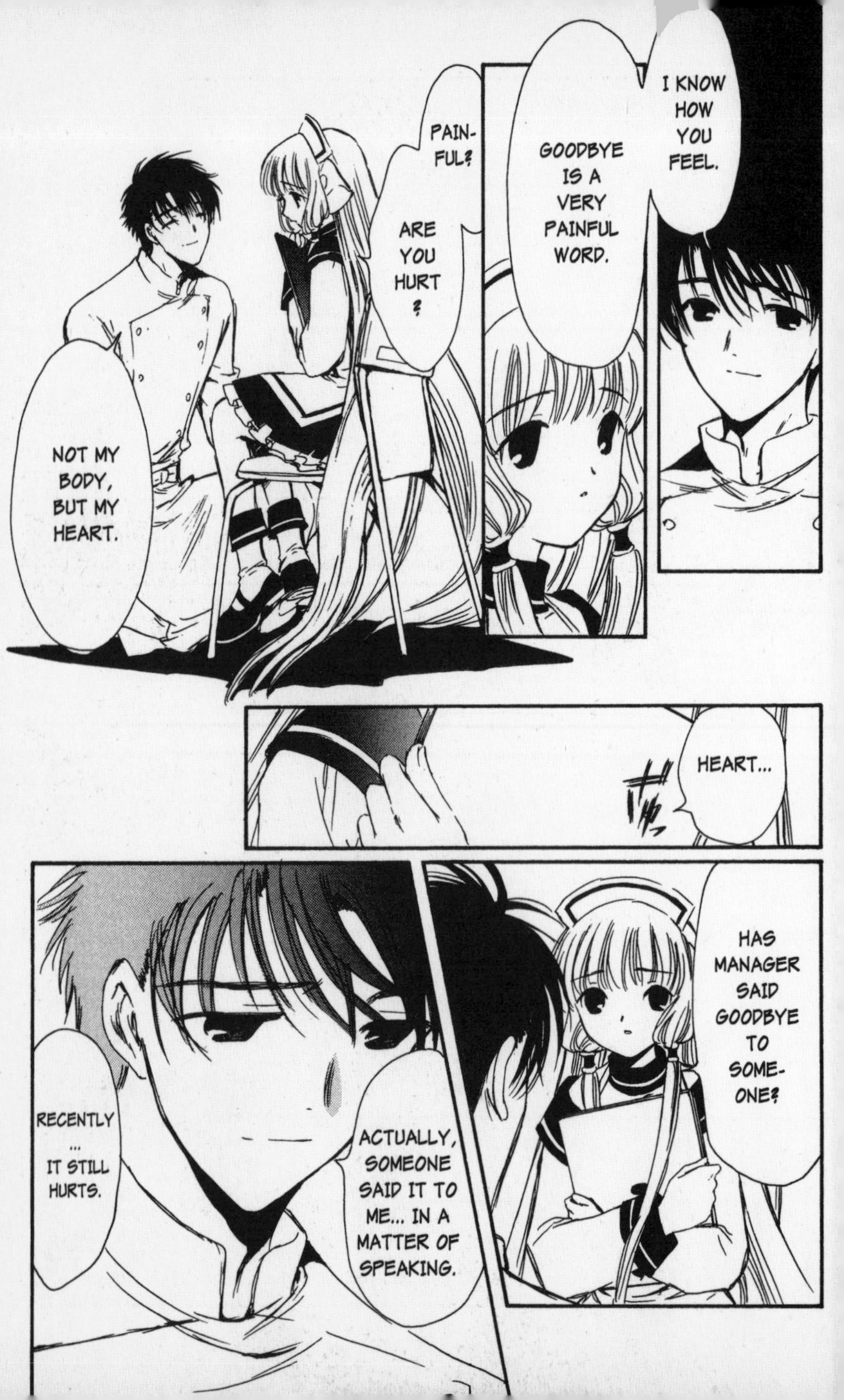
I KNOW HOW YOU FEEL.
GOODBYE IS A VERY PAINFUL WORD.
PAINFUL?
ARE YOU HURT?
NOT MY BODY, BUT MY HEART.
HEART...
HAS MANAGER SAID GOODBYE TO SOMEONE?
ACTUALLY, SOMEONE SAID IT TO ME... IN A MATTER OF SPEAKING.
RECENTLY... IT STILL HURTS.

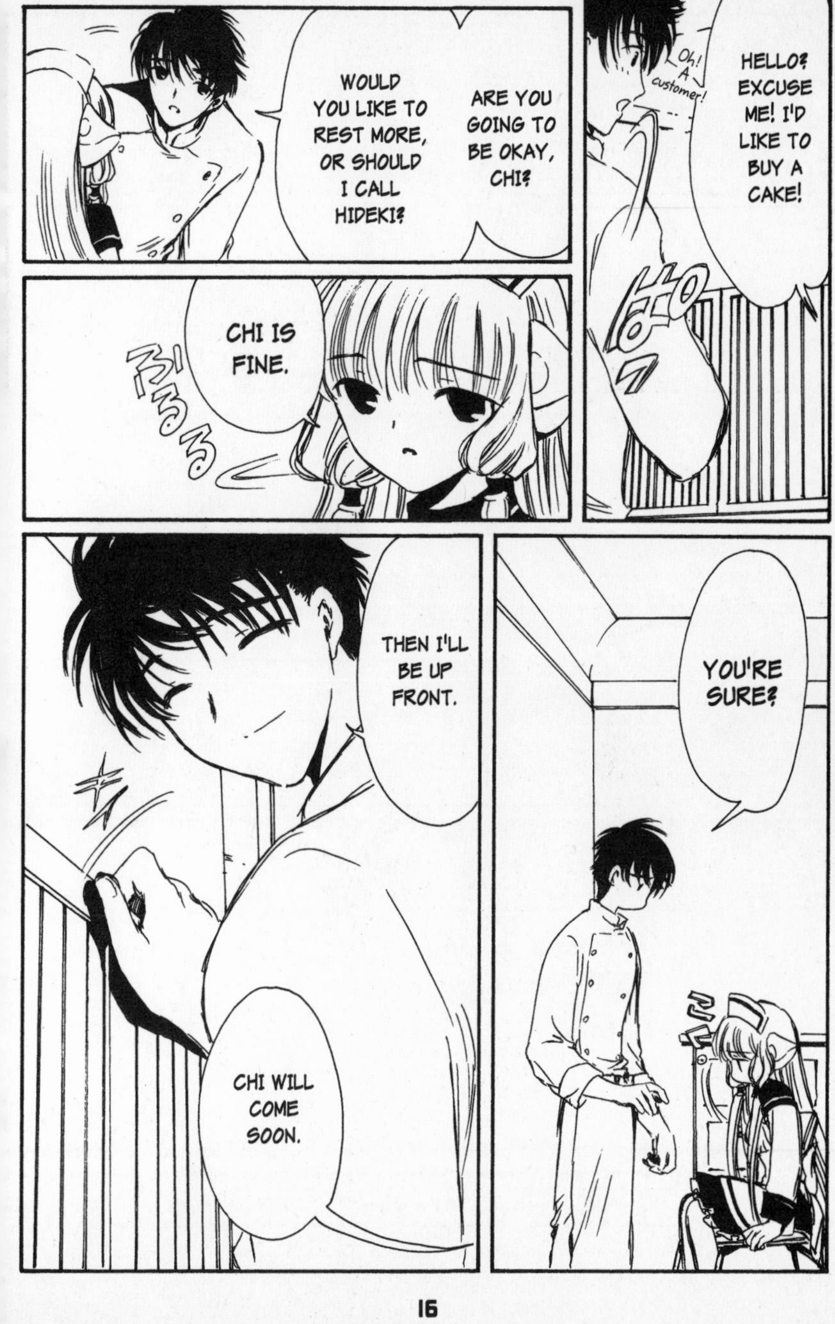
Oh! A customer!
HELLO? EXCUSE ME! I'D LIKE TO BUY A CAKE!
ARE YOU GOING TO BE OKAY, CHI?
WOULD YOU LIKE TO REST MORE, OR SHOULD I CALL HIDEKI?
CHI IS FINE.
YOU'RE SURE?
THEN I'LL BE UP FRONT.
CHI WILL COME SOON.

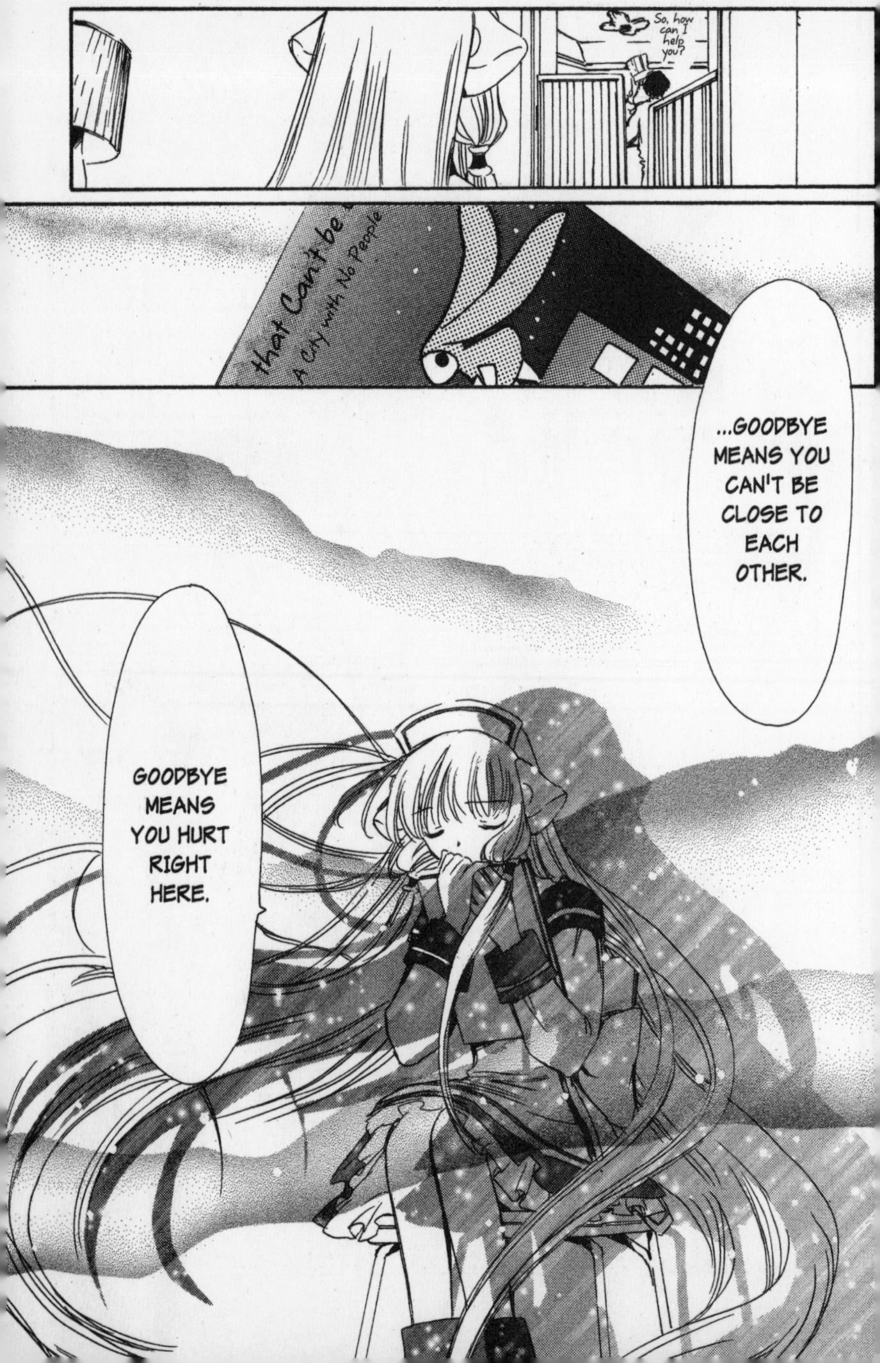
So, how can I help you?
that Can't be
A City with No People
...GOODBYE MEANS YOU CAN'T BE CLOSE TO EACH OTHER.
GOODBYE MEANS YOU HURT RIGHT HERE.

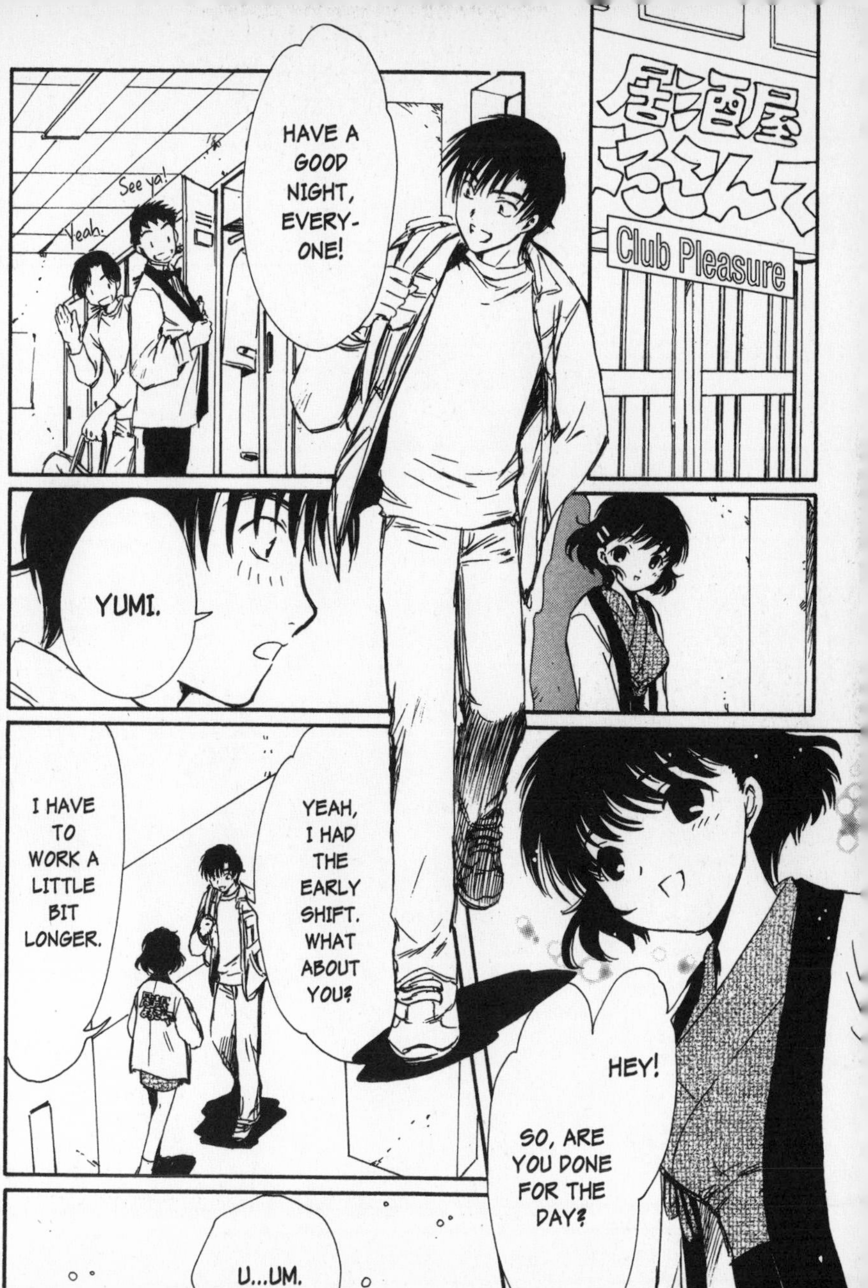
居酒屋
Club Pleasure
HAVE A GOOD NIGHT, EVERY-ONE!
See ya!
Yeah.
YUMI.
HEY!
SO, ARE YOU DONE FOR THE DAY?
YEAH, I HAD THE EARLY SHIFT. WHAT ABOUT YOU?
I HAVE TO WORK A LITTLE BIT LONGER.
U...UM.

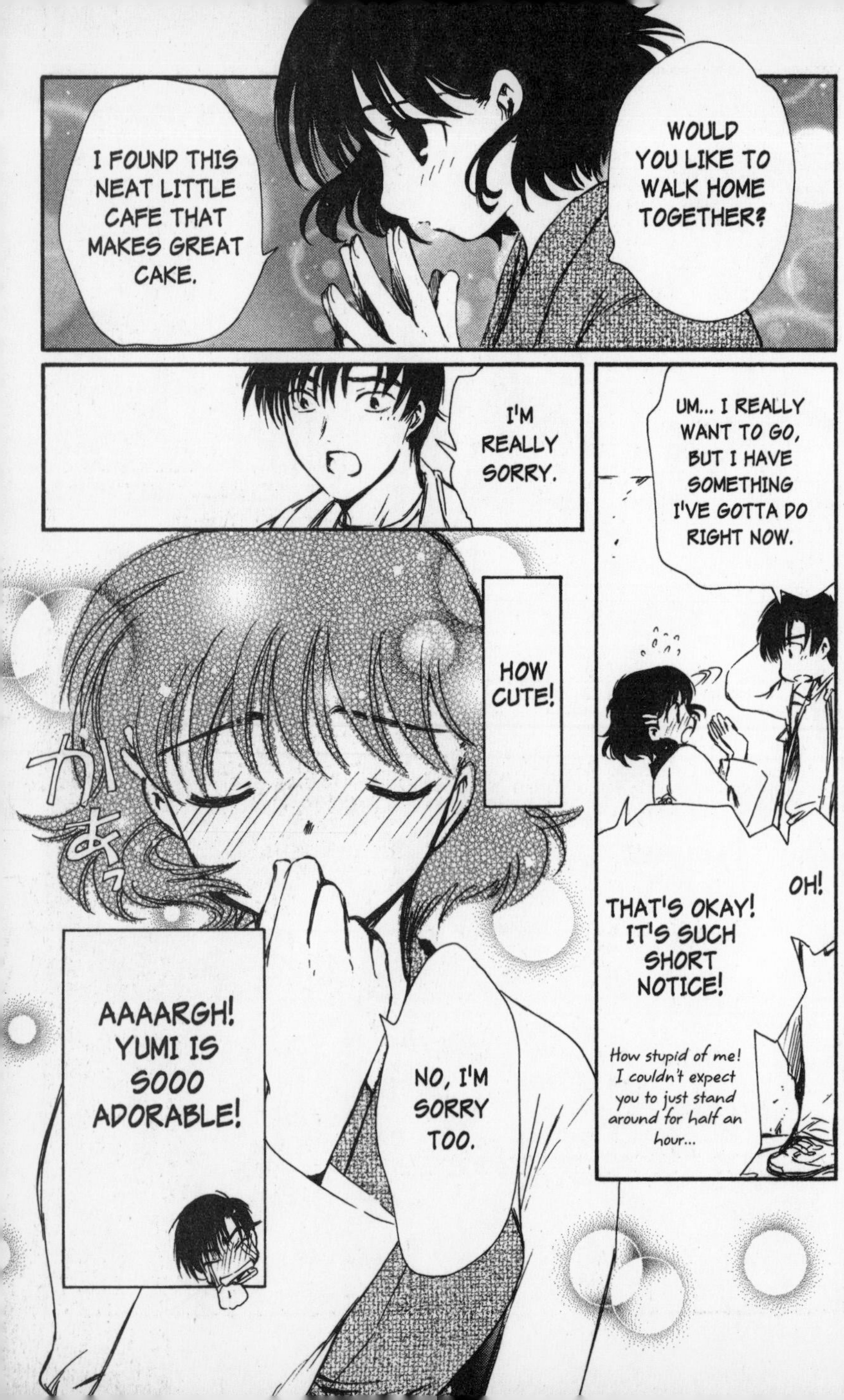
WOULD YOU LIKE TO WALK HOME TOGETHER?
I FOUND THIS NEAT LITTLE CAFE THAT MAKES GREAT CAKE.
UM... I REALLY WANT TO GO, BUT I HAVE SOMETHING I'VE GOTTA DO RIGHT NOW.
OH!
THAT'S OKAY! IT'S SUCH SHORT NOTICE!
How stupid of me! I couldn't expect you to just stand around for half an hour...
I'M REALLY SORRY.
HOW CUTE!
わあっ
NO, I'M SORRY TOO.
AAAARGH! YUMI IS SOOO ADORABLE!

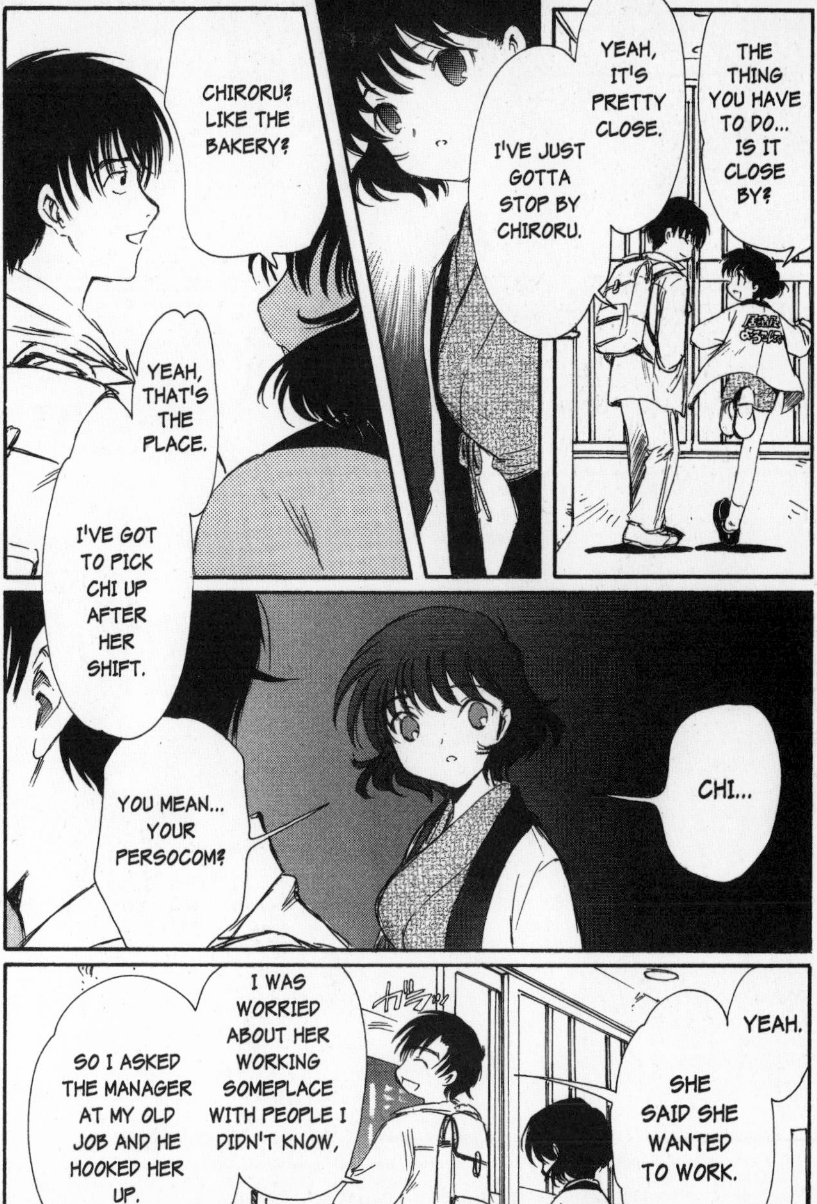
THE THING YOU HAVE TO DO... IS IT CLOSE BY?
YEAH, IT'S PRETTY CLOSE.
I'VE JUST GOTTA STOP BY CHIRORU.
CHIRORU? LIKE THE BAKERY?
YEAH, THAT'S THE PLACE.
I'VE GOT TO PICK CHI UP AFTER HER SHIFT.
CHI...
YOU MEAN... YOUR PERSOCOM?
YEAH.
SHE SAID SHE WANTED TO WORK.
I WAS WORRIED ABOUT HER WORKING SOMEPLACE WITH PEOPLE I DIDN'T KNOW,
SO I ASKED THE MANAGER AT MY OLD JOB AND HE HOOKED HER UP.

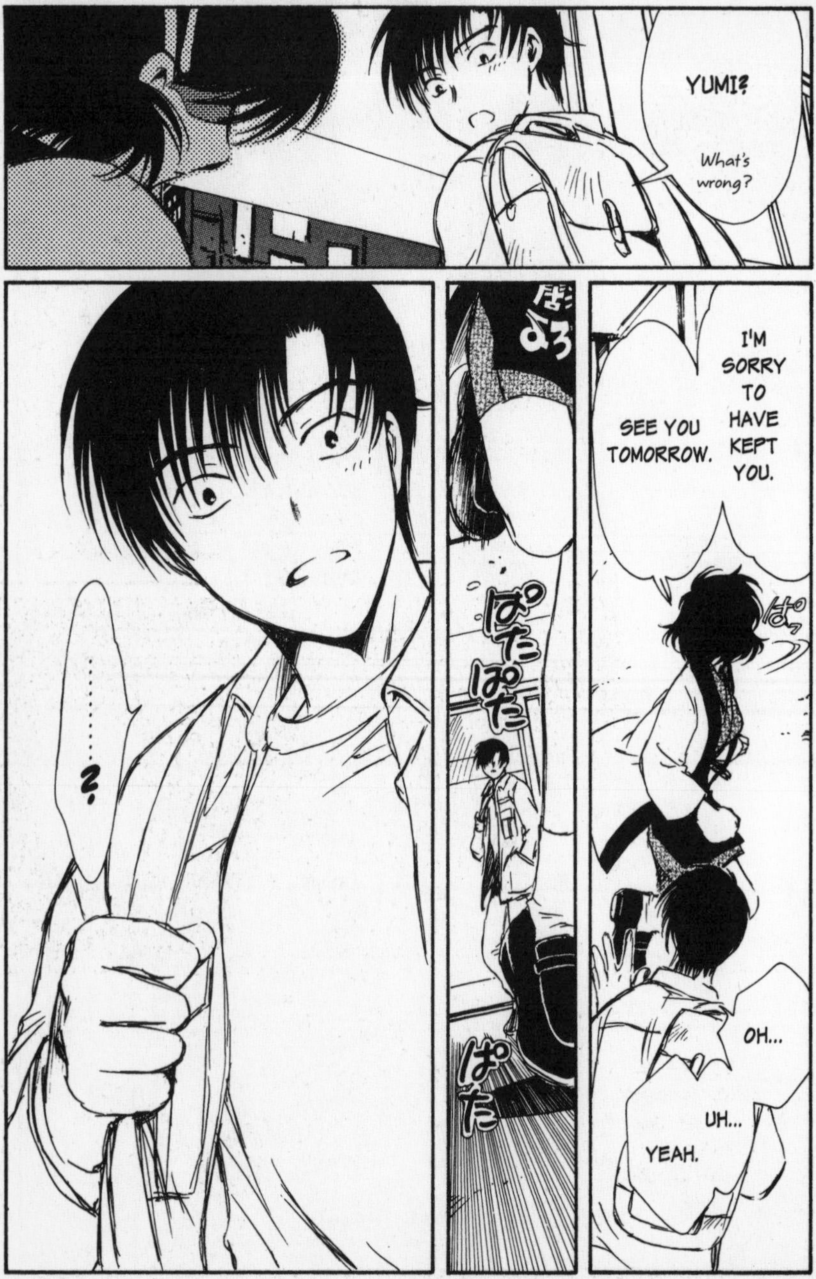
YUMI?
What's wrong?
I'M SORRY TO HAVE KEPT YOU.
SEE YOU TOMORROW.
ぱっ
OH...
UH...
YEAH.
ぱたぱた
ぱた
......?

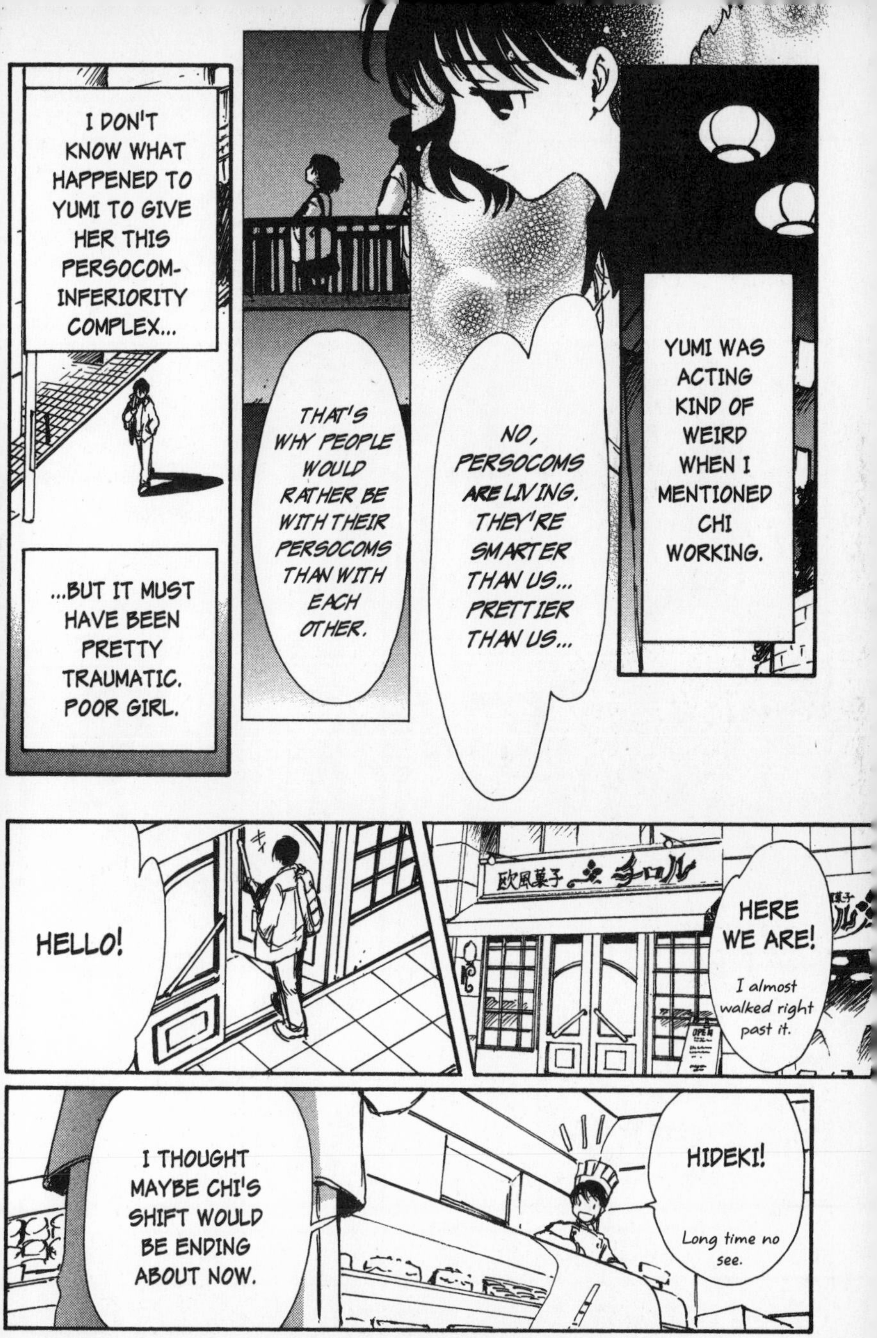
YUMI WAS ACTING KIND OF WEIRD WHEN I MENTIONED CHI WORKING.
NO, PERSOCOMS ARE LIVING. THEY'RE SMARTER THAN US... PRETTIER THAN US...
THAT'S WHY PEOPLE WOULD RATHER BE WITH THEIR PERSOCOMS THAN WITH EACH OTHER.
I DON'T KNOW WHAT HAPPENED TO YUMI TO GIVE HER THIS PERSOCOM-INFERIORITY COMPLEX...
...BUT IT MUST HAVE BEEN PRETTY TRAUMATIC. POOR GIRL.
欧風菓子 チロル
HERE WE ARE!
I almost walked right past it.
HELLO!
HIDEKI!
Long time no see.
I THOUGHT MAYBE CHI'S SHIFT WOULD BE ENDING ABOUT NOW.

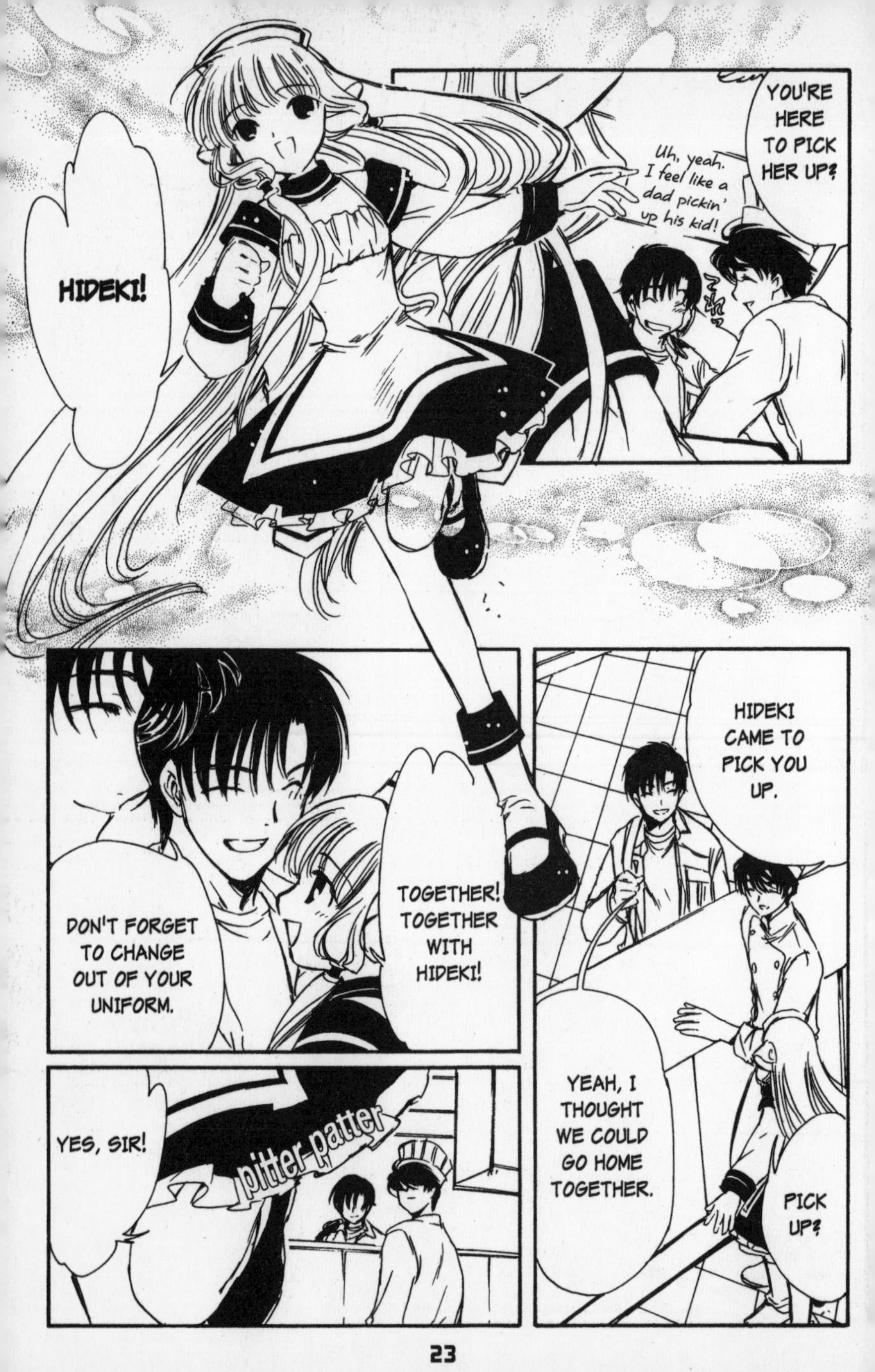
YOU'RE HERE TO PICK HER UP?
Uh, yeah. I feel like a dad pickin' up his kid!
HIDEKI!
HIDEKI CAME TO PICK YOU UP.
PICK UP?
YEAH, I THOUGHT WE COULD GO HOME TOGETHER.
TOGETHER! TOGETHER WITH HIDEKI!
DON'T FORGET TO CHANGE OUT OF YOUR UNIFORM.
pitter-patter
YES, SIR!

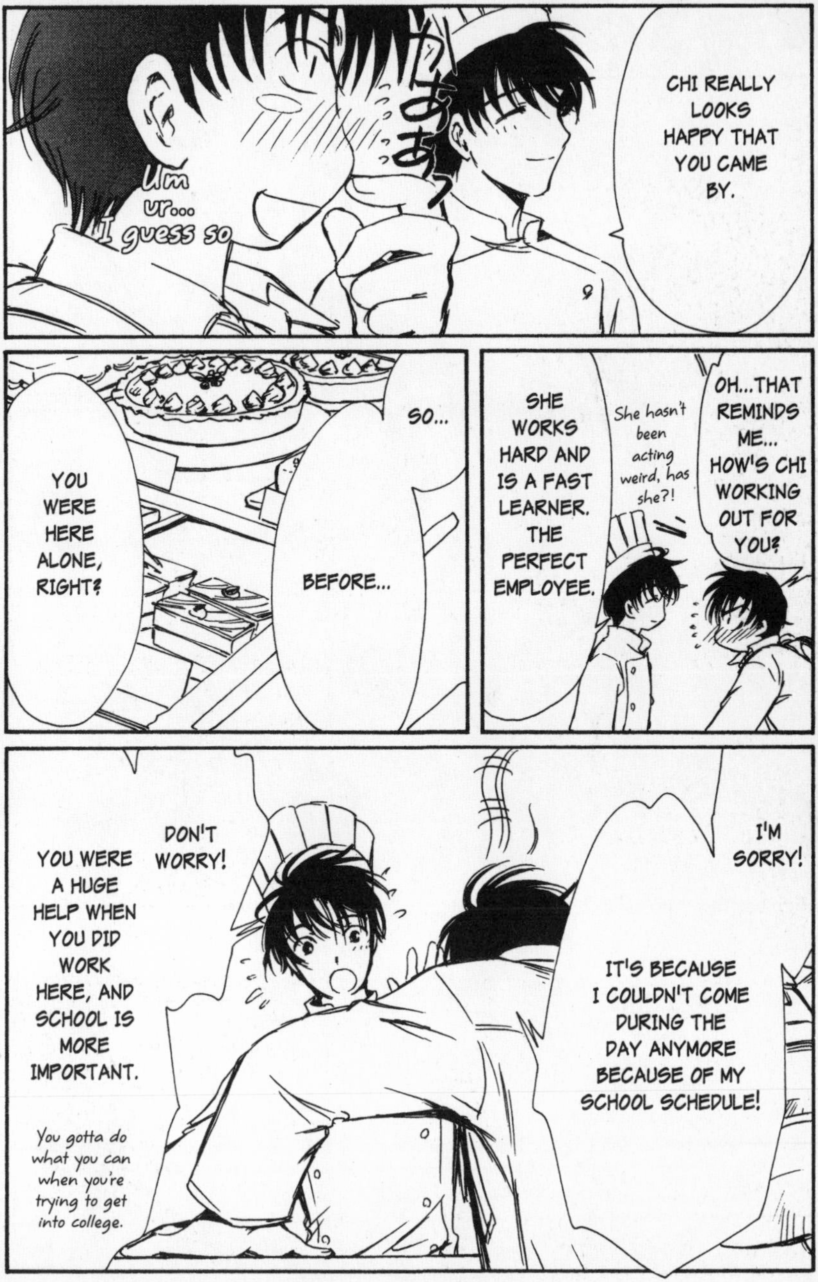
CHI REALLY LOOKS HAPPY THAT YOU CAME BY.
Um ur... I guess so
OH...THAT REMINDS ME... HOW'S CHI WORKING OUT FOR YOU?
She hasn't been acting weird, has she?!
SHE WORKS HARD AND IS A FAST LEARNER. THE PERFECT EMPLOYEE.
SO...
BEFORE...
YOU WERE HERE ALONE, RIGHT?
I'M SORRY!
IT'S BECAUSE I COULDN'T COME DURING THE DAY ANYMORE BECAUSE OF MY SCHOOL SCHEDULE!
DON'T WORRY!
YOU WERE A HUGE HELP WHEN YOU DID WORK HERE, AND SCHOOL IS MORE IMPORTANT.
You gotta do what you can when you're trying to get into college.

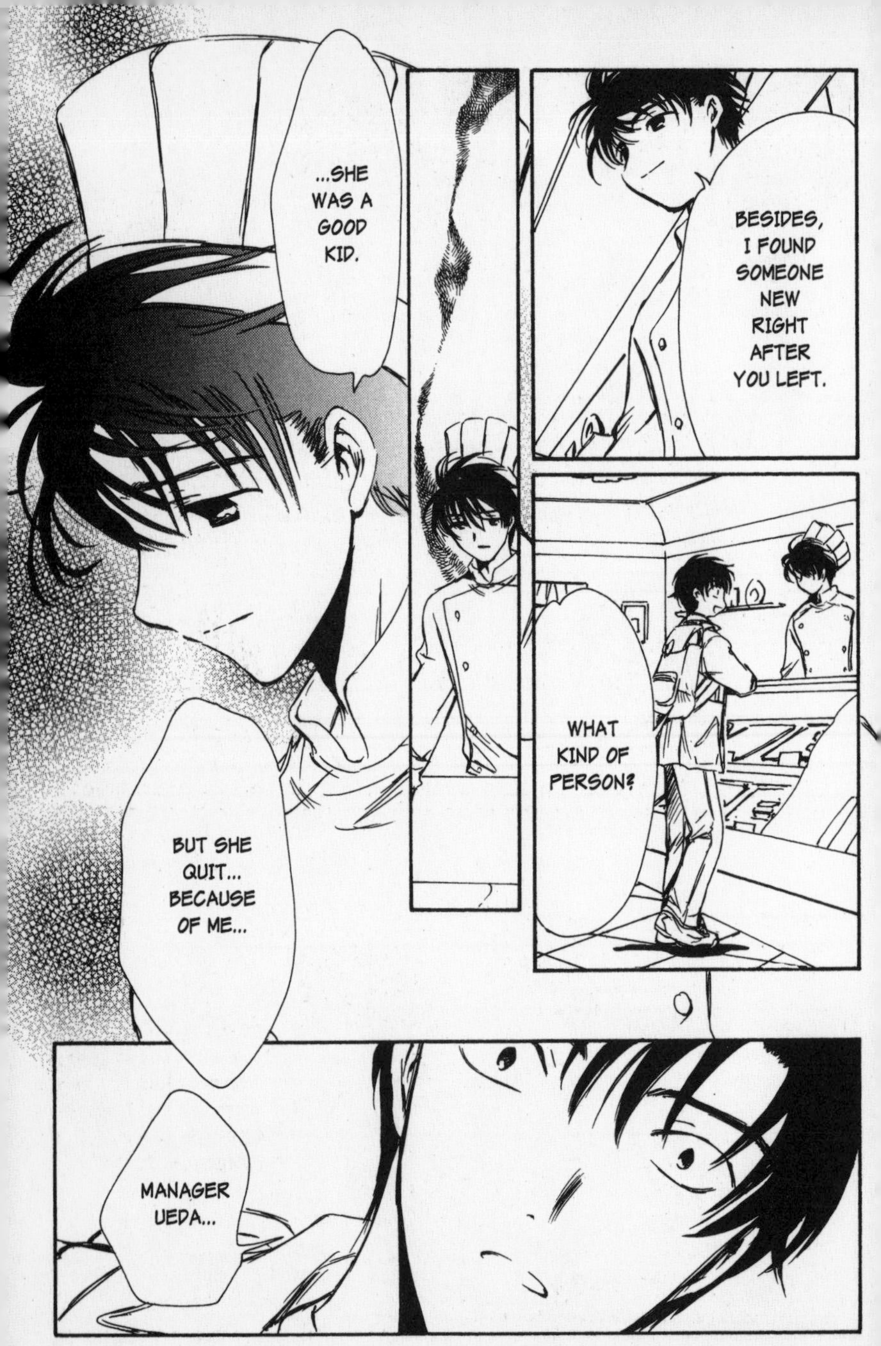
BESIDES, I FOUND SOMEONE NEW RIGHT AFTER YOU LEFT.
WHAT KIND OF PERSON?
...SHE WAS A GOOD KID.
BUT SHE QUIT... BECAUSE OF ME...
MANAGER UEDA...

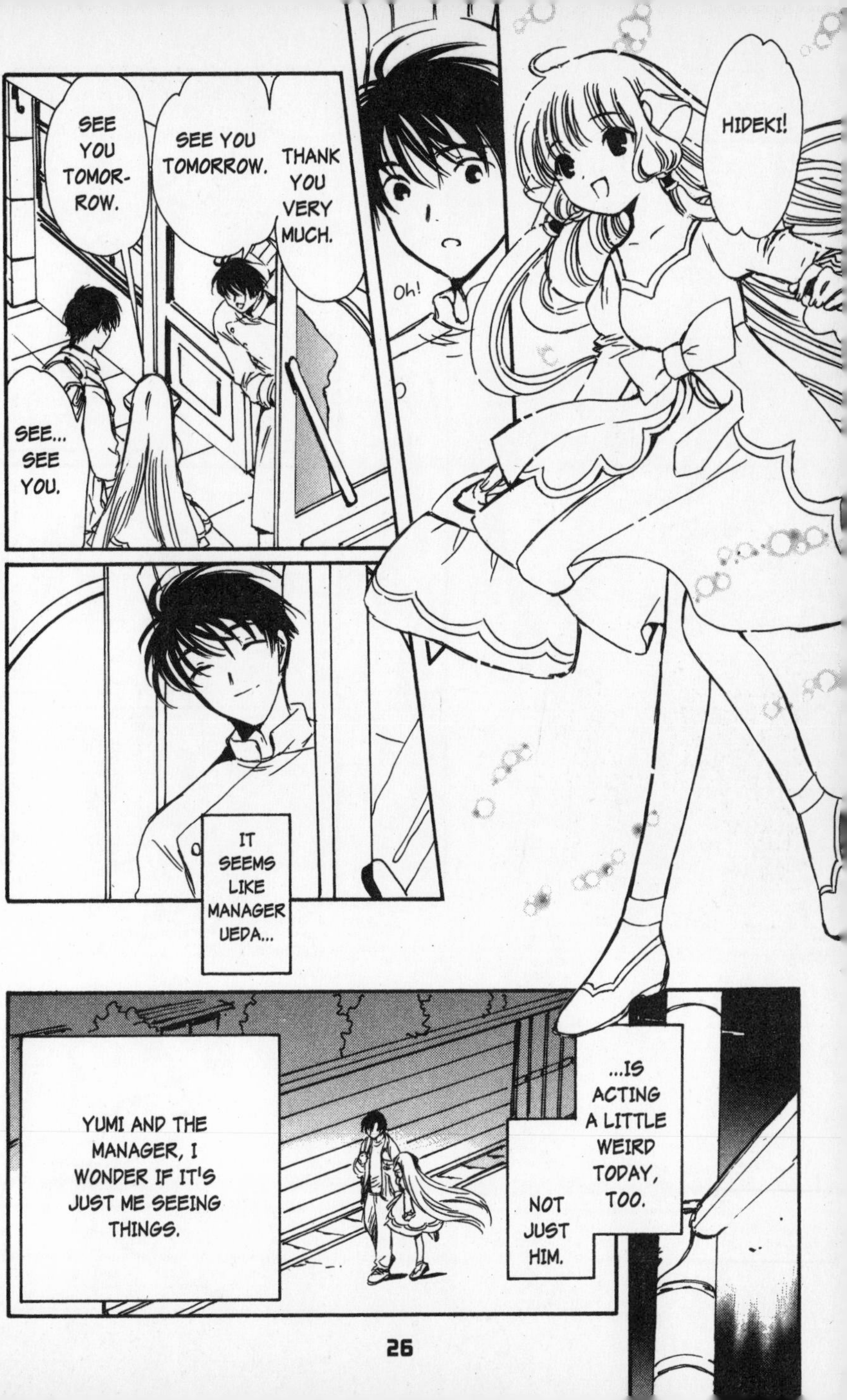
HIDEKI!
Oh!
THANK YOU VERY MUCH.
SEE YOU TOMORROW.
SEE YOU TOMOR-ROW.
SEE... SEE YOU.
IT SEEMS LIKE MANAGER UEDA...
...IS ACTING A LITTLE WEIRD TODAY, TOO.
NOT JUST HIM.
YUMI AND THE MANAGER, I WONDER IF IT'S JUST ME SEEING THINGS.

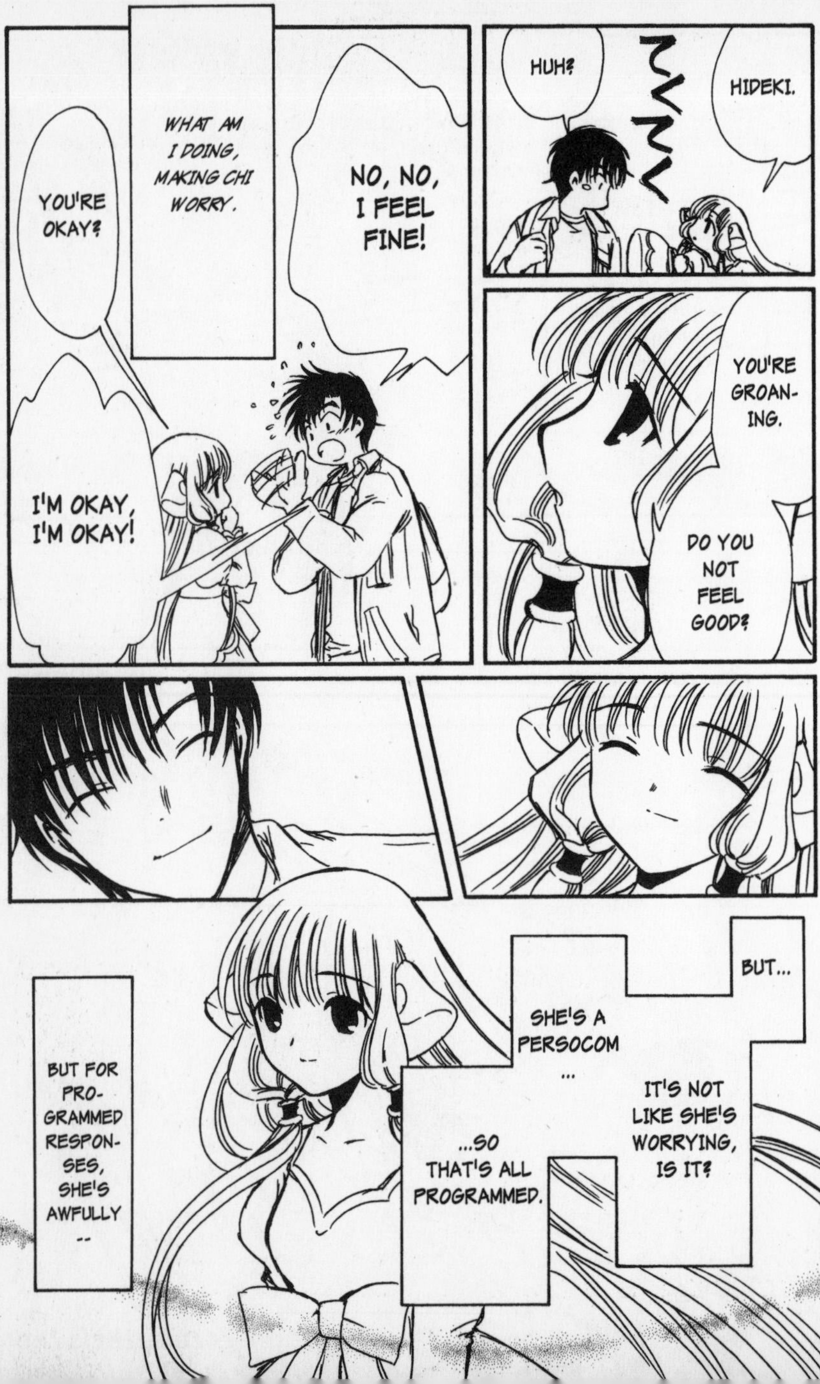
HIDEKI.
HUH?
YOU'RE GROAN-ING.
DO YOU NOT FEEL GOOD?
NO, NO, I FEEL FINE!
WHAT AM I DOING, MAKING CHI WORRY.
YOU'RE OKAY?
I'M OKAY, I'M OKAY!
BUT...
IT'S NOT LIKE SHE'S WORRYING, IS IT?
SHE'S A PERSOCOM ...
...SO THAT'S ALL PROGRAMMED.
BUT FOR PRO-GRAMMED RESPON-SES, SHE'S AWFULLY --

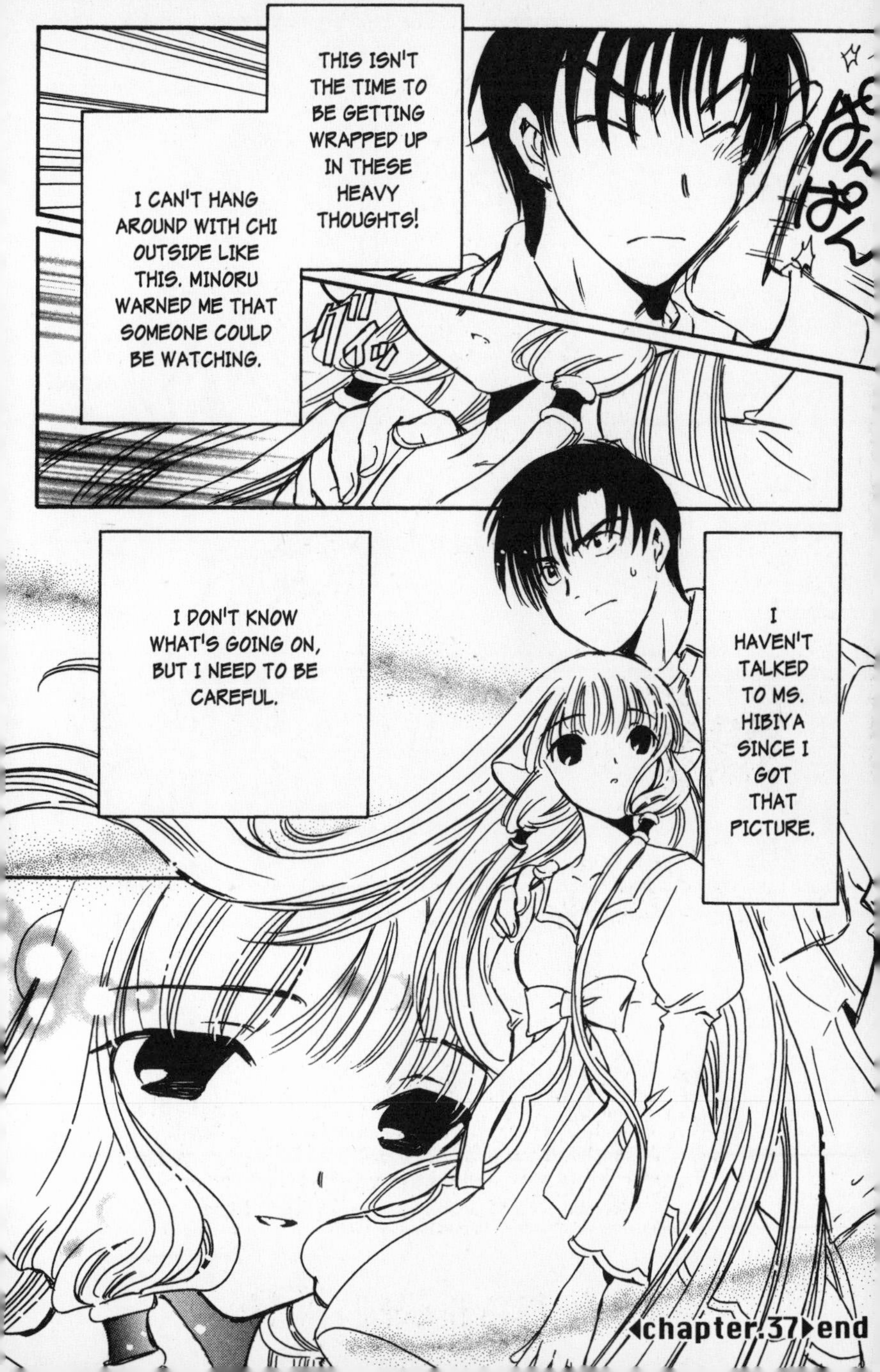
ぽんぽん
THIS ISN'T THE TIME TO BE GETTING WRAPPED UP IN THESE HEAVY THOUGHTS!
I CAN'T HANG AROUND WITH CHI OUTSIDE LIKE THIS. MINORU WARNED ME THAT SOMEONE COULD BE WATCHING.
I HAVEN'T TALKED TO MS. HIBIYA SINCE I GOT THAT PICTURE.
I DON'T KNOW WHAT'S GOING ON, BUT I NEED TO BE CAREFUL.
◀chapter.37▶end

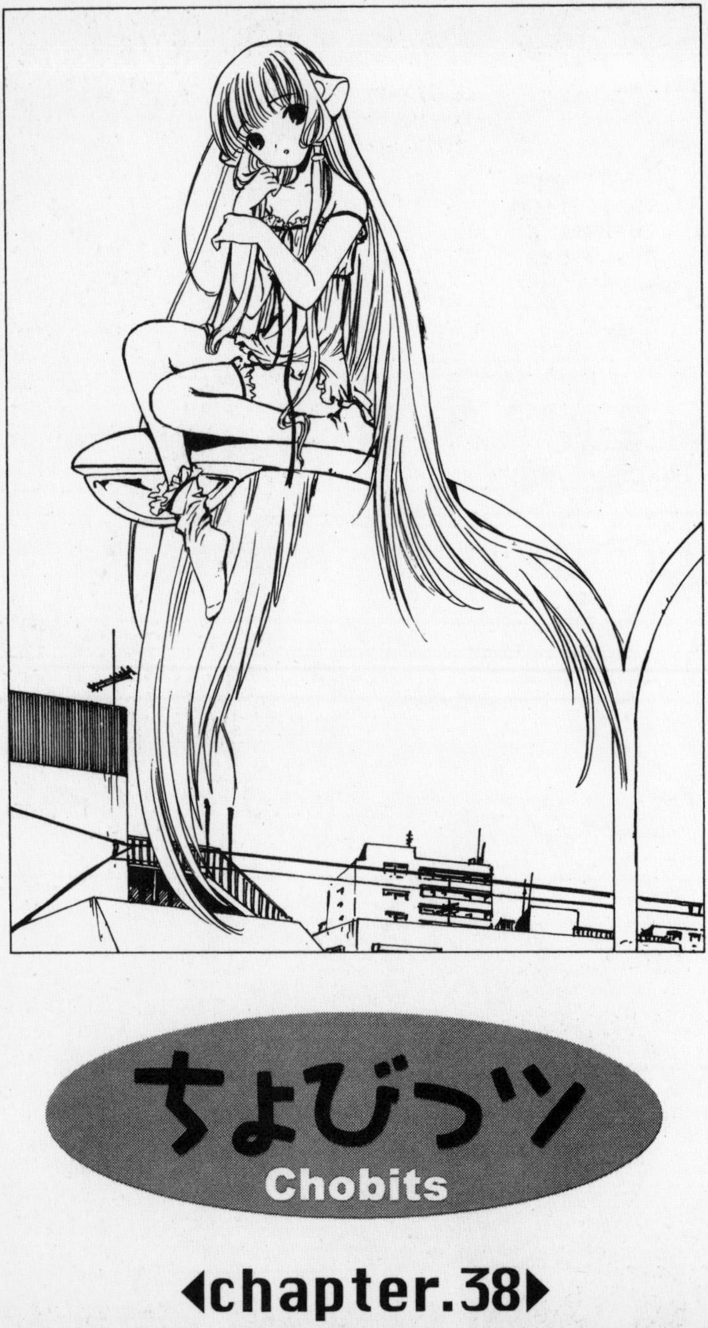

ちょびっツ
Chobits

◀chapter.38▶

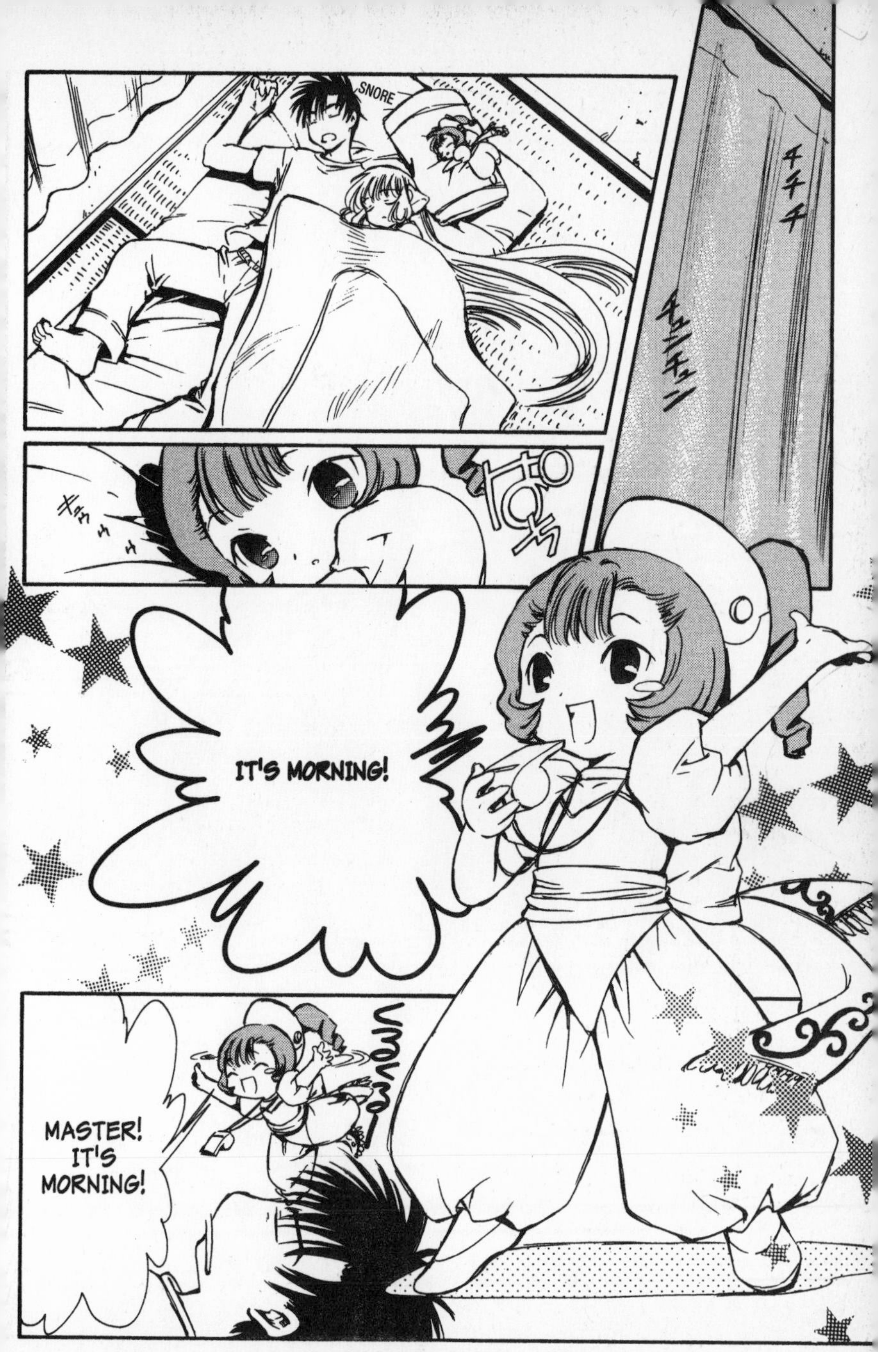

SNORE
チチチ
チュンチュン
ぱちっ
IT'S MORNING!
MASTER! IT'S MORNING!

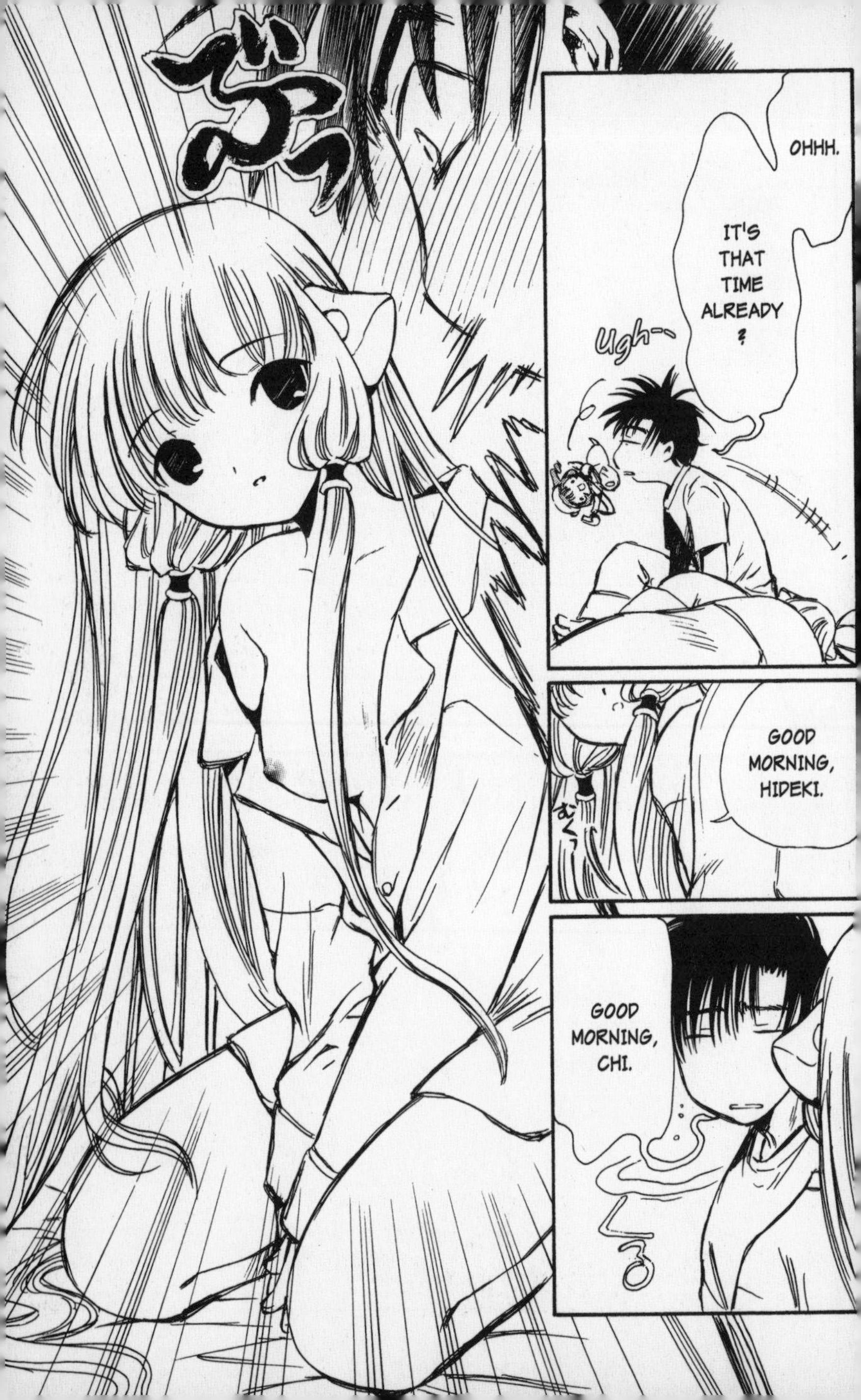
OHHH.
IT'S THAT TIME ALREADY?
Ugh--
GOOD MORNING, HIDEKI.
GOOD MORNING, CHI.

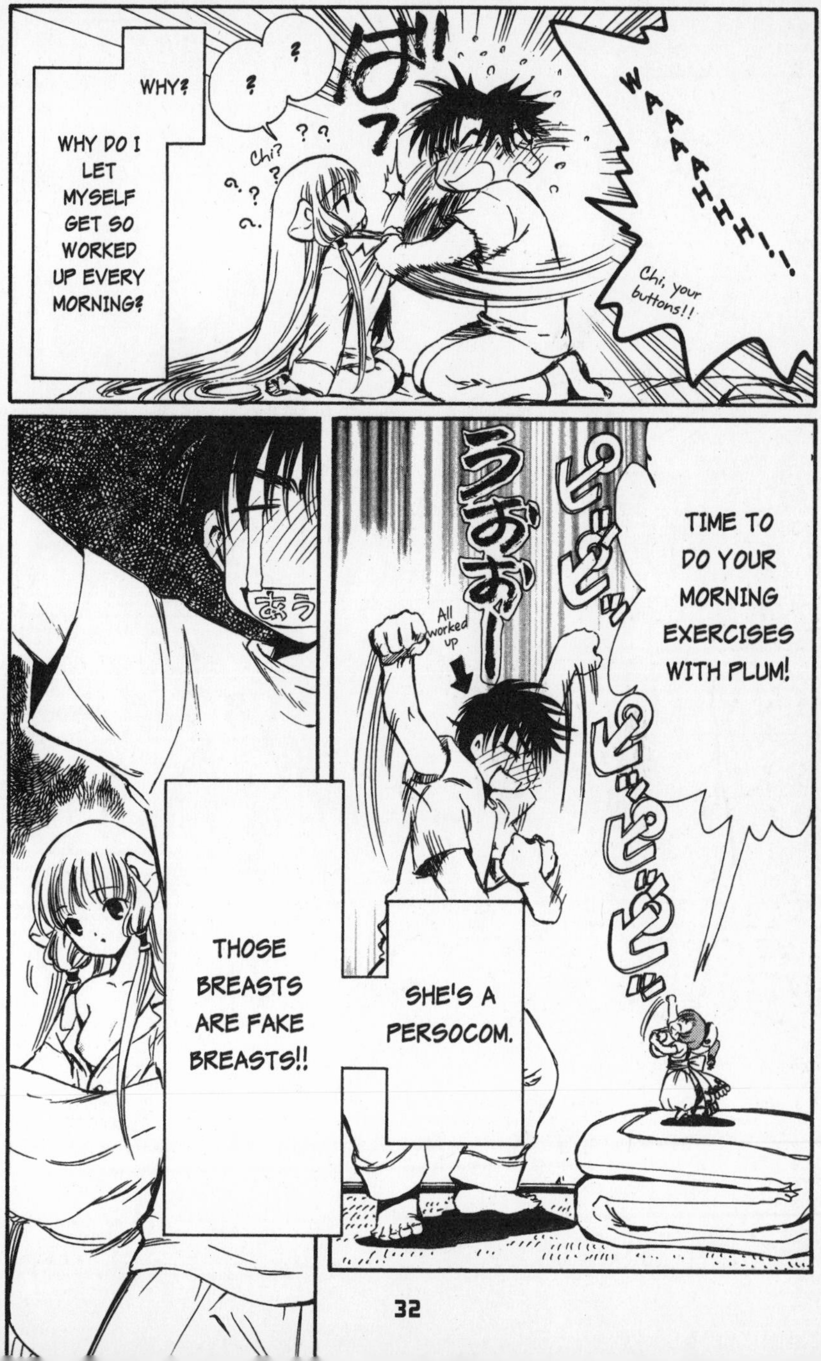
WAAAAHHHH!!!
Chi, your buttons!!
ぱっ
Chi?
WHY?
WHY DO I LET MYSELF GET SO WORKED UP EVERY MORNING?
TIME TO DO YOUR MORNING EXERCISES WITH PLUM!
ピッピッ
ピッピッピッ
うおおー
All worked up
SHE'S A PERSOCOM.
あう
THOSE BREASTS ARE FAKE BREASTS!!

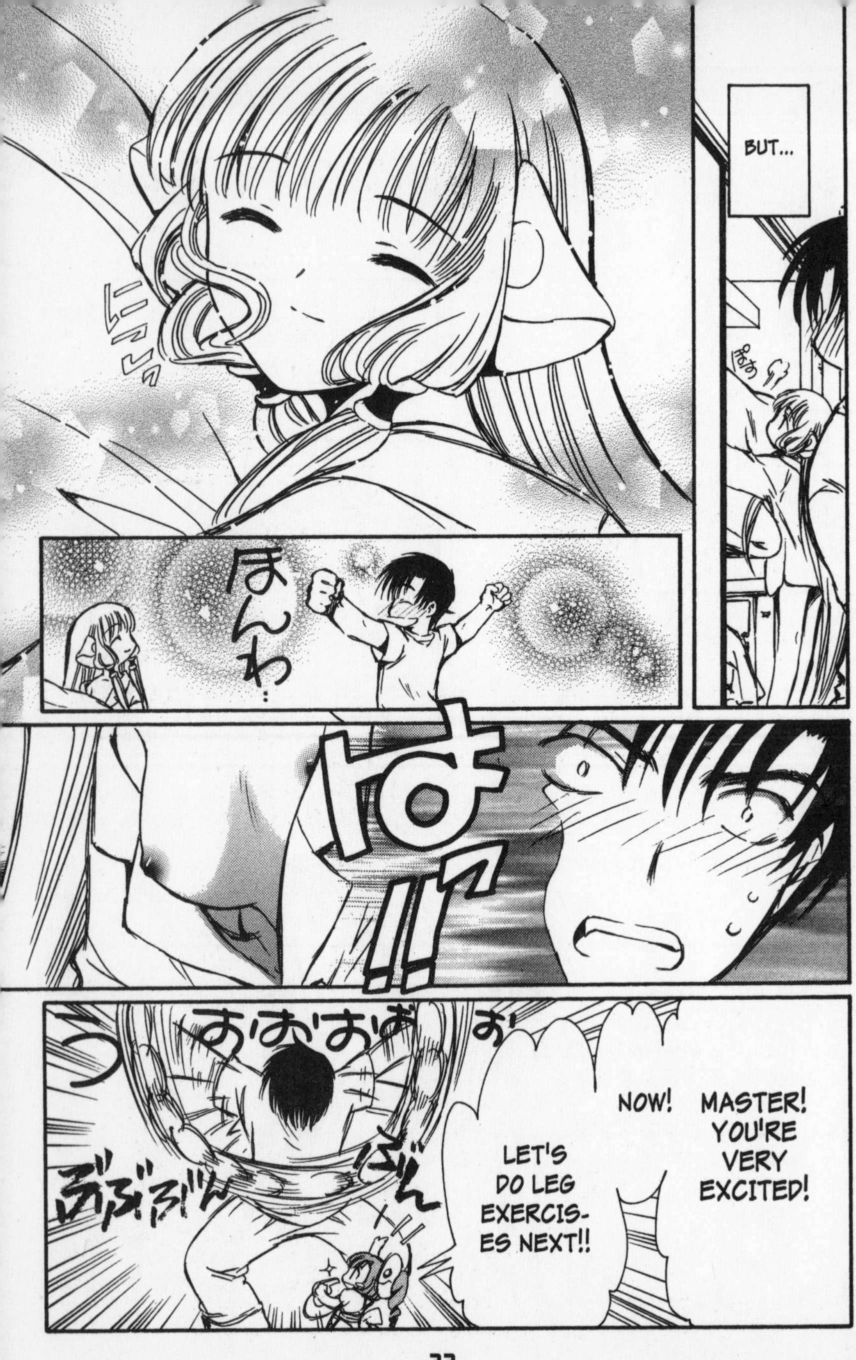
BUT...
ほんわ…
はっ!!
MASTER! YOU'RE VERY EXCITED!
NOW!
LET'S DO LEG EXERCIS-ES NEXT!!

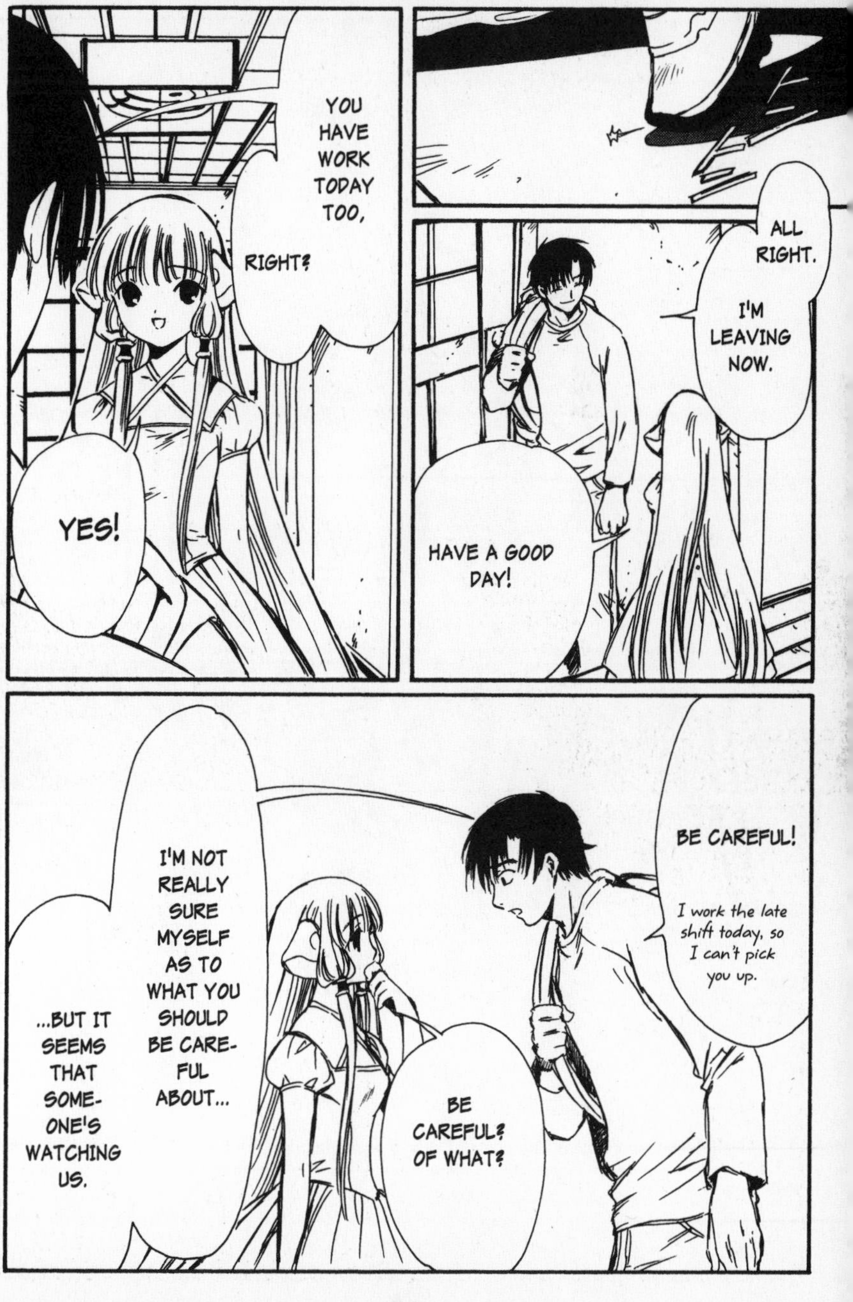
ALL RIGHT. I'M LEAVING NOW.
HAVE A GOOD DAY!
YOU HAVE WORK TODAY TOO,
RIGHT?
YES!
BE CAREFUL!
I work the late shift today, so I can't pick you up.
BE CAREFUL? OF WHAT?
I'M NOT REALLY SURE MYSELF AS TO WHAT YOU SHOULD BE CARE-FUL ABOUT...
...BUT IT SEEMS THAT SOME-ONE'S WATCHING US.

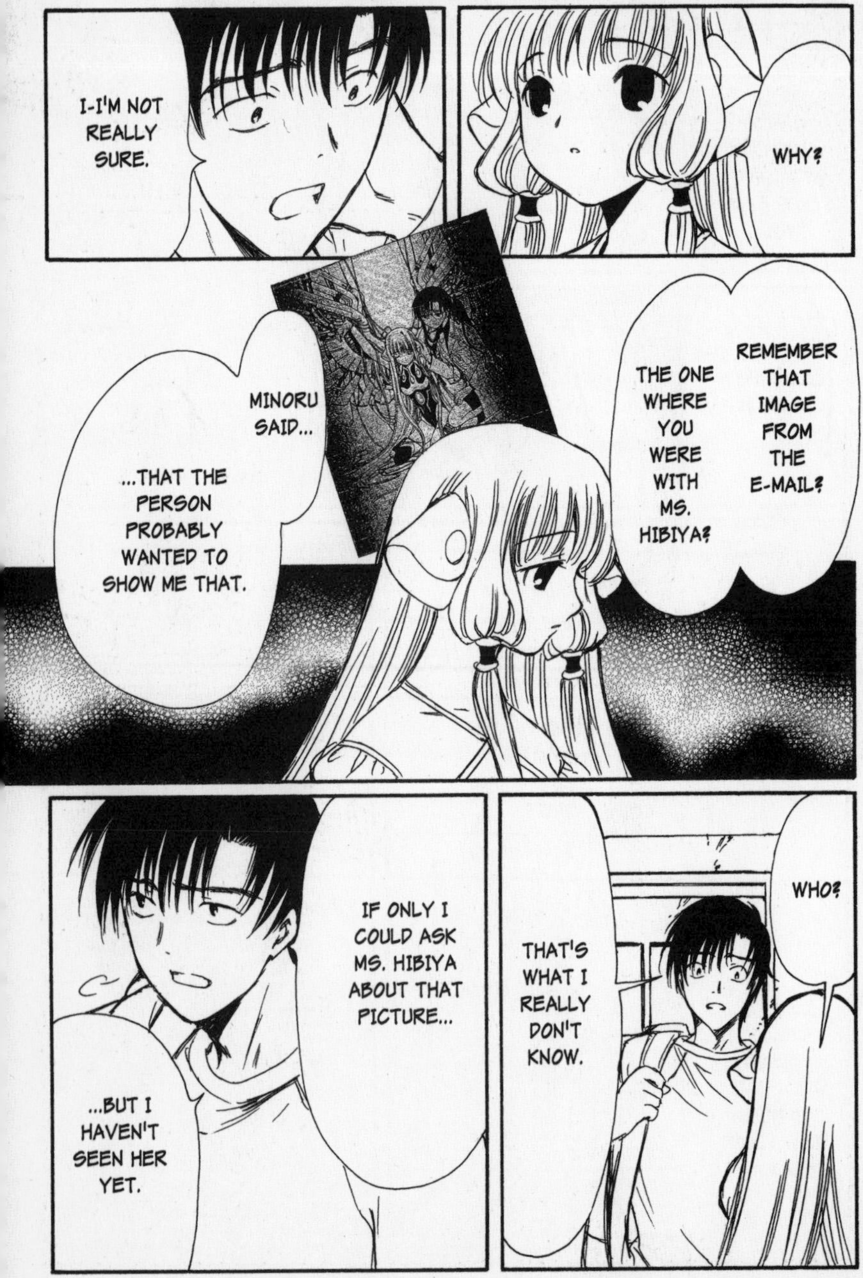
WHY?
I-I'M NOT REALLY SURE.
REMEMBER THAT IMAGE FROM THE E-MAIL?
THE ONE WHERE YOU WERE WITH MS. HIBIYA?
MINORU SAID...
...THAT THE PERSON PROBABLY WANTED TO SHOW ME THAT.
WHO?
THAT'S WHAT I REALLY DON'T KNOW.
IF ONLY I COULD ASK MS. HIBIYA ABOUT THAT PICTURE...
...BUT I HAVEN'T SEEN HER YET.

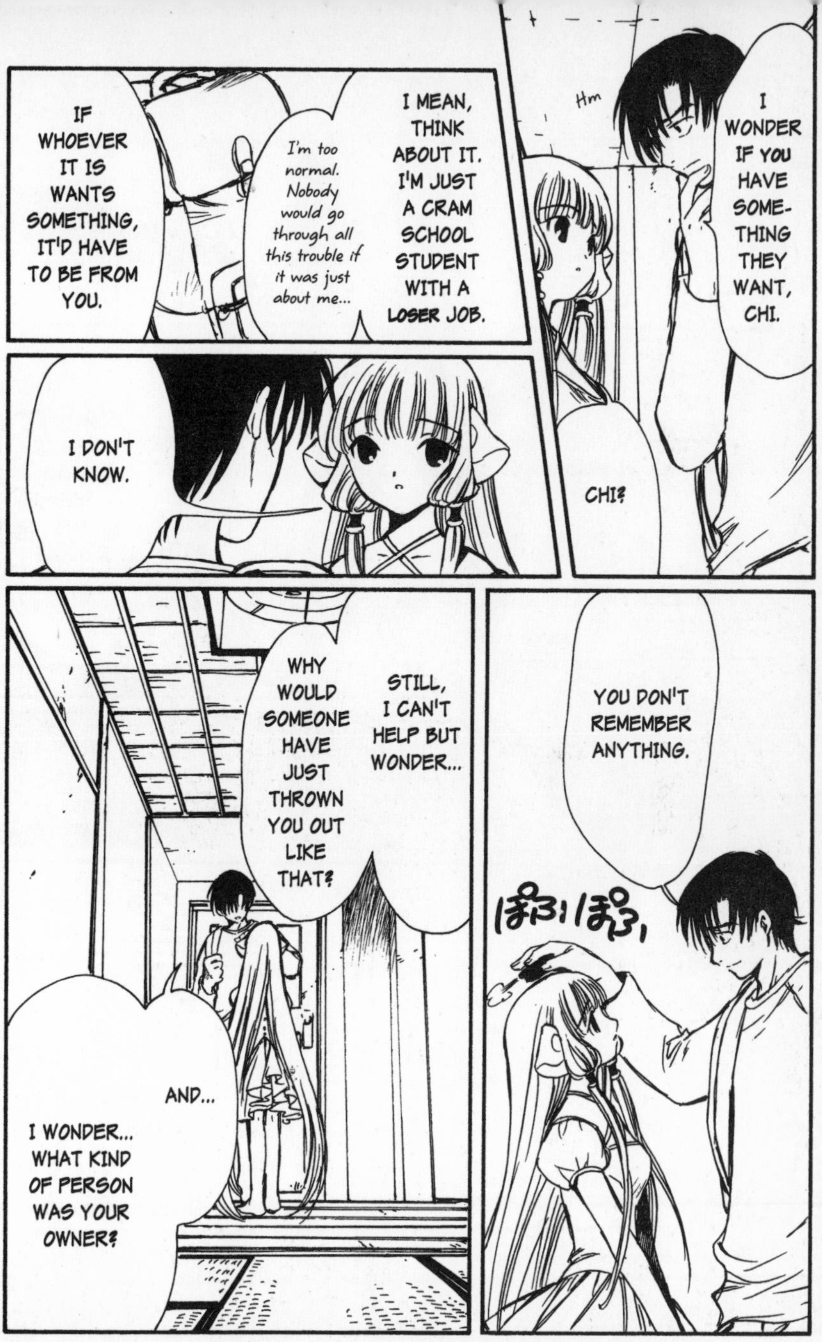
Hm
I WONDER IF YOU HAVE SOMETHING THEY WANT, CHI.
CHI?
I MEAN, THINK ABOUT IT. I'M JUST A CRAM SCHOOL STUDENT WITH A LOSER JOB.
I'm too normal. Nobody would go through all this trouble if it was just about me...
IF WHOEVER IT IS WANTS SOMETHING, IT'D HAVE TO BE FROM YOU.
I DON'T KNOW.
YOU DON'T REMEMBER ANYTHING.
ぽふぽふ
STILL, I CAN'T HELP BUT WONDER...
WHY WOULD SOMEONE HAVE JUST THROWN YOU OUT LIKE THAT?
AND...
I WONDER... WHAT KIND OF PERSON WAS YOUR OWNER?

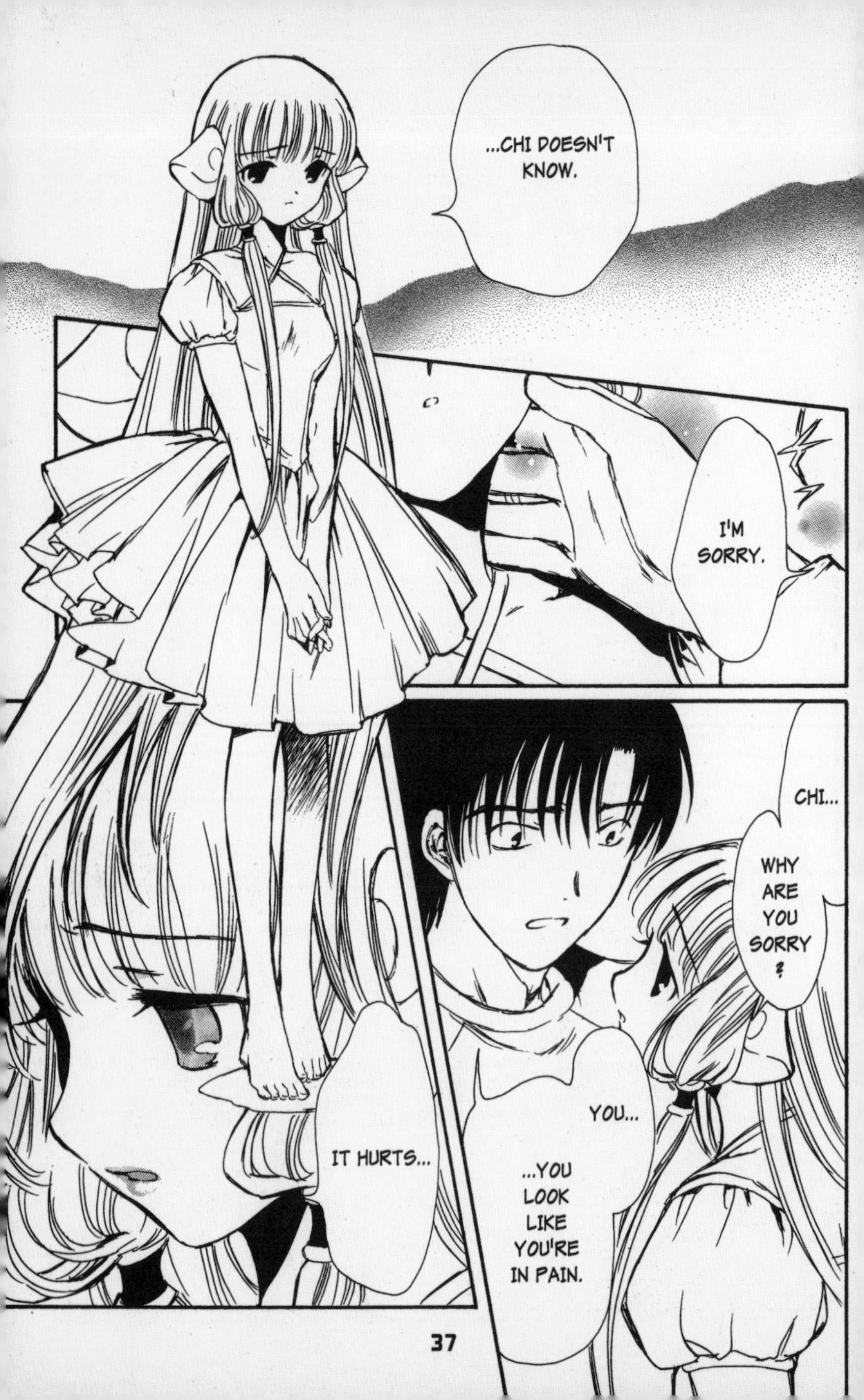
...CHI DOESN'T KNOW.
I'M SORRY.
CHI...
WHY ARE YOU SORRY?
YOU...
...YOU LOOK LIKE YOU'RE IN PAIN.
IT HURTS...

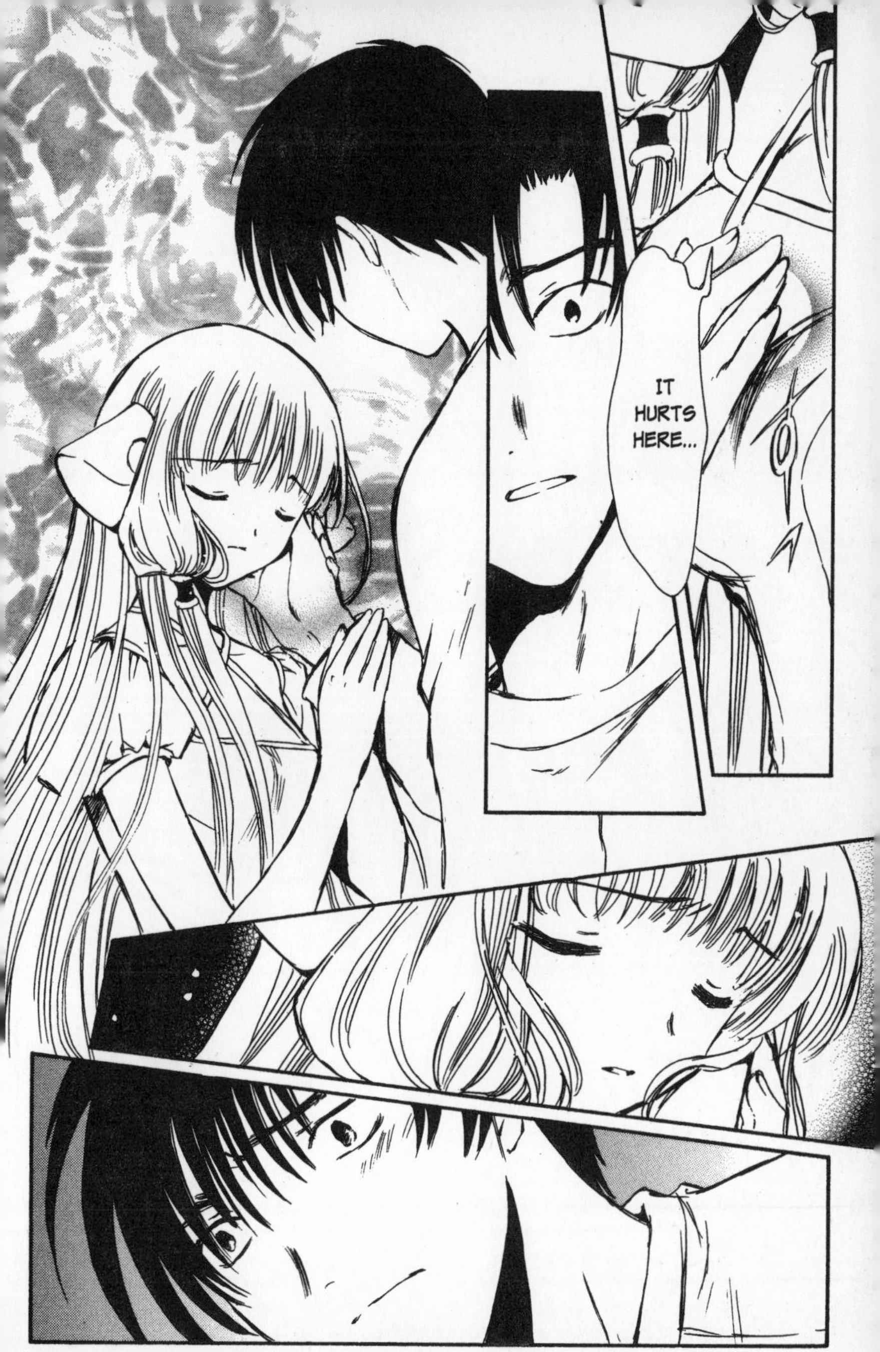
IT HURTS HERE...

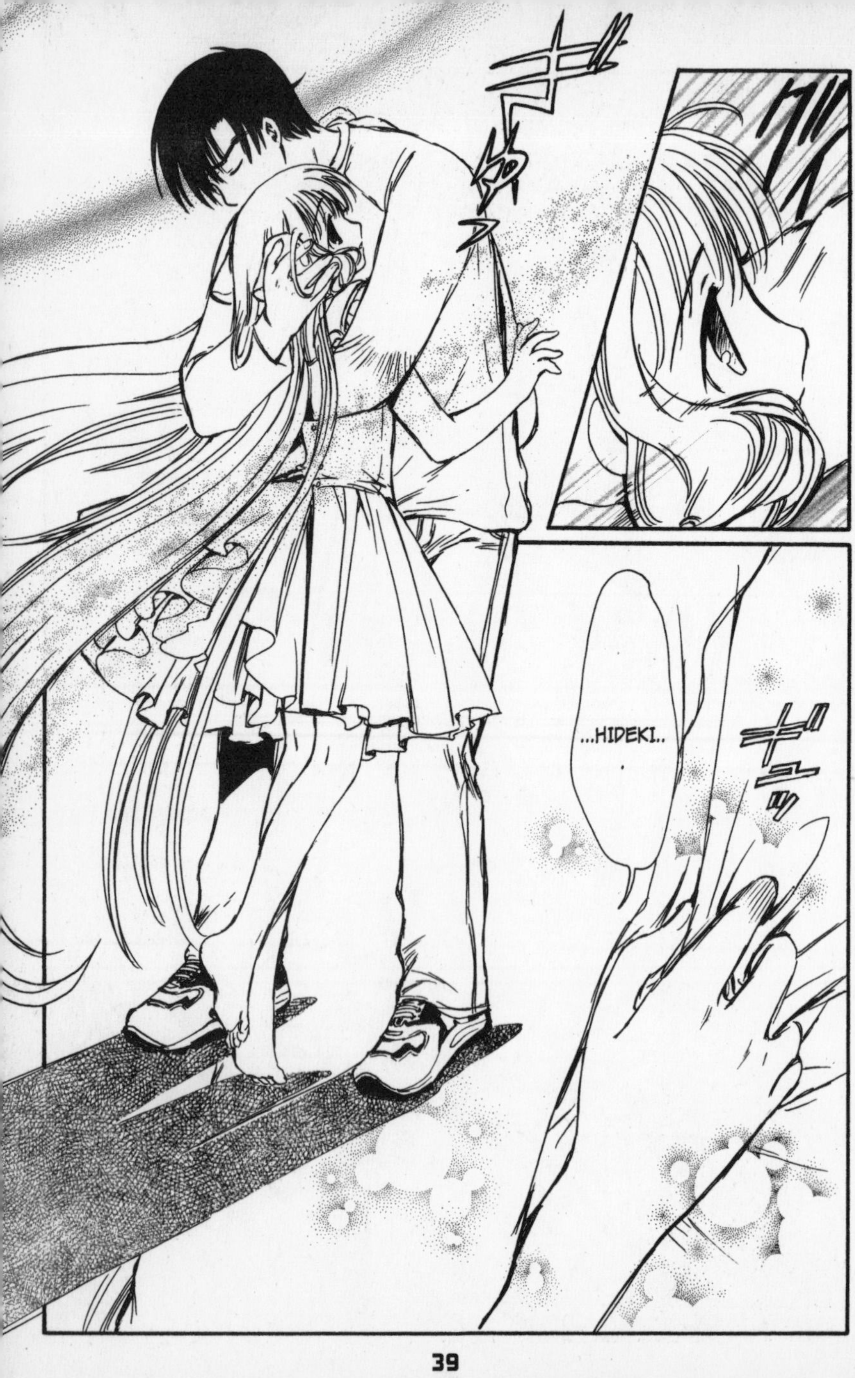
...HIDEKI...

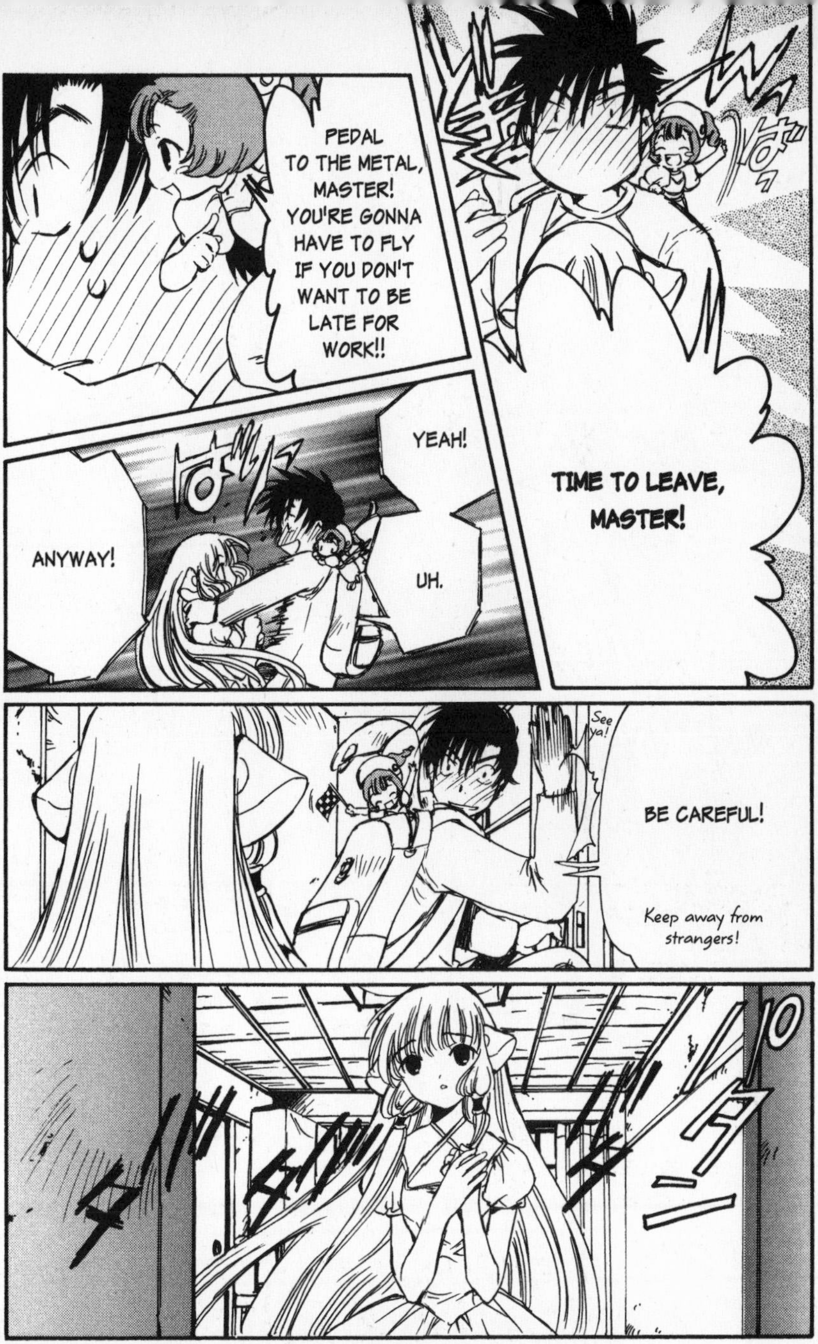
TIME TO LEAVE, MASTER!
PEDAL TO THE METAL, MASTER! YOU'RE GONNA HAVE TO FLY IF YOU DON'T WANT TO BE LATE FOR WORK!!
YEAH!
UH.
ANYWAY!
See ya!
BE CAREFUL!
Keep away from strangers!

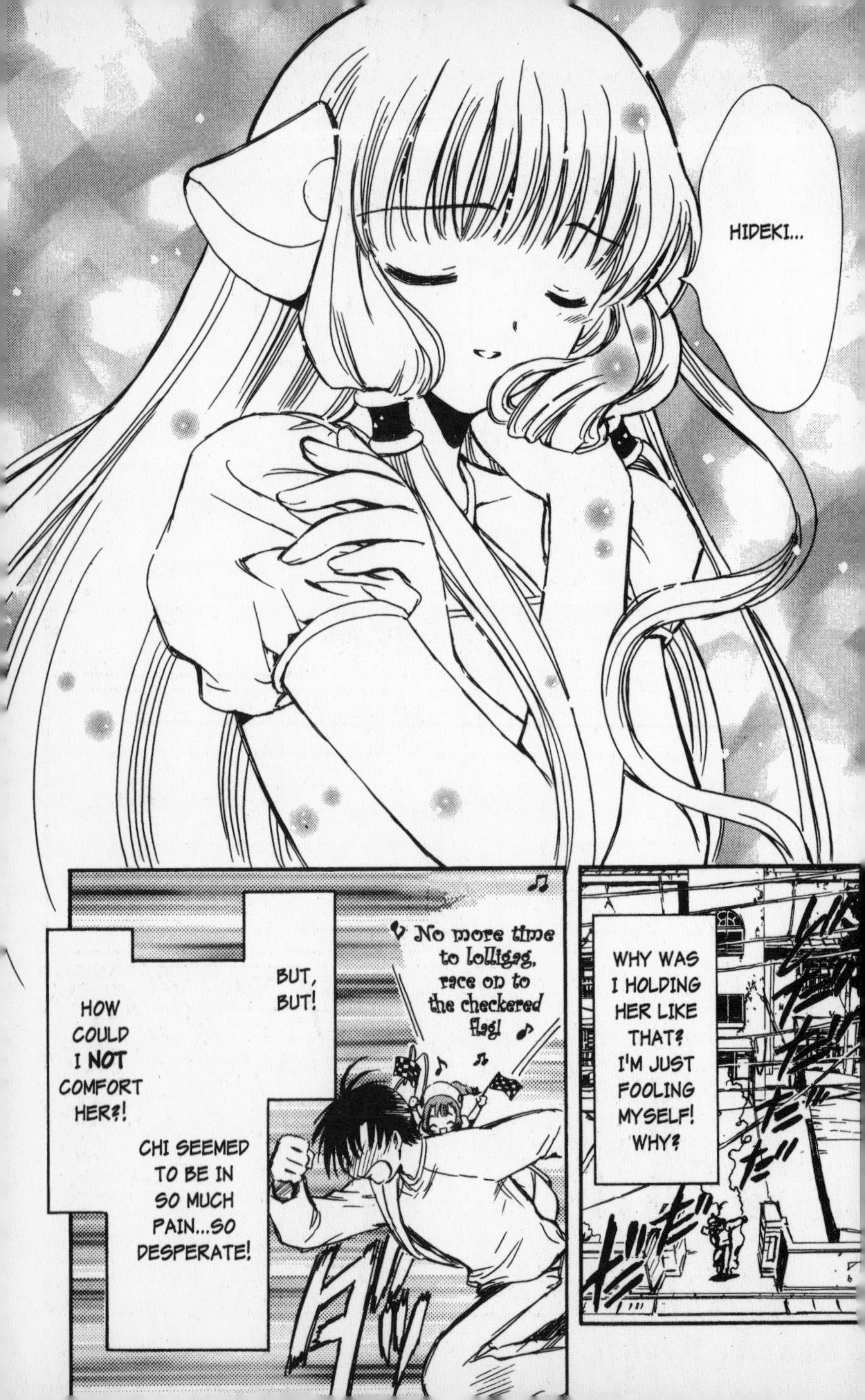
HIDEKI...
WHY WAS I HOLDING HER LIKE THAT? I'M JUST FOOLING MYSELF! WHY?
No more time to lolligag, race on to the checkered flag!
BUT, BUT!
HOW COULD I NOT COMFORT HER?!
CHI SEEMED TO BE IN SO MUCH PAIN...SO DESPERATE!

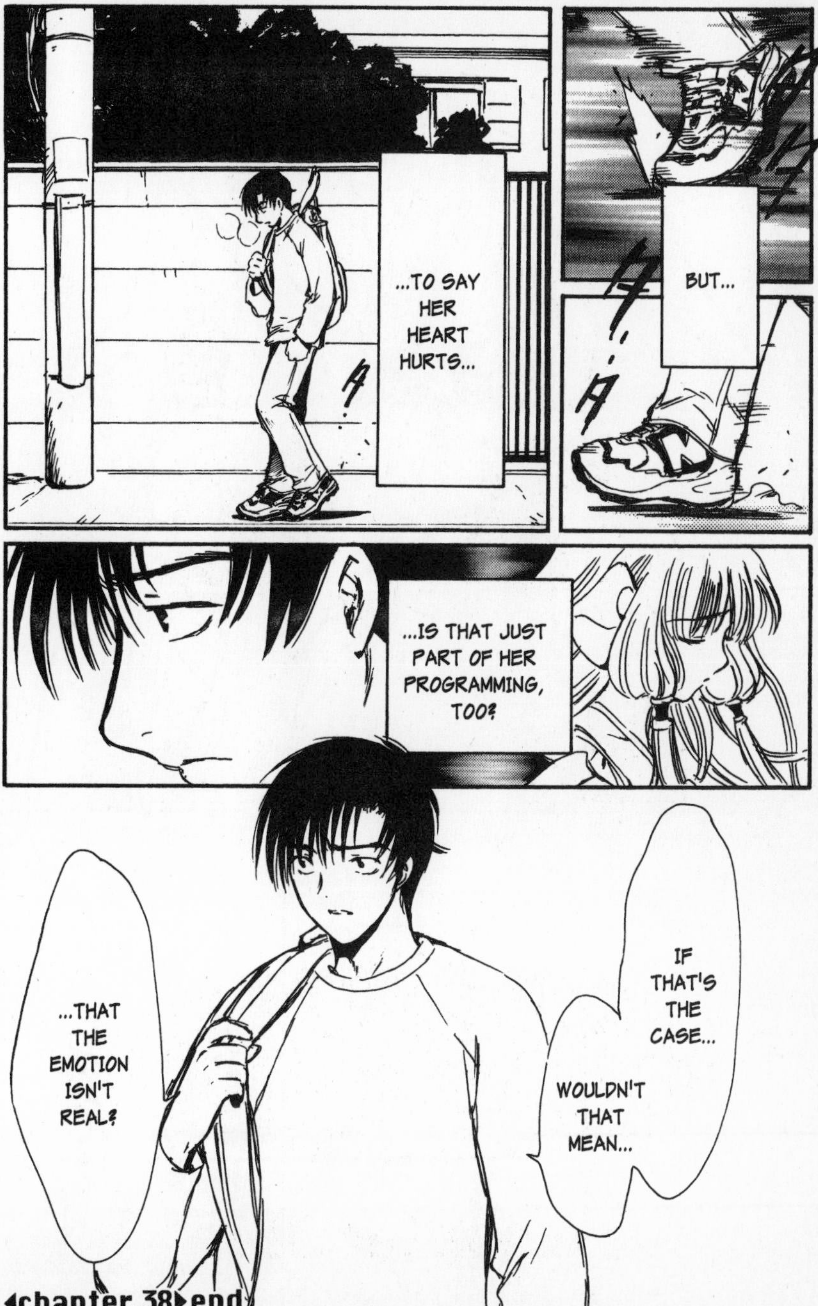
BUT...
...TO SAY HER HEART HURTS...
...IS THAT JUST PART OF HER PROGRAMMING, TOO?
IF THAT'S THE CASE...
WOULDN'T THAT MEAN...
...THAT THE EMOTION ISN'T REAL?

◀chapter..38▶ end

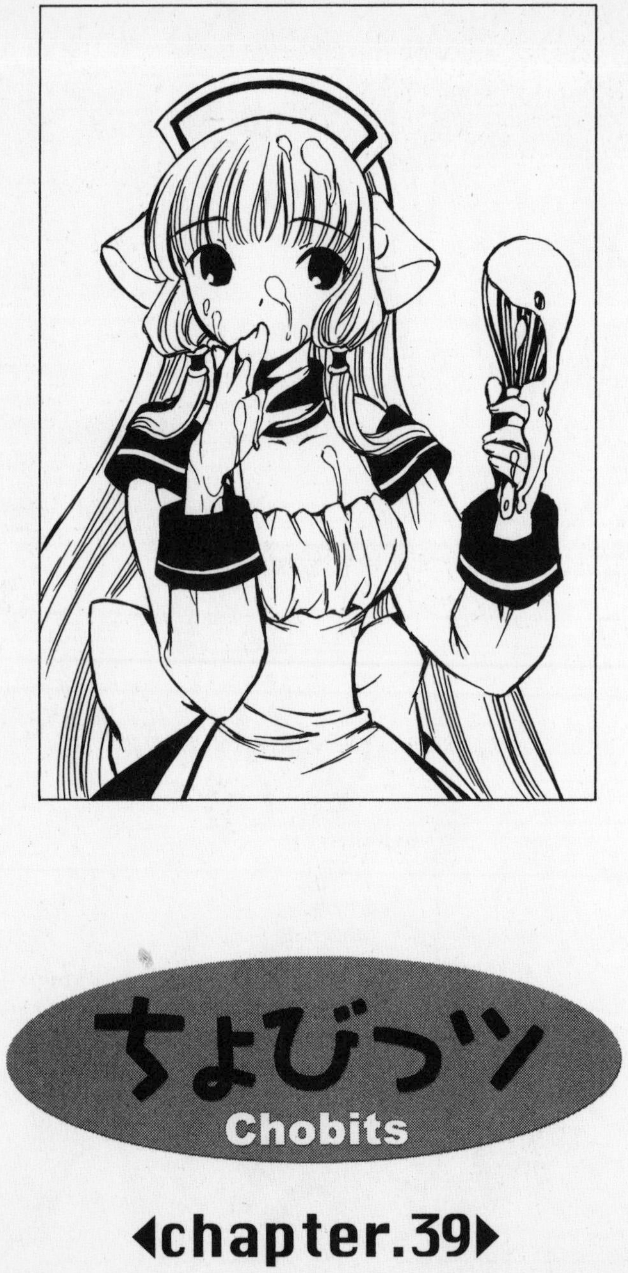

ちょびっツ
Chobits

chapter.39

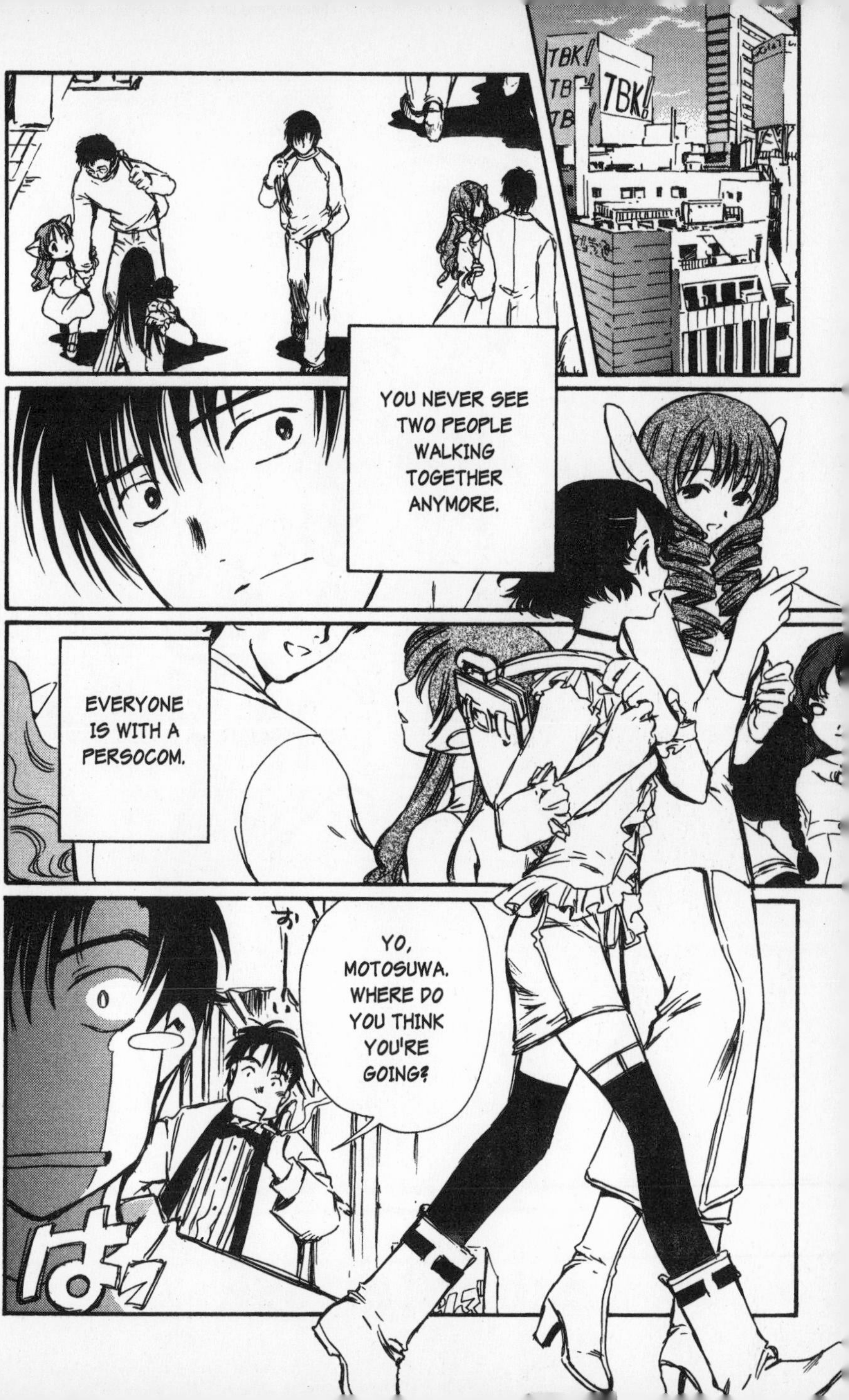
YOU NEVER SEE TWO PEOPLE WALKING TOGETHER ANYMORE.
EVERYONE IS WITH A PERSOCOM.
YO, MOTOSUWA. WHERE DO YOU THINK YOU'RE GOING?
は

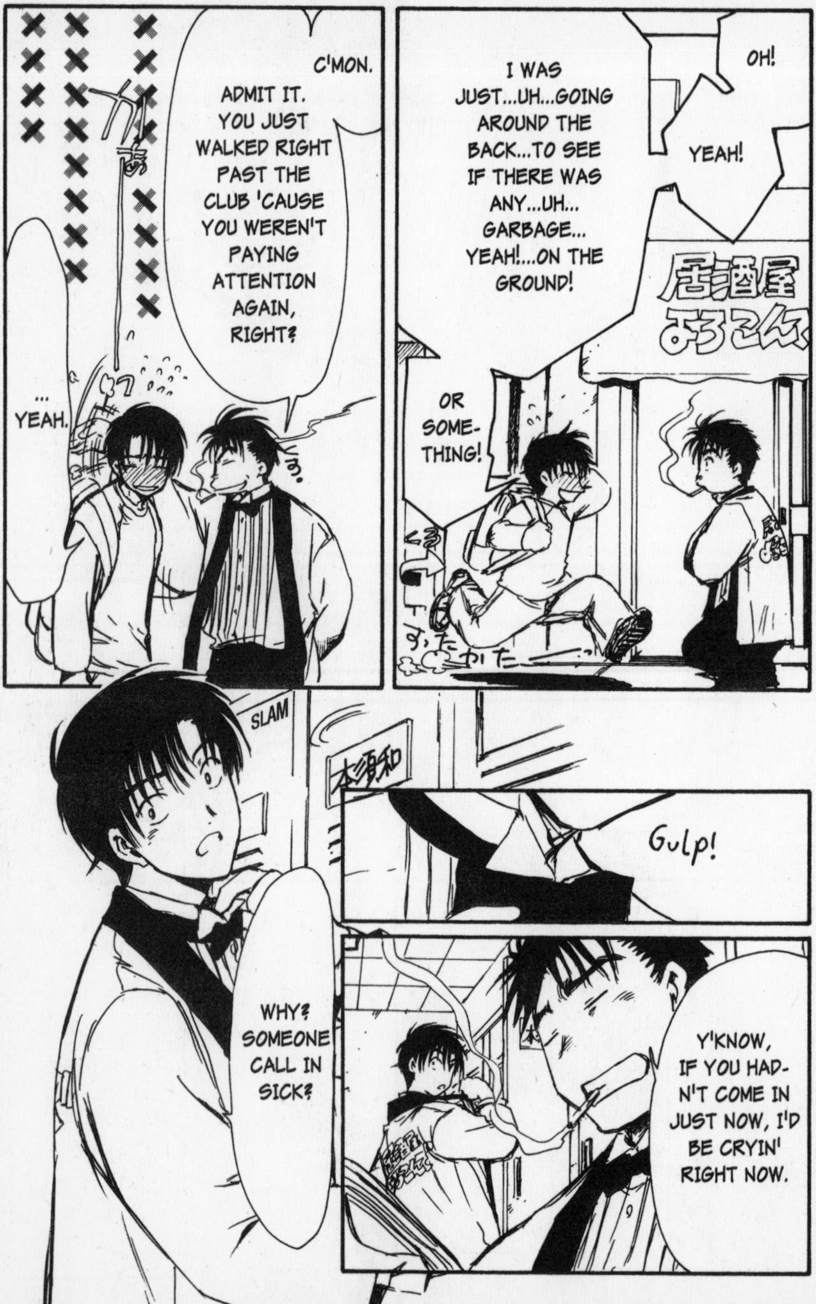
OH!
YEAH!
I WAS JUST...UH...GOING AROUND THE BACK...TO SEE IF THERE WAS ANY...UH... GARBAGE... YEAH!...ON THE GROUND!
居酒屋
OR SOME-THING!
C'MON.
ADMIT IT. YOU JUST WALKED RIGHT PAST THE CLUB 'CAUSE YOU WEREN'T PAYING ATTENTION AGAIN, RIGHT?
... YEAH.
Gulp!
Y'KNOW, IF YOU HAD-N'T COME IN JUST NOW, I'D BE CRYIN' RIGHT NOW.
SLAM
本須和
WHY? SOMEONE CALL IN SICK?

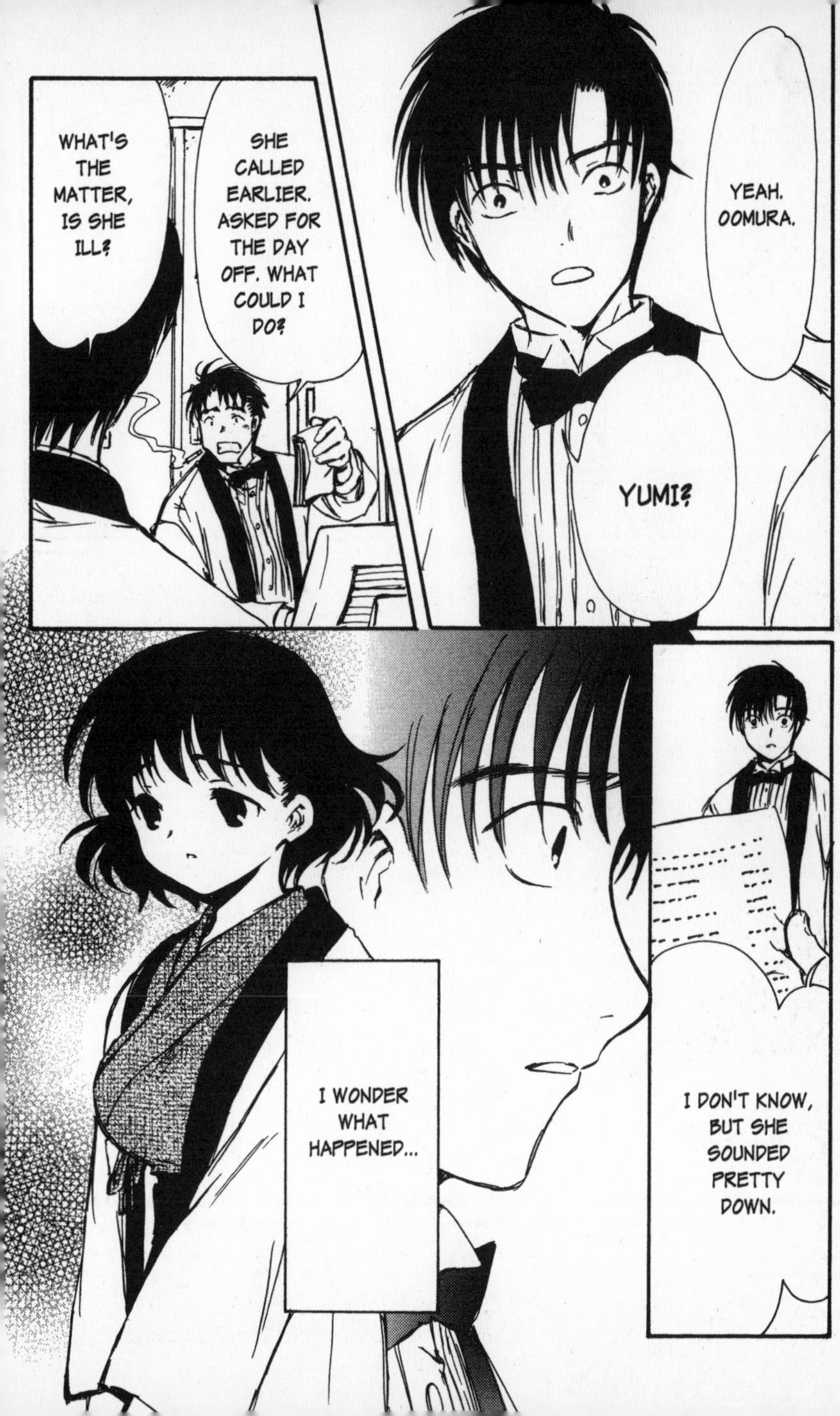
YEAH. OOMURA.
YUMI?
SHE CALLED EARLIER. ASKED FOR THE DAY OFF. WHAT COULD I DO?
WHAT'S THE MATTER, IS SHE ILL?
I DON'T KNOW, BUT SHE SOUNDED PRETTY DOWN.
I WONDER WHAT HAPPENED...

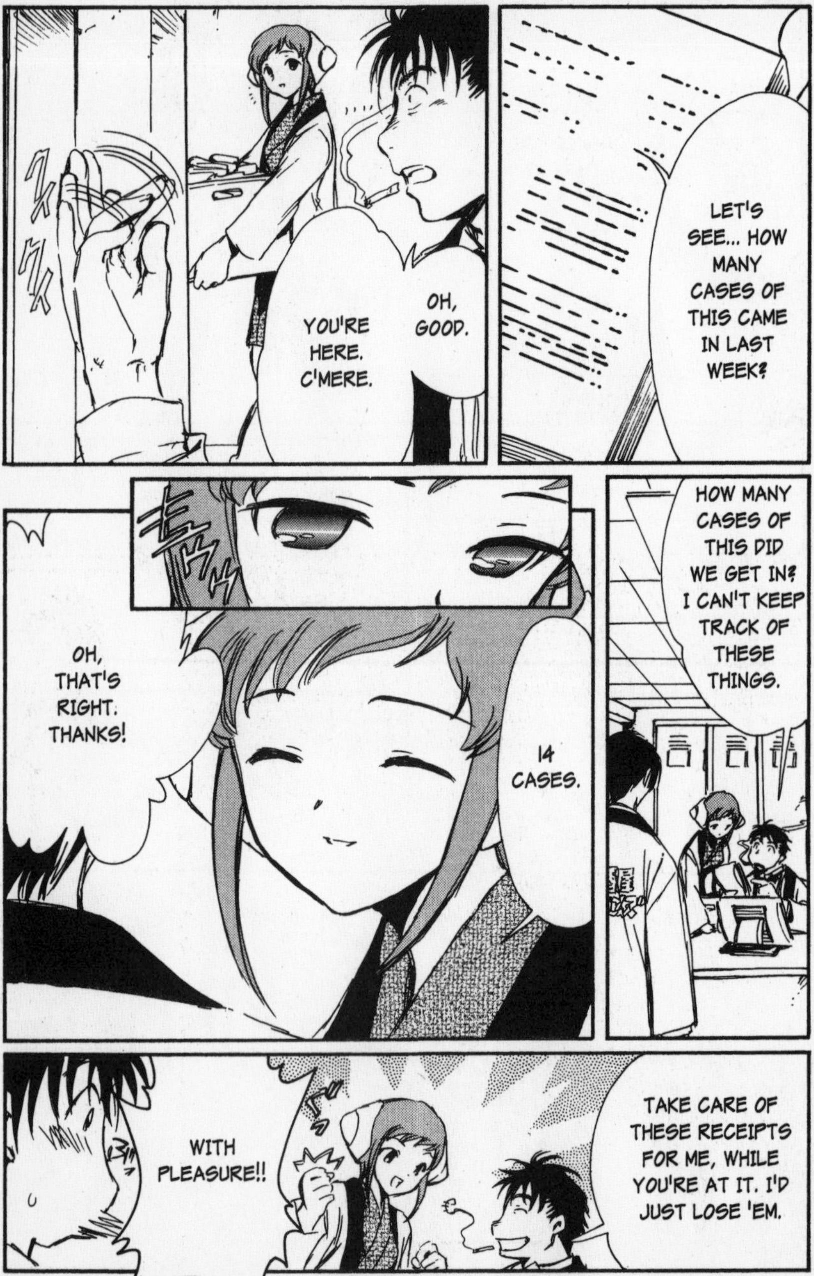
LET'S SEE... HOW MANY CASES OF THIS CAME IN LAST WEEK?
OH, GOOD.
YOU'RE HERE. C'MERE.
HOW MANY CASES OF THIS DID WE GET IN? I CAN'T KEEP TRACK OF THESE THINGS.
14 CASES.
OH, THAT'S RIGHT. THANKS!
TAKE CARE OF THESE RECEIPTS FOR ME, WHILE YOU'RE AT IT. I'D JUST LOSE 'EM.
WITH PLEASURE!!

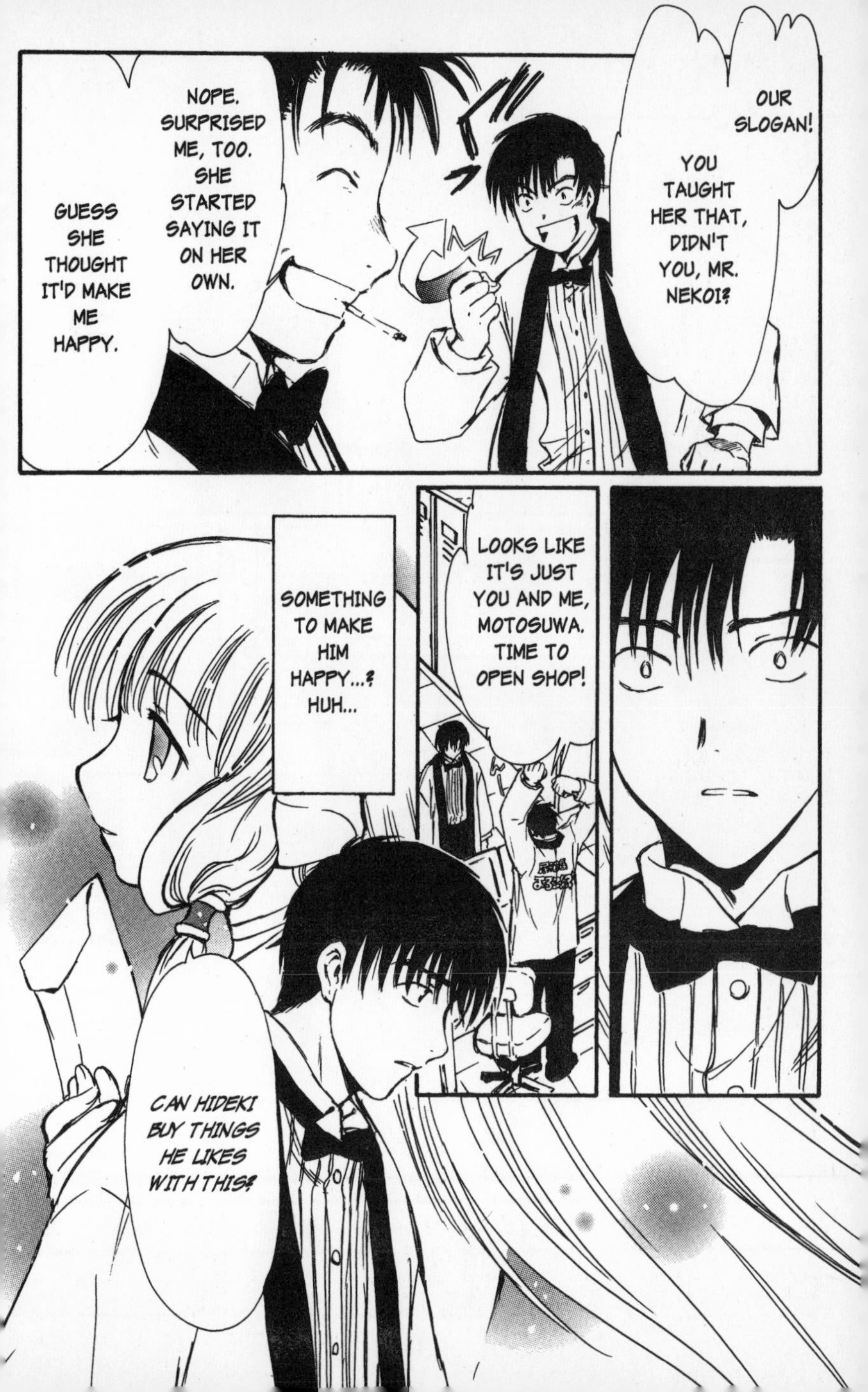
OUR SLOGAN!
YOU TAUGHT HER THAT, DIDN'T YOU, MR. NEKOI?
NOPE. SURPRISED ME, TOO. SHE STARTED SAYING IT ON HER OWN.
GUESS SHE THOUGHT IT'D MAKE ME HAPPY.
LOOKS LIKE IT'S JUST YOU AND ME, MOTOSUWA. TIME TO OPEN SHOP!
SOMETHING TO MAKE HIM HAPPY...? HUH...
CAN HIDEKI BUY THINGS HE LIKES WITH THIS?

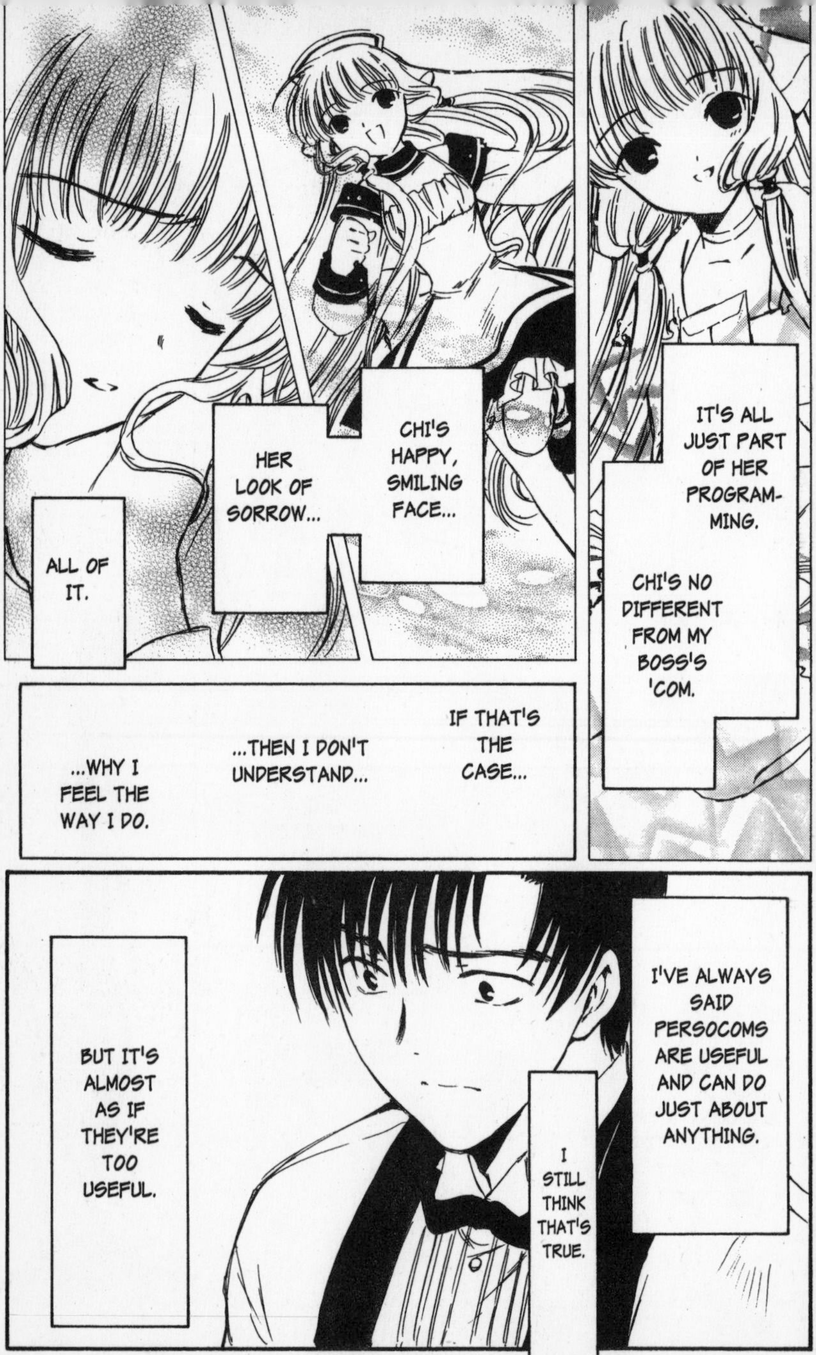
IT'S ALL JUST PART OF HER PROGRAMMING.
CHI'S NO DIFFERENT FROM MY BOSS'S 'COM.
CHI'S HAPPY, SMILING FACE...
HER LOOK OF SORROW...
ALL OF IT.
IF THAT'S THE CASE...
...THEN I DON'T UNDERSTAND...
...WHY I FEEL THE WAY I DO.
I'VE ALWAYS SAID PERSOCOMS ARE USEFUL AND CAN DO JUST ABOUT ANYTHING.
I STILL THINK THAT'S TRUE.
BUT IT'S ALMOST AS IF THEY'RE TOO USEFUL.

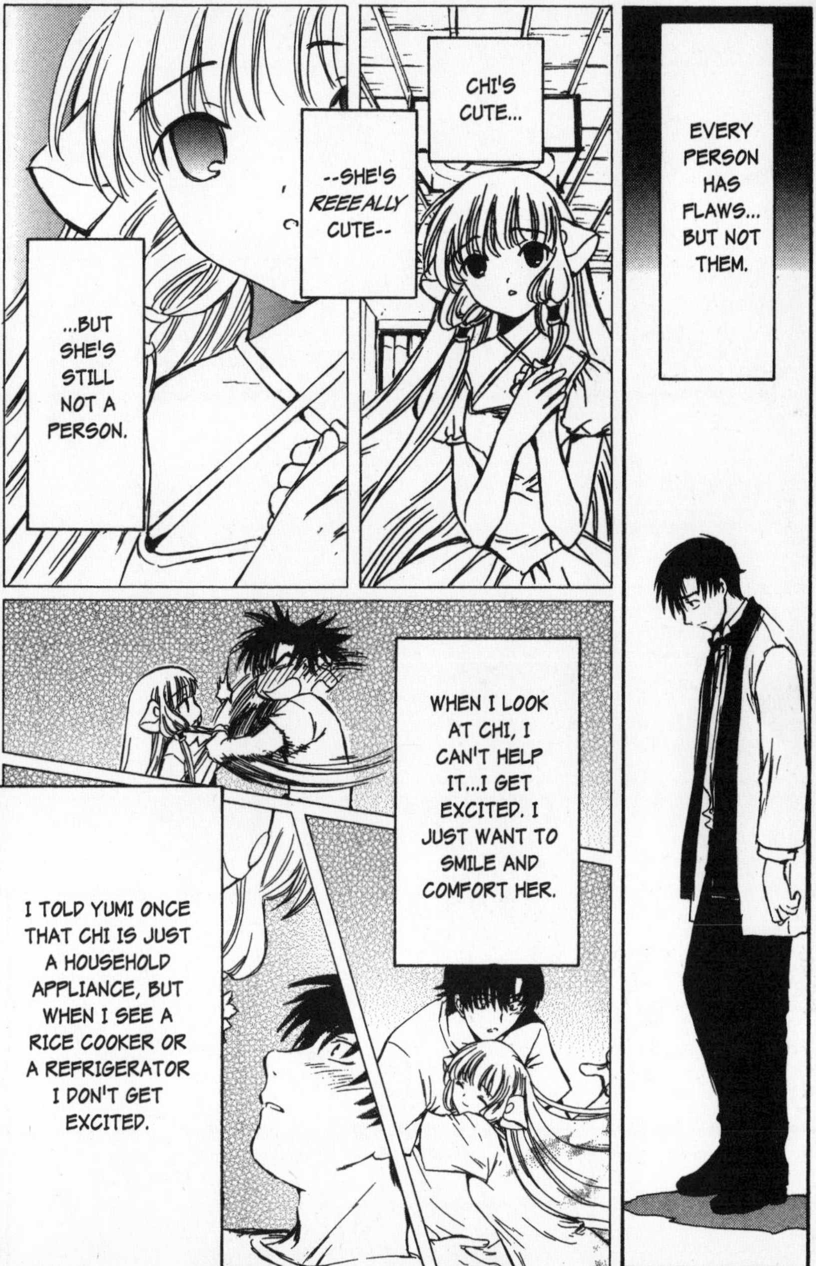
EVERY PERSON HAS FLAWS... BUT NOT THEM.
CHI'S CUTE...
--SHE'S *REEEALLY* CUTE--
...BUT SHE'S STILL NOT A PERSON.
WHEN I LOOK AT CHI, I CAN'T HELP IT...I GET EXCITED. I JUST WANT TO SMILE AND COMFORT HER.
I TOLD YUMI ONCE THAT CHI IS JUST A HOUSEHOLD APPLIANCE, BUT WHEN I SEE A RICE COOKER OR A REFRIGERATOR I DON'T GET EXCITED.

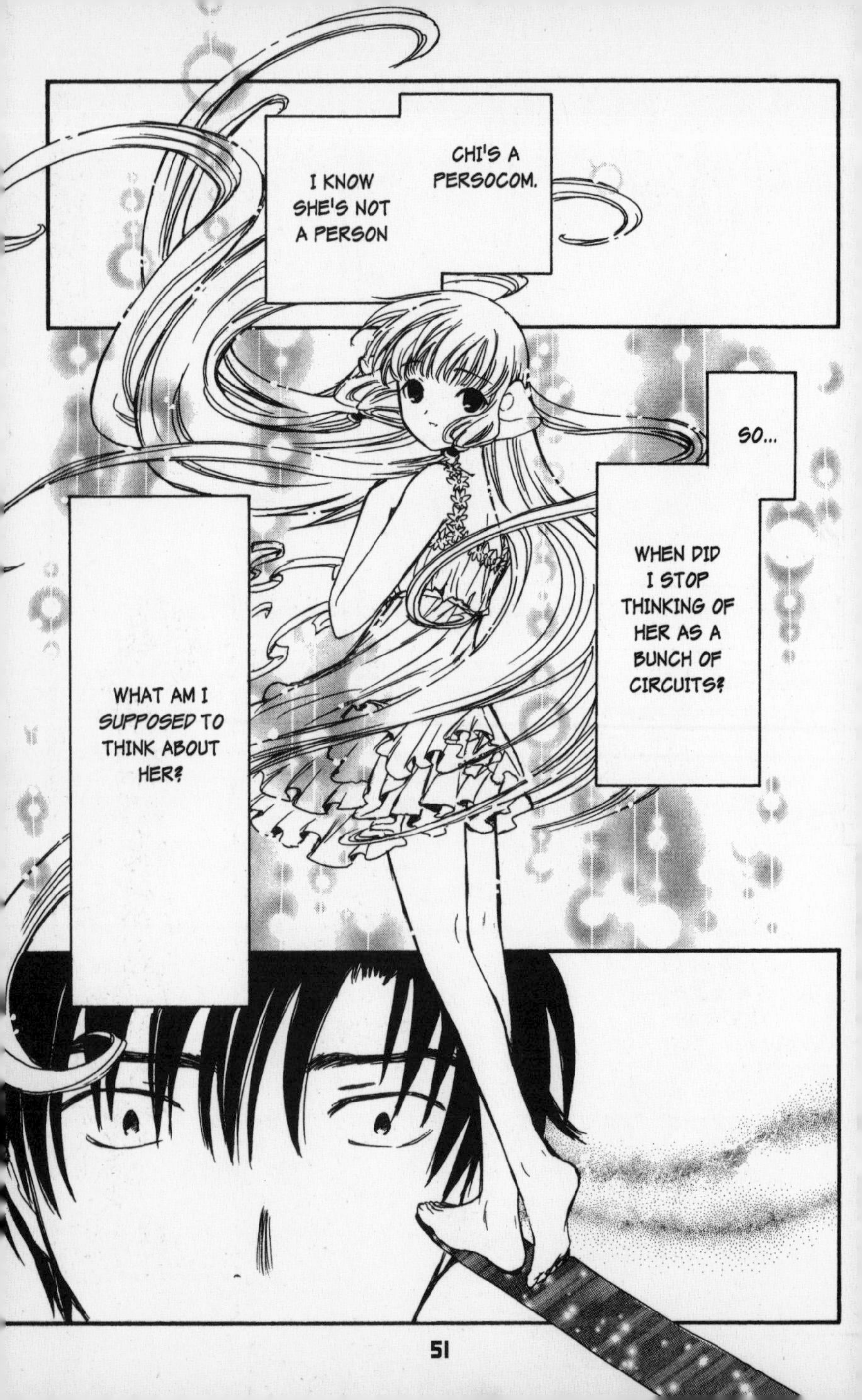
CHI'S A PERSOCOM.
I KNOW SHE'S NOT A PERSON
SO...
WHEN DID I STOP THINKING OF HER AS A BUNCH OF CIRCUITS?
WHAT AM I SUPPOSED TO THINK ABOUT HER?

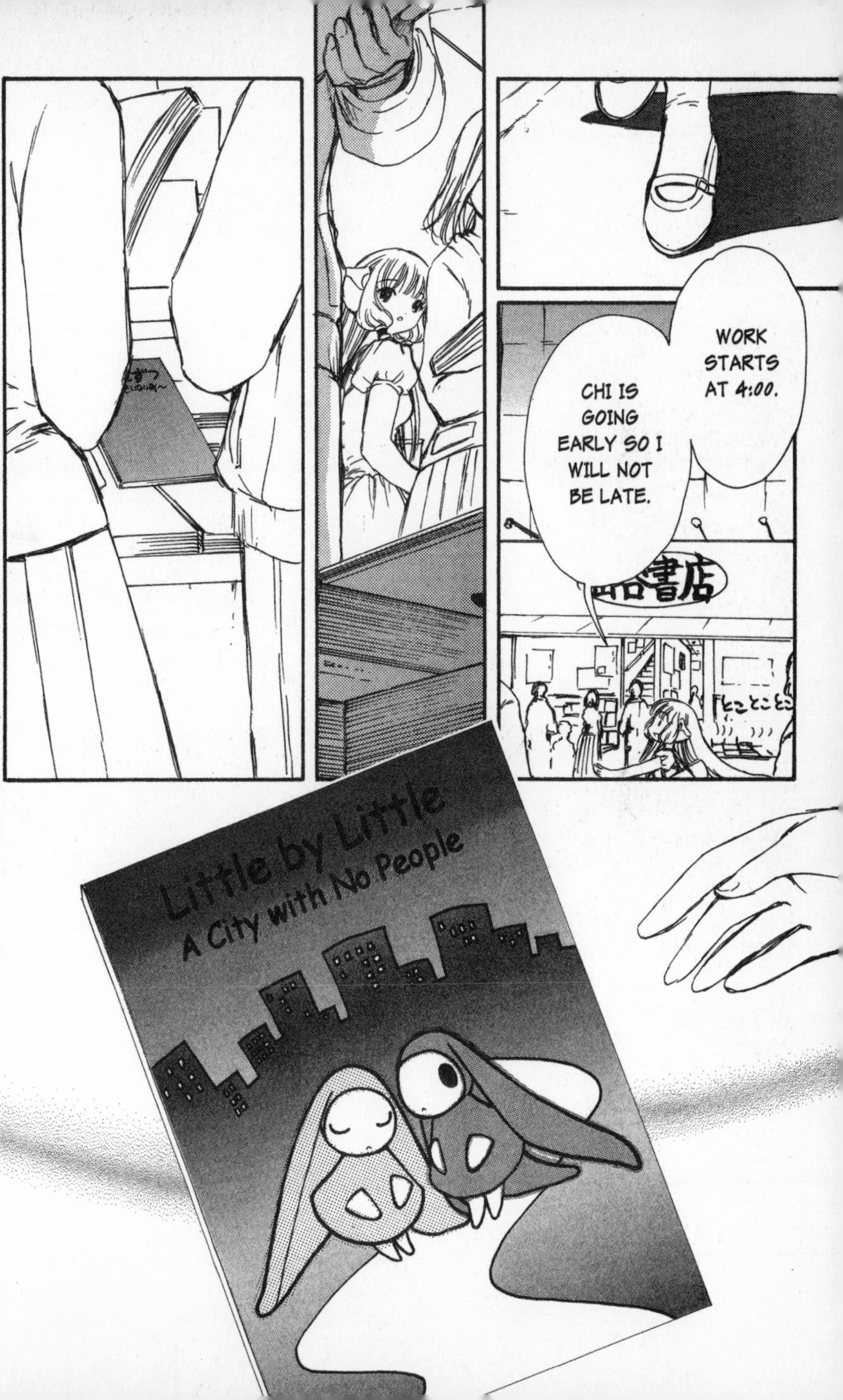
WORK STARTS AT 4:00.
CHI IS GOING EARLY SO I WILL NOT BE LATE.
書店
とことこと
Little by Little
A City with No People

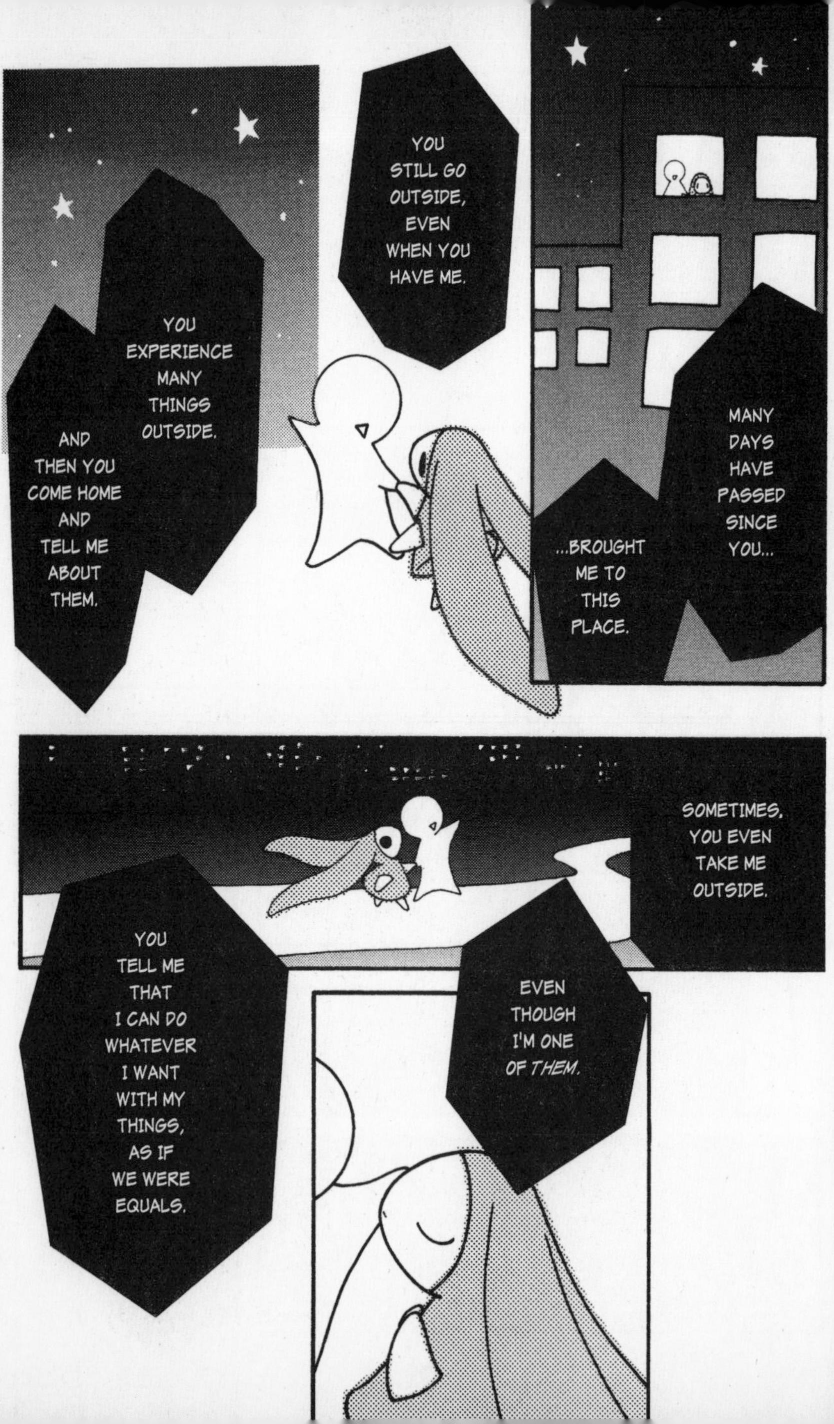
MANY DAYS HAVE PASSED SINCE YOU...
...BROUGHT ME TO THIS PLACE.
YOU STILL GO OUTSIDE, EVEN WHEN YOU HAVE ME.
YOU EXPERIENCE MANY THINGS OUTSIDE.
AND THEN YOU COME HOME AND TELL ME ABOUT THEM.
SOMETIMES, YOU EVEN TAKE ME OUTSIDE.
YOU TELL ME THAT I CAN DO WHATEVER I WANT WITH MY THINGS, AS IF WE WERE EQUALS.
EVEN THOUGH I'M ONE OF *THEM*.

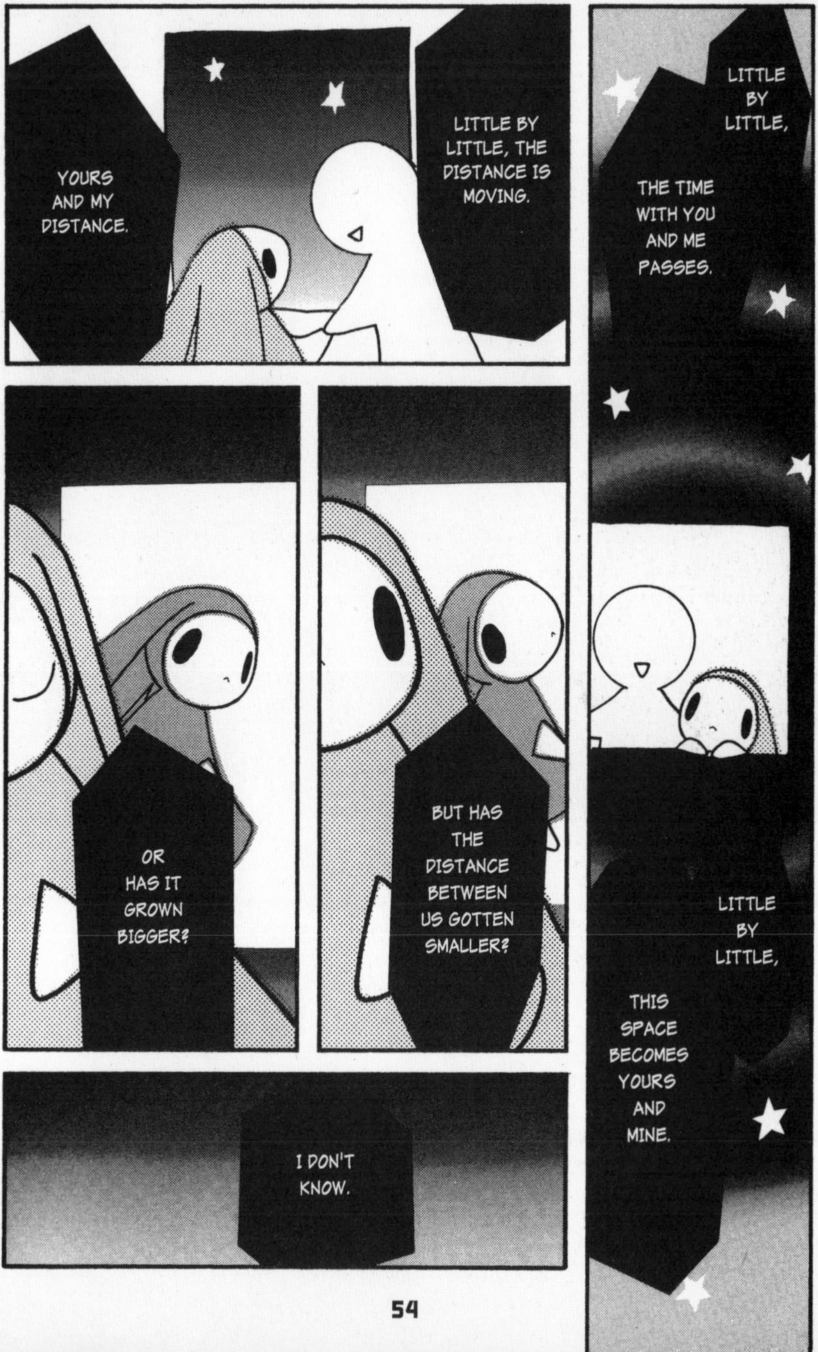
LITTLE BY LITTLE,
THE TIME WITH YOU AND ME PASSES.
LITTLE BY LITTLE,
THIS SPACE BECOMES YOURS AND MINE.
LITTLE BY LITTLE, THE DISTANCE IS MOVING.
YOURS AND MY DISTANCE.
BUT HAS THE DISTANCE BETWEEN US GOTTEN SMALLER?
OR HAS IT GROWN BIGGER?
I DON'T KNOW.

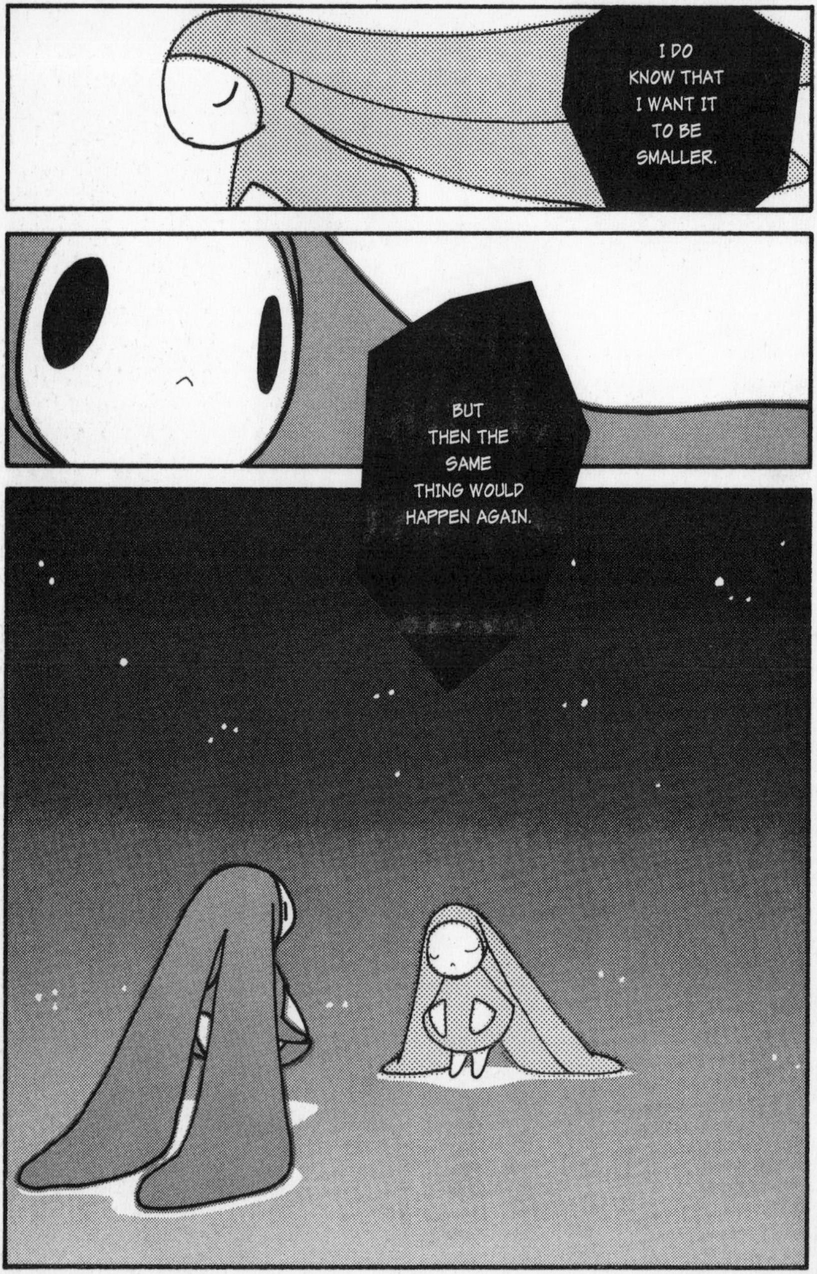
I DO KNOW THAT I WANT IT TO BE SMALLER.
BUT THEN THE SAME THING WOULD HAPPEN AGAIN.

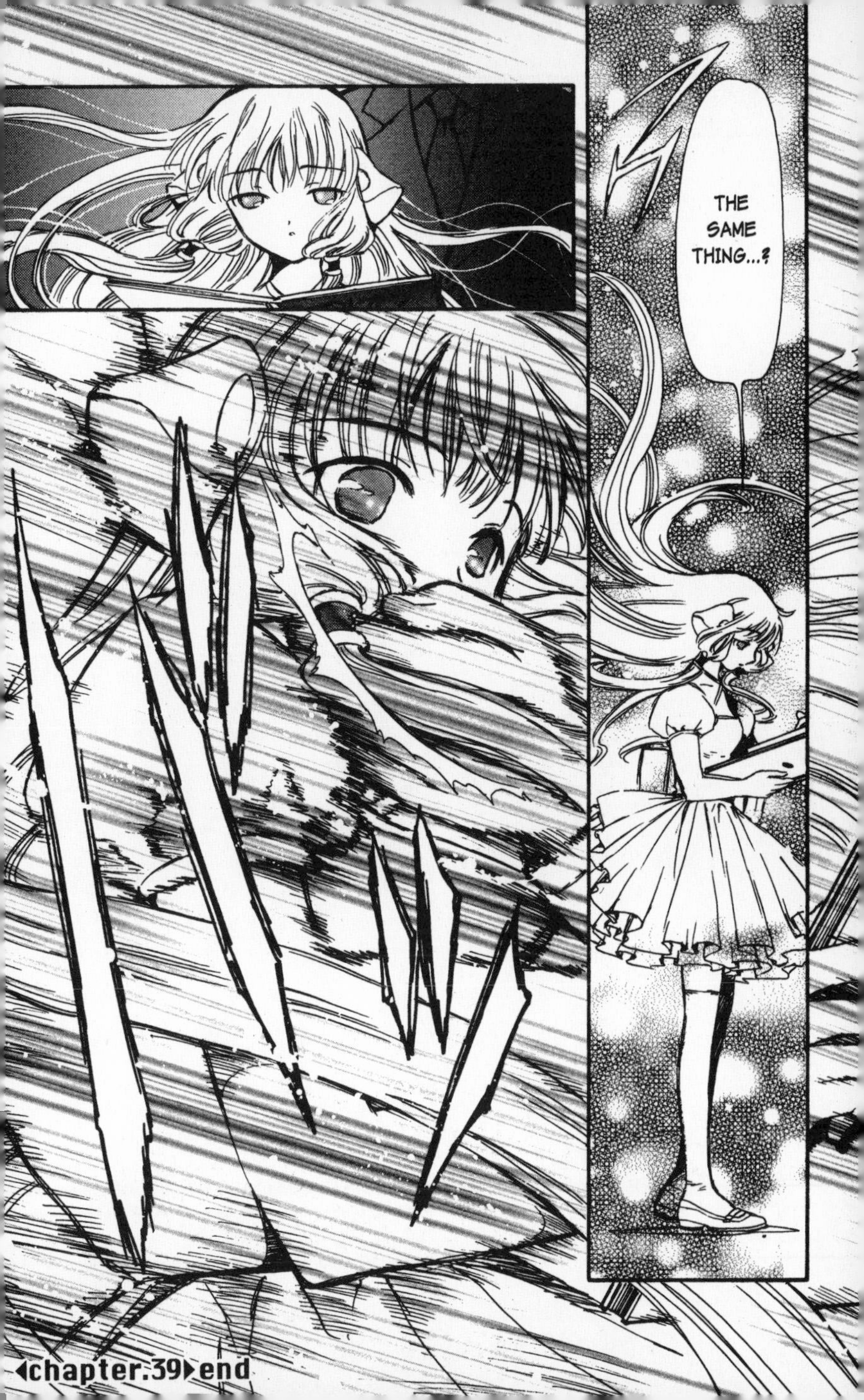
THE SAME THING...?
chapter.39 end

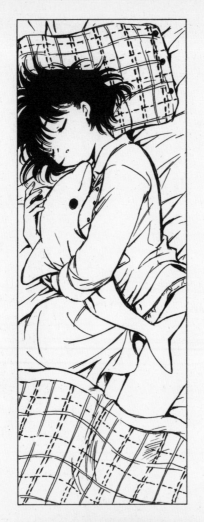

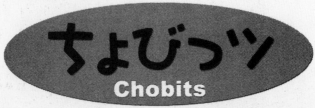

ちょびっツ
Chobits

◀chapter.40▶

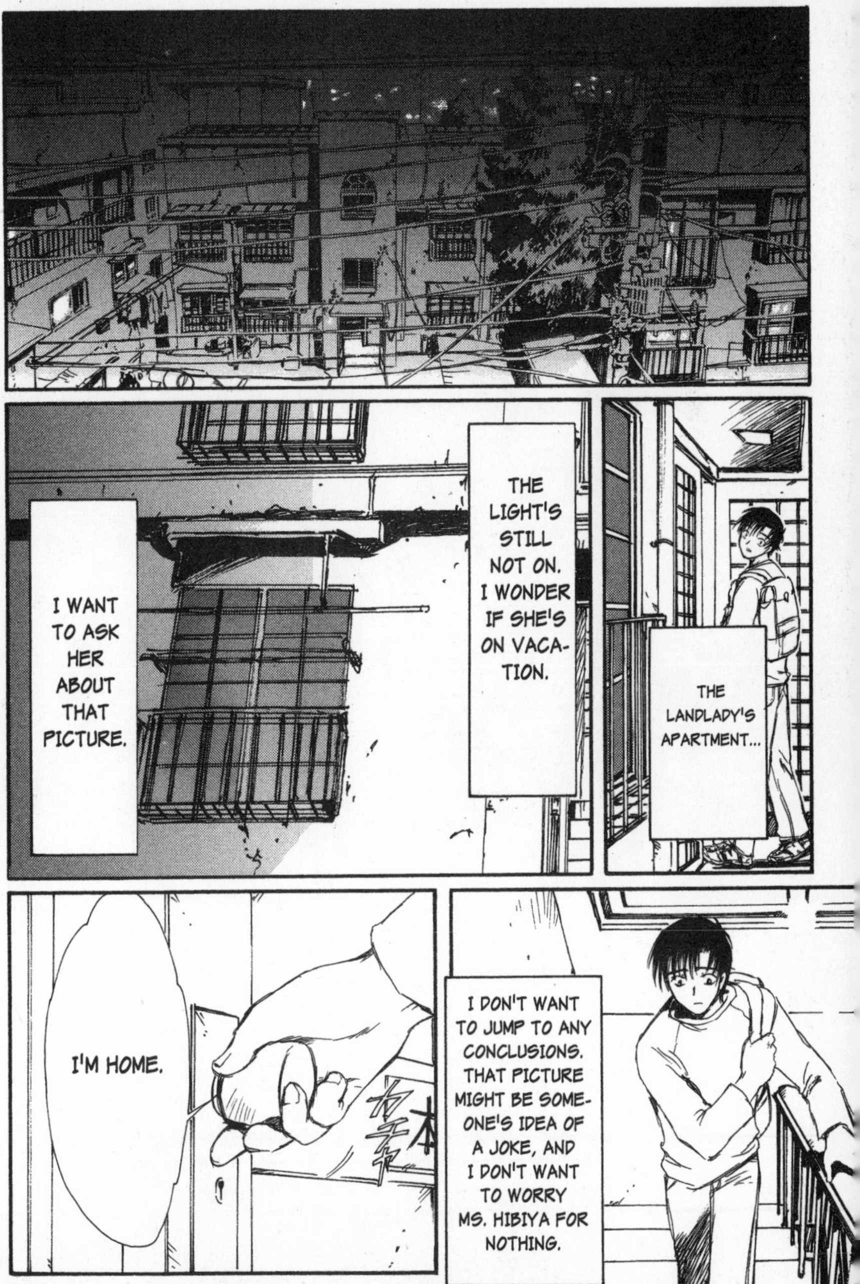
THE LANDLADY'S APARTMENT...
THE LIGHT'S STILL NOT ON. I WONDER IF SHE'S ON VACA- TION.
I WANT TO ASK HER ABOUT THAT PICTURE.
I DON'T WANT TO JUMP TO ANY CONCLUSIONS. THAT PICTURE MIGHT BE SOME- ONE'S IDEA OF A JOKE, AND I DON'T WANT TO WORRY MS. HIBIYA FOR NOTHING.
カチャ
I'M HOME.

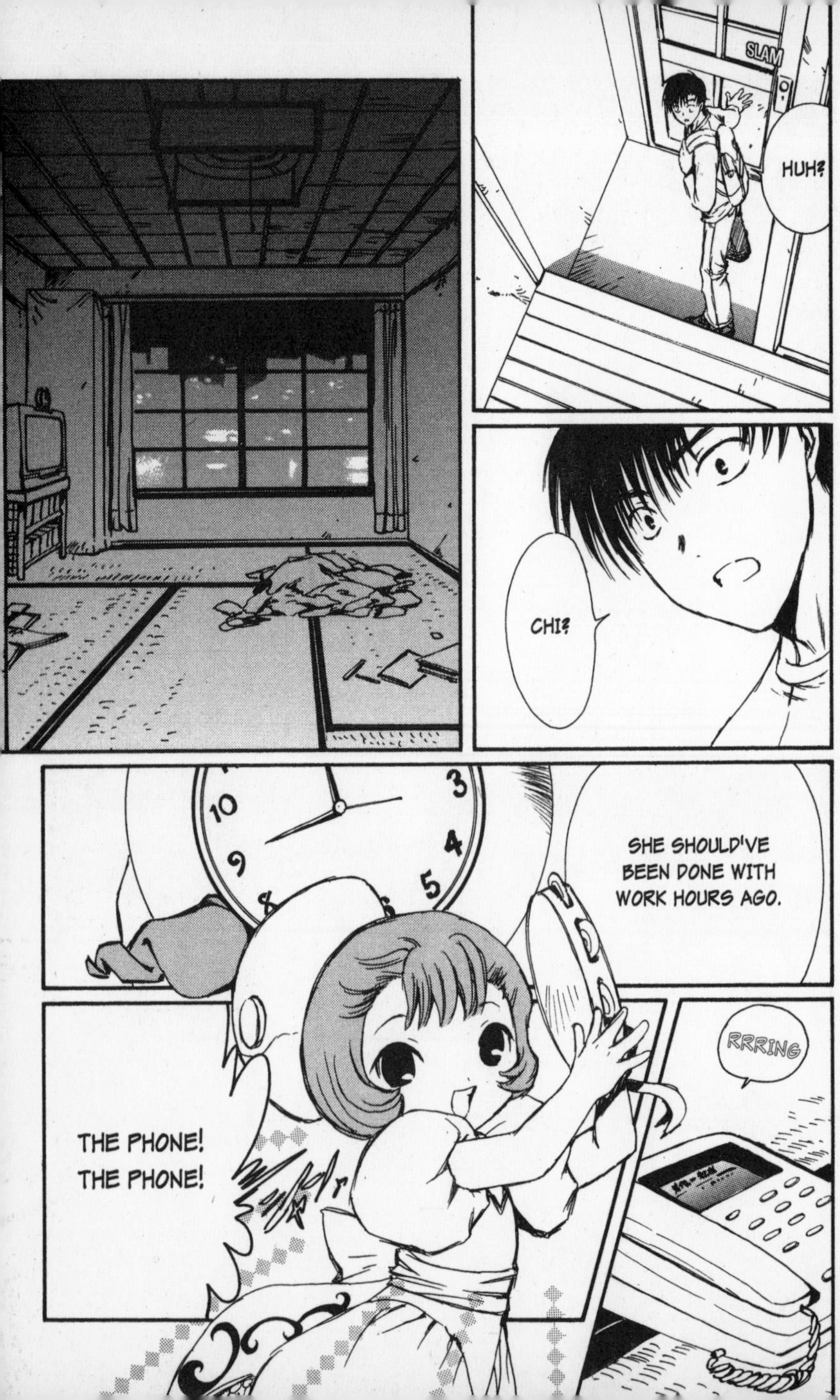
SLAM
HUH?
CHI?
SHE SHOULD'VE BEEN DONE WITH WORK HOURS AGO.
RRRING
THE PHONE! THE PHONE!

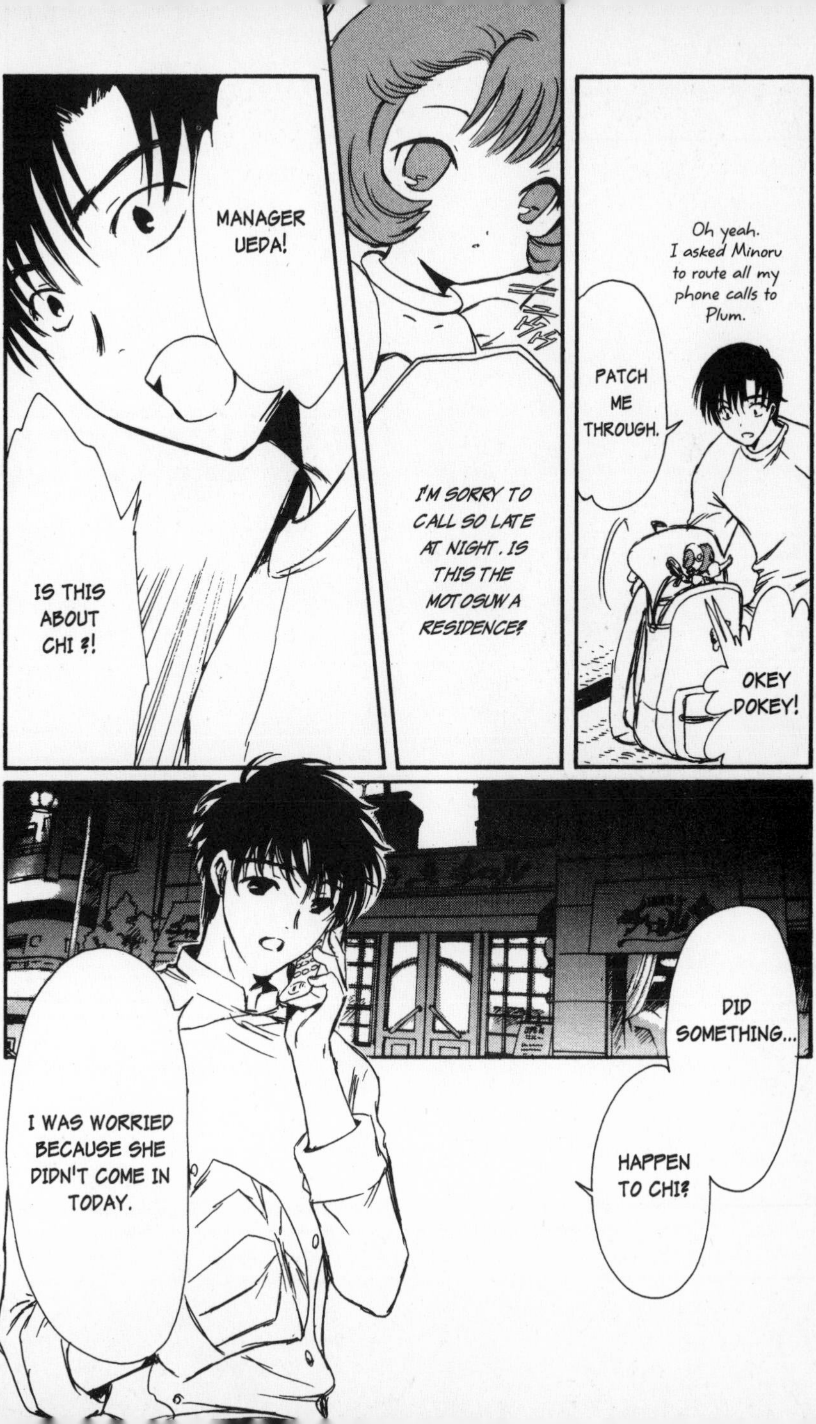

Oh yeah. I asked Minoru to route all my phone calls to Plum.
PATCH ME THROUGH.
OKEY DOKEY!
I'M SORRY TO CALL SO LATE AT NIGHT. IS THIS THE MOTOSUWA RESIDENCE?
MANAGER UEDA!
IS THIS ABOUT CHI ?!
DID SOMETHING...
HAPPEN TO CHI?
I WAS WORRIED BECAUSE SHE DIDN'T COME IN TODAY.

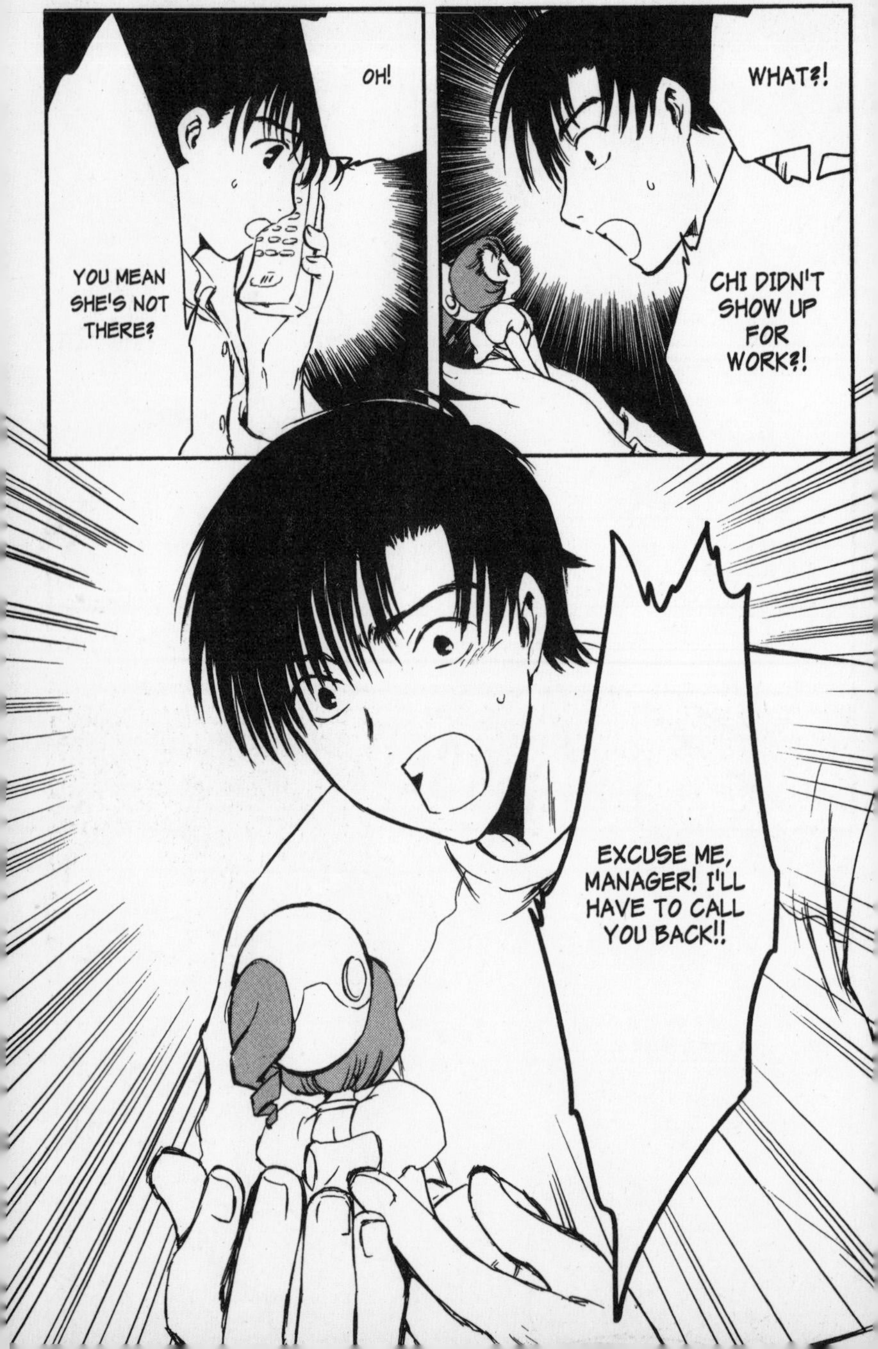
WHAT?!
CHI DIDN'T SHOW UP FOR WORK?!
OH!
YOU MEAN SHE'S NOT THERE?
EXCUSE ME, MANAGER! I'LL HAVE TO CALL YOU BACK!!

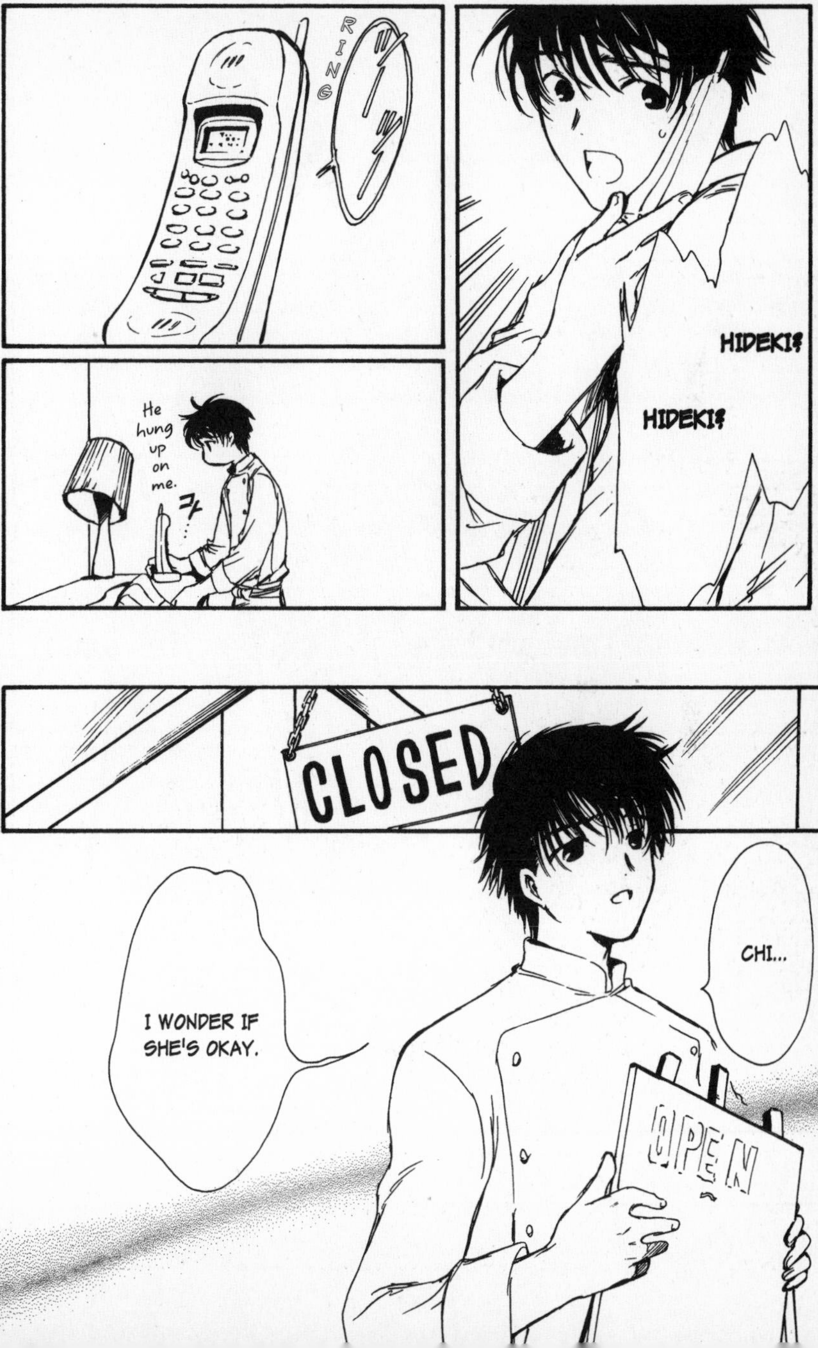
HIDEKI?
HIDEKI?
RING
He hung up on me.
CLOSED
CHI...
I WONDER IF SHE'S OKAY.
OPEN

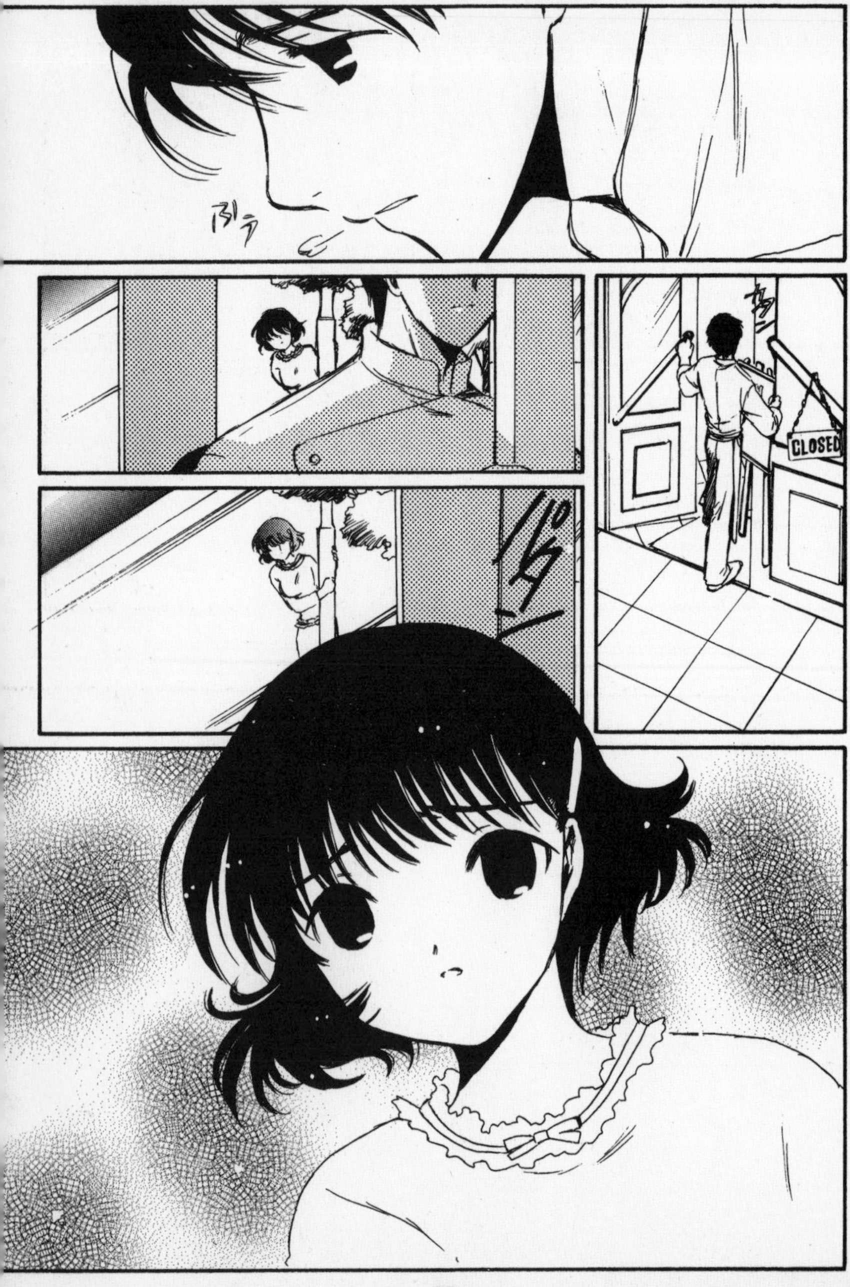
CLOSED

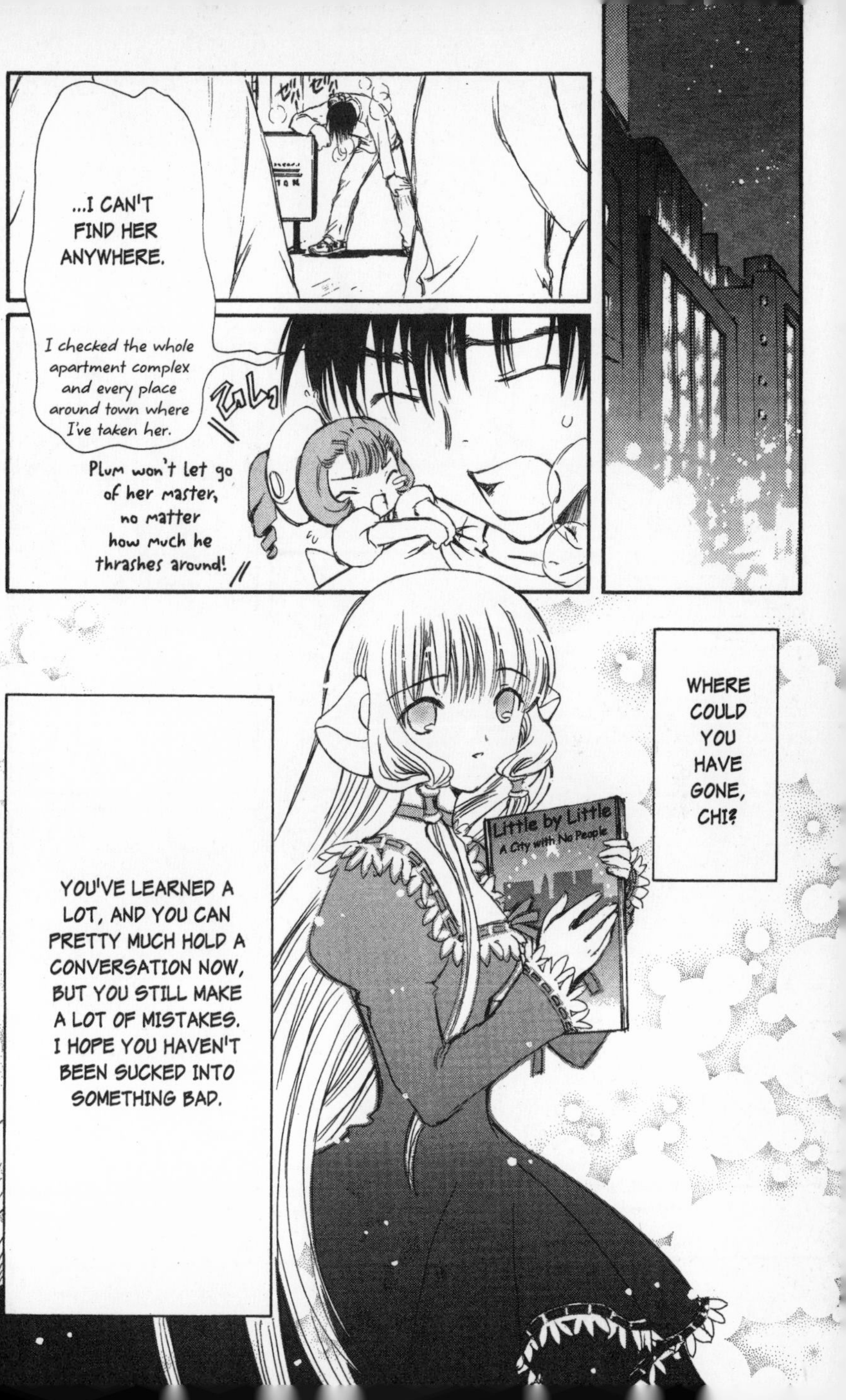
...I CAN'T FIND HER ANYWHERE.
I checked the whole apartment complex and every place around town where I've taken her.
Plum won't let go of her master, no matter how much he thrashes around!
WHERE COULD YOU HAVE GONE, CHI?
Little by Little
A City with No People
YOU'VE LEARNED A LOT, AND YOU CAN PRETTY MUCH HOLD A CONVERSATION NOW, BUT YOU STILL MAKE A LOT OF MISTAKES. I HOPE YOU HAVEN'T BEEN SUCKED INTO SOMETHING BAD.

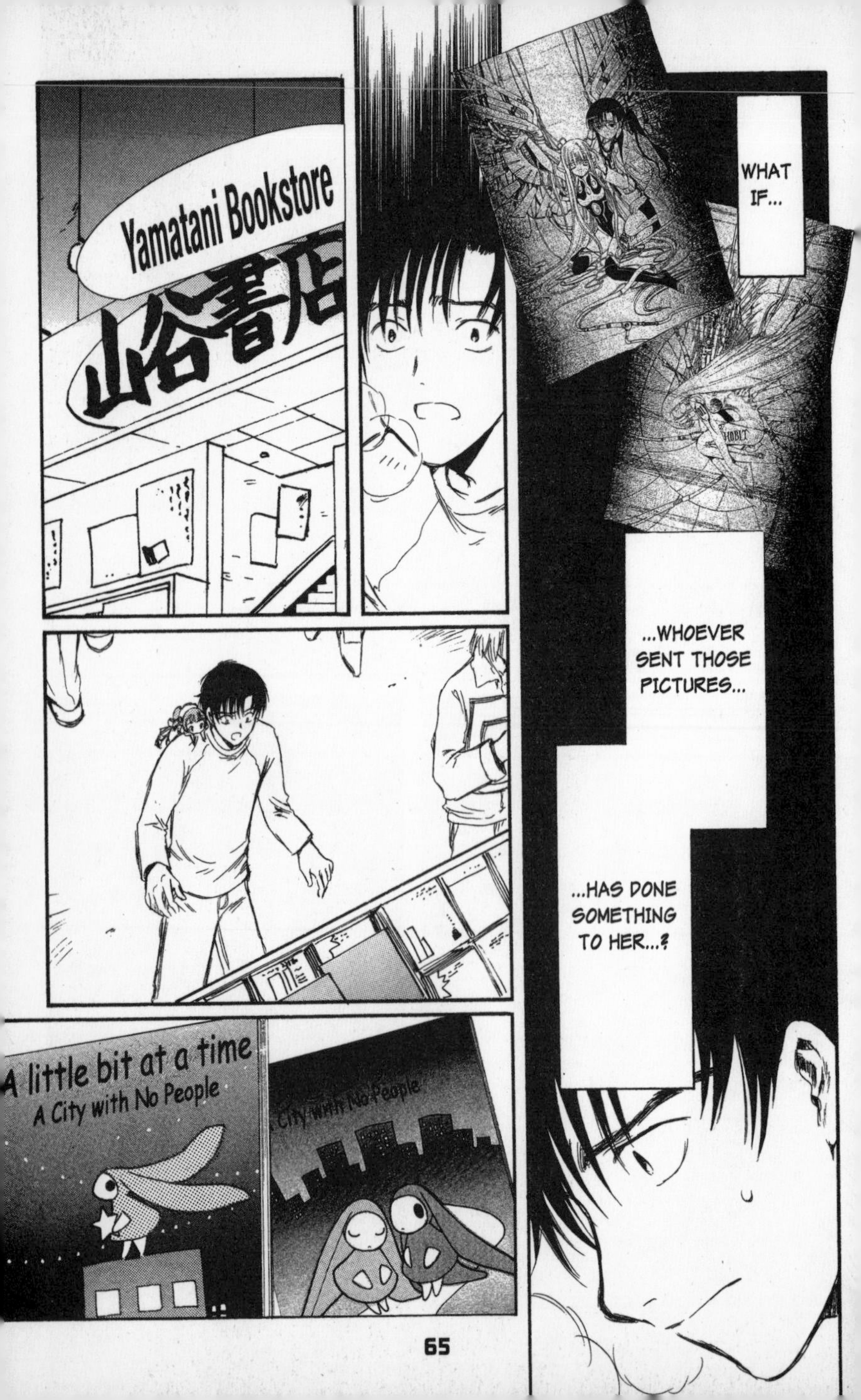
WHAT IF...
...WHOEVER SENT THOSE PICTURES...
...HAS DONE SOMETHING TO HER...?
Yamatani Bookstore
山谷書店
City with No People
A little bit at a time
A City with No People

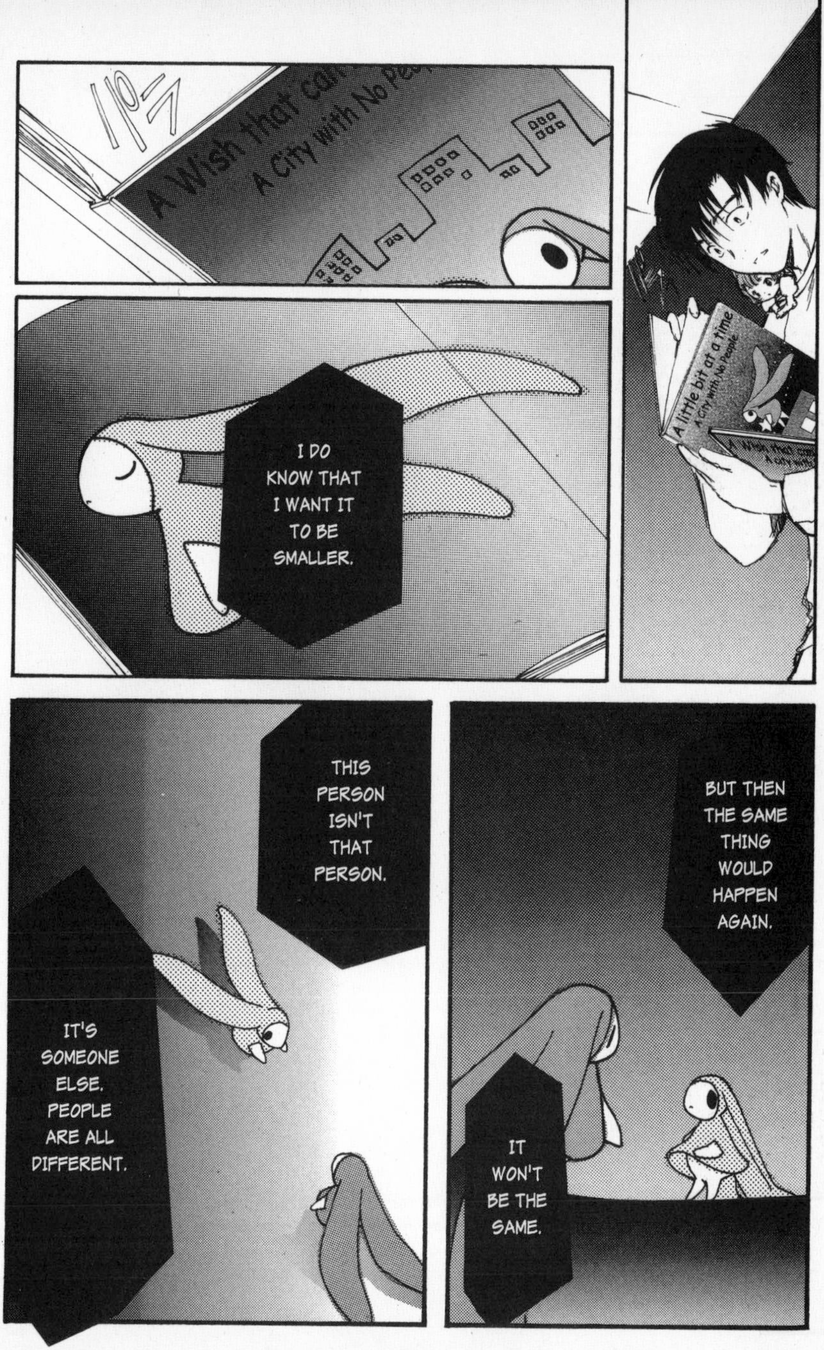
A little bit at a time
A City with No People
パラ
I DO KNOW THAT I WANT IT TO BE SMALLER.
BUT THEN THE SAME THING WOULD HAPPEN AGAIN.
IT WON'T BE THE SAME.
THIS PERSON ISN'T THAT PERSON.
IT'S SOMEONE ELSE. PEOPLE ARE ALL DIFFERENT.

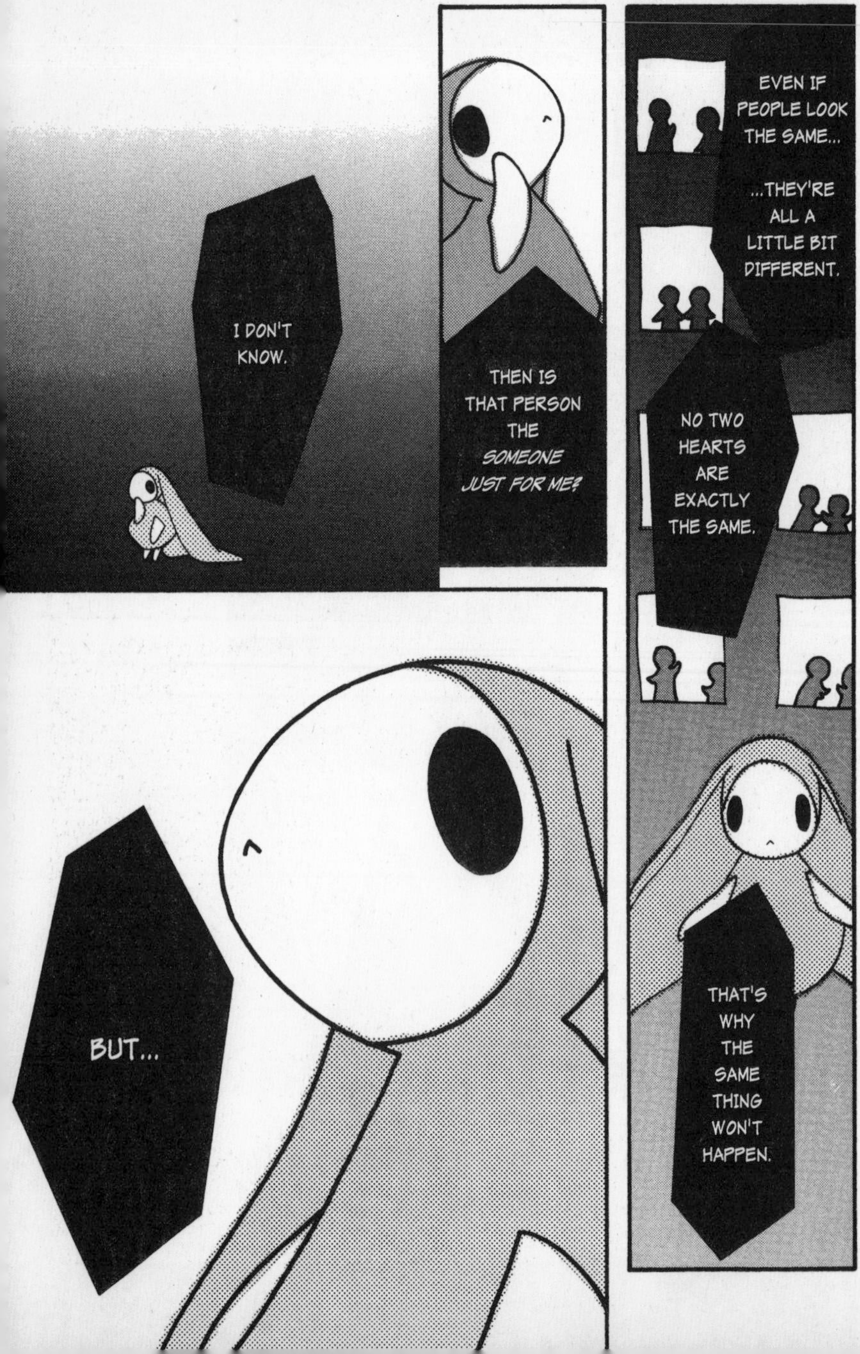
EVEN IF PEOPLE LOOK THE SAME...
...THEY'RE ALL A LITTLE BIT DIFFERENT.
NO TWO HEARTS ARE EXACTLY THE SAME.
THAT'S WHY THE SAME THING WON'T HAPPEN.
THEN IS THAT PERSON THE *SOMEONE JUST FOR ME?*
I DON'T KNOW.
BUT...

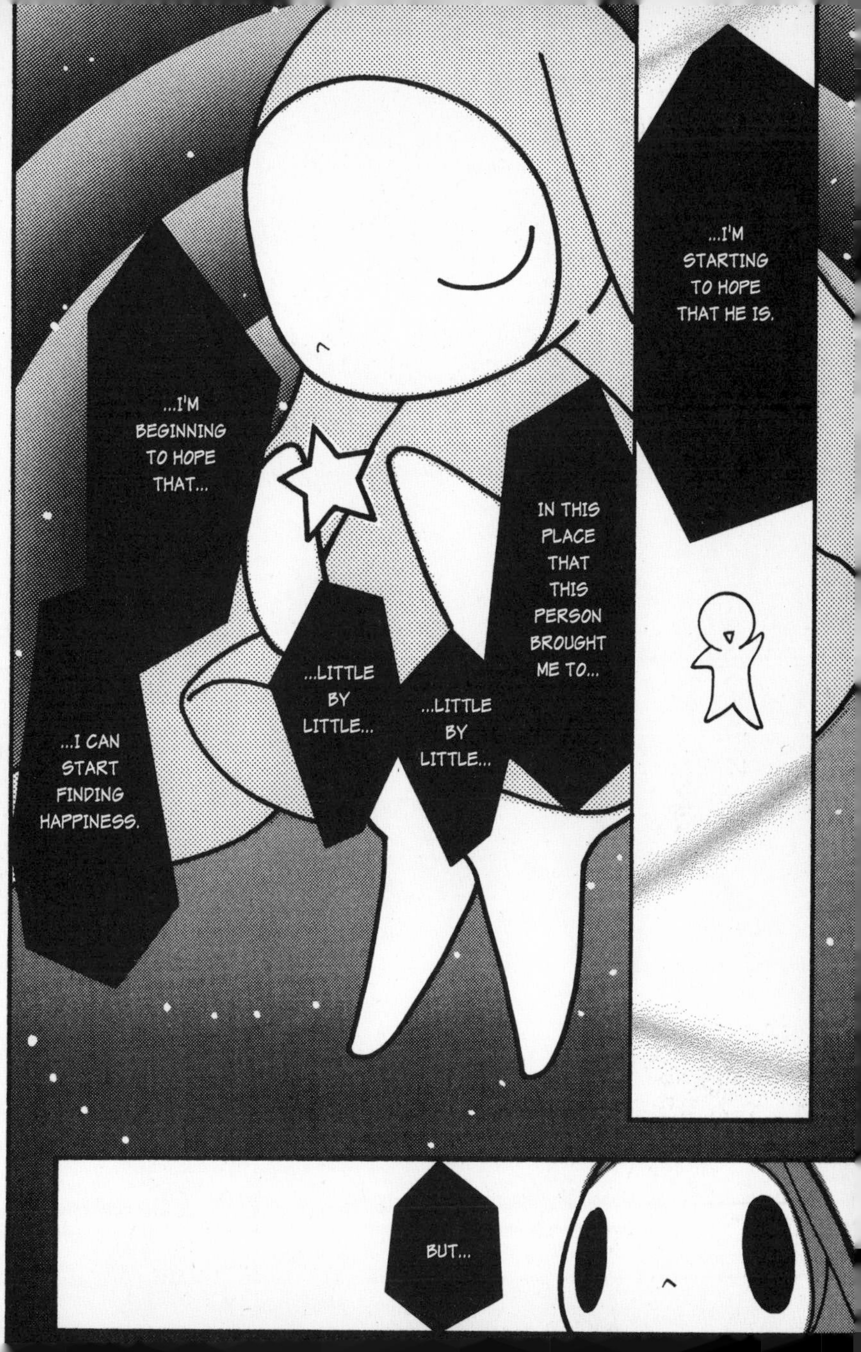
...I'M STARTING TO HOPE THAT HE IS.
IN THIS PLACE THAT THIS PERSON BROUGHT ME TO...
...I'M BEGINNING TO HOPE THAT...
...LITTLE BY LITTLE...
...LITTLE BY LITTLE...
...I CAN START FINDING HAPPINESS.
BUT...

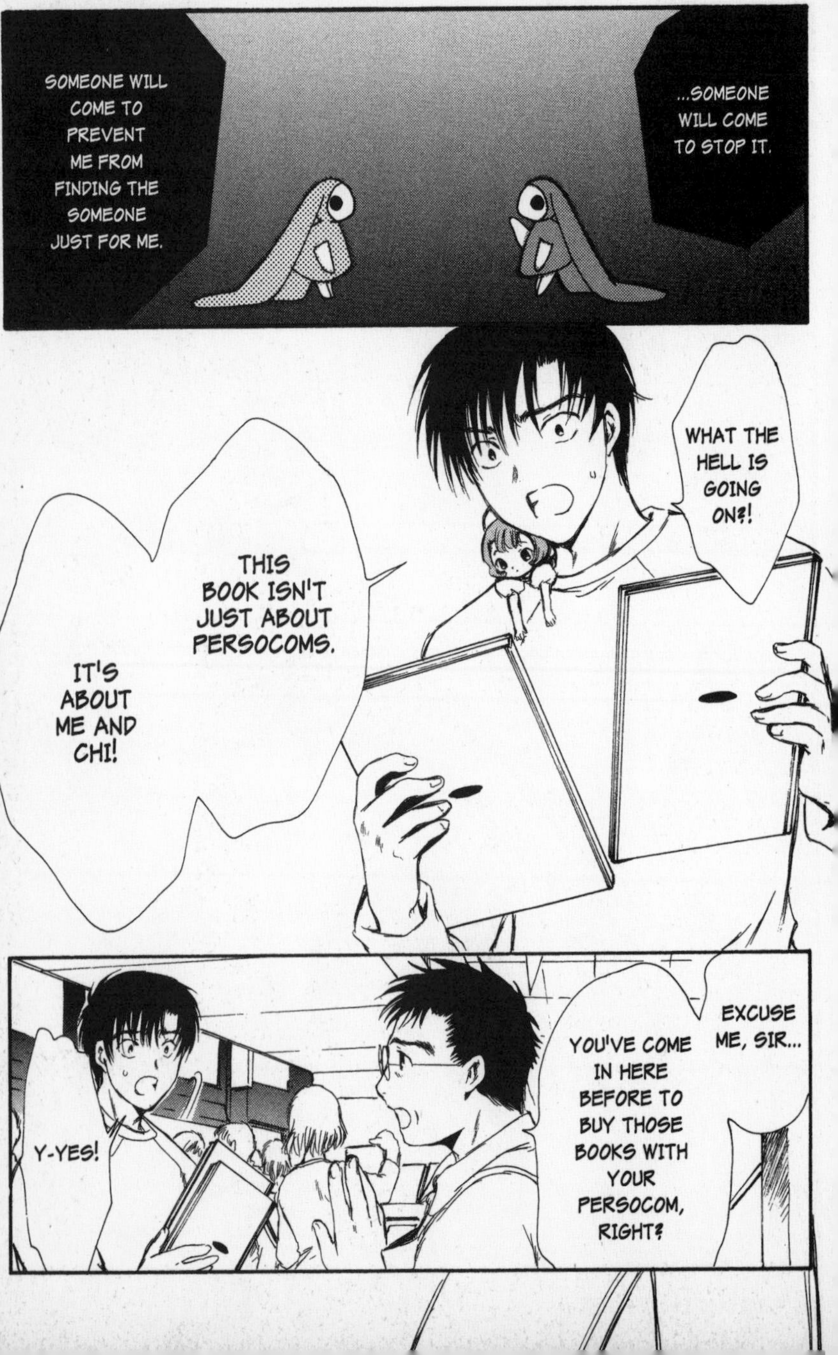
...SOMEONE WILL COME TO STOP IT.
SOMEONE WILL COME TO PREVENT ME FROM FINDING THE SOMEONE JUST FOR ME.
WHAT THE HELL IS GOING ON?!
THIS BOOK ISN'T JUST ABOUT PERSOCOMS.
IT'S ABOUT ME AND CHI!
EXCUSE ME, SIR...
YOU'VE COME IN HERE BEFORE TO BUY THOSE BOOKS WITH YOUR PERSOCOM, RIGHT?
Y-YES!

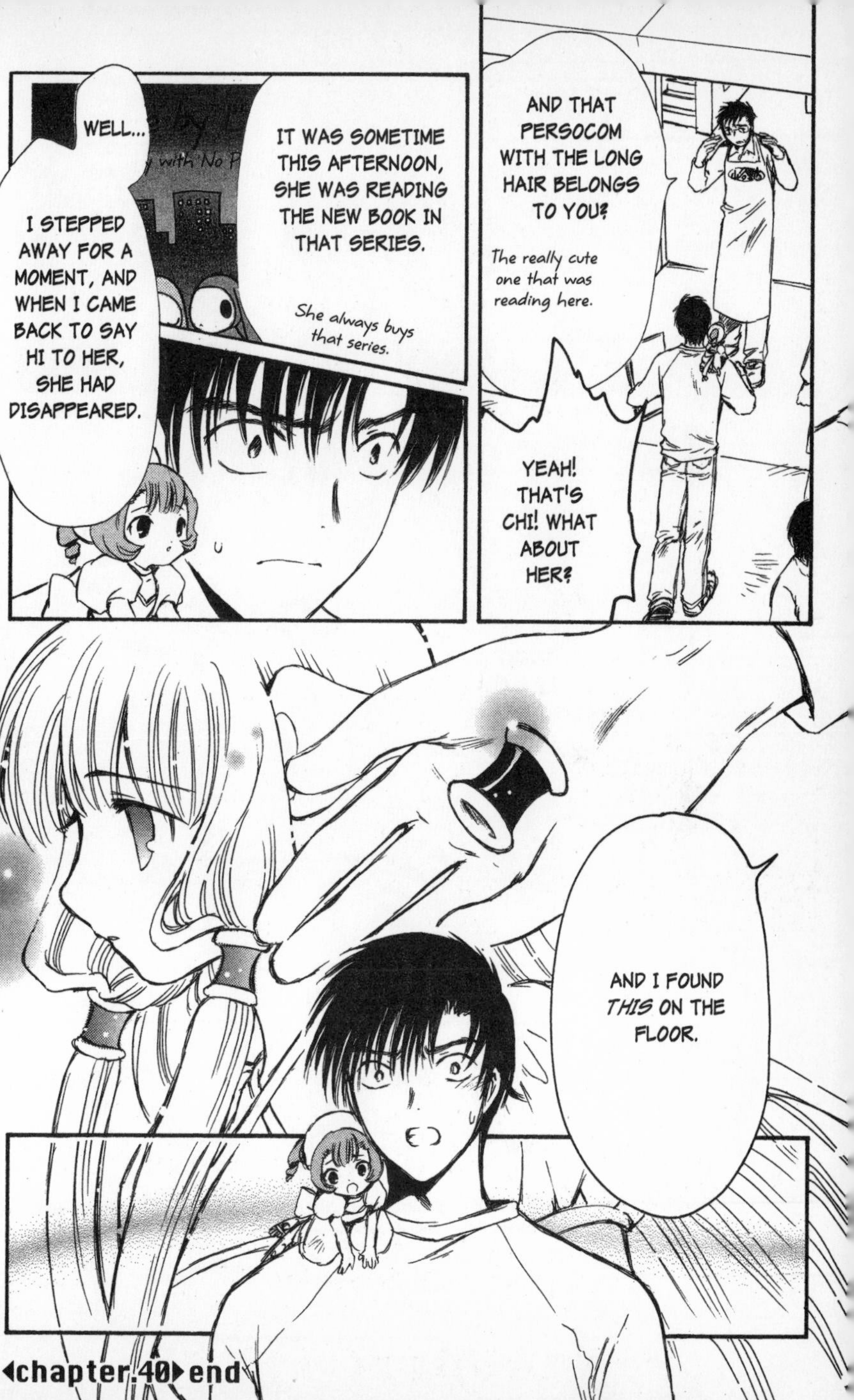
AND THAT PERSOCOM WITH THE LONG HAIR BELONGS TO YOU?
The really cute one that was reading here.
YEAH! THAT'S CHI! WHAT ABOUT HER?
IT WAS SOMETIME THIS AFTERNOON, SHE WAS READING THE NEW BOOK IN THAT SERIES.
She always buys that series.
WELL...
I STEPPED AWAY FOR A MOMENT, AND WHEN I CAME BACK TO SAY HI TO HER, SHE HAD DISAPPEARED.
AND I FOUND *THIS* ON THE FLOOR.

◀chapter.40▶ end

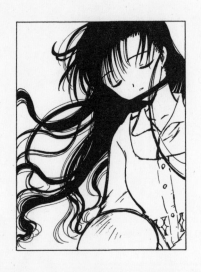

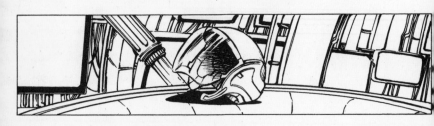

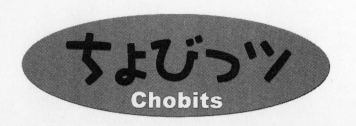

ちょびっツ

Chobits

◀chapter.41▶

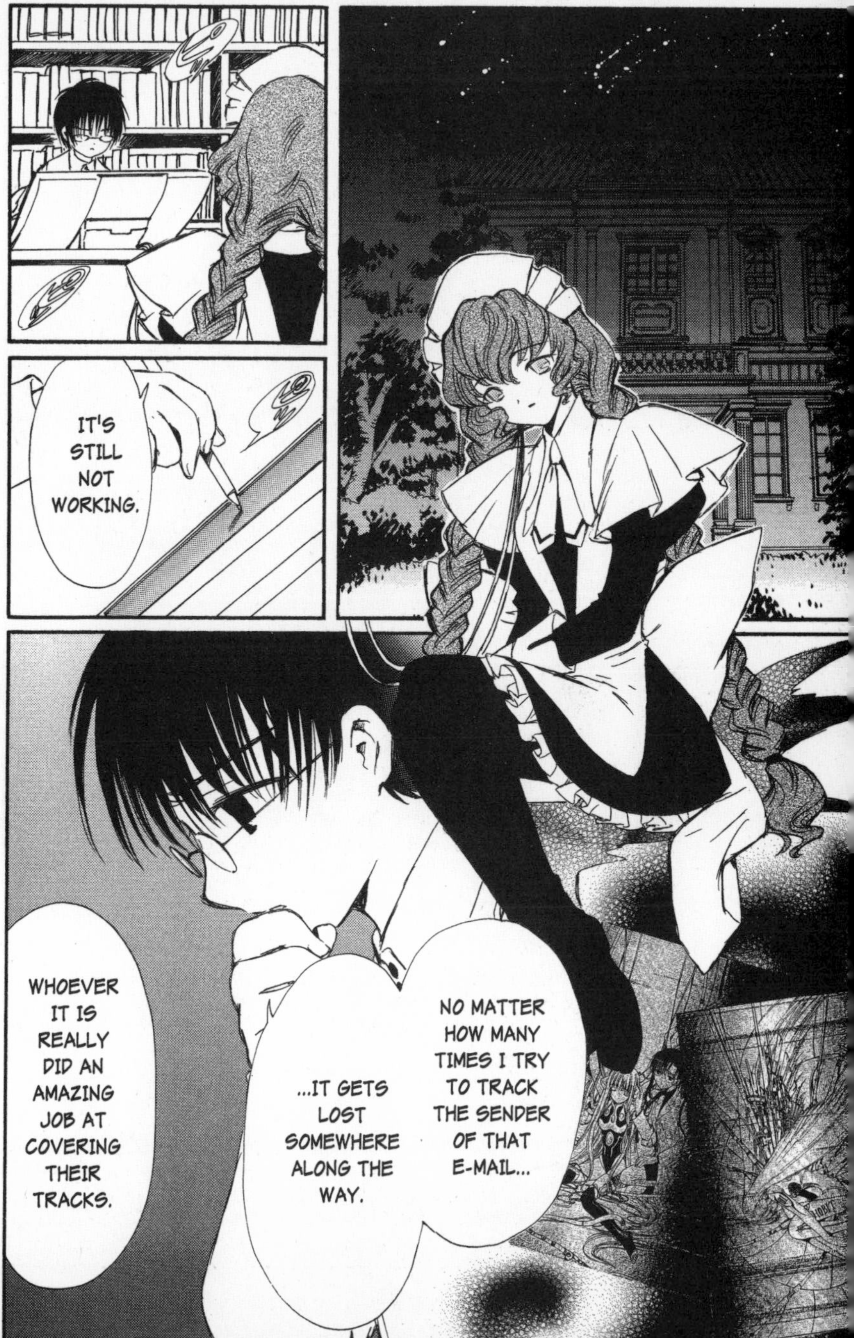
IT'S STILL NOT WORKING.
NO MATTER HOW MANY TIMES I TRY TO TRACK THE SENDER OF THAT E-MAIL...
...IT GETS LOST SOMEWHERE ALONG THE WAY.
WHOEVER IT IS REALLY DID AN AMAZING JOB AT COVERING THEIR TRACKS.

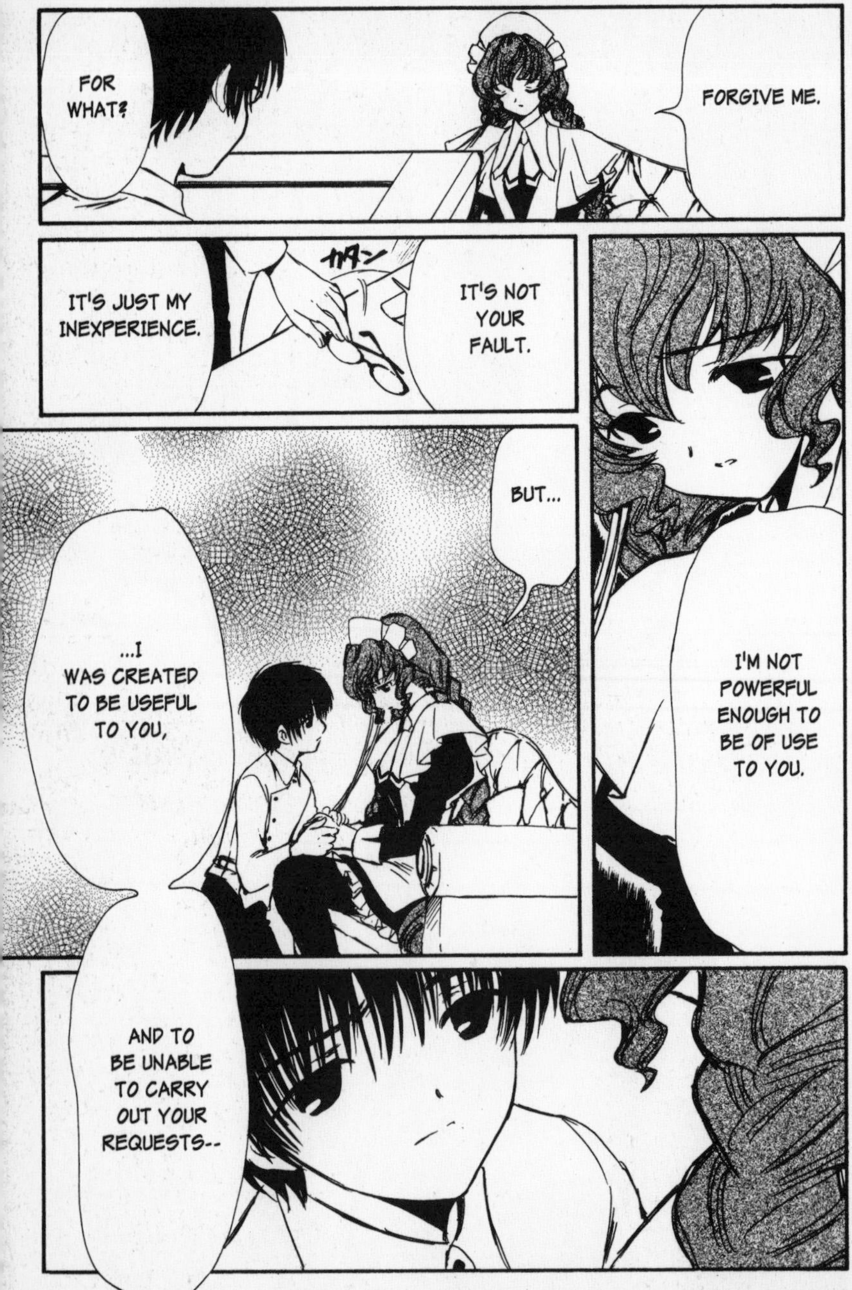
FORGIVE ME.
FOR WHAT?
I'M NOT POWERFUL ENOUGH TO BE OF USE TO YOU.
IT'S NOT YOUR FAULT.
カタン
IT'S JUST MY INEXPERIENCE.
BUT...
...I WAS CREATED TO BE USEFUL TO YOU,
AND TO BE UNABLE TO CARRY OUT YOUR REQUESTS--

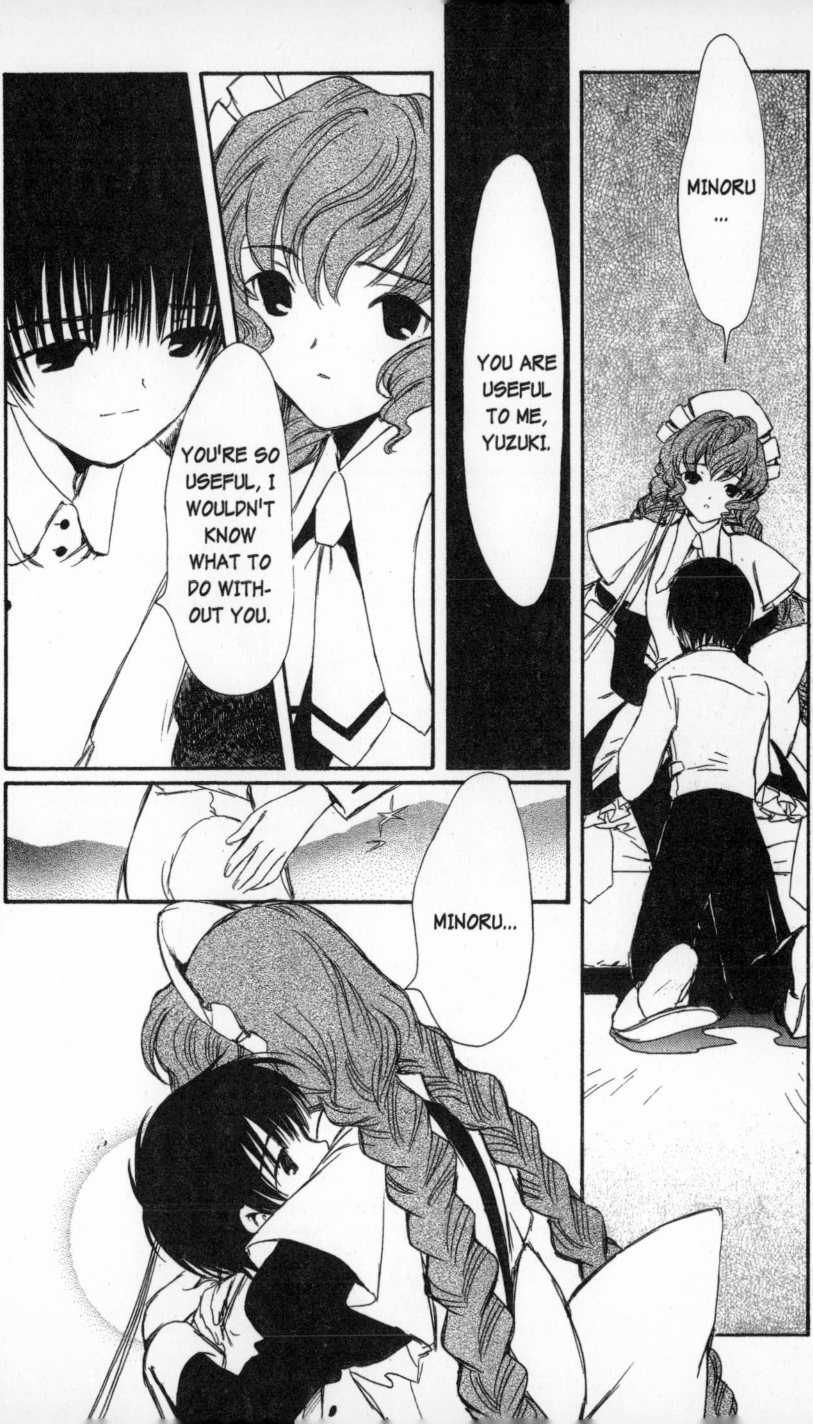
MINORU ...
YOU ARE USEFUL TO ME, YUZUKI.
YOU'RE SO USEFUL, I WOULDN'T KNOW WHAT TO DO WITH-OUT YOU.
MINORU...

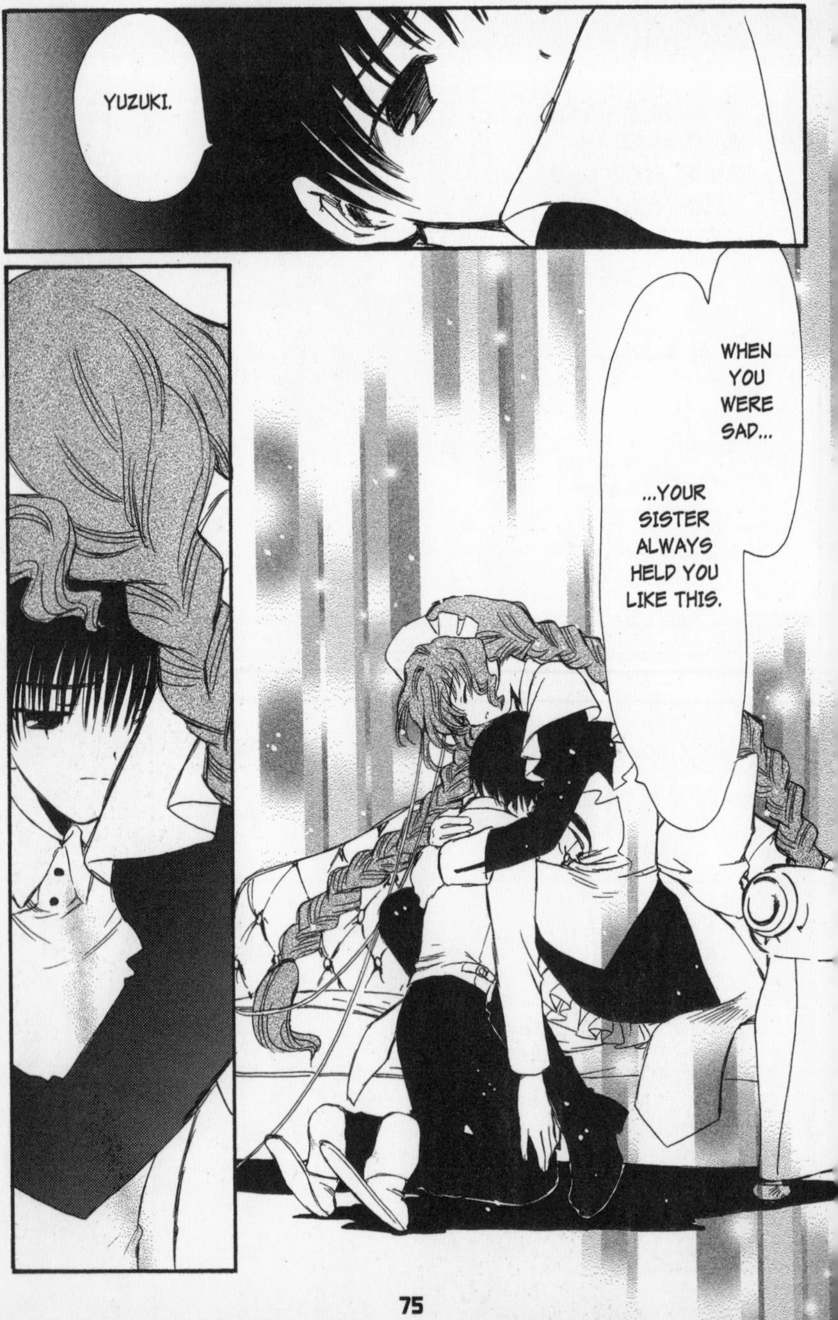
YUZUKI.
WHEN YOU WERE SAD...
...YOUR SISTER ALWAYS HELD YOU LIKE THIS.

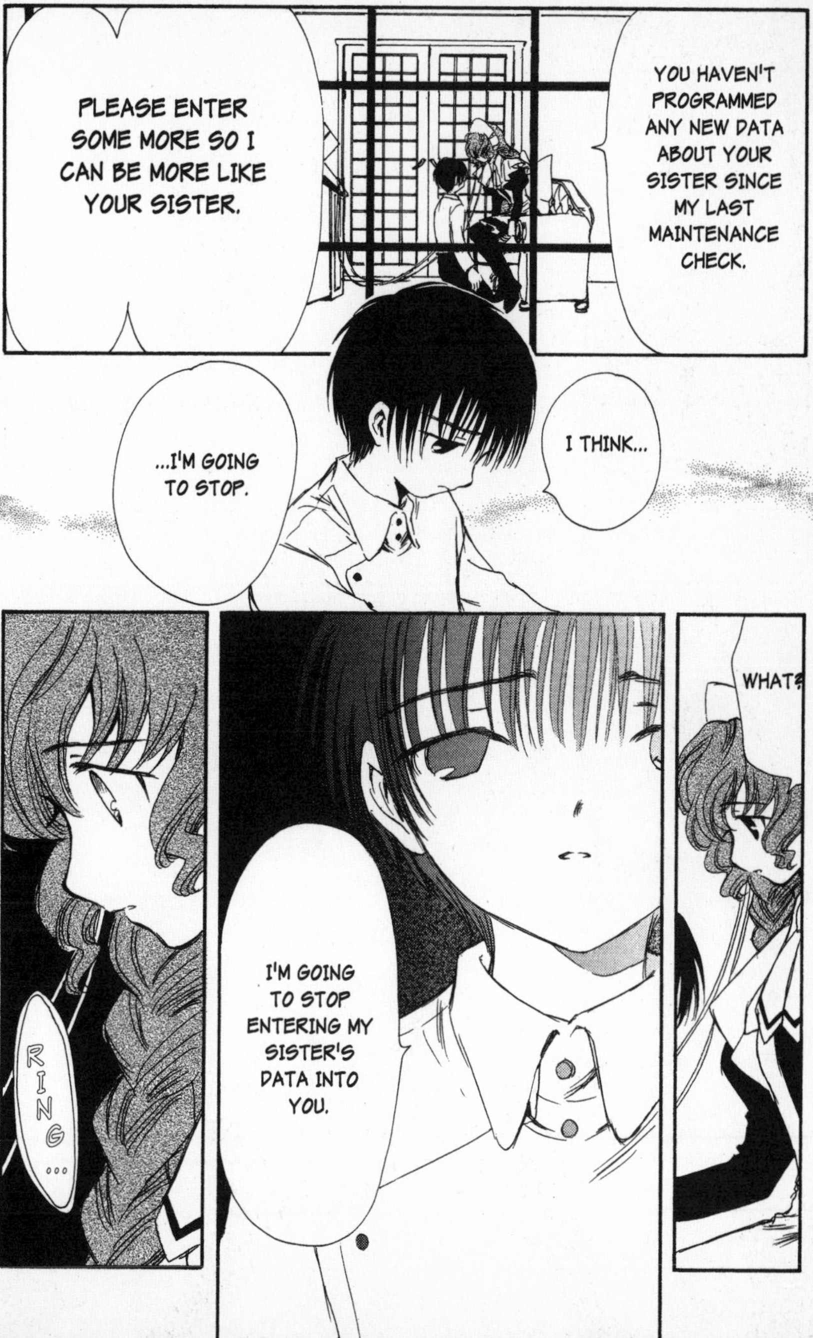
YOU HAVEN'T PROGRAMMED ANY NEW DATA ABOUT YOUR SISTER SINCE MY LAST MAINTENANCE CHECK.
PLEASE ENTER SOME MORE SO I CAN BE MORE LIKE YOUR SISTER.
I THINK...
...I'M GOING TO STOP.
WHAT?
I'M GOING TO STOP ENTERING MY SISTER'S DATA INTO YOU.
RING...

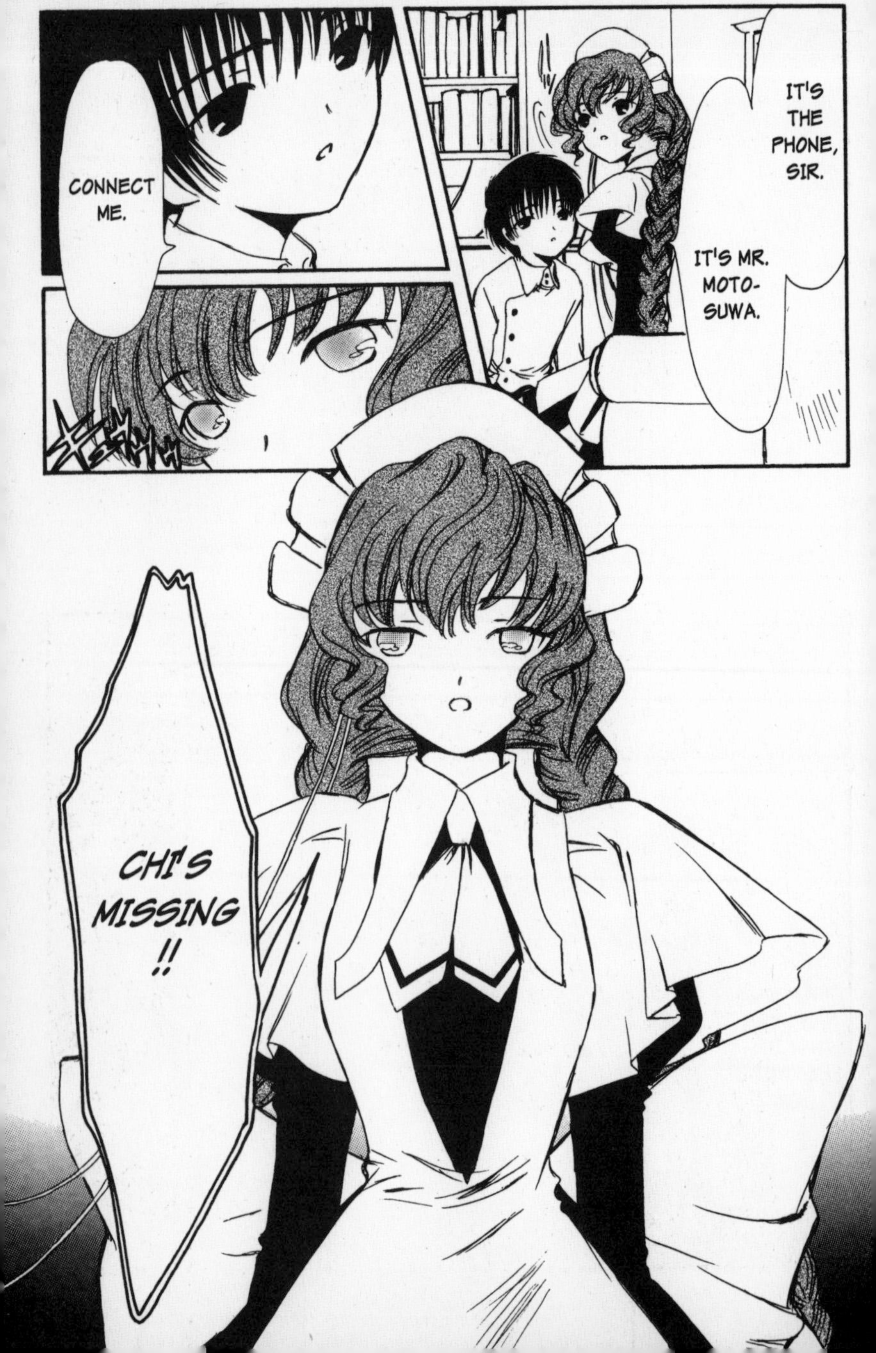
IT'S THE PHONE, SIR.
IT'S MR. MOTO-SUWA.
CONNECT ME.
CHI'S MISSING !!

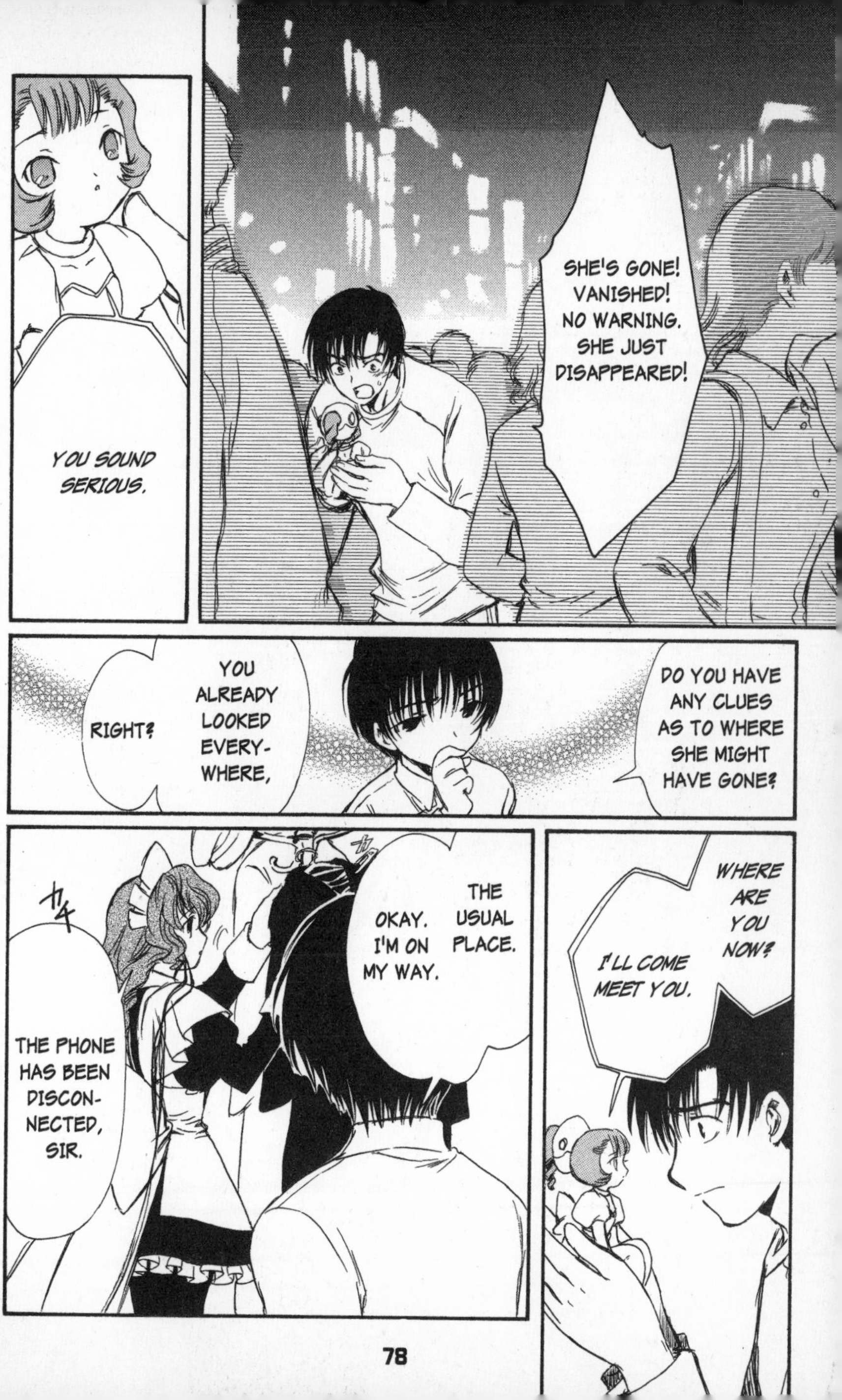
SHE'S GONE! VANISHED! NO WARNING. SHE JUST DISAPPEARED!
YOU SOUND SERIOUS.
DO YOU HAVE ANY CLUES AS TO WHERE SHE MIGHT HAVE GONE?
YOU ALREADY LOOKED EVERY-WHERE,
RIGHT?
WHERE ARE YOU NOW?
I'LL COME MEET YOU.
THE USUAL PLACE.
OKAY. I'M ON MY WAY.
THE PHONE HAS BEEN DISCON-NECTED, SIR.

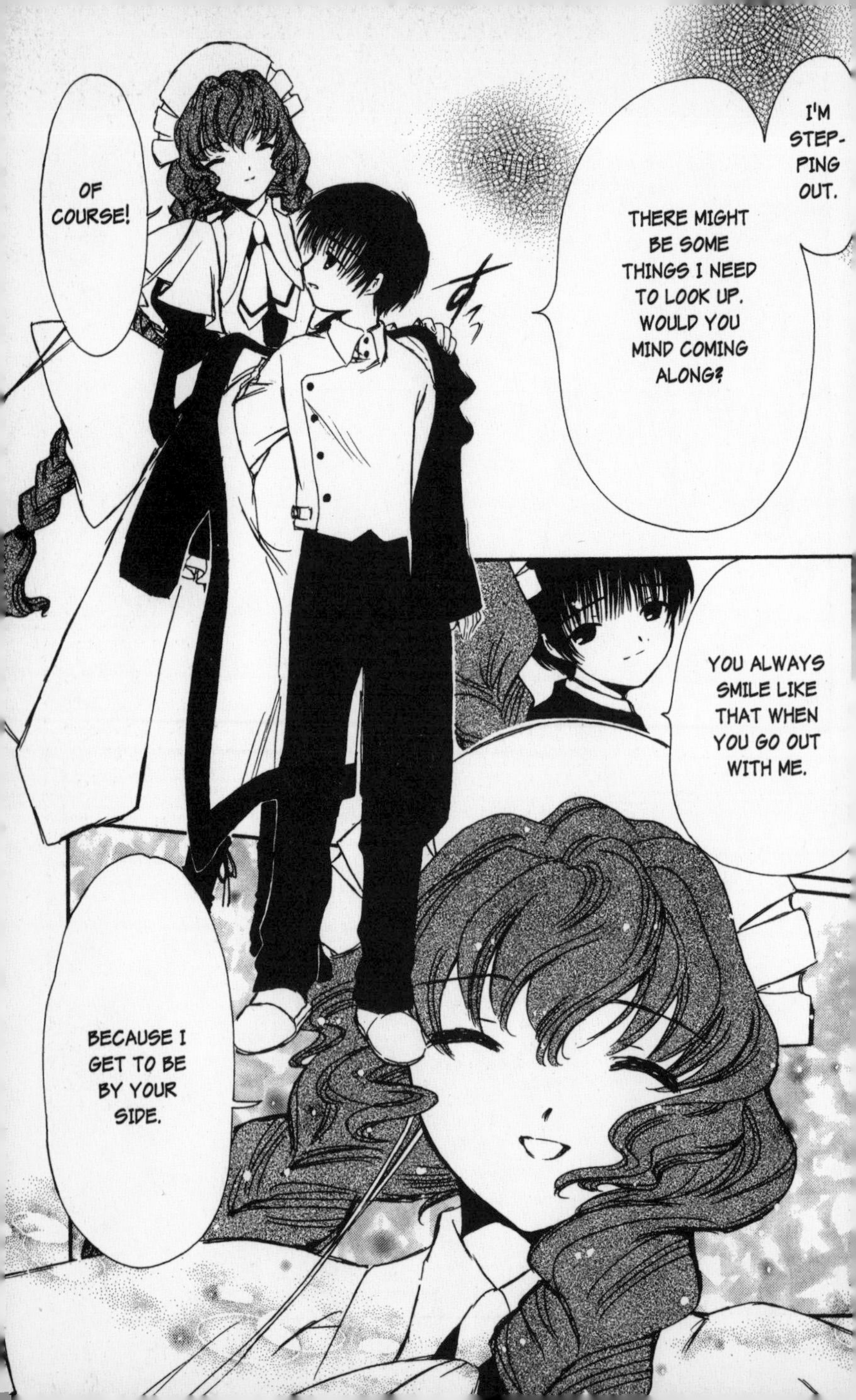
I'M STEP-PING OUT.
THERE MIGHT BE SOME THINGS I NEED TO LOOK UP. WOULD YOU MIND COMING ALONG?
OF COURSE!
YOU ALWAYS SMILE LIKE THAT WHEN YOU GO OUT WITH ME.
BECAUSE I GET TO BE BY YOUR SIDE.

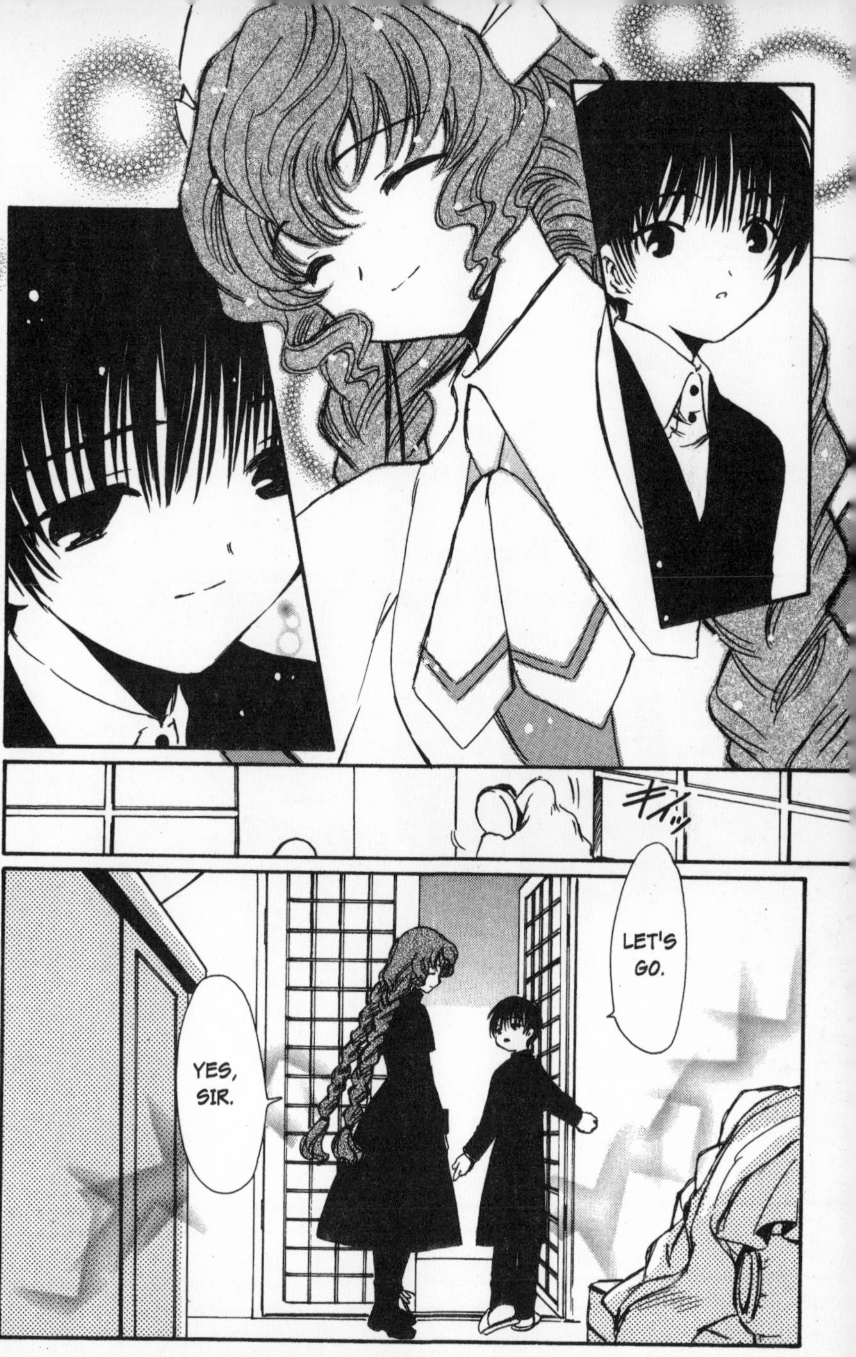
キィッ
LET'S GO.
YES, SIR.

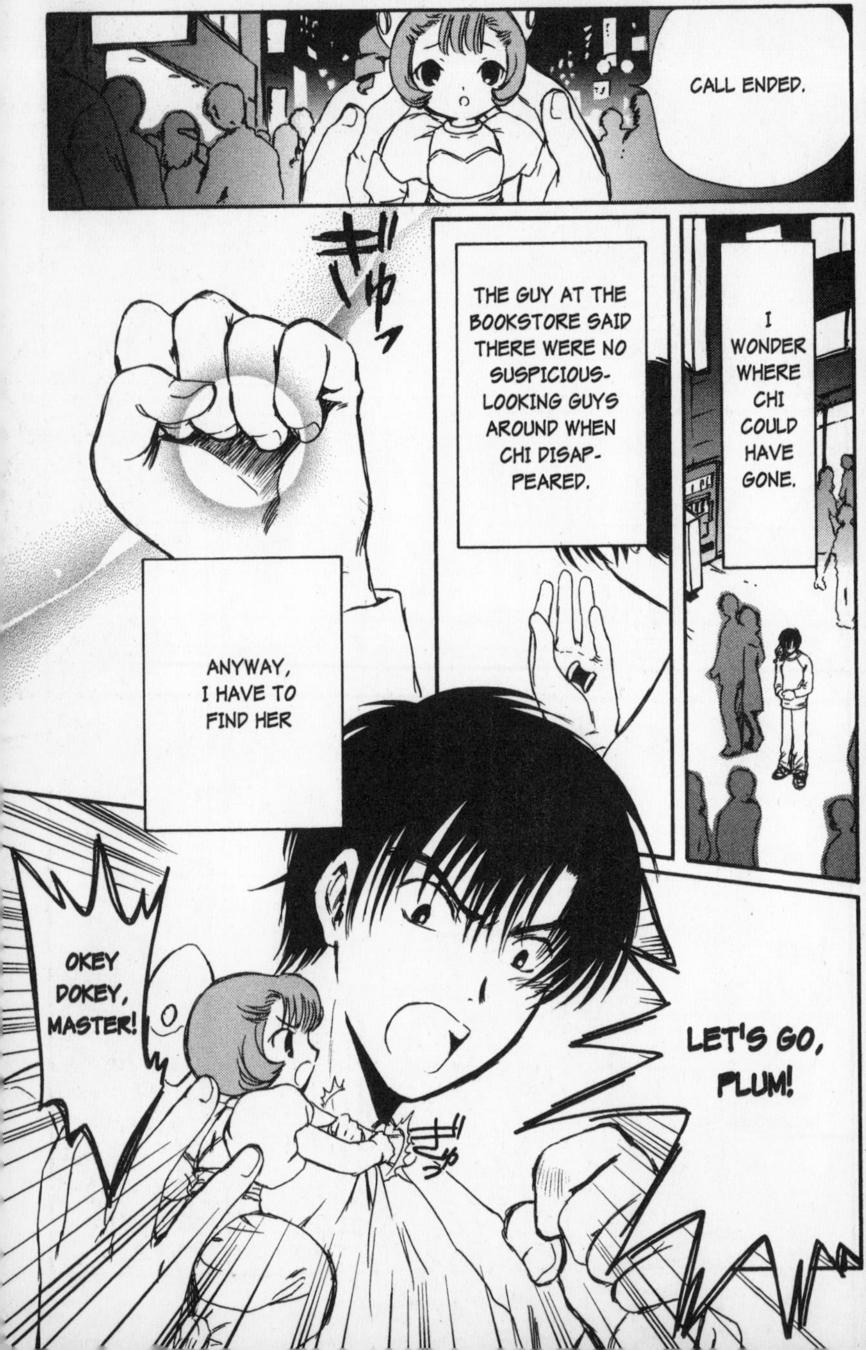
CALL ENDED.
I WONDER WHERE CHI COULD HAVE GONE.
THE GUY AT THE BOOKSTORE SAID THERE WERE NO SUSPICIOUS-LOOKING GUYS AROUND WHEN CHI DISAP-PEARED.
ぎゅっ
ANYWAY, I HAVE TO FIND HER
LET'S GO, PLUM!
OKEY DOKEY, MASTER!
ぎゅ

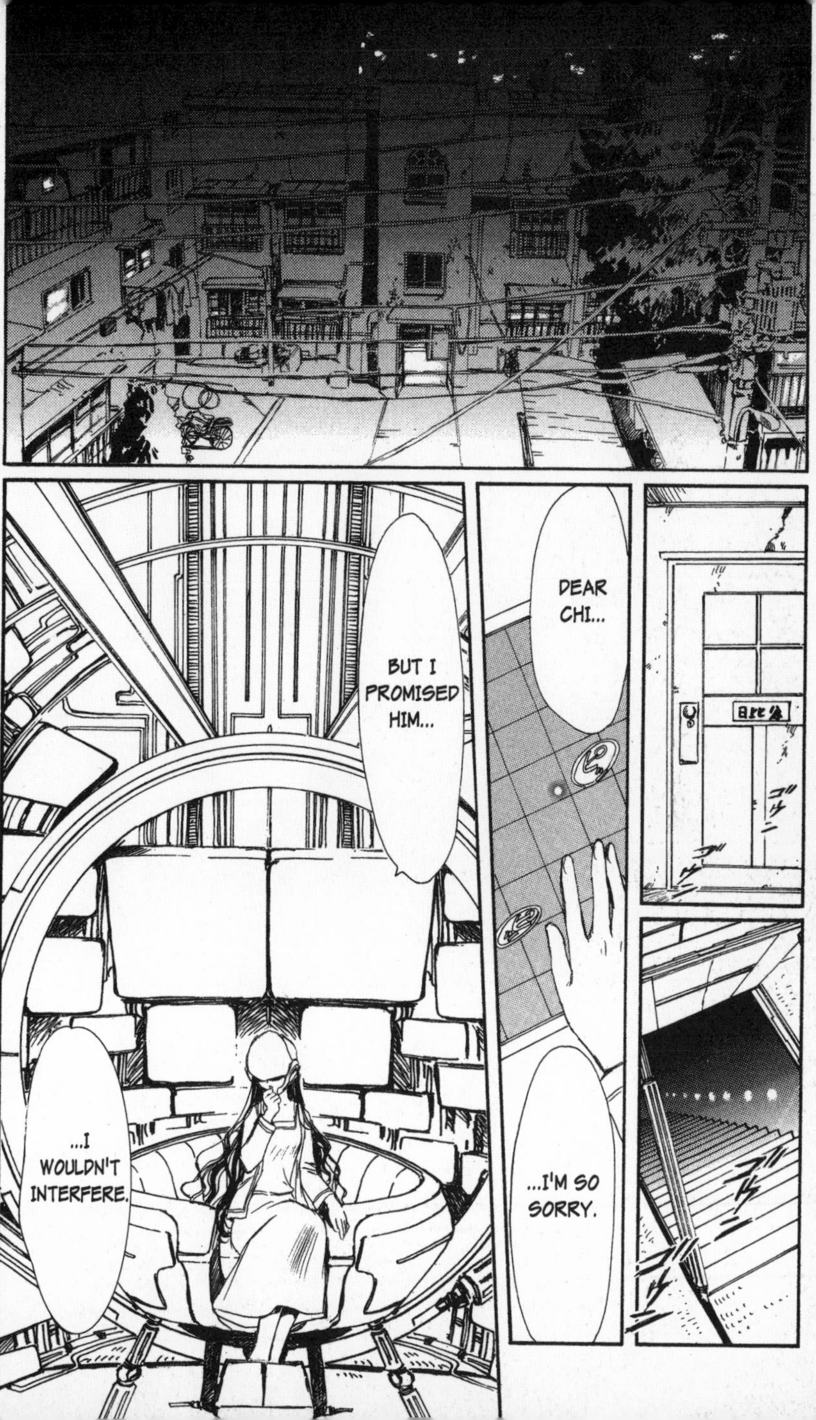
DEAR CHI...
...I'M SO SORRY.
BUT I PROMISED HIM...
...I WOULDN'T INTERFERE.

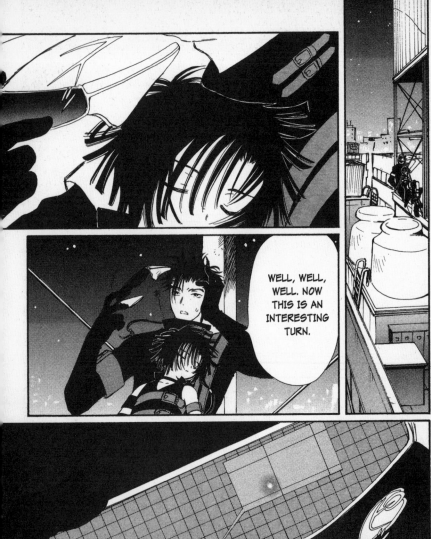

WELL, WELL, WELL. NOW THIS IS AN INTERESTING TURN.

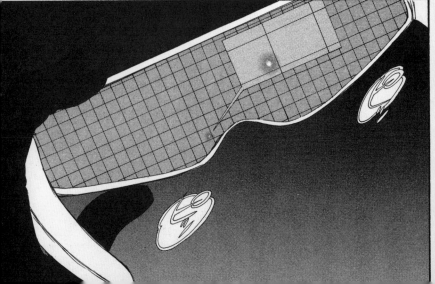

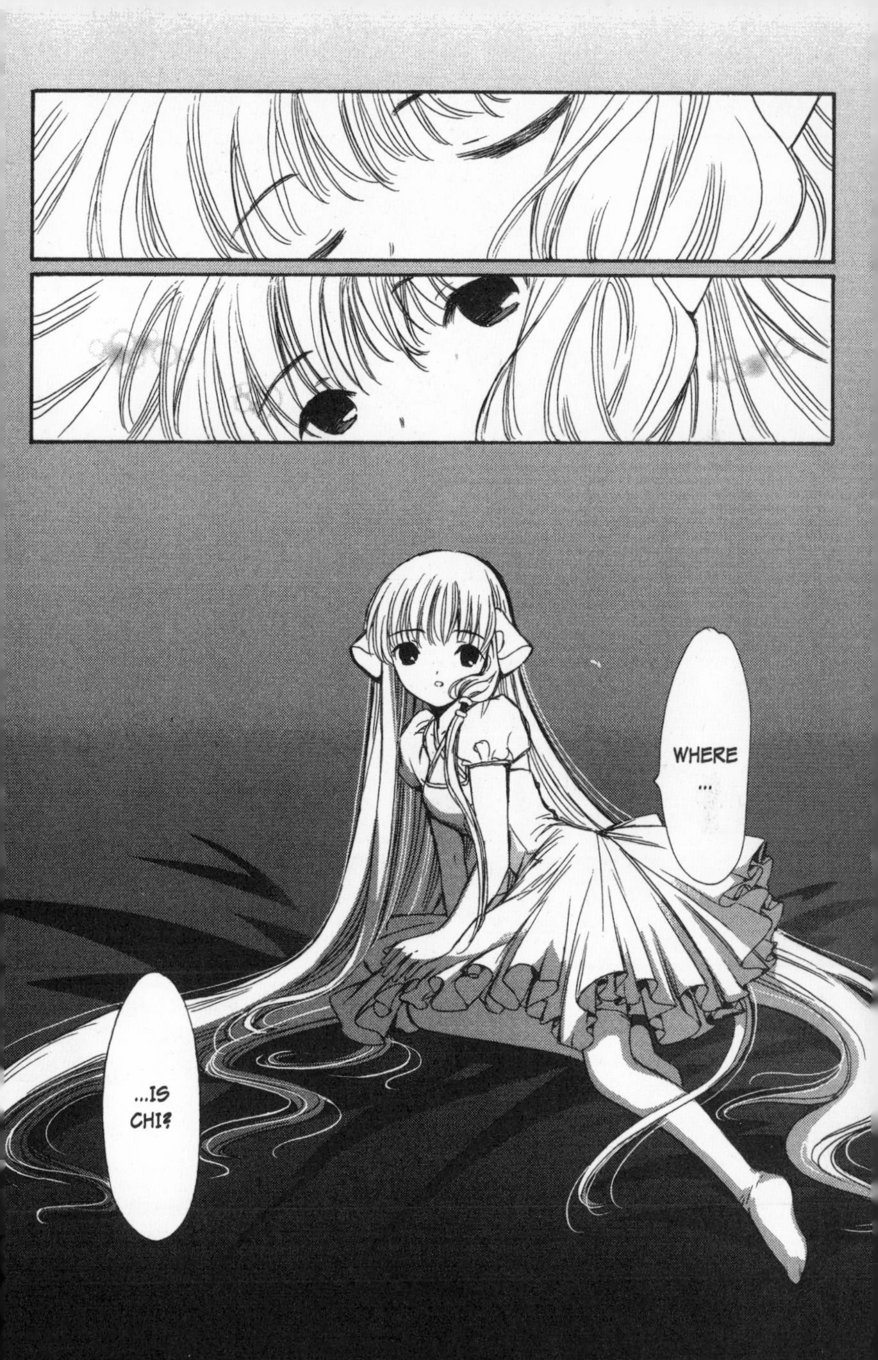
WHERE ...
...IS CHI?

◂chapter.41▸end

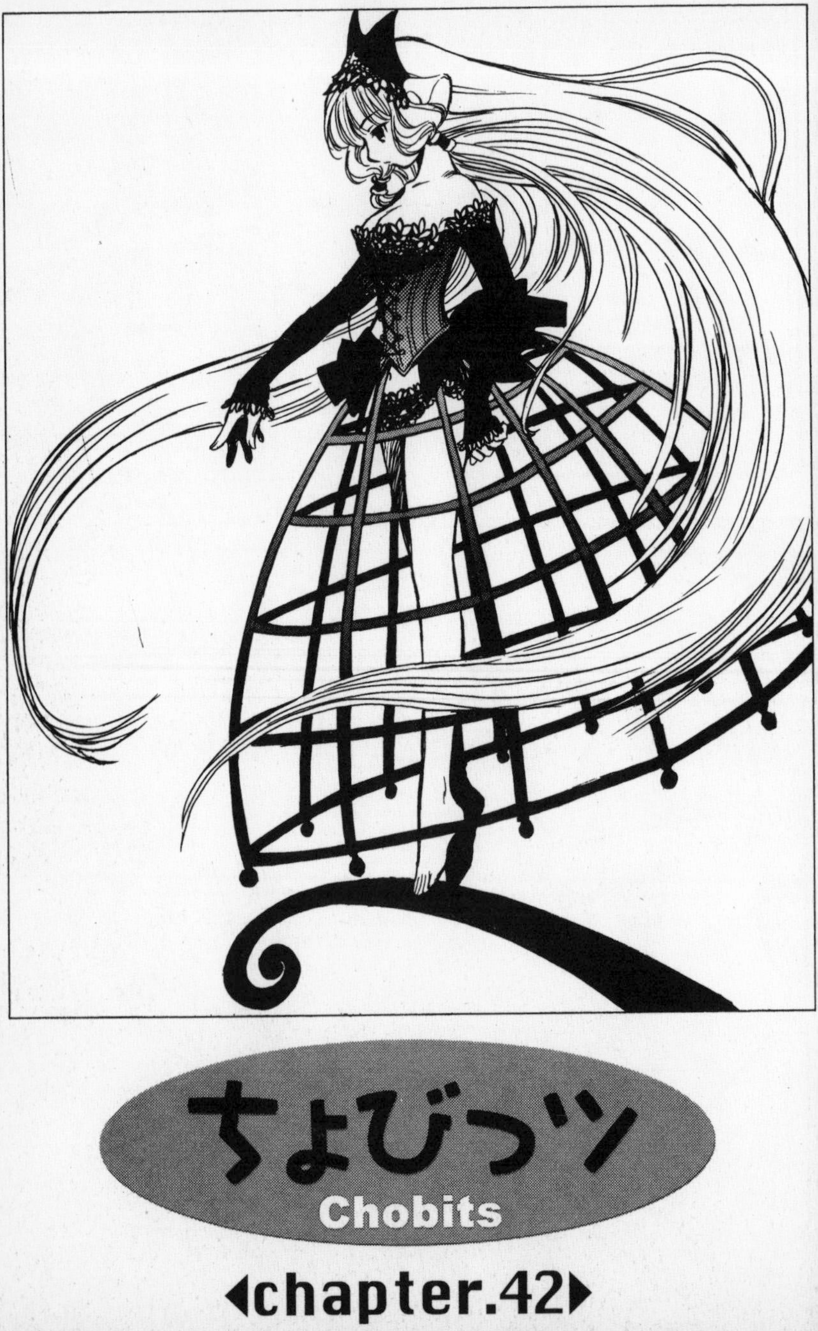

ちょびっツ

Chobits

◀chapter.42▶

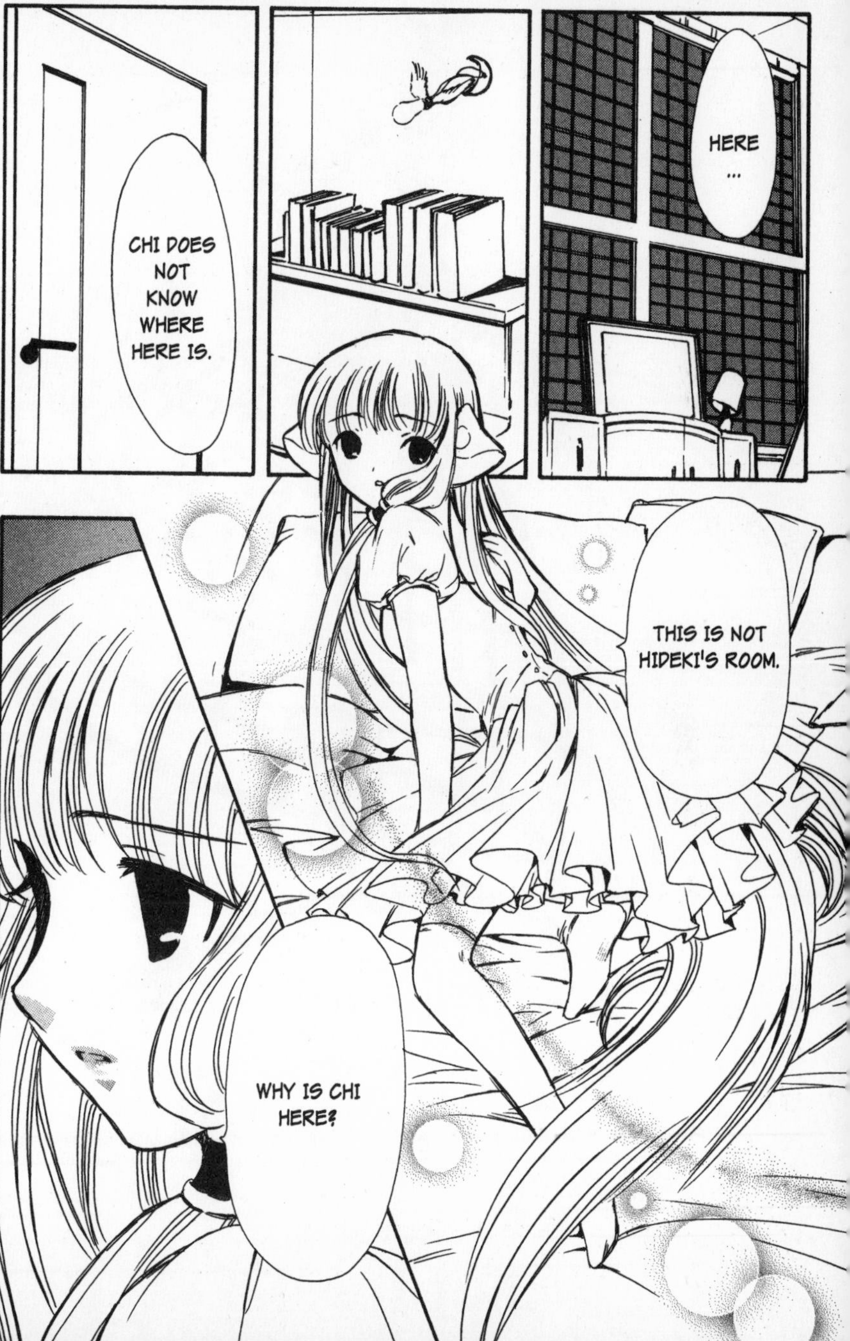
HERE ...
CHI DOES NOT KNOW WHERE HERE IS.
THIS IS NOT HIDEKI'S ROOM.
WHY IS CHI HERE?

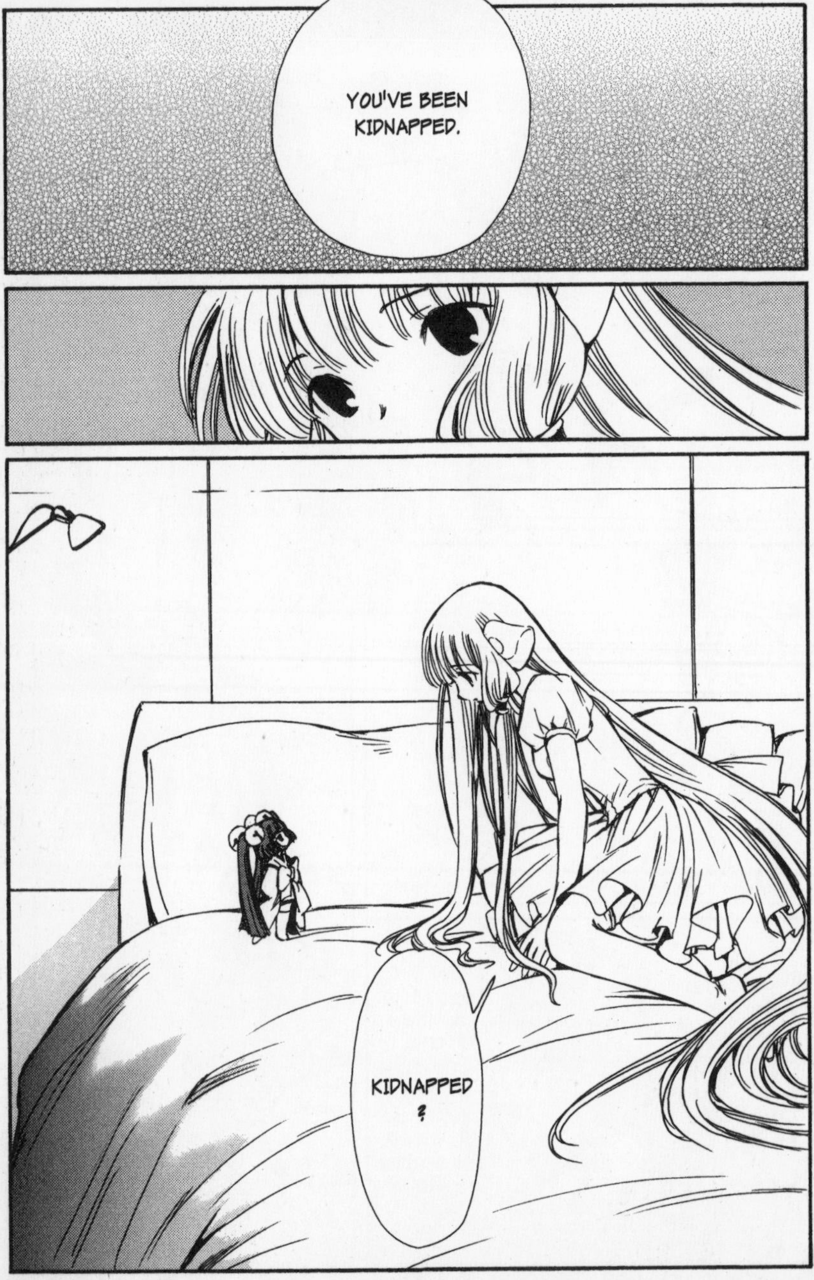
YOU'VE BEEN KIDNAPPED.
KIDNAPPED?

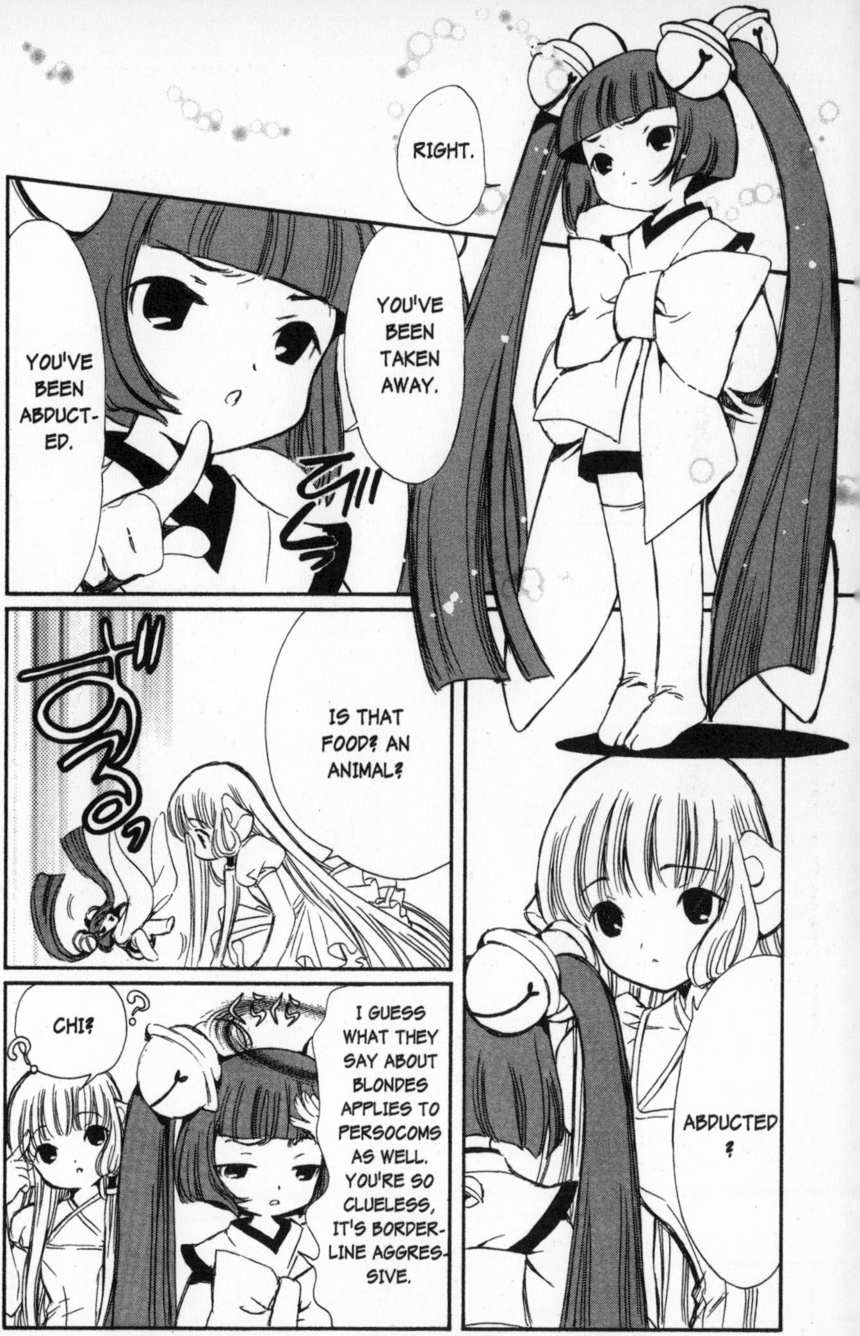
RIGHT.
YOU'VE BEEN TAKEN AWAY.
YOU'VE BEEN ABDUCTED.
ABDUCTED?
IS THAT FOOD? AN ANIMAL?
I GUESS WHAT THEY SAY ABOUT BLONDES APPLIES TO PERSOCOMS AS WELL. YOU'RE SO CLUELESS, IT'S BORDERLINE AGGRESSIVE.
CHI?

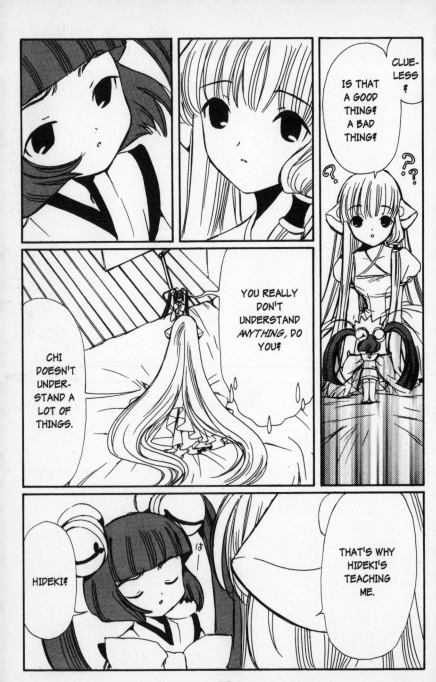

CLUELESS?

IS THAT A GOOD THING? A BAD THING?

YOU REALLY DON'T UNDERSTAND *ANYTHING*, DO YOU?

CHI DOESN'T UNDERSTAND A LOT OF THINGS.

THAT'S WHY HIDEKI'S TEACHING ME.

HIDEKI?

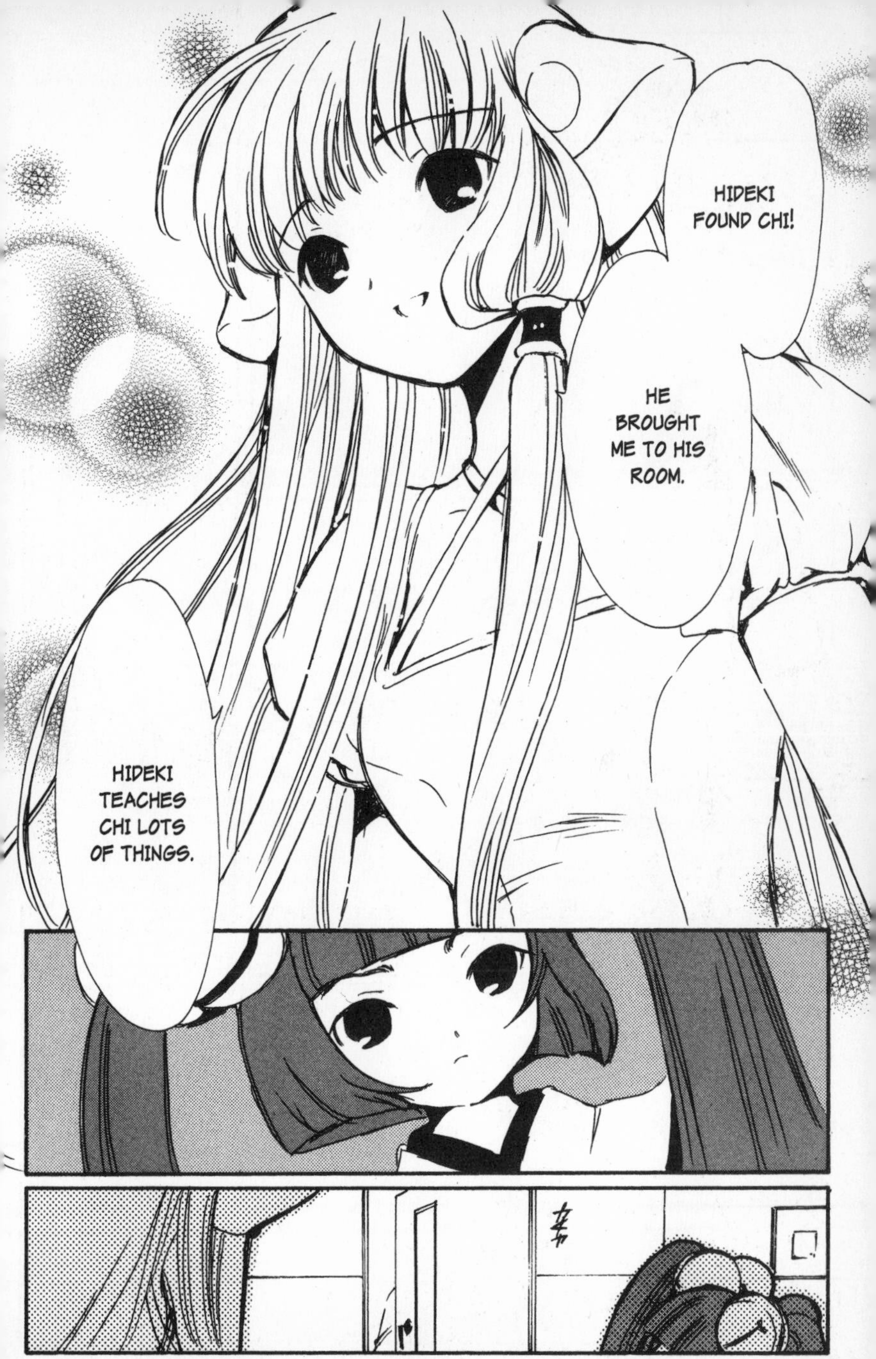
HIDEKI FOUND CHI!
HE BROUGHT ME TO HIS ROOM.
HIDEKI TEACHES CHI LOTS OF THINGS.

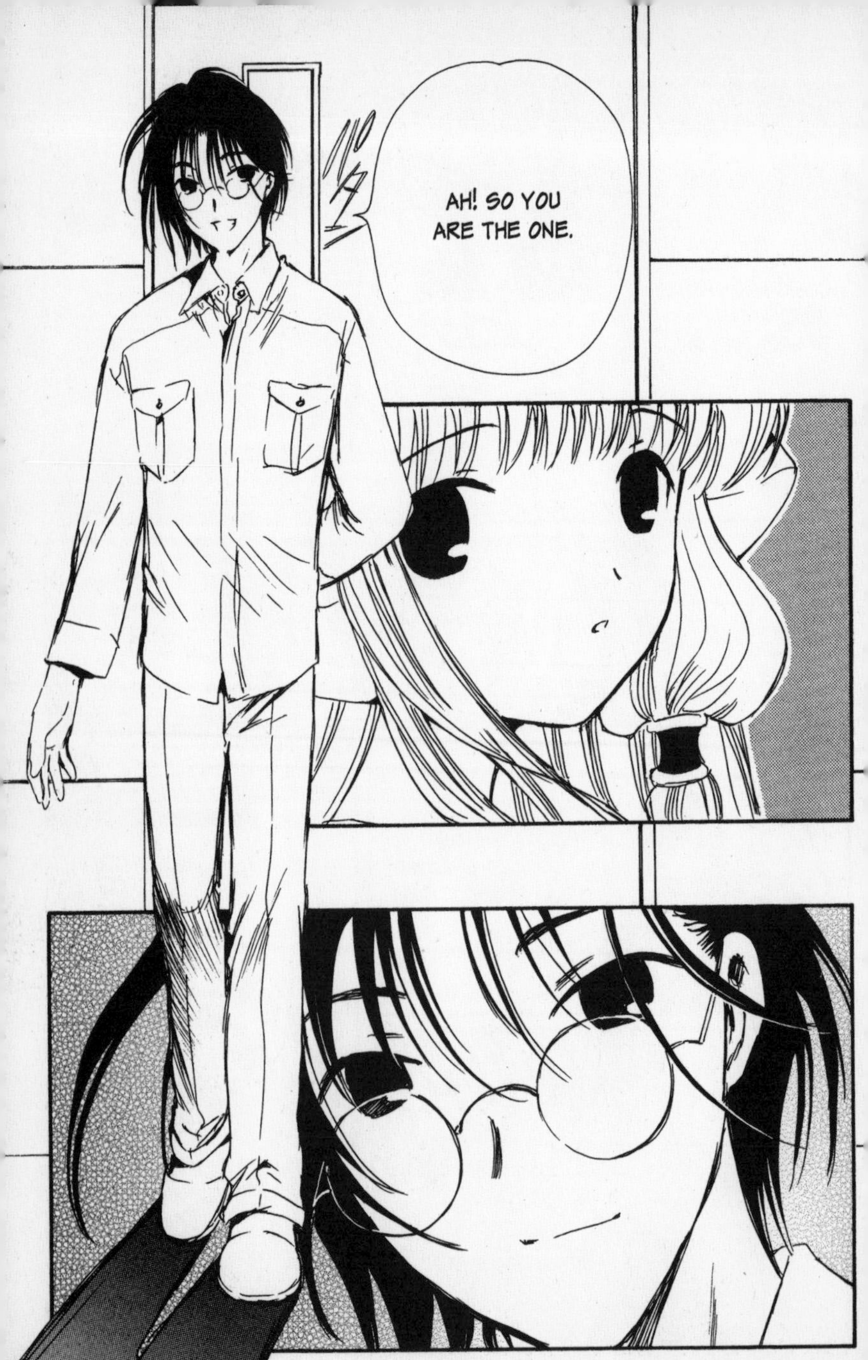
AH! SO YOU ARE THE ONE.

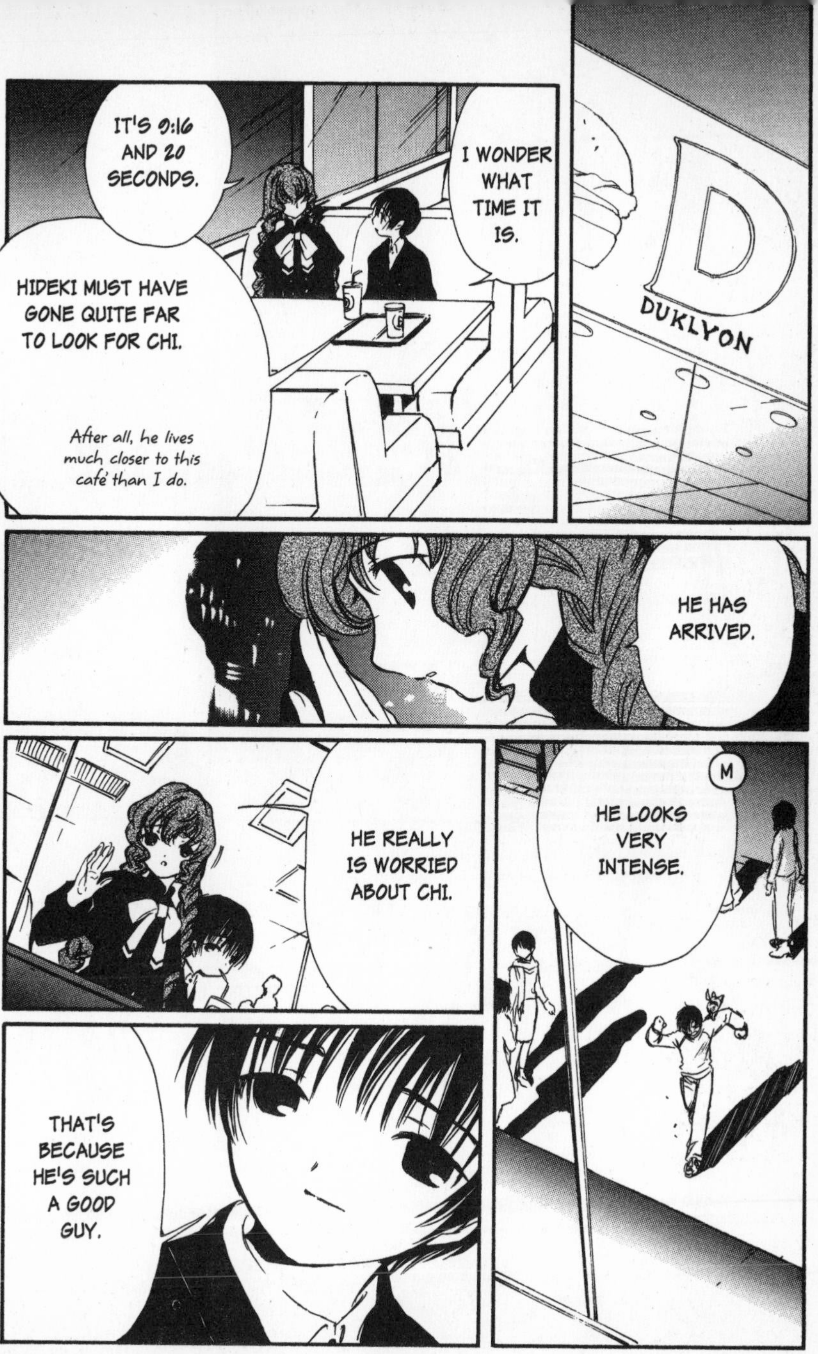
D
DUKLYON
I WONDER WHAT TIME IT IS.
IT'S 9:16 AND 20 SECONDS.
HIDEKI MUST HAVE GONE QUITE FAR TO LOOK FOR CHI.
After all, he lives much closer to this café than I do.
HE HAS ARRIVED.
M
HE LOOKS VERY INTENSE.
HE REALLY IS WORRIED ABOUT CHI.
THAT'S BECAUSE HE'S SUCH A GOOD GUY.

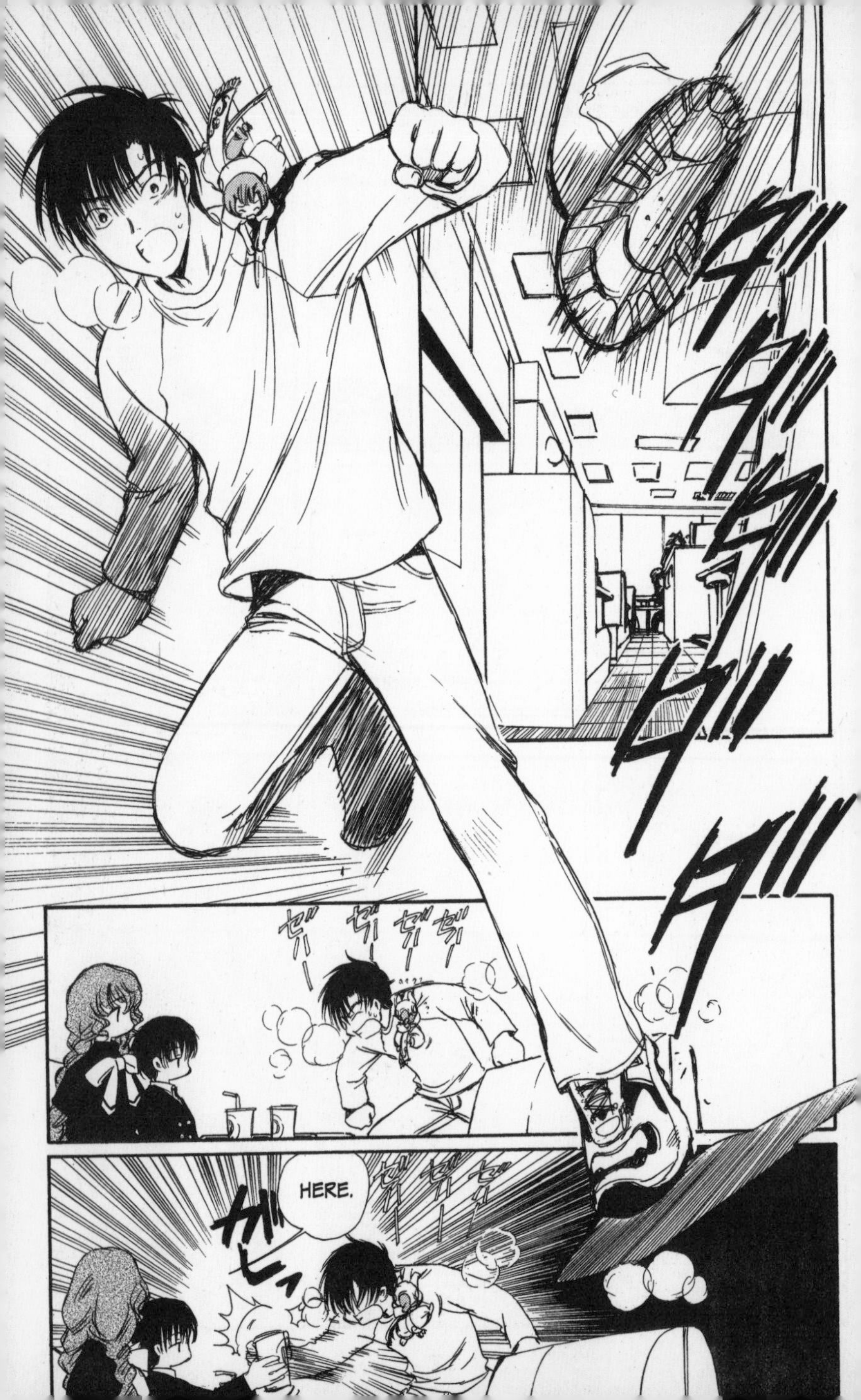
ダダダダダダ
ぜーぜーぜーぜー
ぜーぜーぜー
HERE.

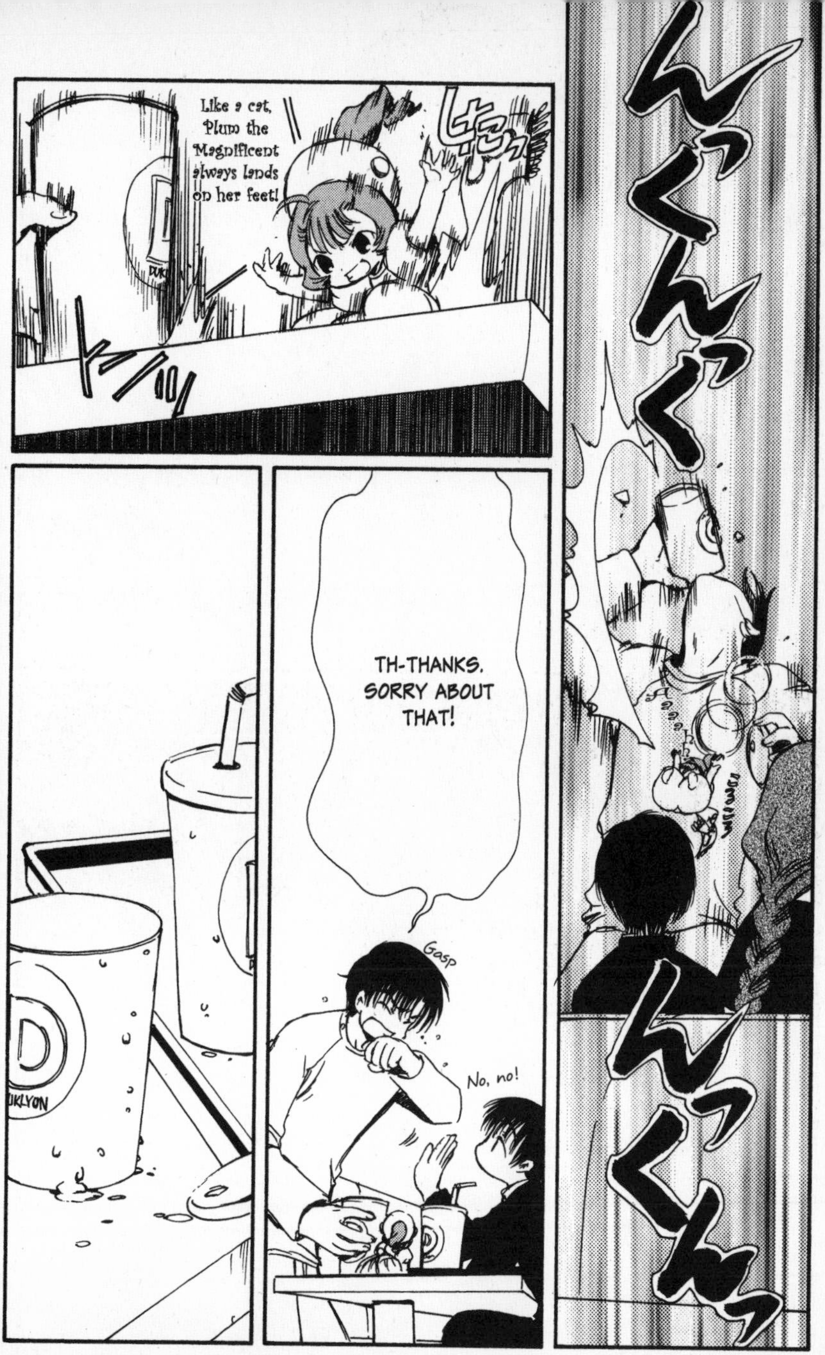
Like a cat, Plum the Magnificent always lands on her feet!
TH-THANKS. SORRY ABOUT THAT!
Gasp
No, no!

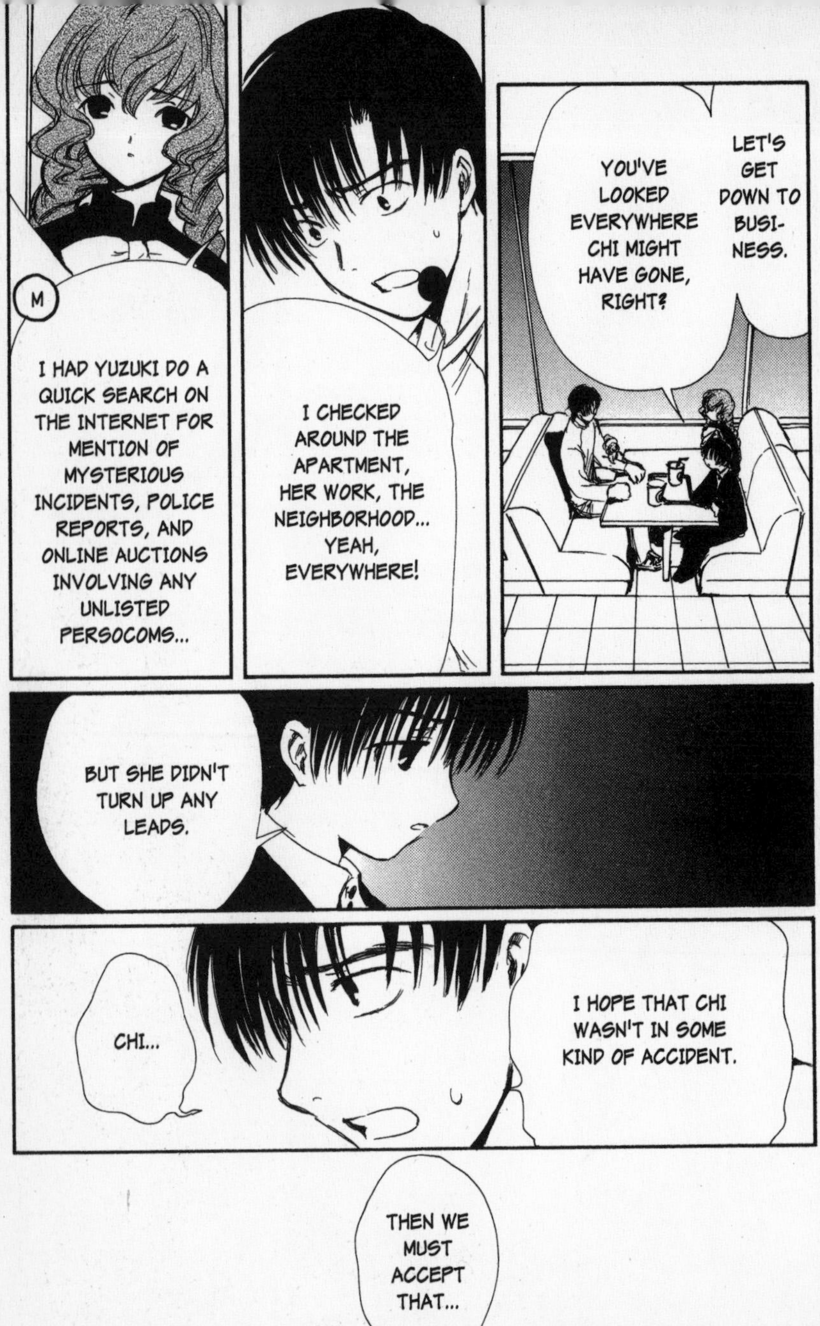
LET'S GET DOWN TO BUSI-NESS.
YOU'VE LOOKED EVERYWHERE CHI MIGHT HAVE GONE, RIGHT?
I CHECKED AROUND THE APARTMENT, HER WORK, THE NEIGHBORHOOD... YEAH, EVERYWHERE!
I HAD YUZUKI DO A QUICK SEARCH ON THE INTERNET FOR MENTION OF MYSTERIOUS INCIDENTS, POLICE REPORTS, AND ONLINE AUCTIONS INVOLVING ANY UNLISTED PERSOCOMS...
BUT SHE DIDN'T TURN UP ANY LEADS.
I HOPE THAT CHI WASN'T IN SOME KIND OF ACCIDENT.
CHI...
THEN WE MUST ACCEPT THAT...

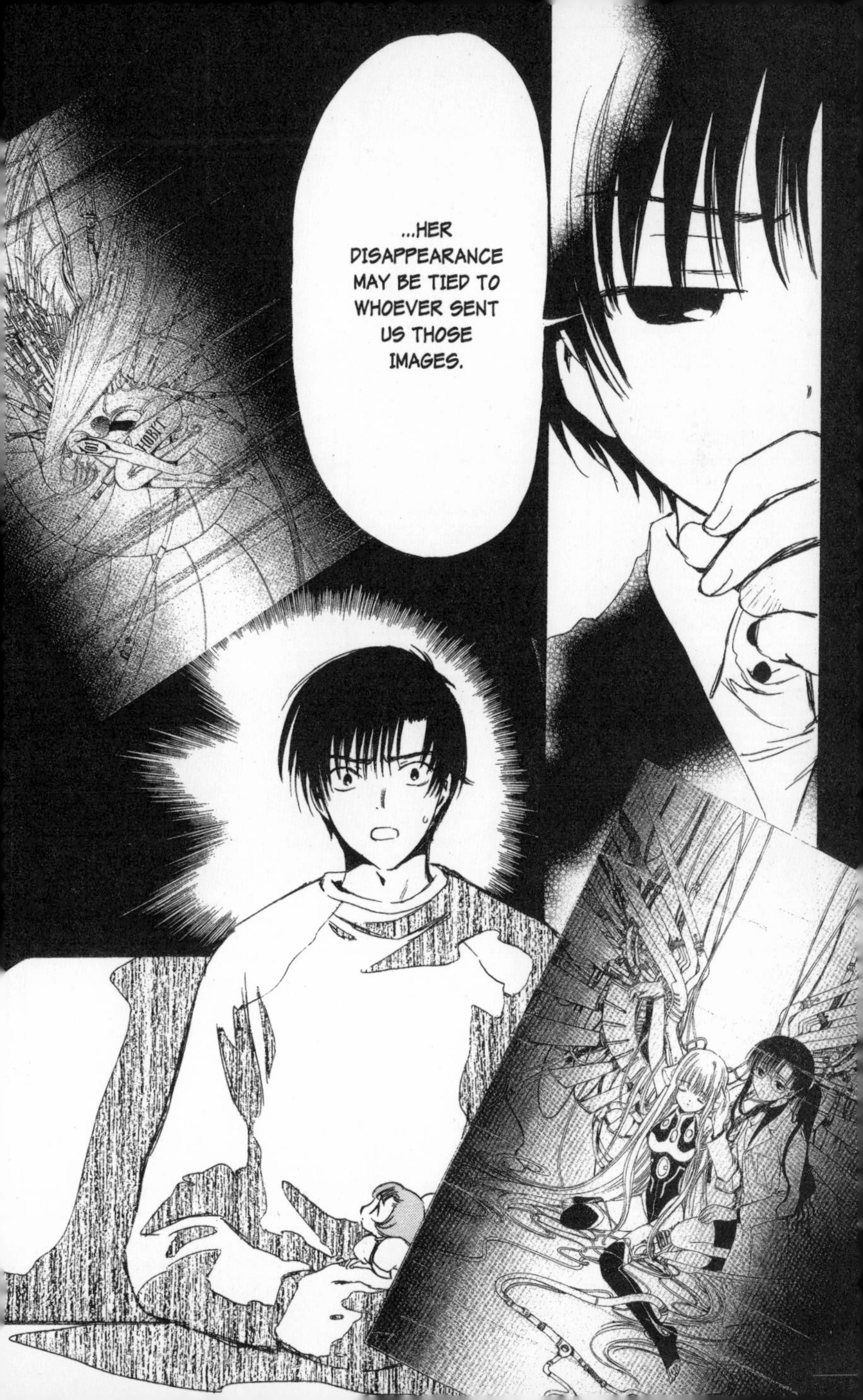
...HER DISAPPEARANCE MAY BE TIED TO WHOEVER SENT US THOSE IMAGES.

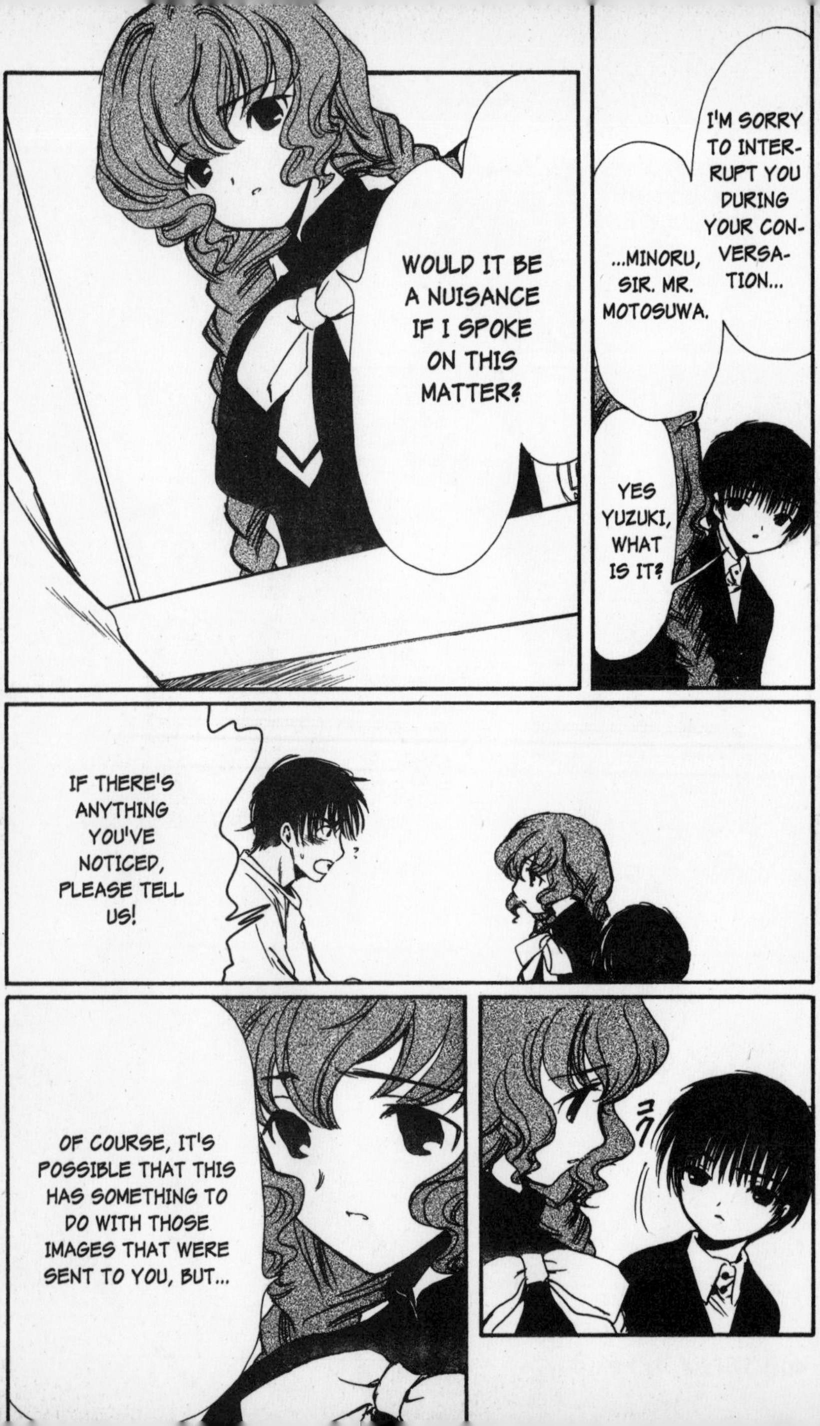
I'M SORRY TO INTER- RUPT YOU DURING YOUR CON- VERSA- TION...
...MINORU, SIR. MR. MOTOSUWA.
YES YUZUKI, WHAT IS IT?
WOULD IT BE A NUISANCE IF I SPOKE ON THIS MATTER?
IF THERE'S ANYTHING YOU'VE NOTICED, PLEASE TELL US!
コク
OF COURSE, IT'S POSSIBLE THAT THIS HAS SOMETHING TO DO WITH THOSE IMAGES THAT WERE SENT TO YOU, BUT...

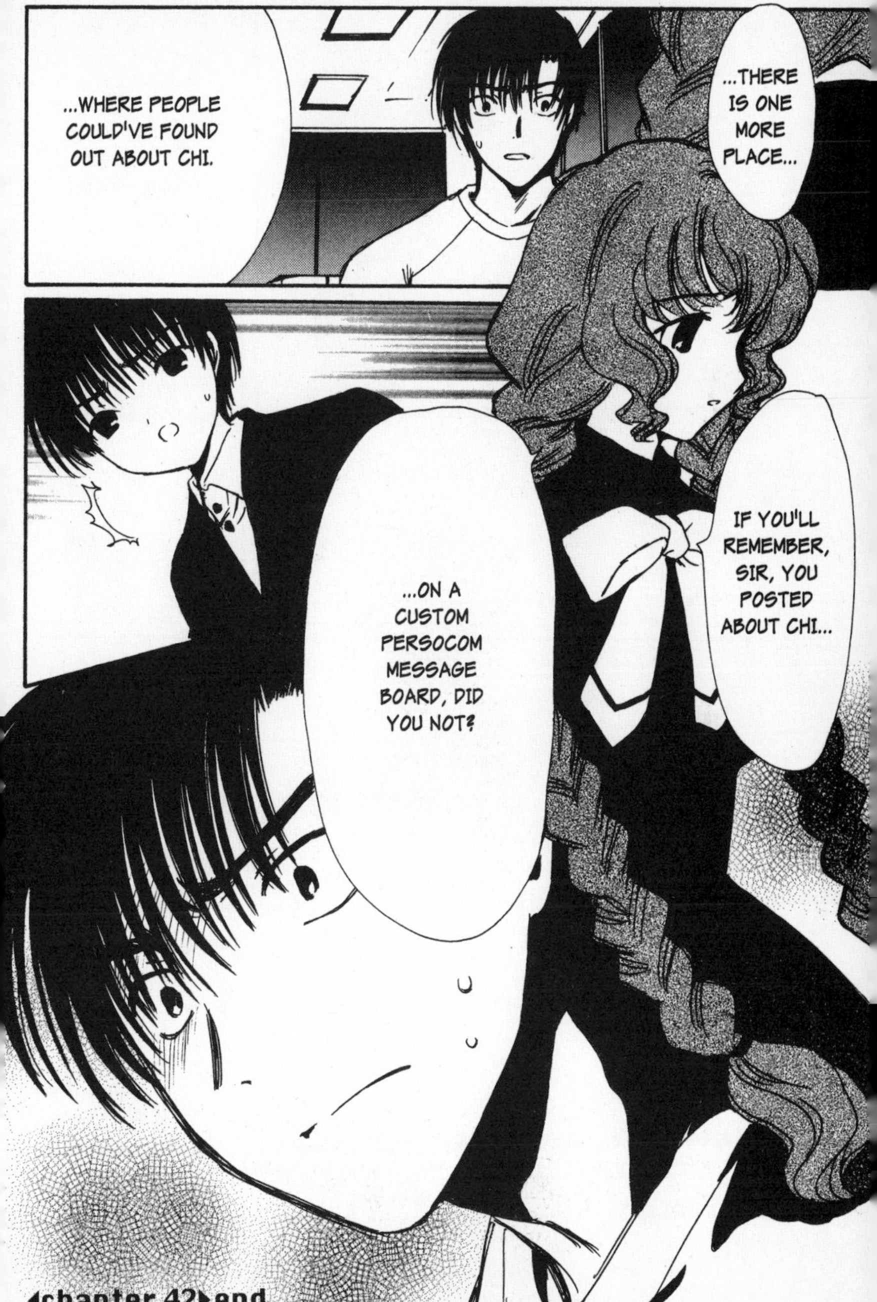
...THERE IS ONE MORE PLACE...
...WHERE PEOPLE COULD'VE FOUND OUT ABOUT CHI.
IF YOU'LL REMEMBER, SIR, YOU POSTED ABOUT CHI...
...ON A CUSTOM PERSOCOM MESSAGE BOARD, DID YOU NOT?
‹chapter.42› end

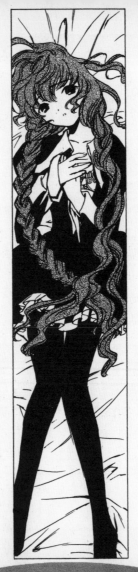

ちょびっツ

Chobits

◀chapter.43▶

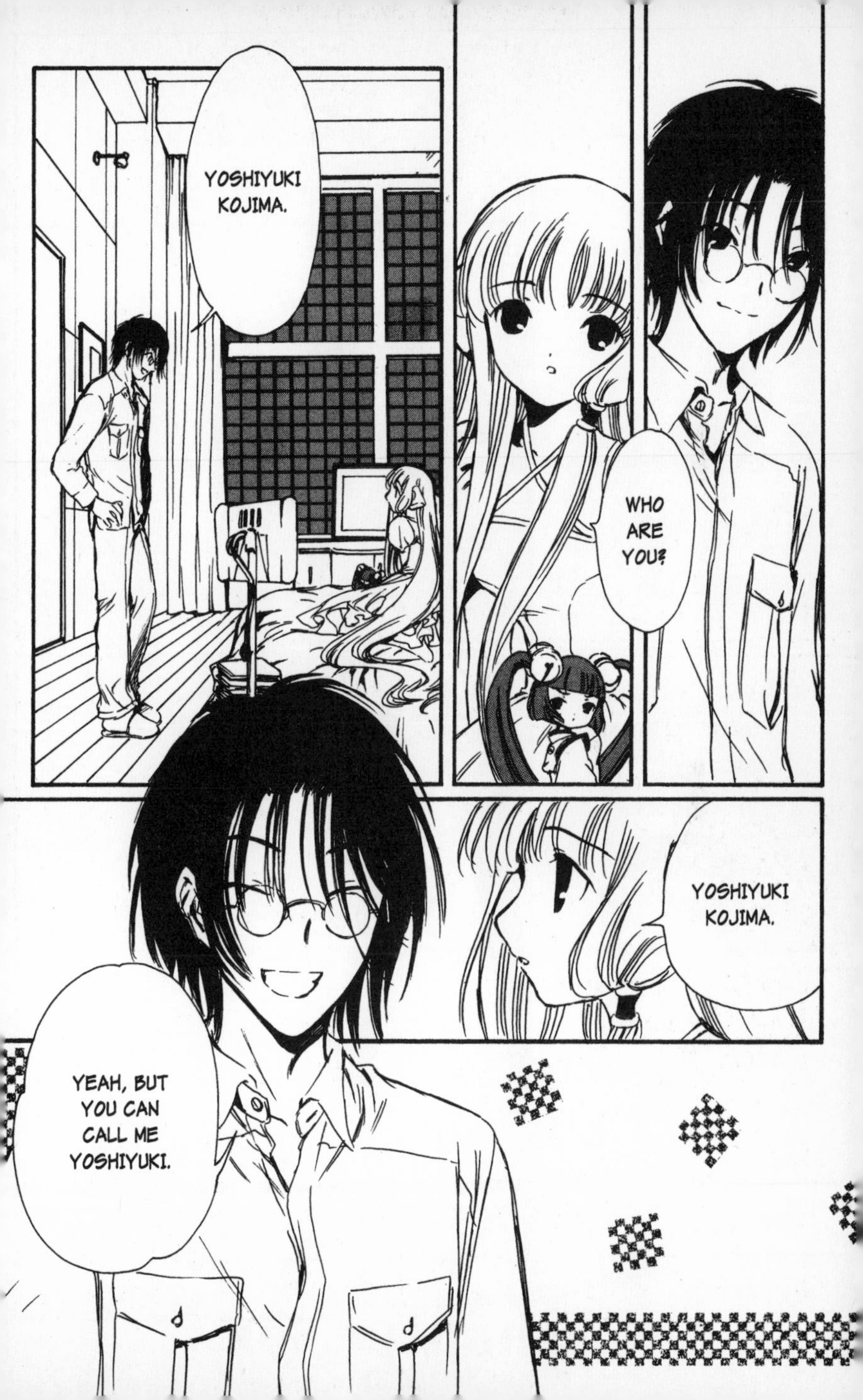
WHO ARE YOU?
YOSHIYUKI KOJIMA.
YOSHIYUKI KOJIMA.
YEAH, BUT YOU CAN CALL ME YOSHIYUKI.

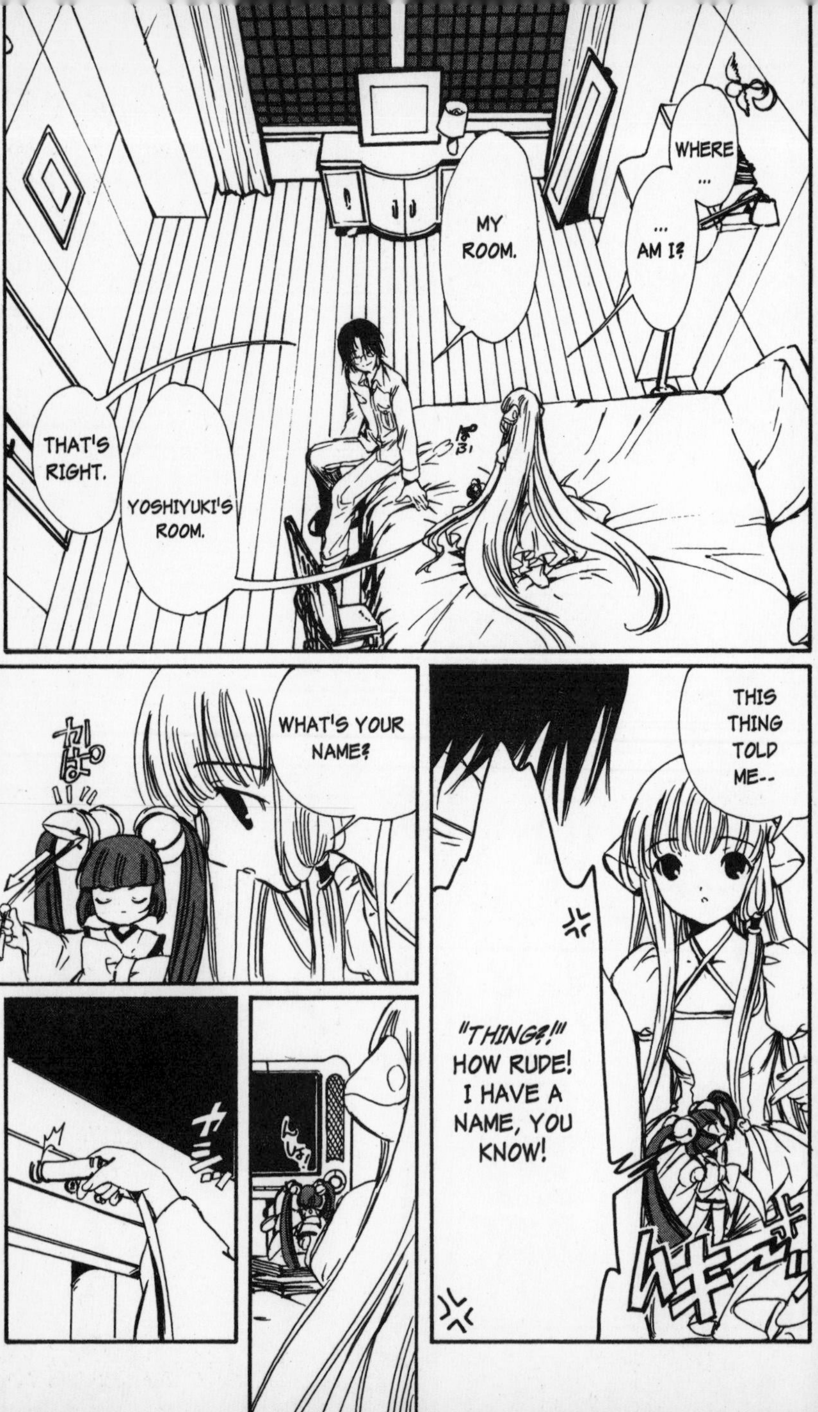
WHERE ... ... AM I?
MY ROOM.
THAT'S RIGHT.
YOSHIYUKI'S ROOM.
THIS THING TOLD ME--
"THING?!" HOW RUDE! I HAVE A NAME, YOU KNOW!
WHAT'S YOUR NAME?

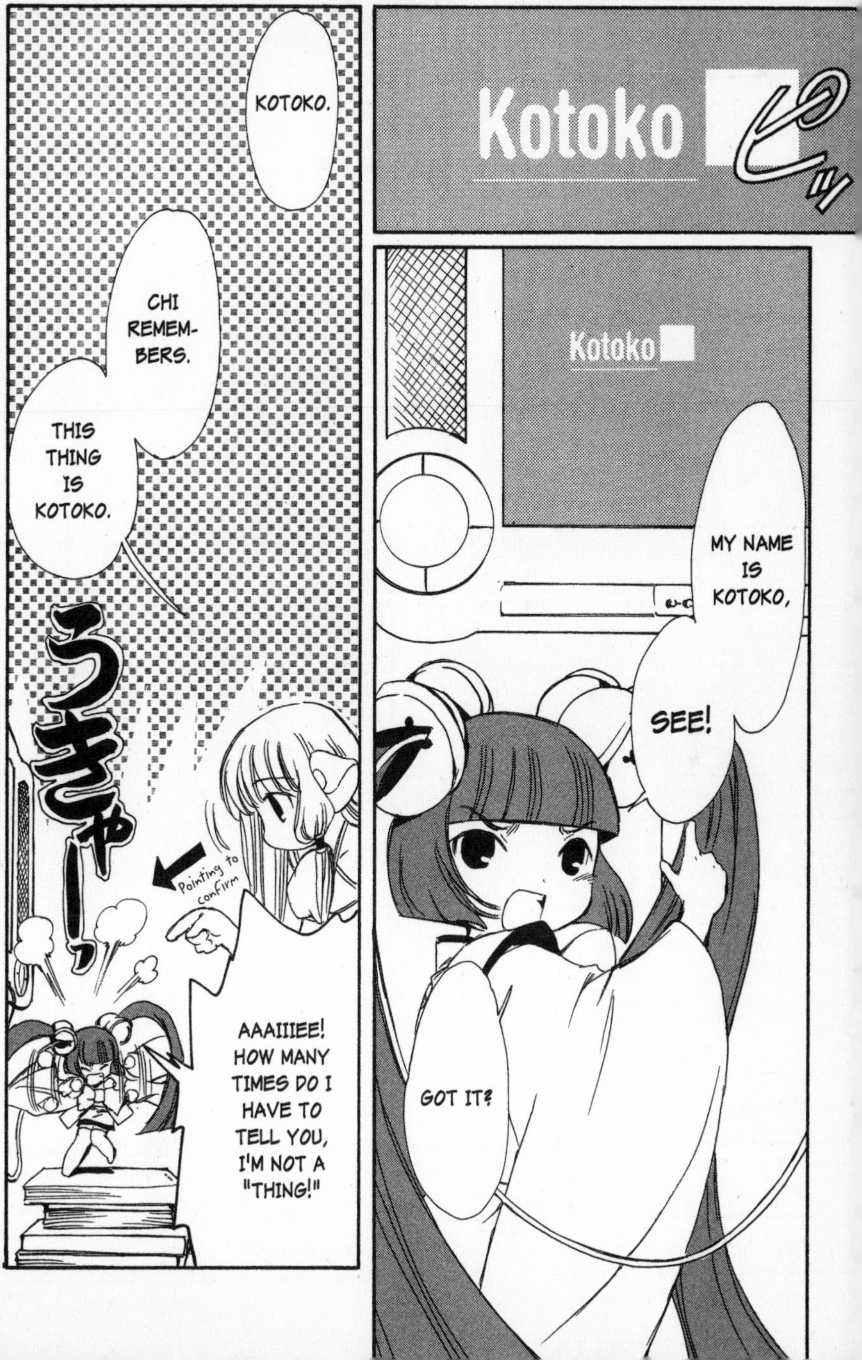
Kotoko
ピッ
Kotoko
MY NAME IS KOTOKO,
SEE!
GOT IT?
KOTOKO.
CHI REMEMBERS.
THIS THING IS KOTOKO.
うきゃー
Pointing to confirm
AAAIIIEE! HOW MANY TIMES DO I HAVE TO TELL YOU, I'M NOT A "THING!"

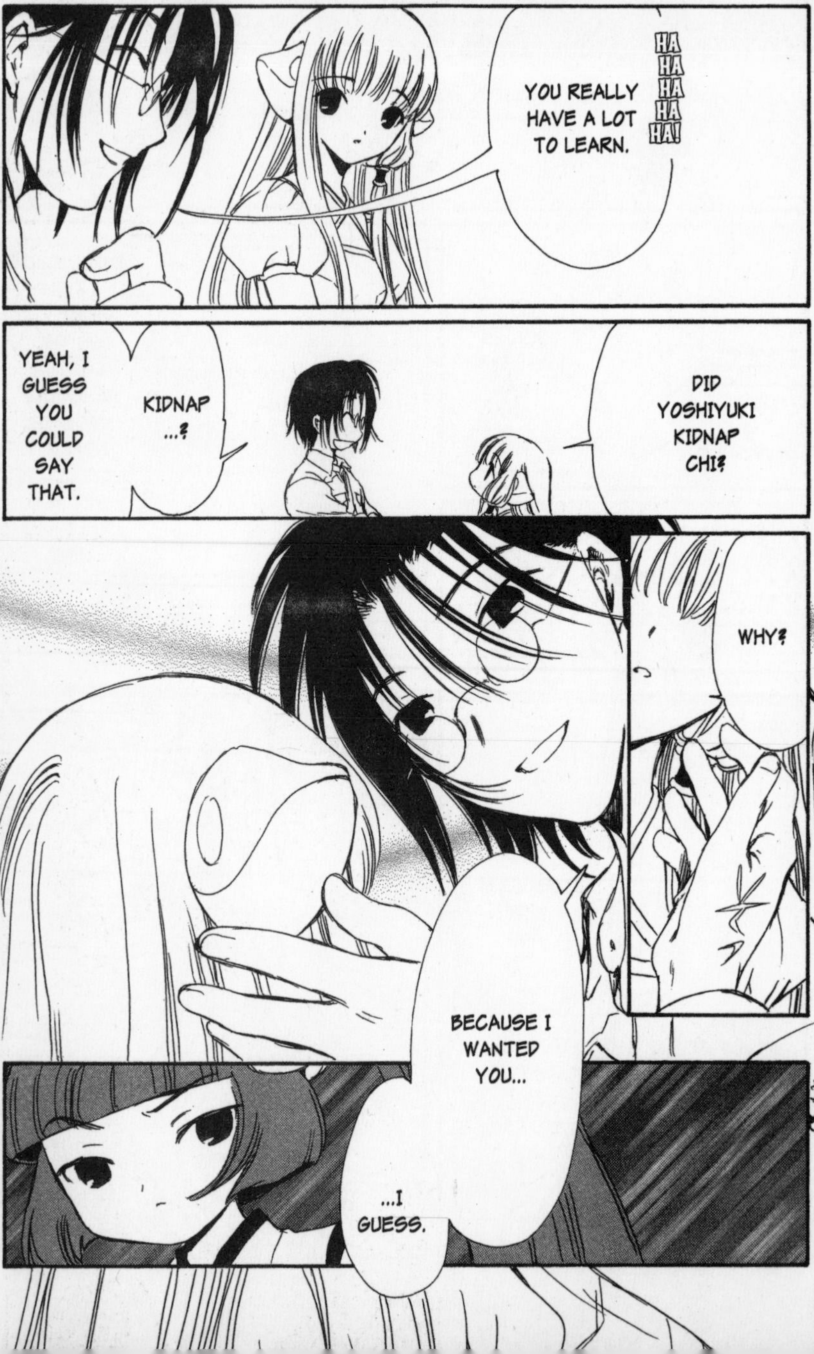
HA HA HA HA HA!
YOU REALLY HAVE A LOT TO LEARN.
DID YOSHIYUKI KIDNAP CHI?
KIDNAP ...?
YEAH, I GUESS YOU COULD SAY THAT.
WHY?
BECAUSE I WANTED YOU...
...I GUESS.

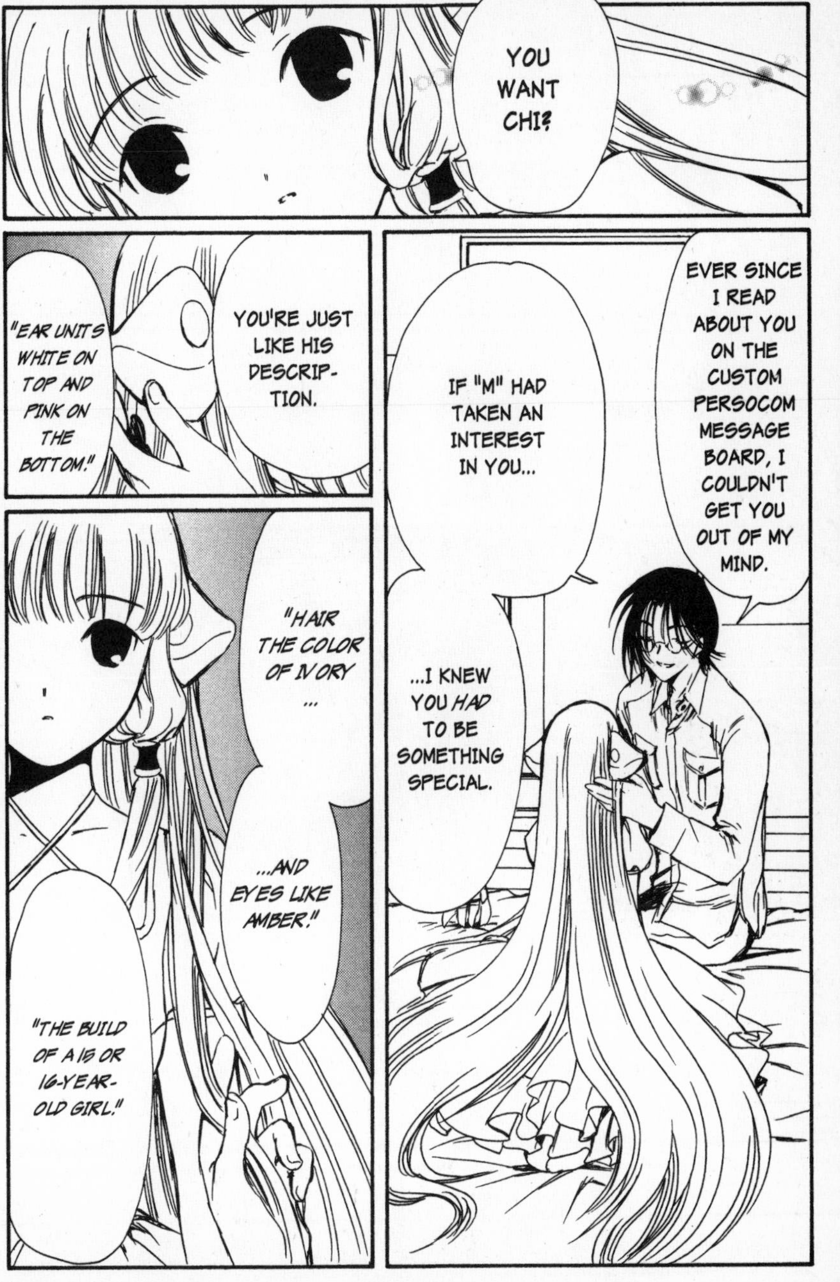
YOU WANT CHI?
EVER SINCE I READ ABOUT YOU ON THE CUSTOM PERSOCOM MESSAGE BOARD, I COULDN'T GET YOU OUT OF MY MIND.
IF "M" HAD TAKEN AN INTEREST IN YOU...
...I KNEW YOU HAD TO BE SOMETHING SPECIAL.
YOU'RE JUST LIKE HIS DESCRIPTION.
"EAR UNITS WHITE ON TOP AND PINK ON THE BOTTOM."
"HAIR THE COLOR OF IVORY...
...AND EYES LIKE AMBER."
"THE BUILD OF A 15 OR 16-YEAR-OLD GIRL."

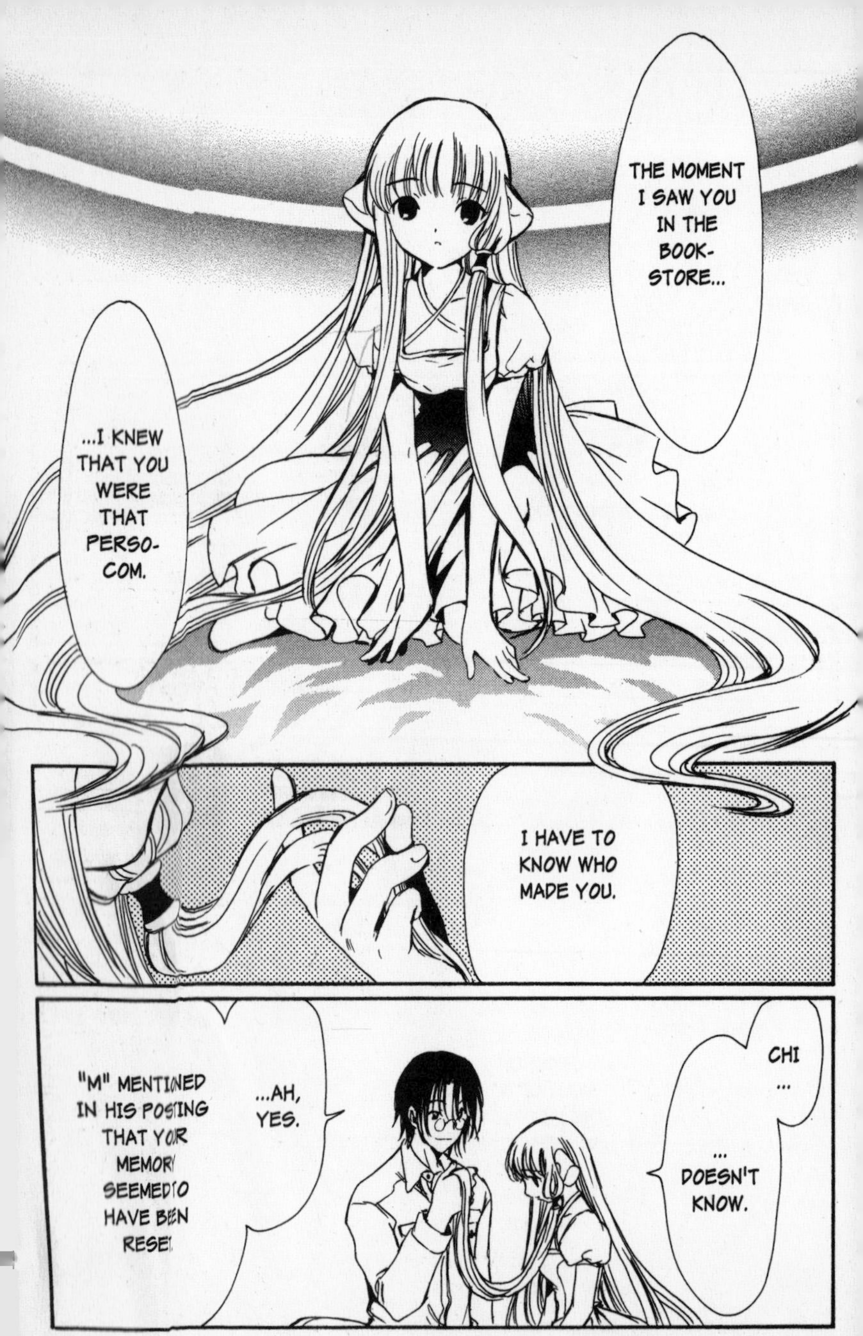
THE MOMENT I SAW YOU IN THE BOOK-STORE...
...I KNEW THAT YOU WERE THAT PERSO-COM.
I HAVE TO KNOW WHO MADE YOU.
CHI ... ... DOESN'T KNOW.
...AH, YES.
"M" MENTIONED IN HIS POSTING THAT YOUR MEMORY SEEMED TO HAVE BEEN RESET.

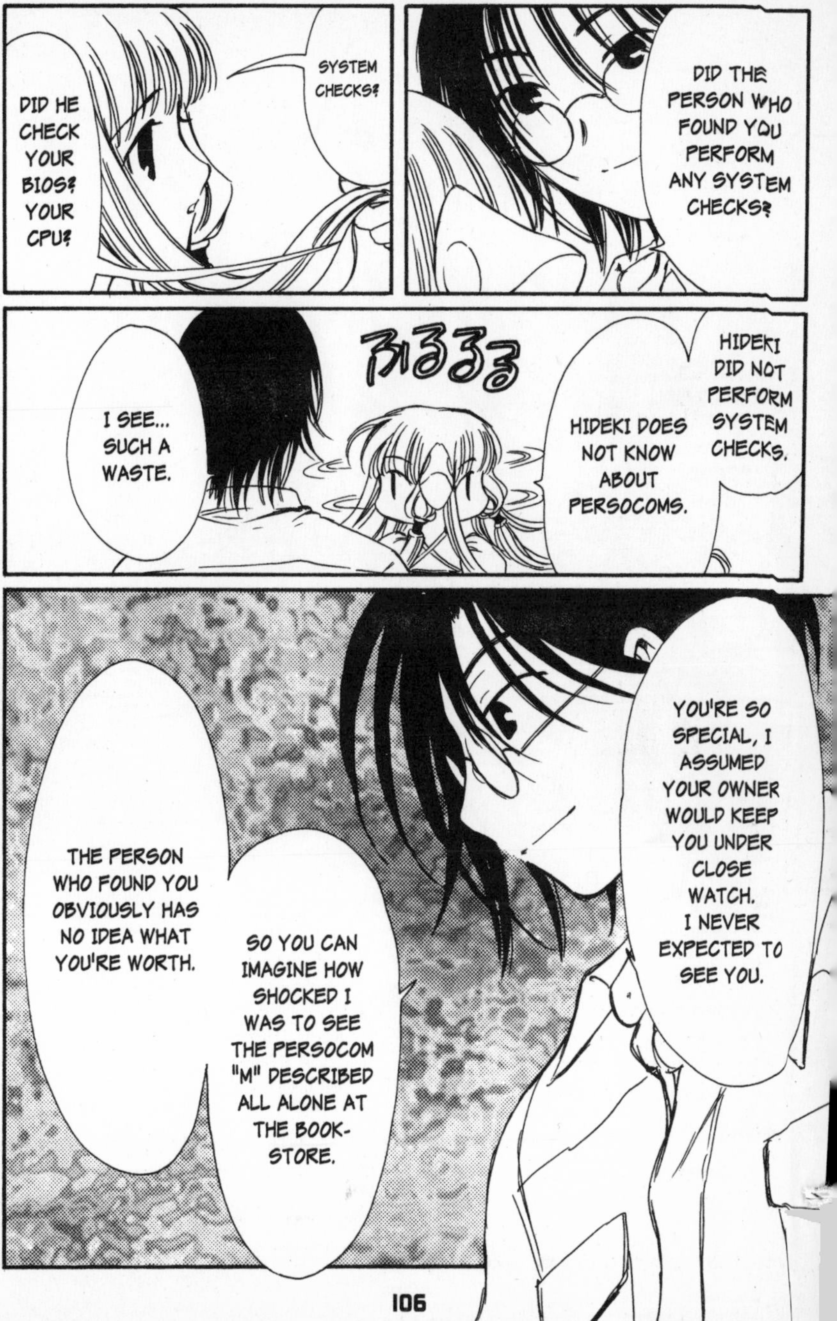
DID THE PERSON WHO FOUND YOU PERFORM ANY SYSTEM CHECKS?
SYSTEM CHECKS?
DID HE CHECK YOUR BIOS? YOUR CPU?
HIDEKI DID NOT PERFORM SYSTEM CHECKS.
HIDEKI DOES NOT KNOW ABOUT PERSOCOMS.
ふるるる
I SEE... SUCH A WASTE.
YOU'RE SO SPECIAL, I ASSUMED YOUR OWNER WOULD KEEP YOU UNDER CLOSE WATCH. I NEVER EXPECTED TO SEE YOU.
THE PERSON WHO FOUND YOU OBVIOUSLY HAS NO IDEA WHAT YOU'RE WORTH.
SO YOU CAN IMAGINE HOW SHOCKED I WAS TO SEE THE PERSOCOM "M" DESCRIBED ALL ALONE AT THE BOOK-STORE.

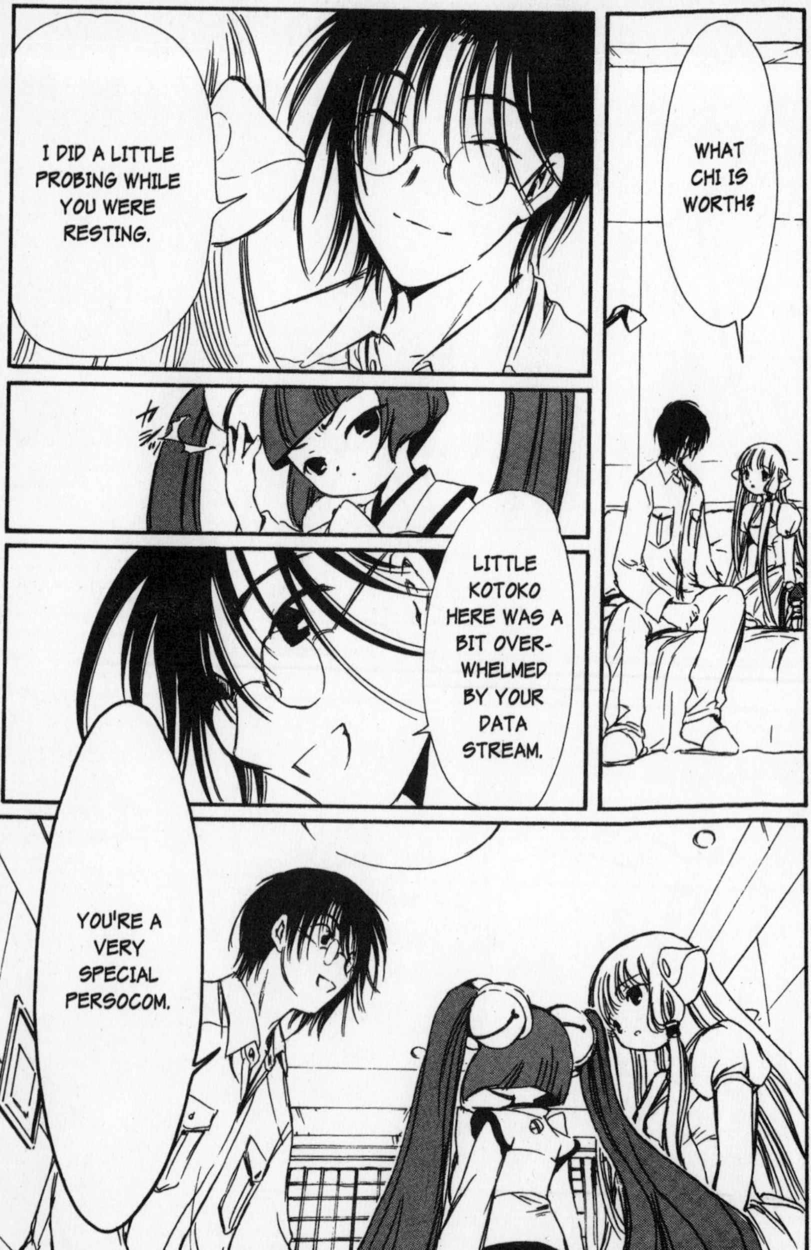
WHAT CHI IS WORTH?
I DID A LITTLE PROBING WHILE YOU WERE RESTING.
LITTLE KOTOKO HERE WAS A BIT OVER-WHELMED BY YOUR DATA STREAM.
YOU'RE A VERY SPECIAL PERSOCOM.

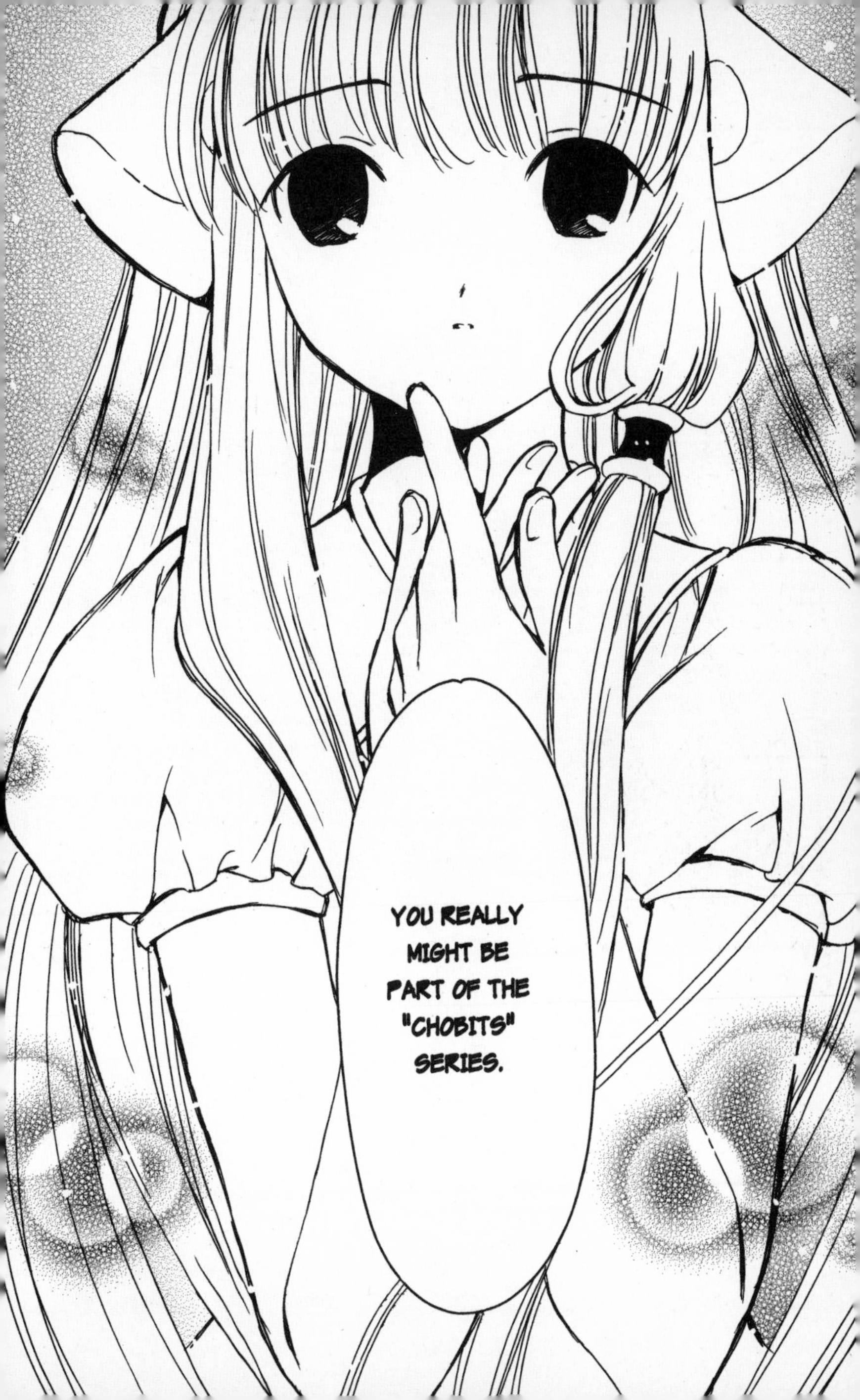
YOU REALLY MIGHT BE PART OF THE "CHOBITS" SERIES.

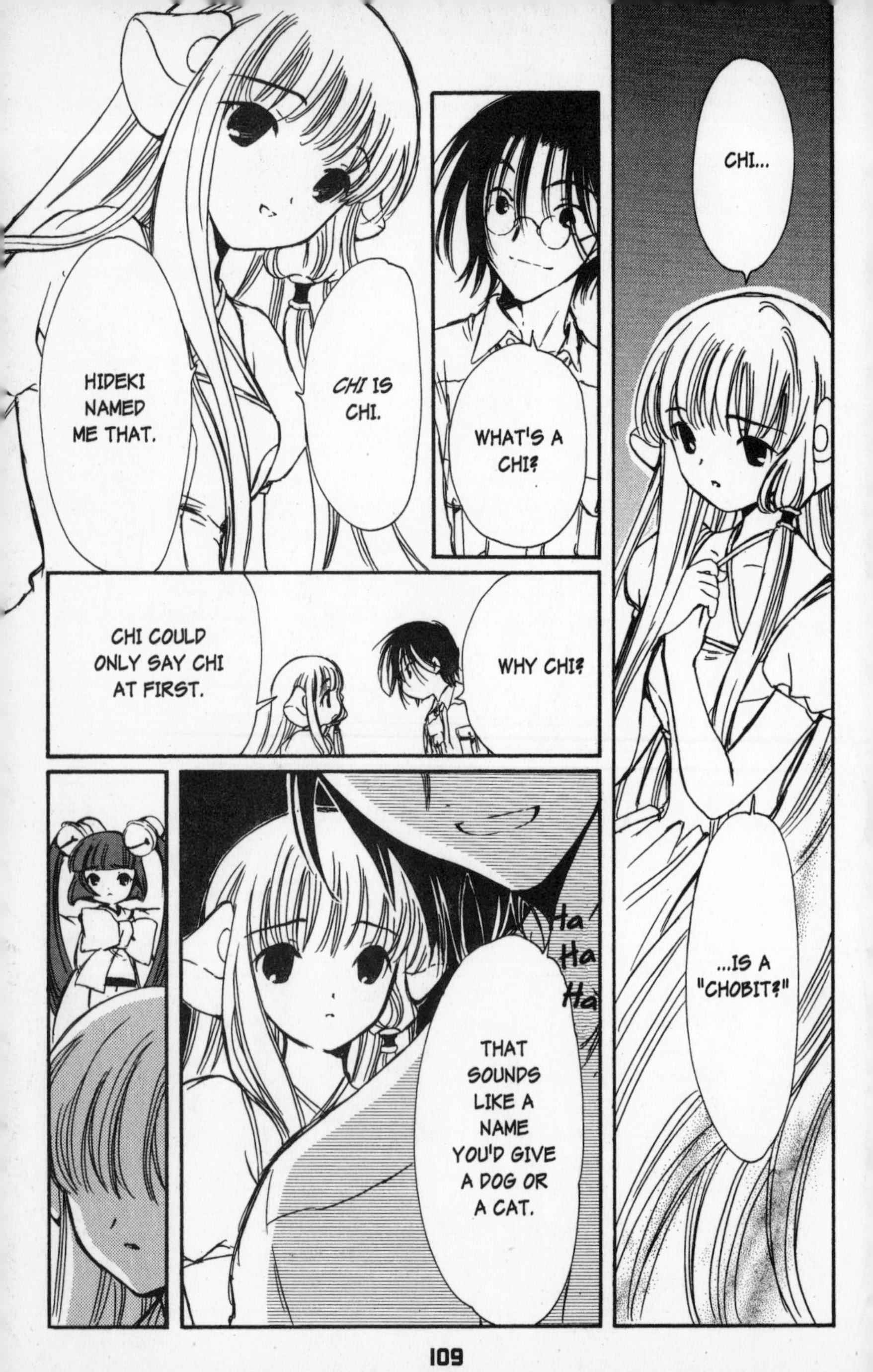

CHI...
...IS A "CHOBIT?"
WHAT'S A CHI?
CHI IS CHI.
HIDEKI NAMED ME THAT.
WHY CHI?
CHI COULD ONLY SAY CHI AT FIRST.
Ha Ha Ha
THAT SOUNDS LIKE A NAME YOU'D GIVE A DOG OR A CAT.

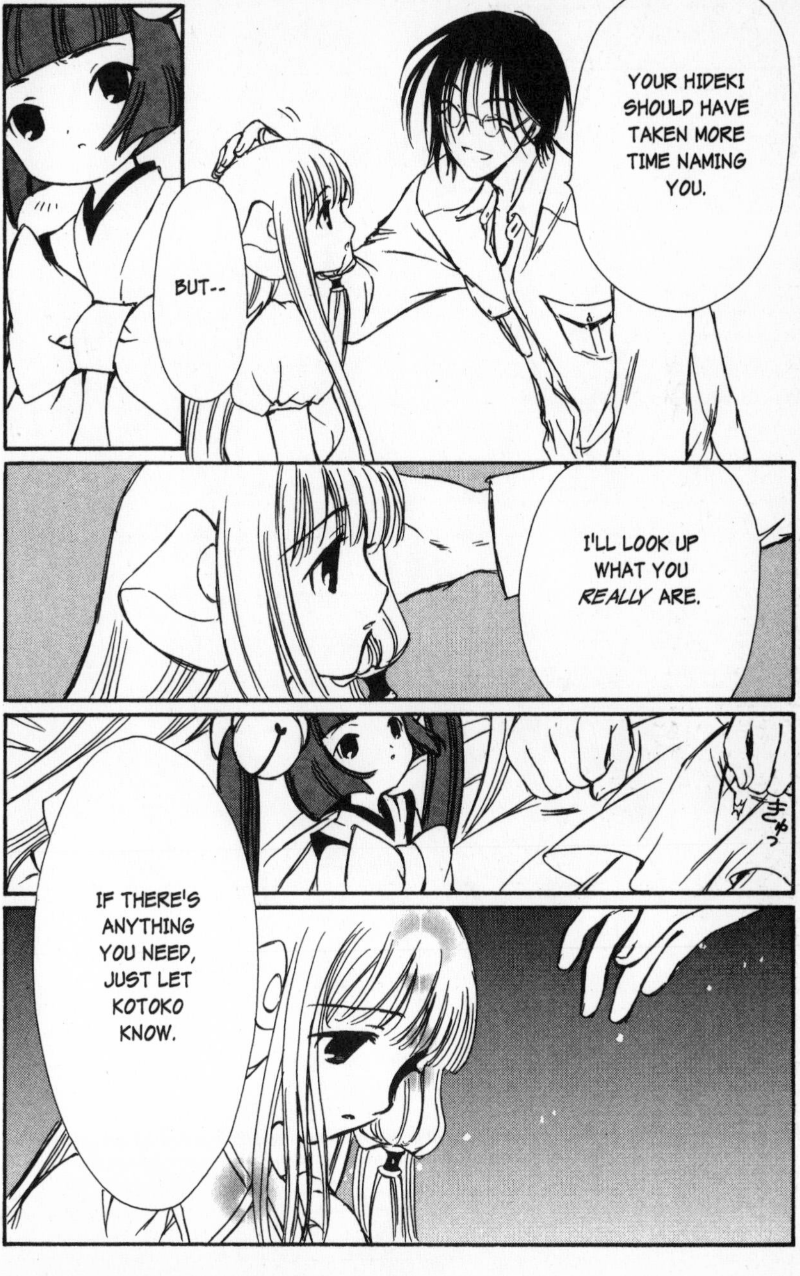
YOUR HIDEKI SHOULD HAVE TAKEN MORE TIME NAMING YOU.
BUT--
I'LL LOOK UP WHAT YOU *REALLY* ARE.
きゅっ
IF THERE'S ANYTHING YOU NEED, JUST LET KOTOKO KNOW.

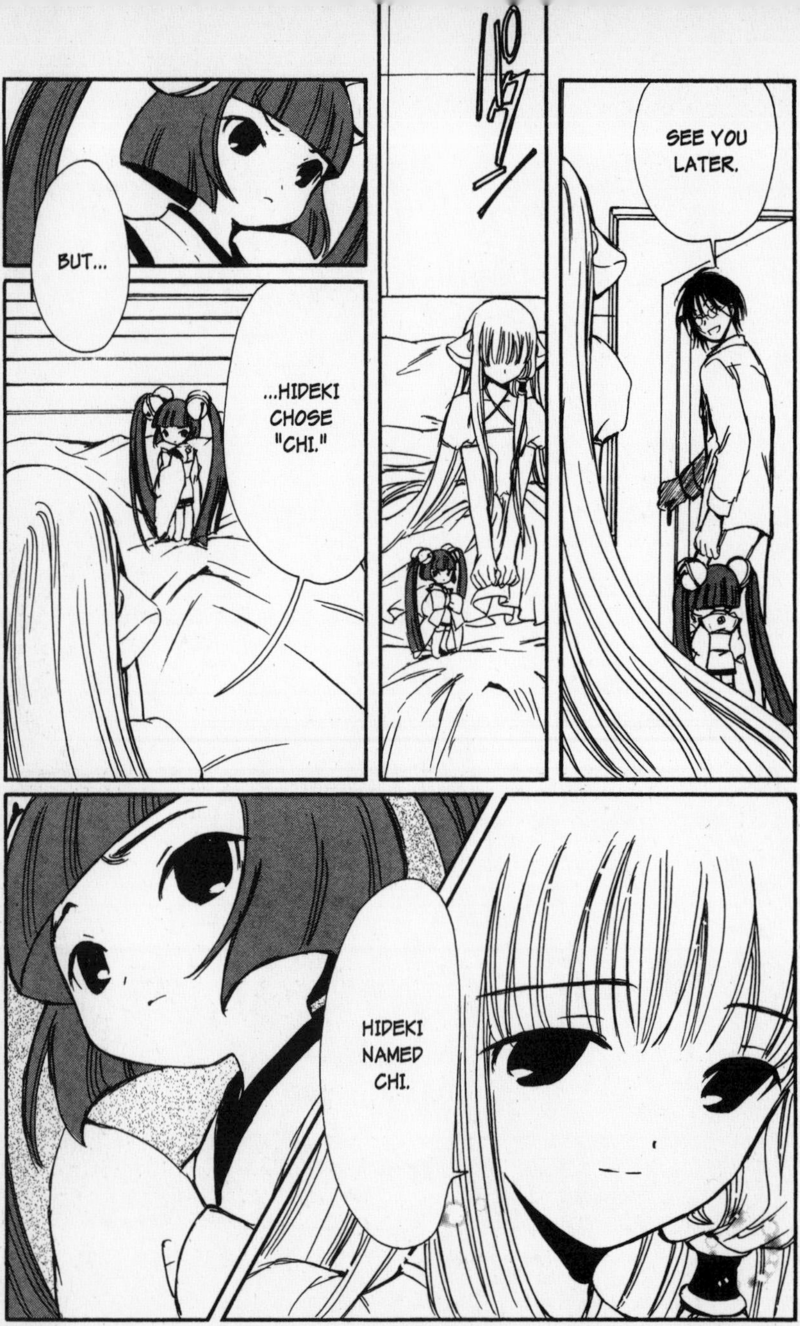
SEE YOU LATER.
BUT...
...HIDEKI CHOSE "CHI."
HIDEKI NAMED CHI.

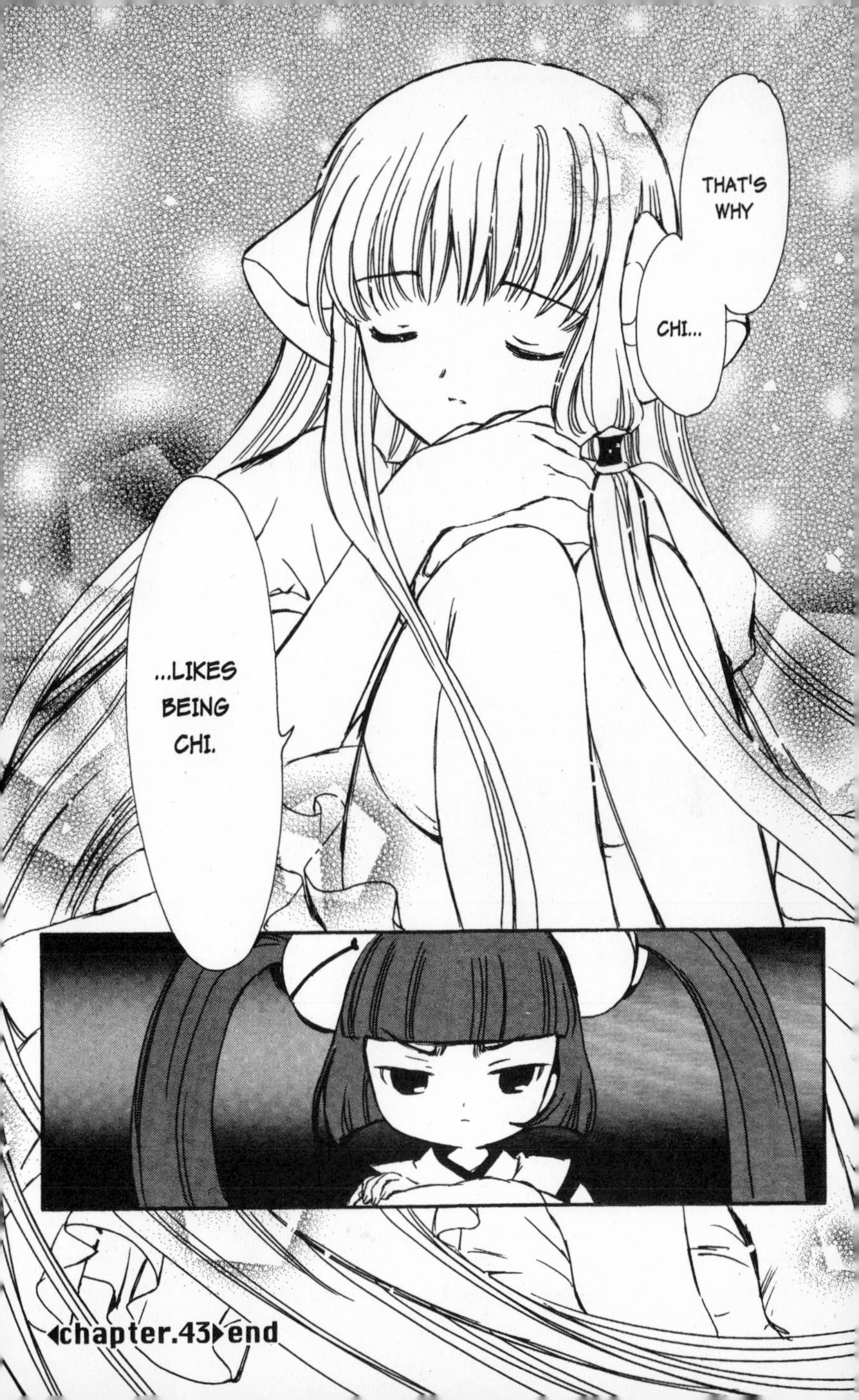
THAT'S WHY
CHI...
...LIKES BEING CHI.
chapter.43 end

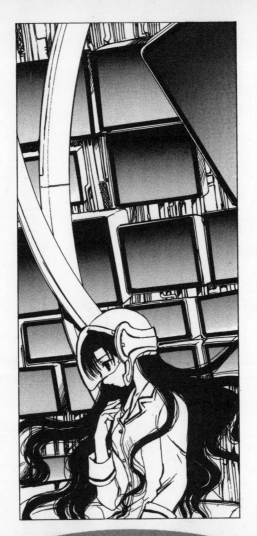

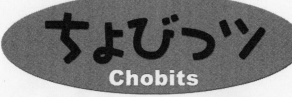

ちょびっツ
Chobits

◀chapter.44▶

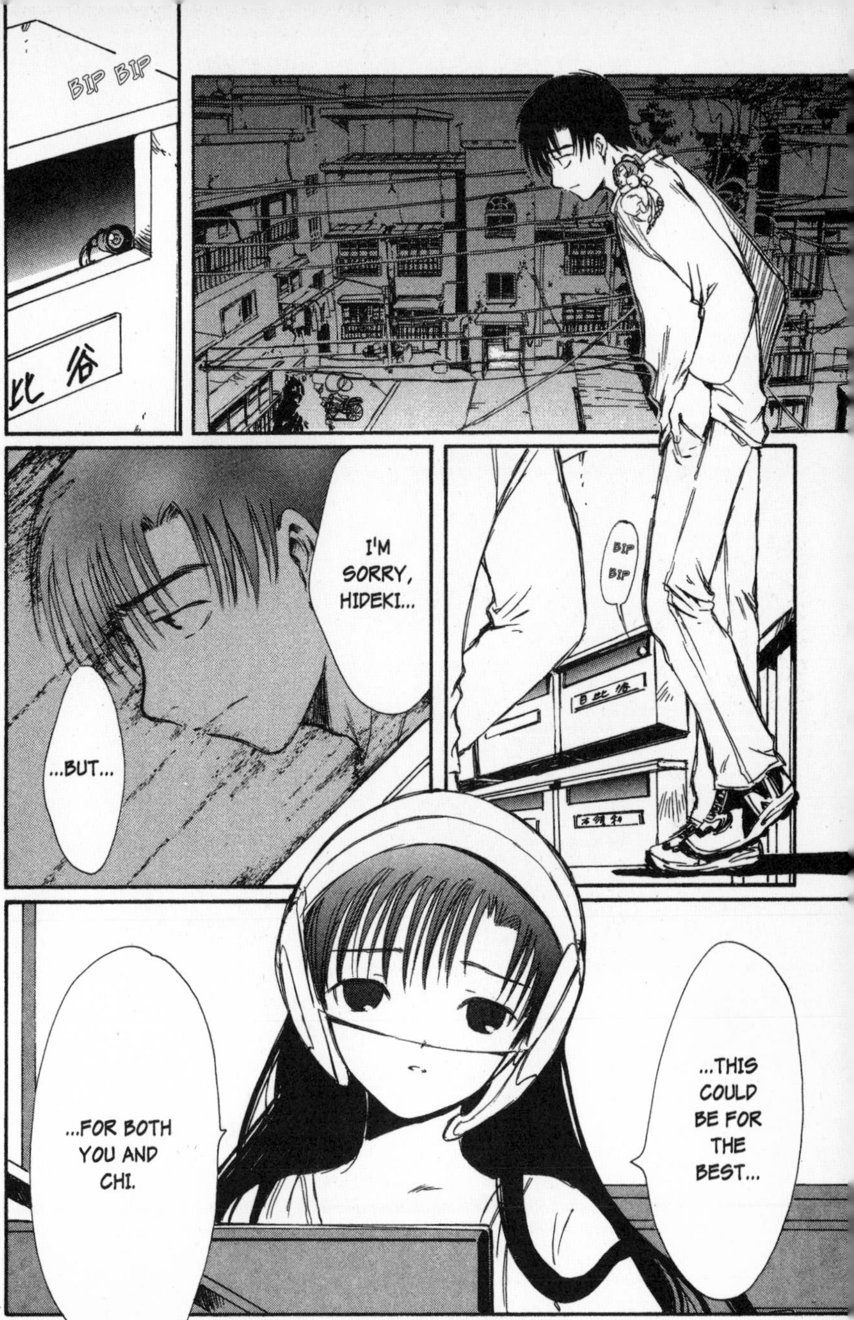
BIP BIP
比谷
BIP BIP
I'M SORRY, HIDEKI...
...BUT...
...THIS COULD BE FOR THE BEST...
...FOR BOTH YOU AND CHI.

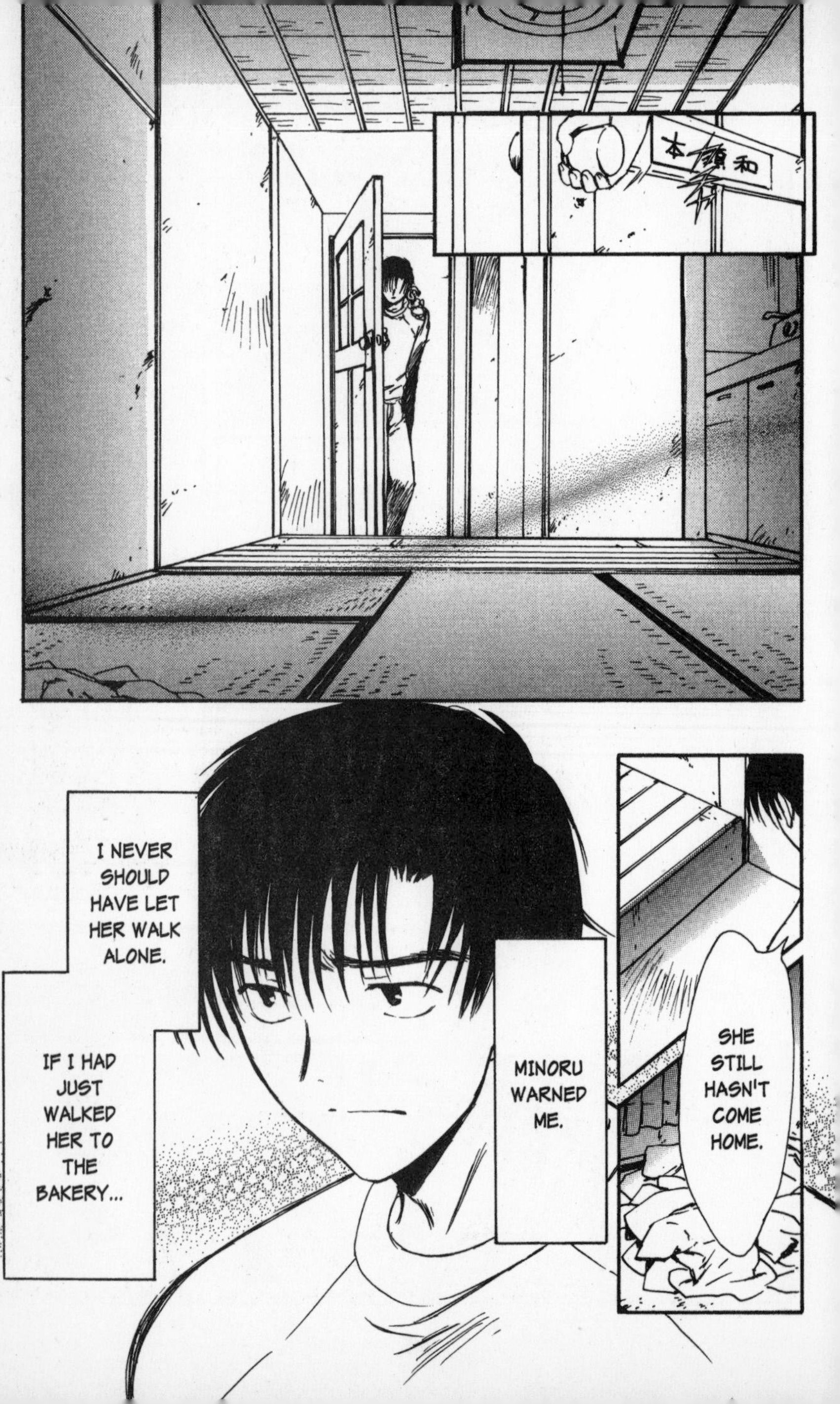
SHE STILL HASN'T COME HOME.
MINORU WARNED ME.
I NEVER SHOULD HAVE LET HER WALK ALONE.
IF I HAD JUST WALKED HER TO THE BAKERY...

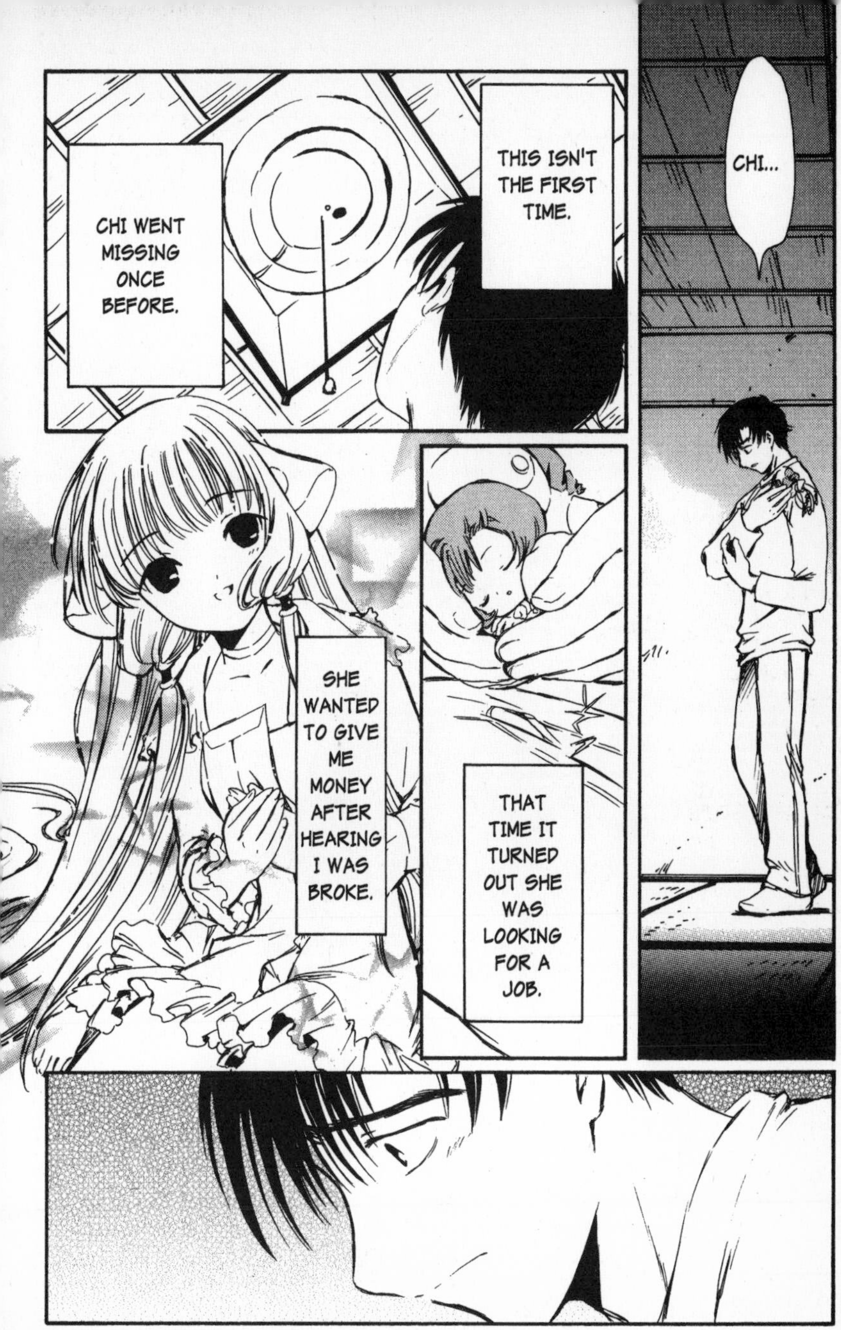
CHI...
THIS ISN'T THE FIRST TIME.
CHI WENT MISSING ONCE BEFORE.
THAT TIME IT TURNED OUT SHE WAS LOOKING FOR A JOB.
SHE WANTED TO GIVE ME MONEY AFTER HEARING I WAS BROKE.

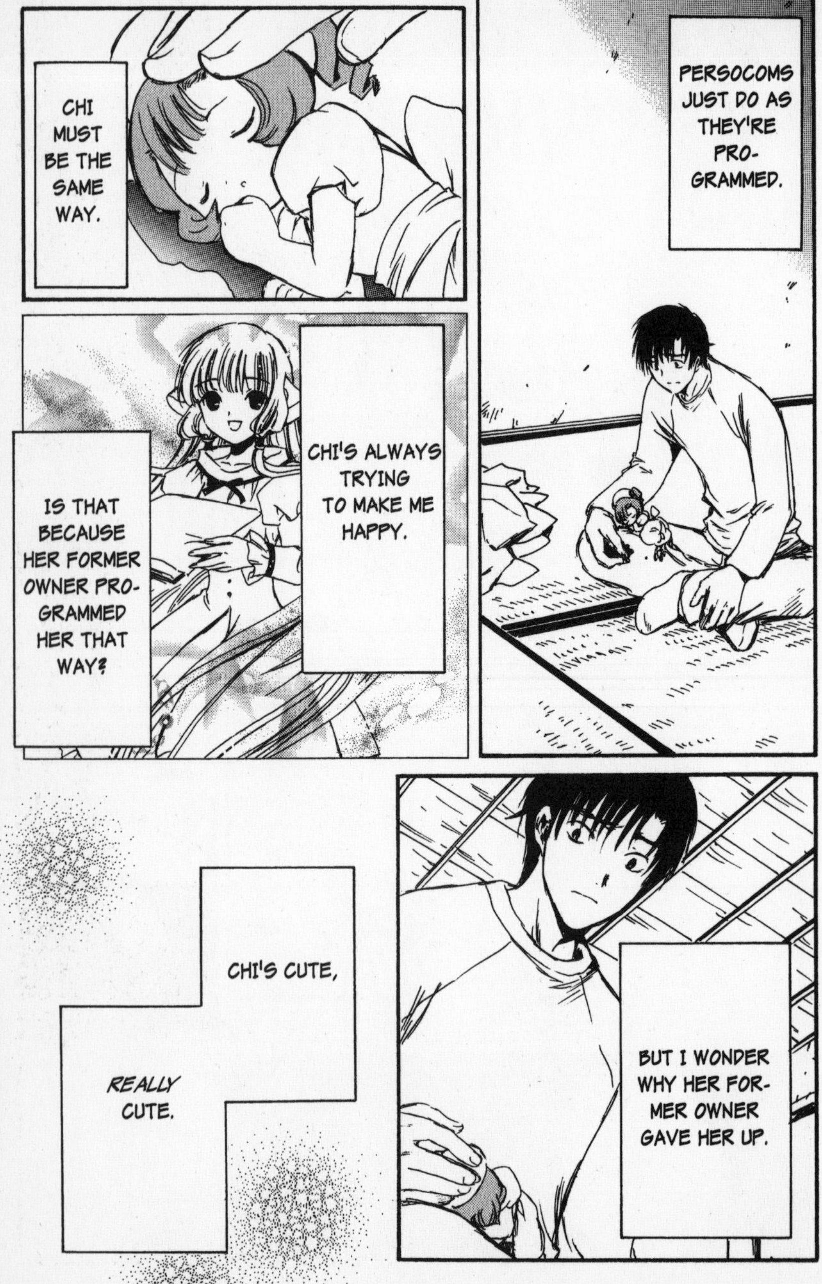
PERSOCOMS JUST DO AS THEY'RE PRO-GRAMMED.
CHI MUST BE THE SAME WAY.
CHI'S ALWAYS TRYING TO MAKE ME HAPPY.
IS THAT BECAUSE HER FORMER OWNER PRO-GRAMMED HER THAT WAY?
BUT I WONDER WHY HER FOR-MER OWNER GAVE HER UP.
CHI'S CUTE,
REALLY CUTE.

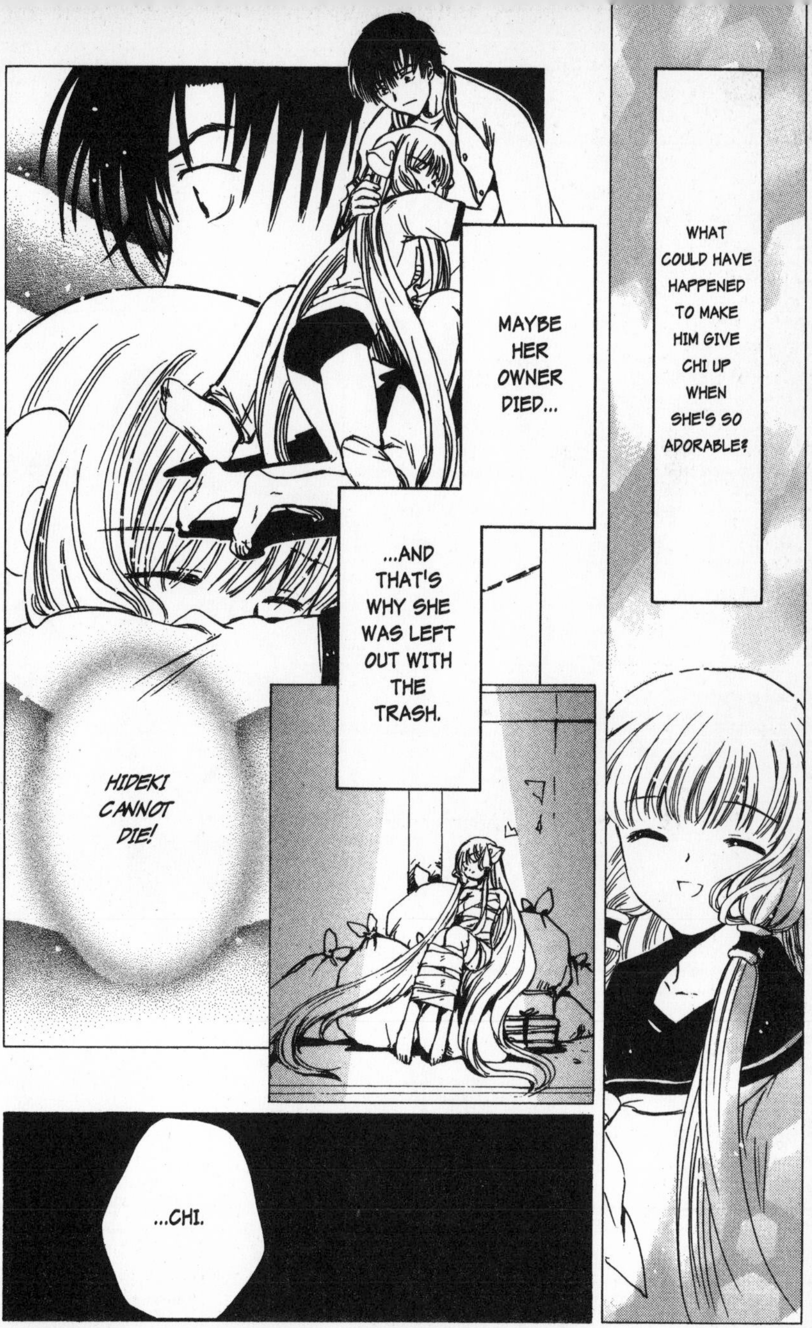
WHAT COULD HAVE HAPPENED TO MAKE HIM GIVE CHI UP WHEN SHE'S SO ADORABLE?
MAYBE HER OWNER DIED...
...AND THAT'S WHY SHE WAS LEFT OUT WITH THE TRASH.
HIDEKI CANNOT DIE!
...CHI.

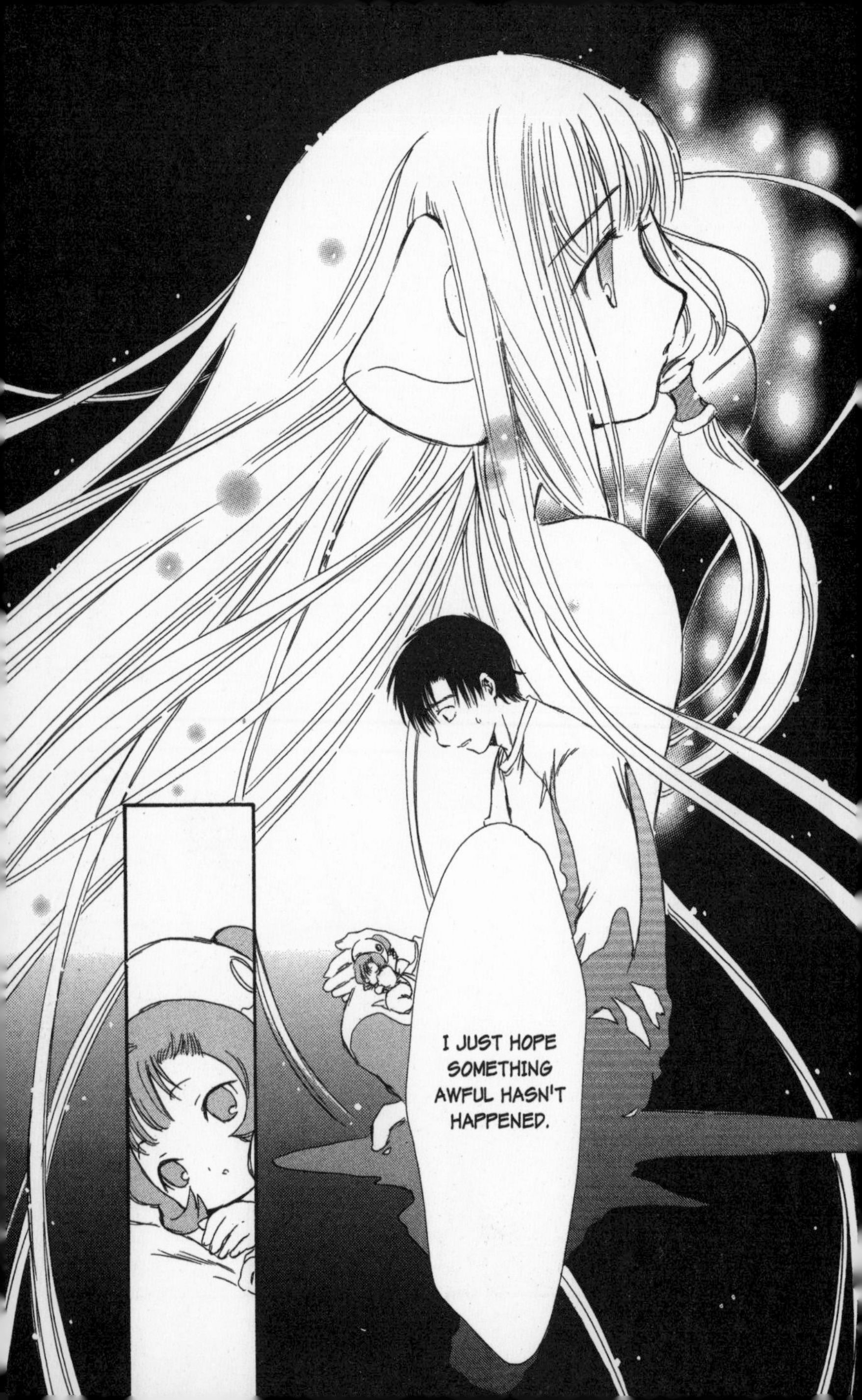
I JUST HOPE SOMETHING AWFUL HASN'T HAPPENED.

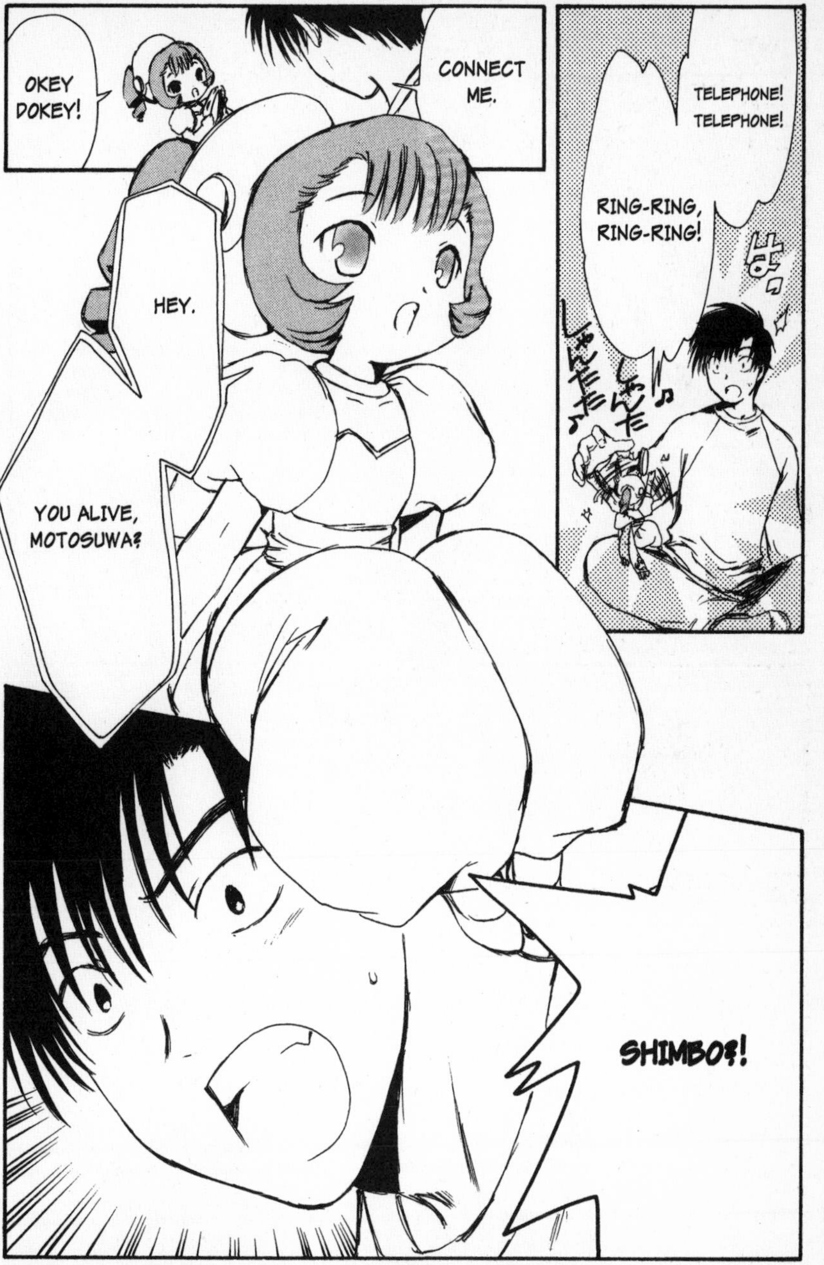
TELEPHONE! TELEPHONE!
RING-RING, RING-RING!
はっ
CONNECT ME.
OKEY DOKEY!
HEY.
YOU ALIVE, MOTOSUWA?
SHIMBO?!

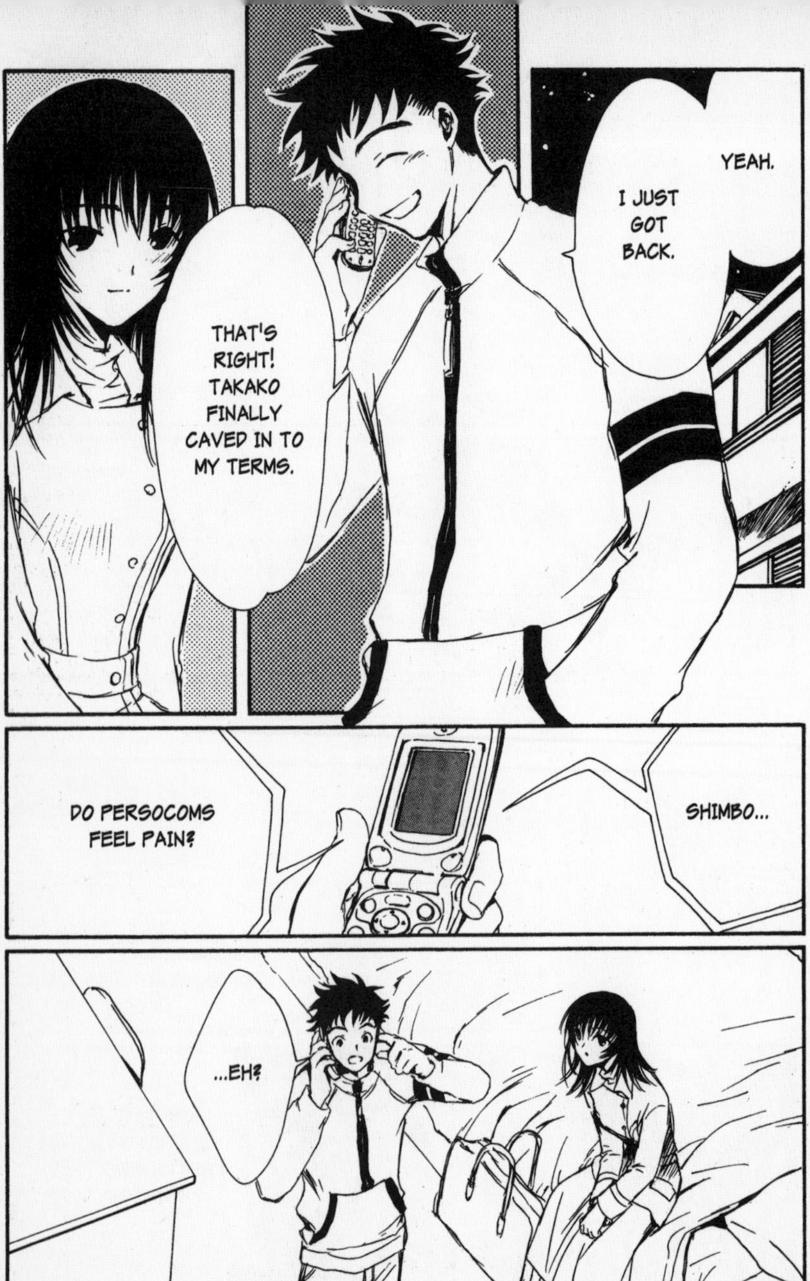
YEAH.
I JUST GOT BACK.
THAT'S RIGHT! TAKAKO FINALLY CAVED IN TO MY TERMS.
SHIMBO...
DO PERSOCOMS FEEL PAIN?
...EH?

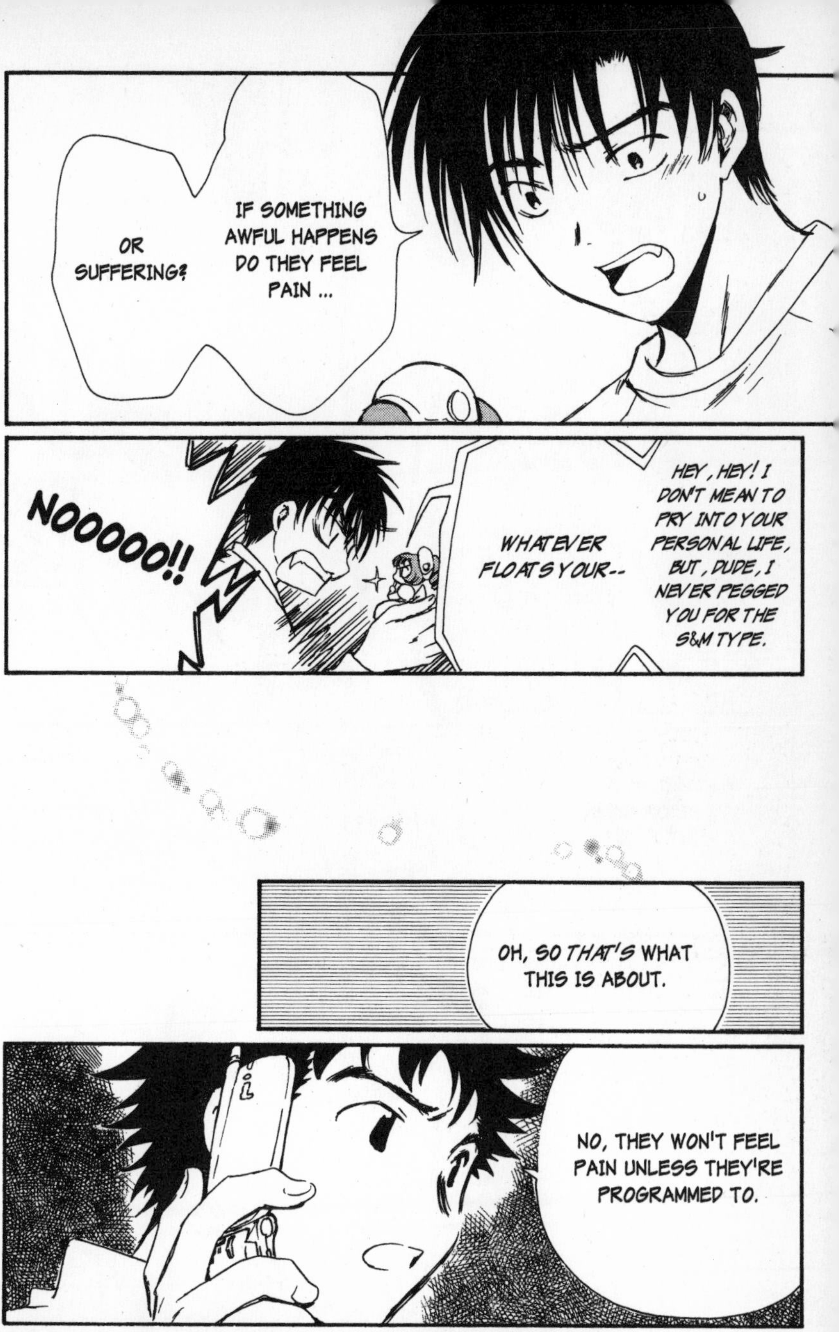
IF SOMETHING AWFUL HAPPENS DO THEY FEEL PAIN ...
OR SUFFERING?
HEY, HEY! I DON'T MEAN TO PRY INTO YOUR PERSONAL LIFE, BUT, DUDE, I NEVER PEGGED YOU FOR THE S&M TYPE.
WHATEVER FLOATS YOUR--
NOOOOO!!
OH, SO THAT'S WHAT THIS IS ABOUT.
NO, THEY WON'T FEEL PAIN UNLESS THEY'RE PROGRAMMED TO.

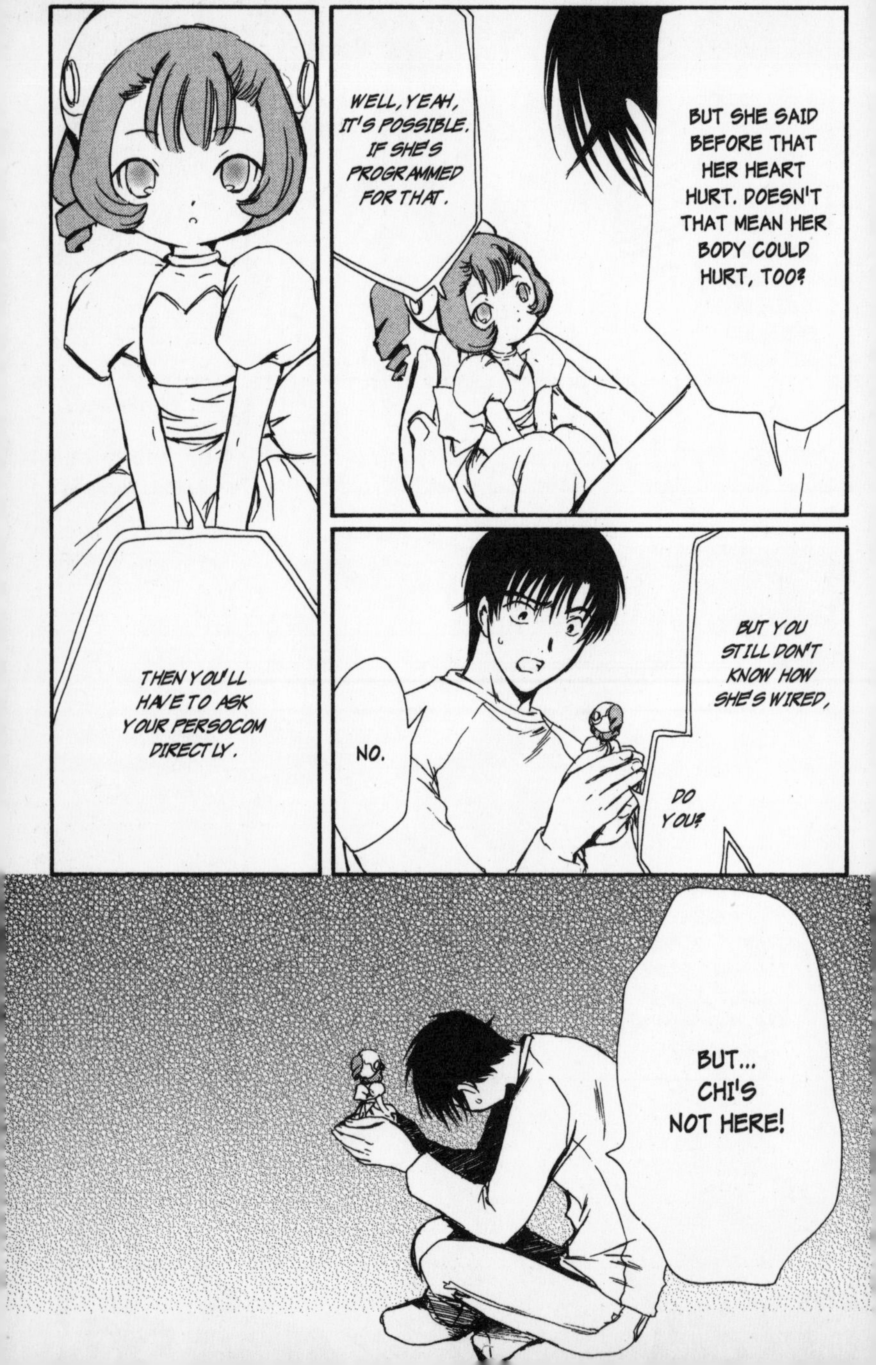
BUT SHE SAID BEFORE THAT HER HEART HURT. DOESN'T THAT MEAN HER BODY COULD HURT, TOO?
WELL, YEAH, IT'S POSSIBLE. IF SHE'S PROGRAMMED FOR THAT.
BUT YOU STILL DON'T KNOW HOW SHE'S WIRED,
DO YOU?
NO.
THEN YOU'LL HAVE TO ASK YOUR PERSOCOM DIRECTLY.
BUT... CHI'S NOT HERE!

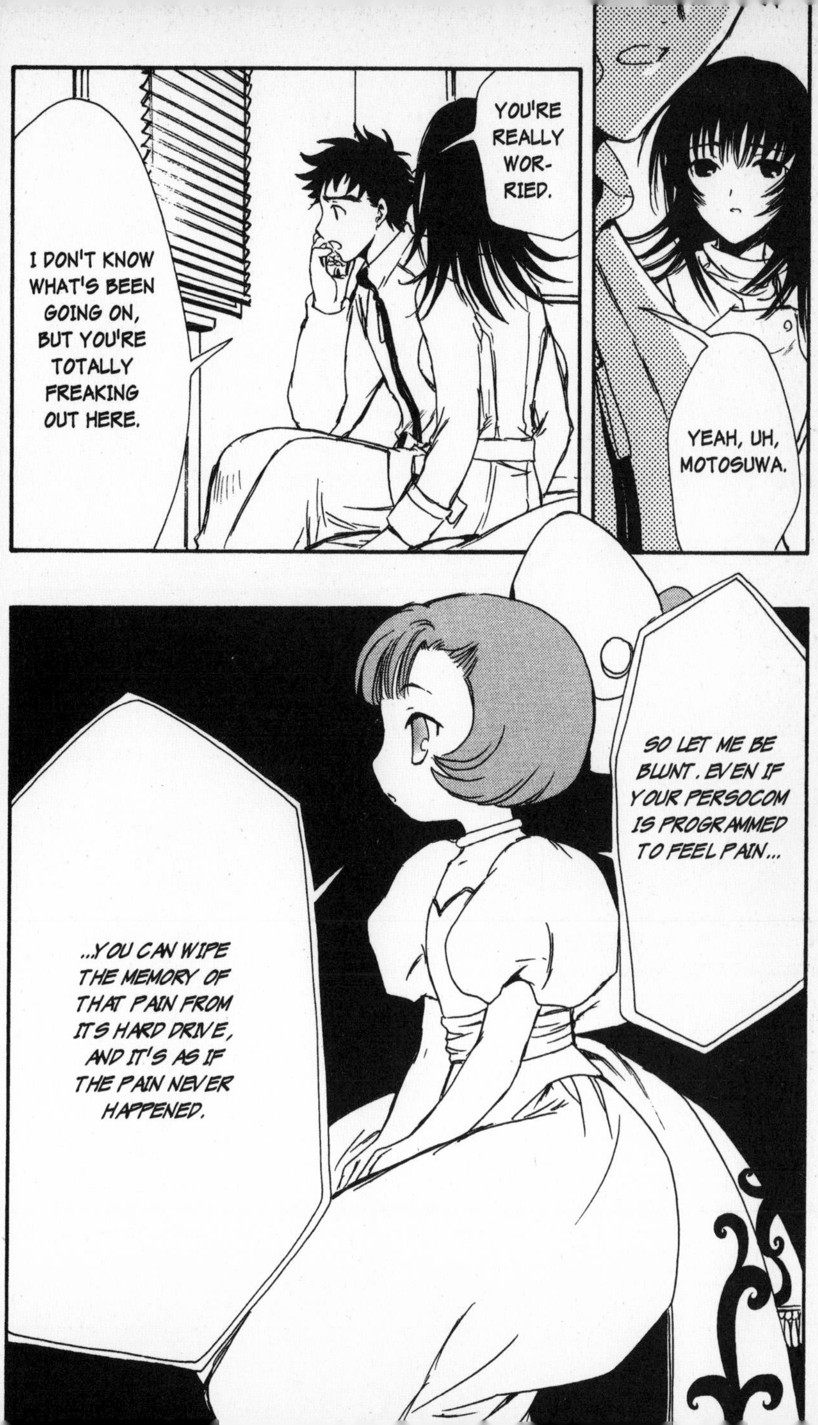
YEAH, UH, MOTOSUWA.
YOU'RE REALLY WOR-RIED.
I DON'T KNOW WHAT'S BEEN GOING ON, BUT YOU'RE TOTALLY FREAKING OUT HERE.
SO LET ME BE BLUNT. EVEN IF YOUR PERSOCOM IS PROGRAMMED TO FEEL PAIN...
...YOU CAN WIPE THE MEMORY OF THAT PAIN FROM ITS HARD DRIVE, AND IT'S AS IF THE PAIN NEVER HAPPENED.

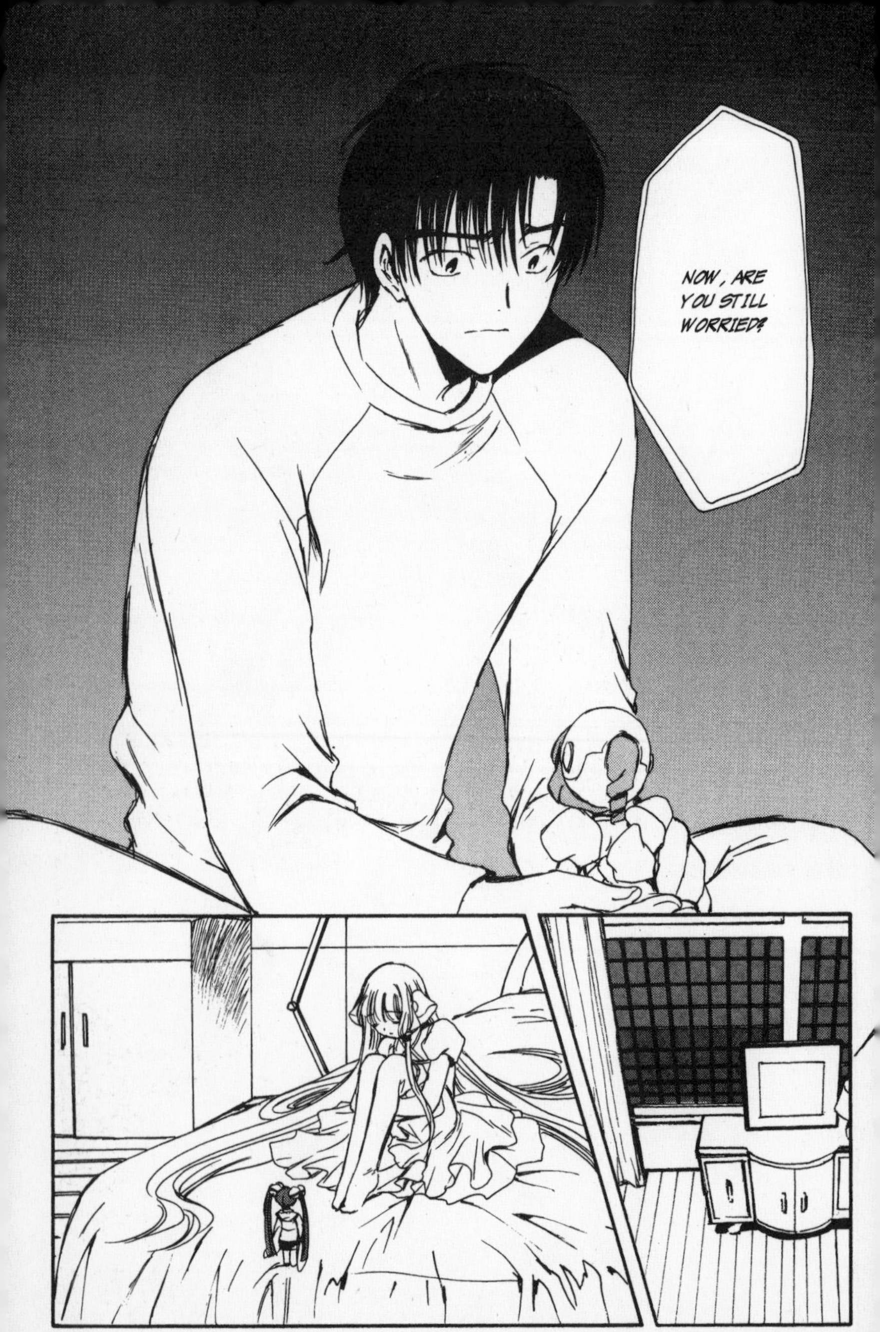
NOW, ARE YOU STILL WORRIED?

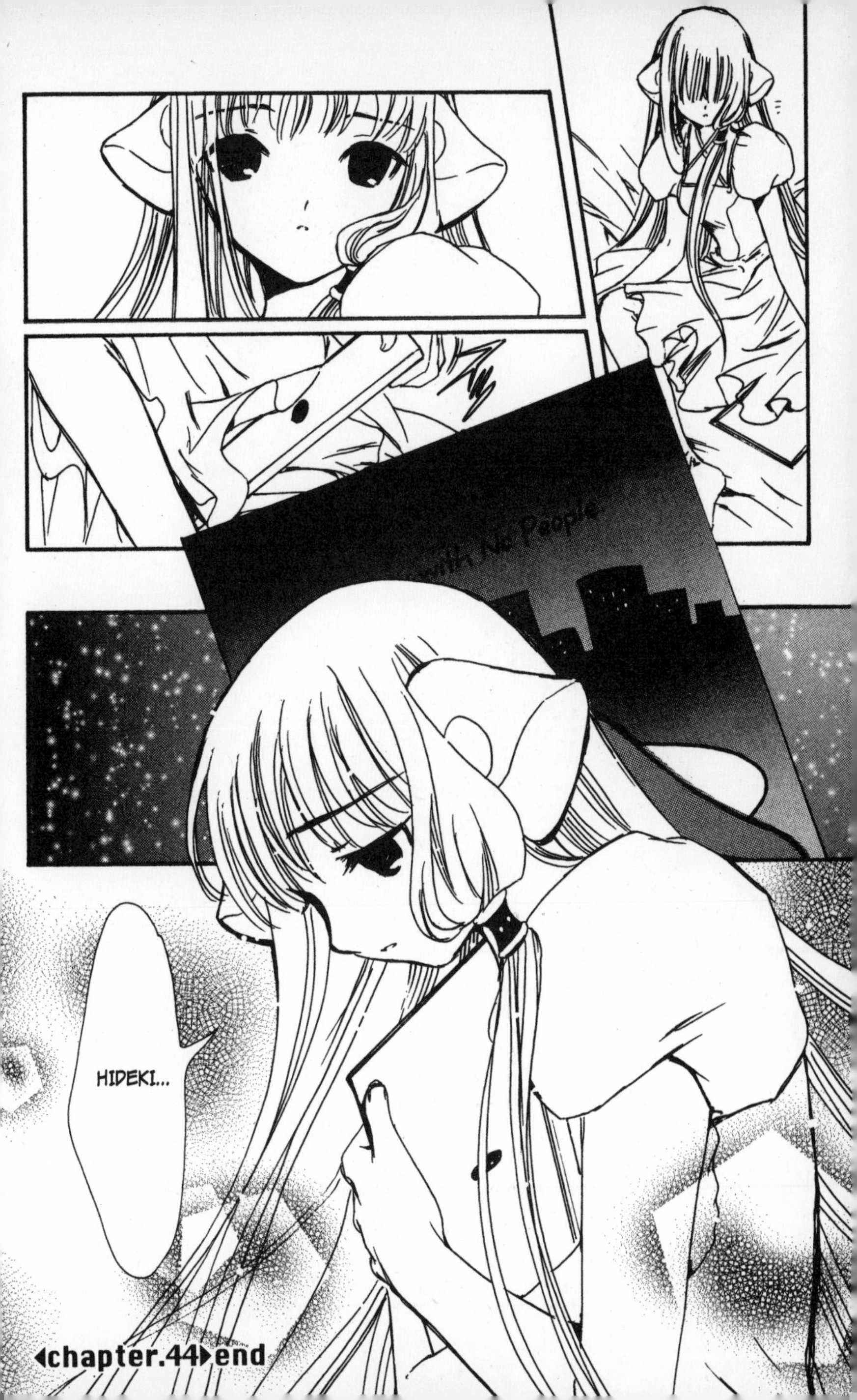
with No People
HIDEKI...
chapter.44 end

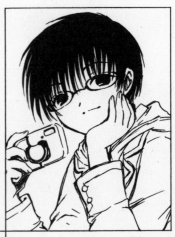

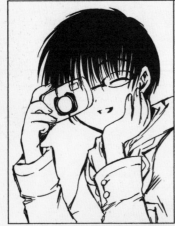

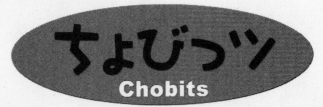

ちょびっツ

Chobits

◀chapter.45▶

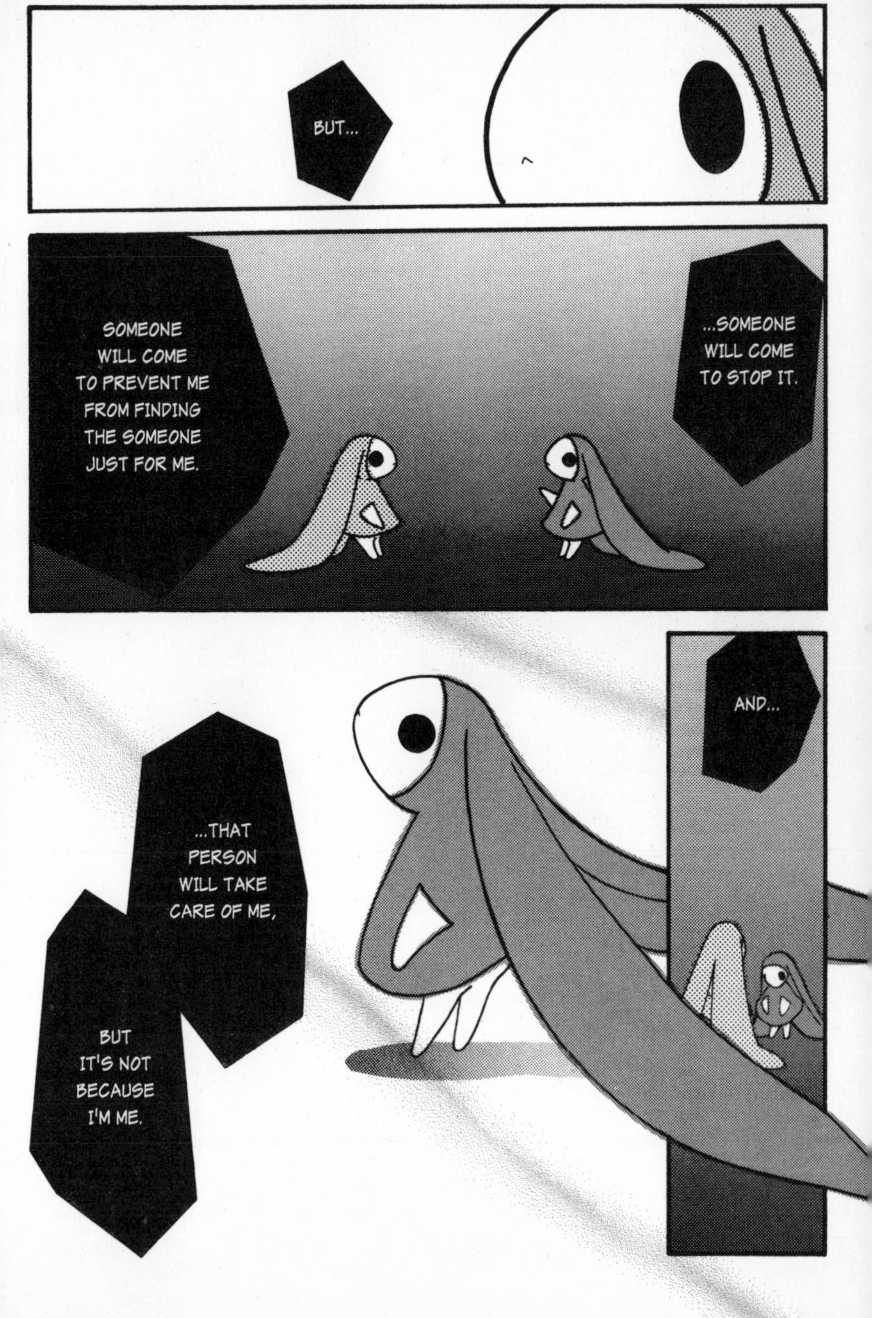
BUT...
...SOMEONE WILL COME TO STOP IT.
SOMEONE WILL COME TO PREVENT ME FROM FINDING THE SOMEONE JUST FOR ME.
AND...
...THAT PERSON WILL TAKE CARE OF ME,
BUT IT'S NOT BECAUSE I'M ME.

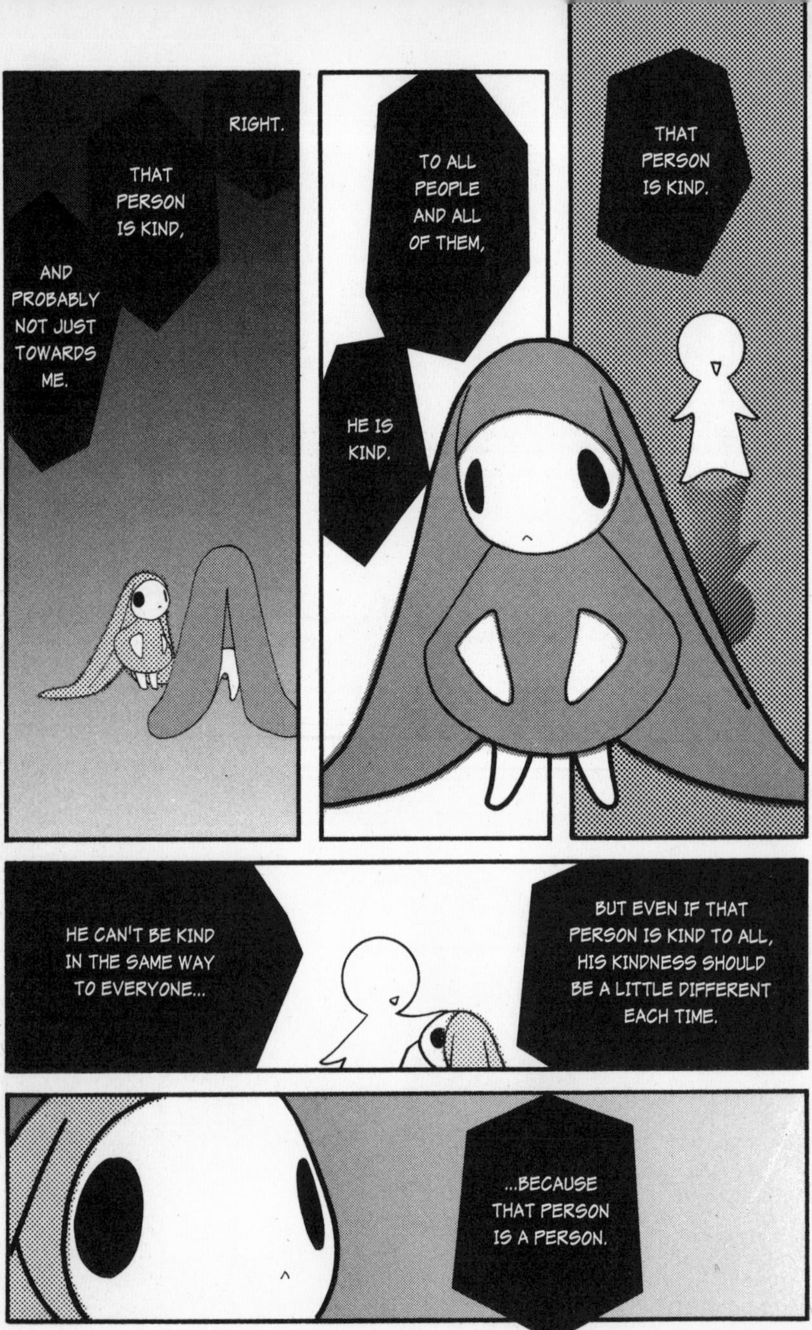
THAT PERSON IS KIND.
TO ALL PEOPLE AND ALL OF THEM,
HE IS KIND.
RIGHT.
THAT PERSON IS KIND,
AND PROBABLY NOT JUST TOWARDS ME.
BUT EVEN IF THAT PERSON IS KIND TO ALL, HIS KINDNESS SHOULD BE A LITTLE DIFFERENT EACH TIME.
HE CAN'T BE KIND IN THE SAME WAY TO EVERYONE...
...BECAUSE THAT PERSON IS A PERSON.

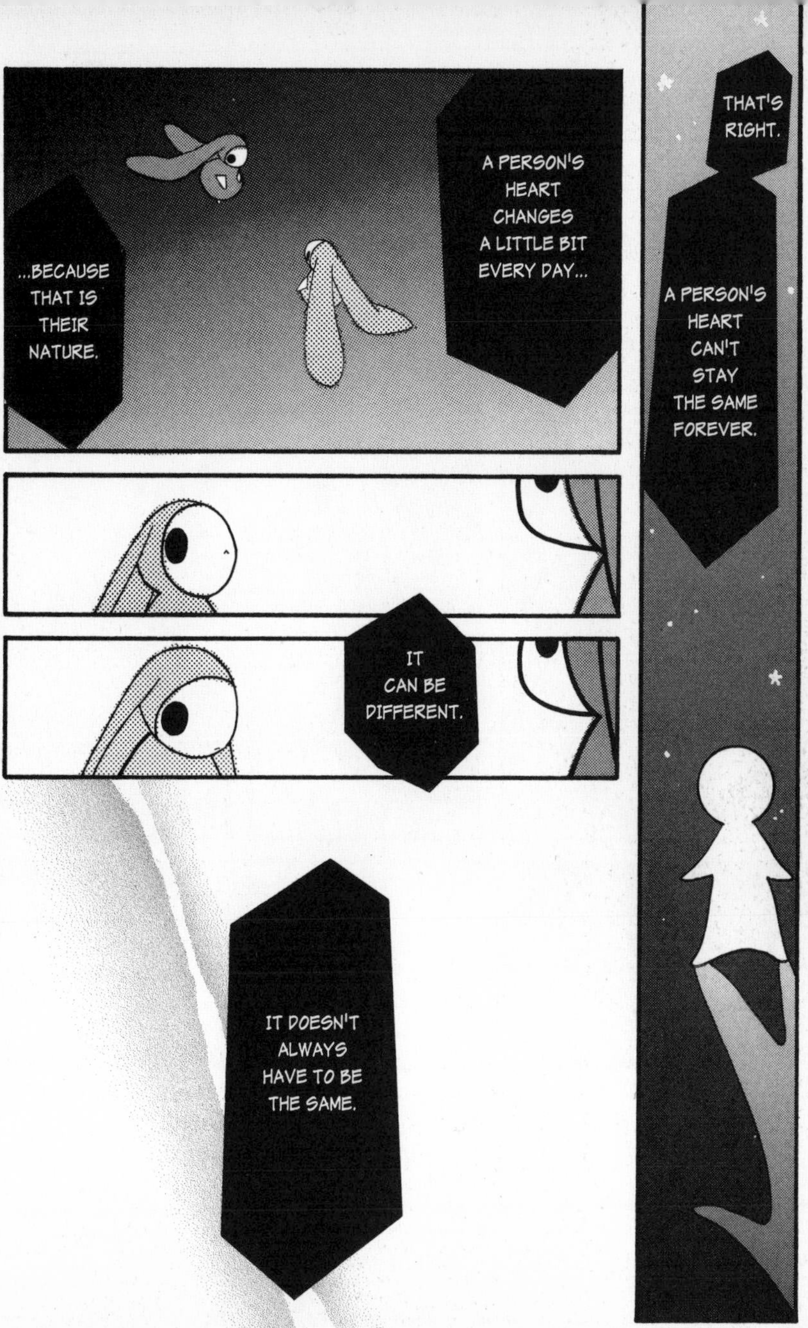
THAT'S RIGHT.
A PERSON'S HEART CAN'T STAY THE SAME FOREVER.
A PERSON'S HEART CHANGES A LITTLE BIT EVERY DAY...
...BECAUSE THAT IS THEIR NATURE.
IT CAN BE DIFFERENT.
IT DOESN'T ALWAYS HAVE TO BE THE SAME.

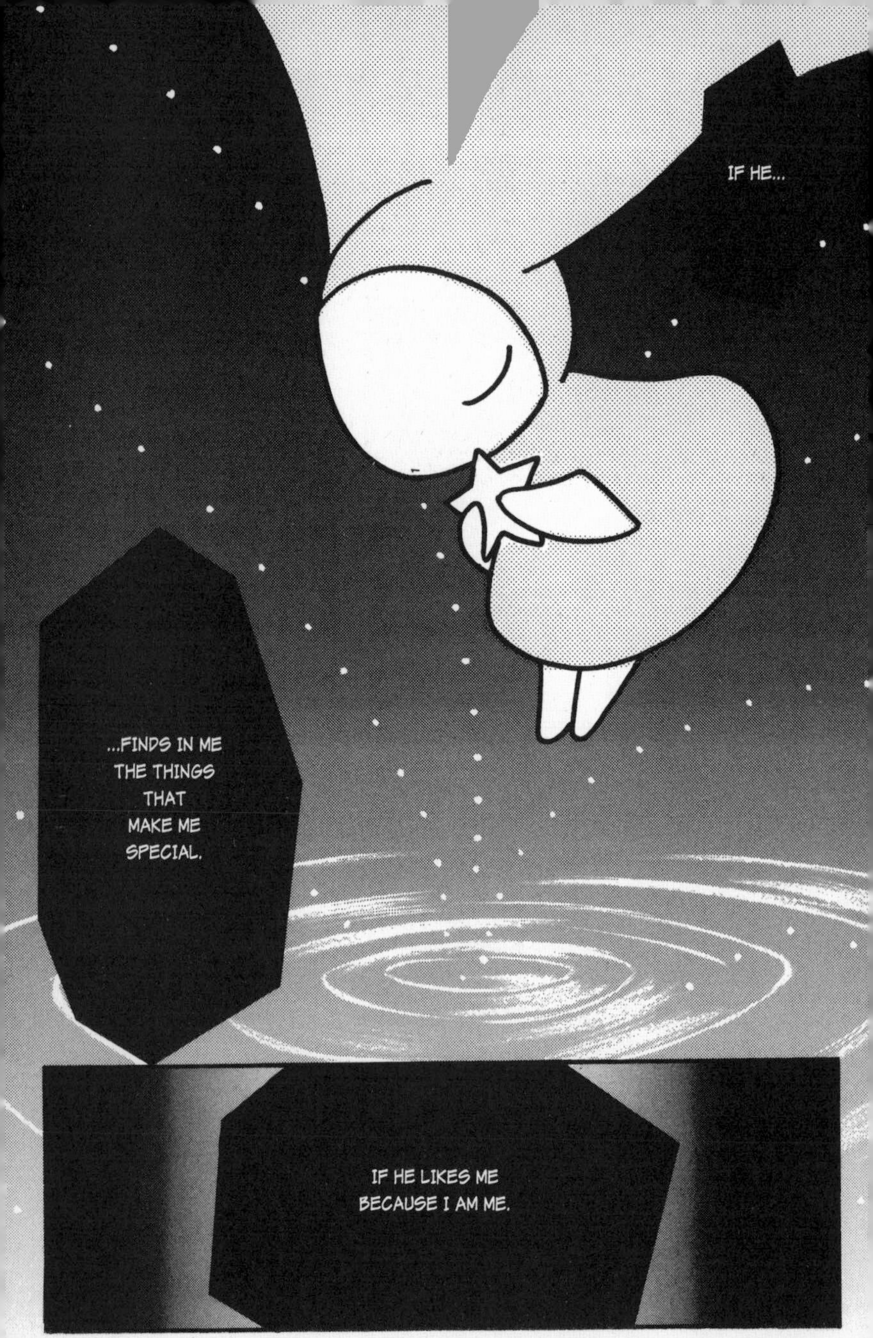
IF HE...
...FINDS IN ME THE THINGS THAT MAKE ME SPECIAL.
IF HE LIKES ME BECAUSE I AM ME.

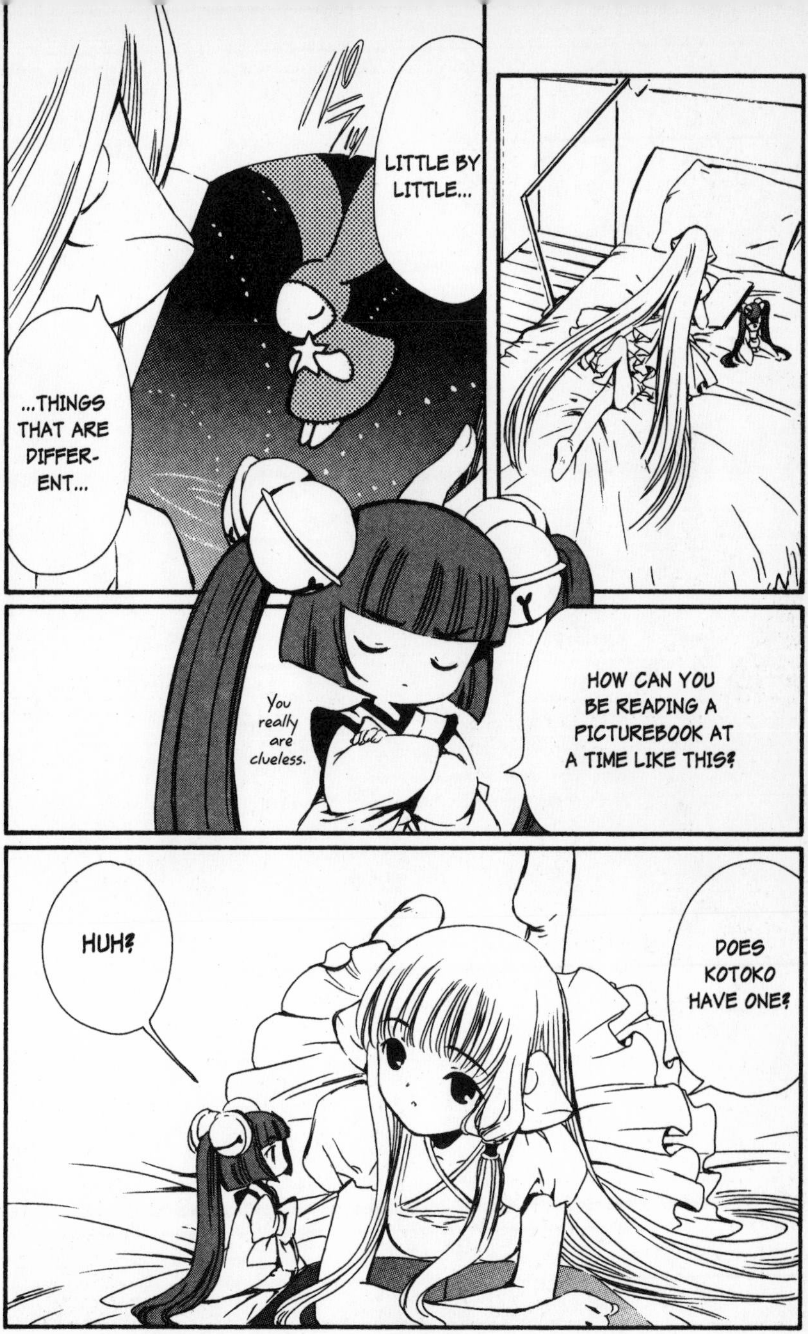
LITTLE BY LITTLE...
...THINGS THAT ARE DIFFER-ENT...
HOW CAN YOU BE READING A PICTUREBOOK AT A TIME LIKE THIS?
You really are clueless.
DOES KOTOKO HAVE ONE?
HUH?

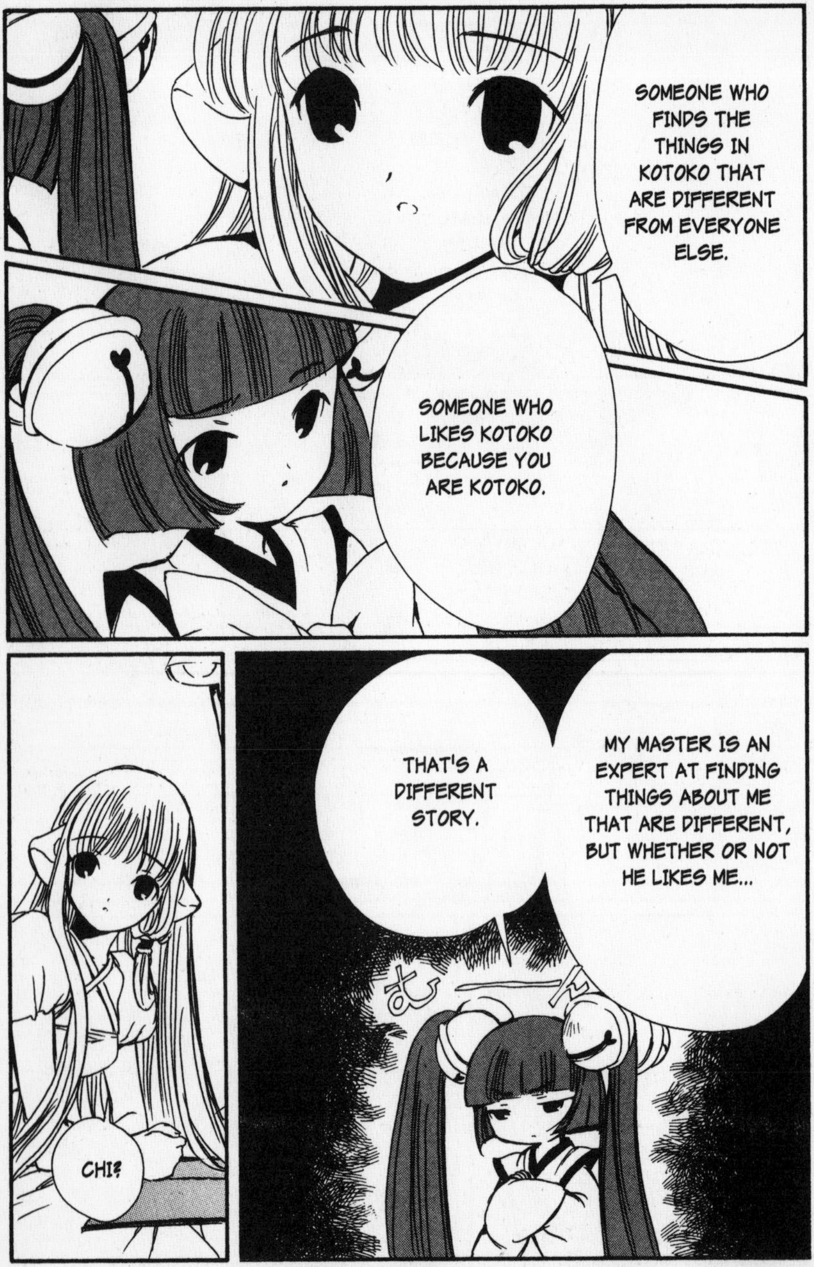
SOMEONE WHO FINDS THE THINGS IN KOTOKO THAT ARE DIFFERENT FROM EVERYONE ELSE.
SOMEONE WHO LIKES KOTOKO BECAUSE YOU ARE KOTOKO.
MY MASTER IS AN EXPERT AT FINDING THINGS ABOUT ME THAT ARE DIFFERENT, BUT WHETHER OR NOT HE LIKES ME...
THAT'S A DIFFERENT STORY.
むーん
CHI?

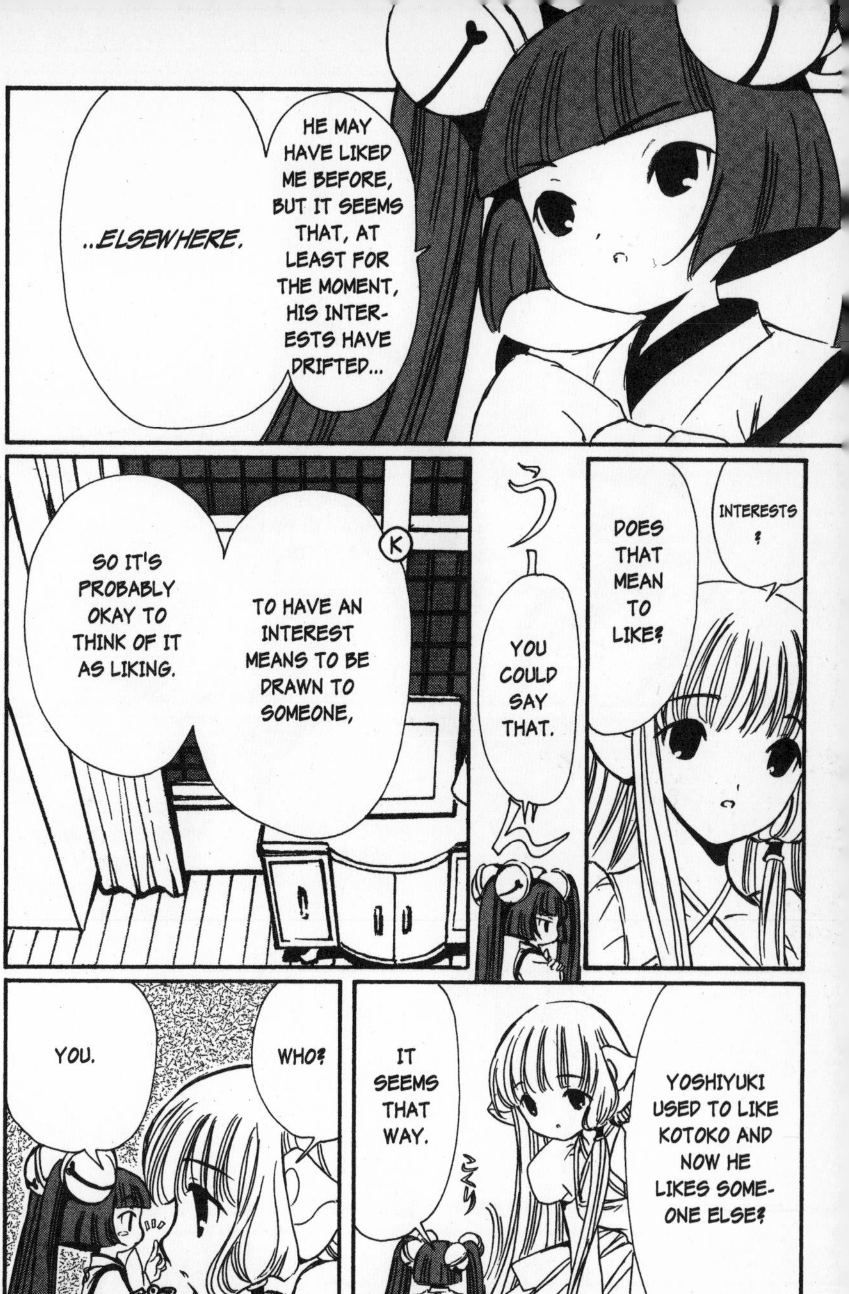
HE MAY HAVE LIKED ME BEFORE, BUT IT SEEMS THAT, AT LEAST FOR THE MOMENT, HIS INTER-ESTS HAVE DRIFTED...
...ELSEWHERE.
INTERESTS?
DOES THAT MEAN TO LIKE?
YOU COULD SAY THAT.
K
TO HAVE AN INTEREST MEANS TO BE DRAWN TO SOMEONE,
SO IT'S PROBABLY OKAY TO THINK OF IT AS LIKING.
YOSHIYUKI USED TO LIKE KOTOKO AND NOW HE LIKES SOME-ONE ELSE?
IT SEEMS THAT WAY.
WHO?
YOU.

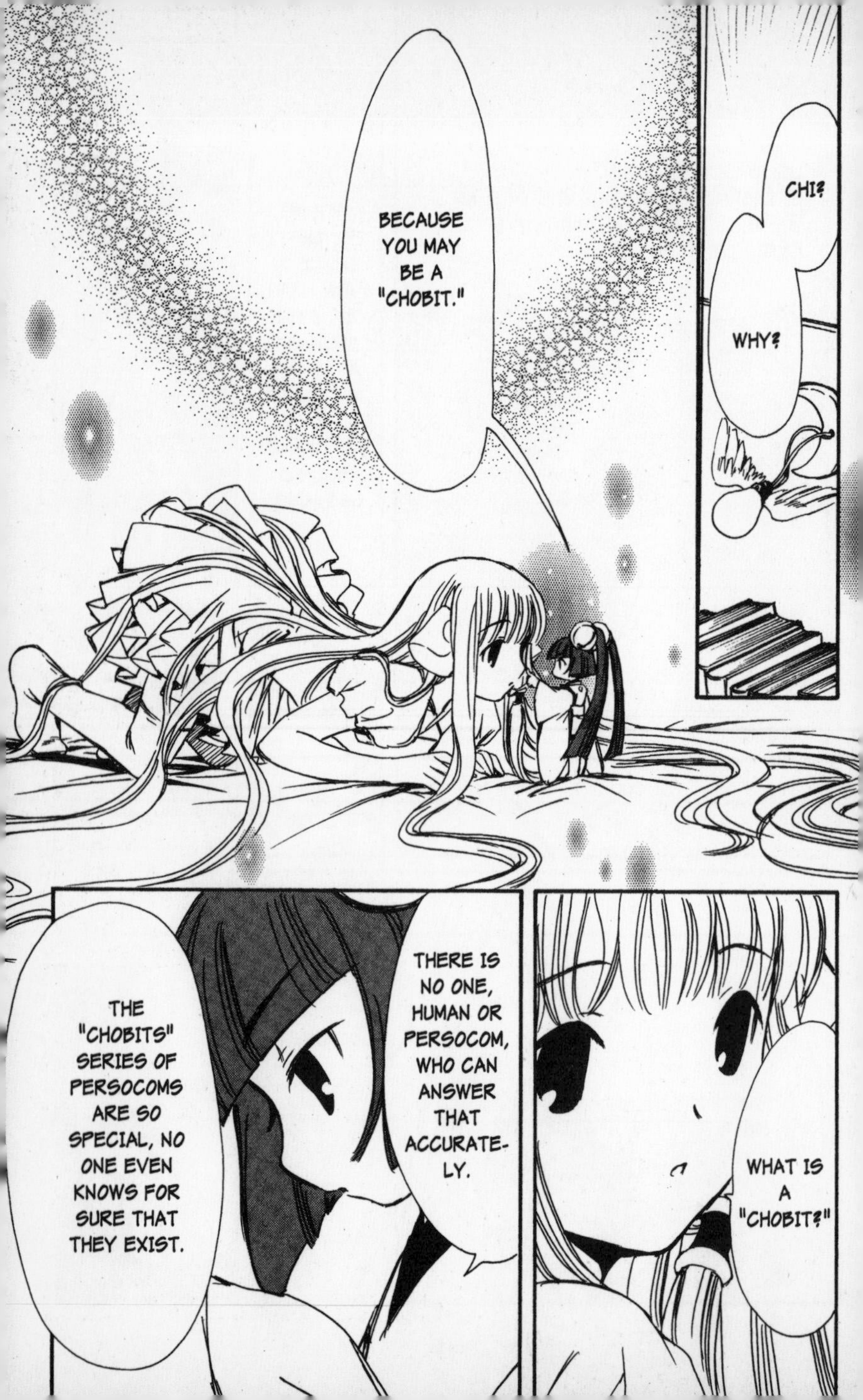
CHI?
WHY?
BECAUSE YOU MAY BE A "CHOBIT."
WHAT IS A "CHOBIT?"
THERE IS NO ONE, HUMAN OR PERSOCOM, WHO CAN ANSWER THAT ACCURATE-LY.
THE "CHOBITS" SERIES OF PERSOCOMS ARE SO SPECIAL, NO ONE EVEN KNOWS FOR SURE THAT THEY EXIST.

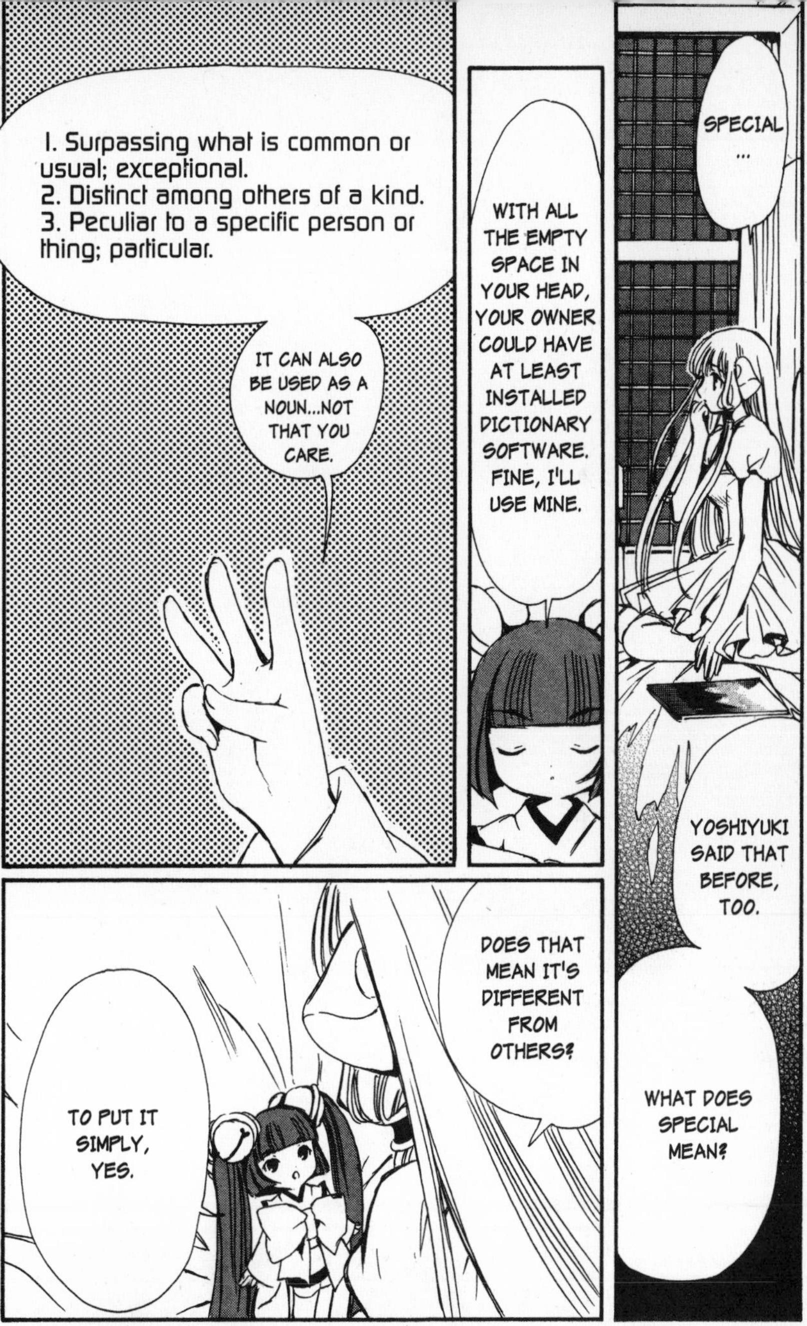
SPECIAL ...
YOSHIYUKI SAID THAT BEFORE, TOO.
WHAT DOES SPECIAL MEAN?
WITH ALL THE EMPTY SPACE IN YOUR HEAD, YOUR OWNER COULD HAVE AT LEAST INSTALLED DICTIONARY SOFTWARE. FINE, I'LL USE MINE.
1. Surpassing what is common or usual; exceptional.
2. Distinct among others of a kind.
3. Peculiar to a specific person or thing; particular.
IT CAN ALSO BE USED AS A NOUN...NOT THAT YOU CARE.
DOES THAT MEAN IT'S DIFFERENT FROM OTHERS?
TO PUT IT SIMPLY, YES.

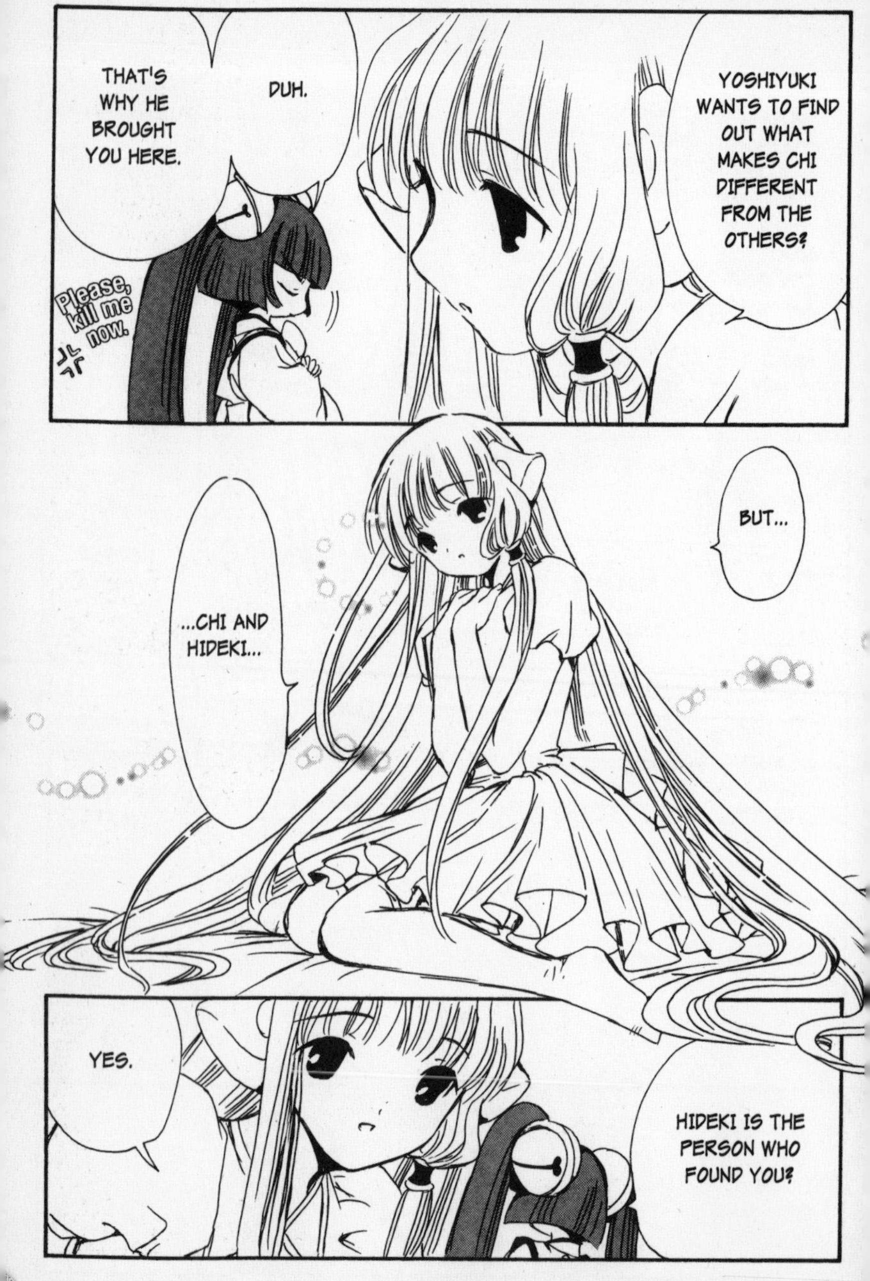
YOSHIYUKI WANTS TO FIND OUT WHAT MAKES CHI DIFFERENT FROM THE OTHERS?
DUH.
THAT'S WHY HE BROUGHT YOU HERE.
Please, kill me now.
BUT...
...CHI AND HIDEKI...
HIDEKI IS THE PERSON WHO FOUND YOU?
YES.

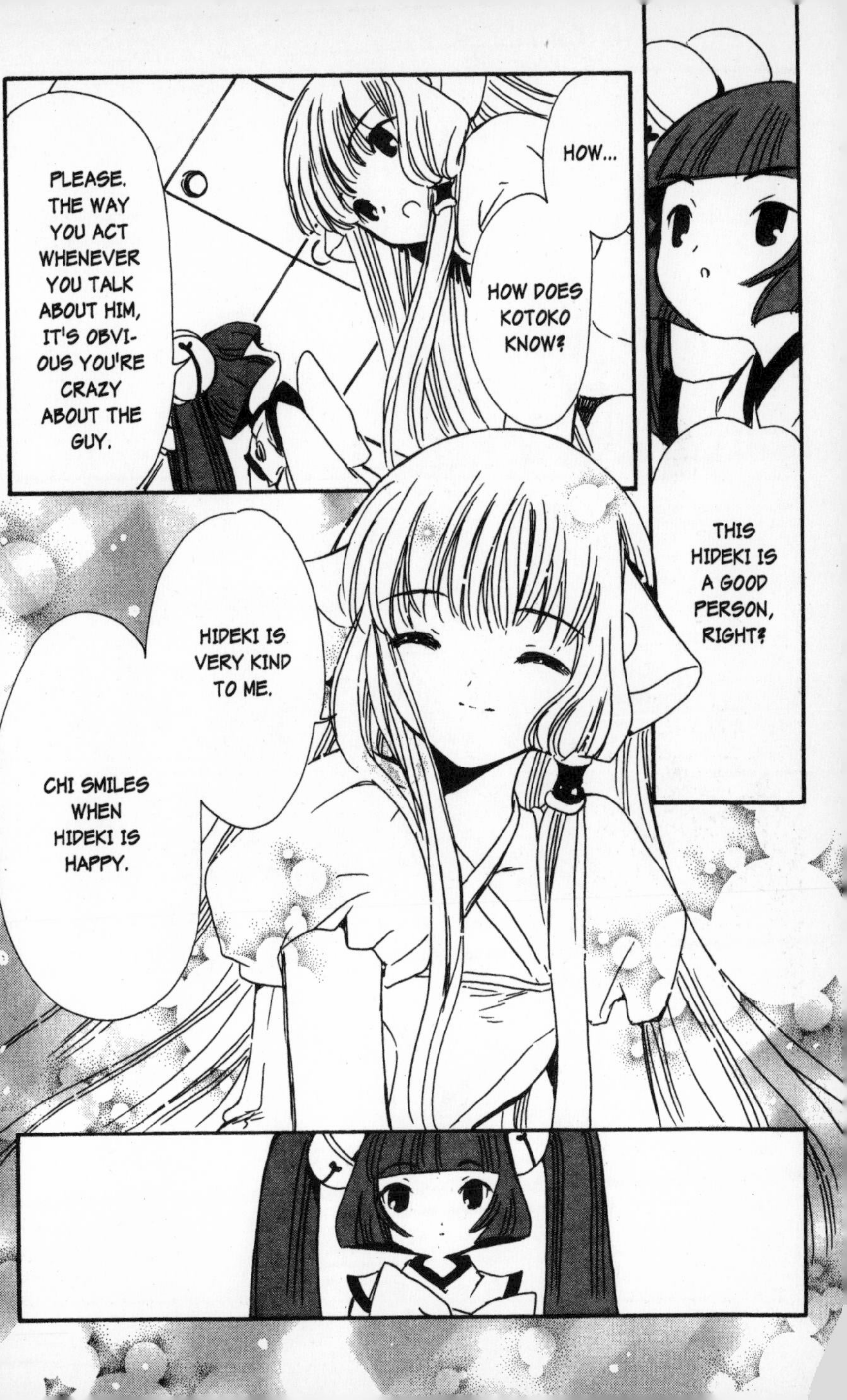

THIS HIDEKI IS A GOOD PERSON, RIGHT?
HOW...
HOW DOES KOTOKO KNOW?
PLEASE. THE WAY YOU ACT WHENEVER YOU TALK ABOUT HIM, IT'S OBVI-OUS YOU'RE CRAZY ABOUT THE GUY.
HIDEKI IS VERY KIND TO ME.
CHI SMILES WHEN HIDEKI IS HAPPY.

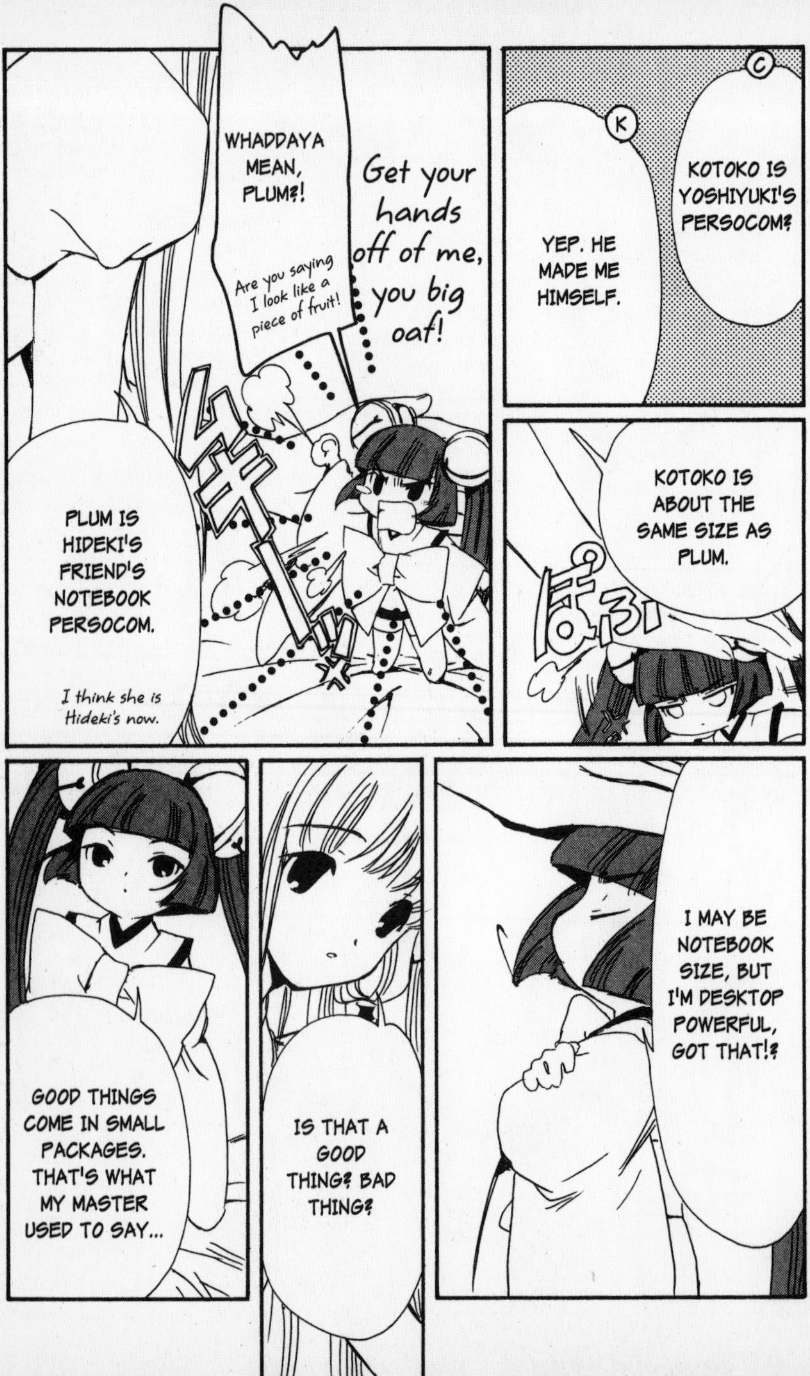
KOTOKO IS YOSHIYUKI'S PERSOCOM?
YEP. HE MADE ME HIMSELF.
KOTOKO IS ABOUT THE SAME SIZE AS PLUM.
ぽふ
Get your hands off of me, you big oaf!
WHADDAYA MEAN, PLUM?!
Are you saying I look like a piece of fruit!
PLUM IS HIDEKI'S FRIEND'S NOTEBOOK PERSOCOM.
I think she is Hideki's now.
I MAY BE NOTEBOOK SIZE, BUT I'M DESKTOP POWERFUL, GOT THAT!?
IS THAT A GOOD THING? BAD THING?
GOOD THINGS COME IN SMALL PACKAGES. THAT'S WHAT MY MASTER USED TO SAY...

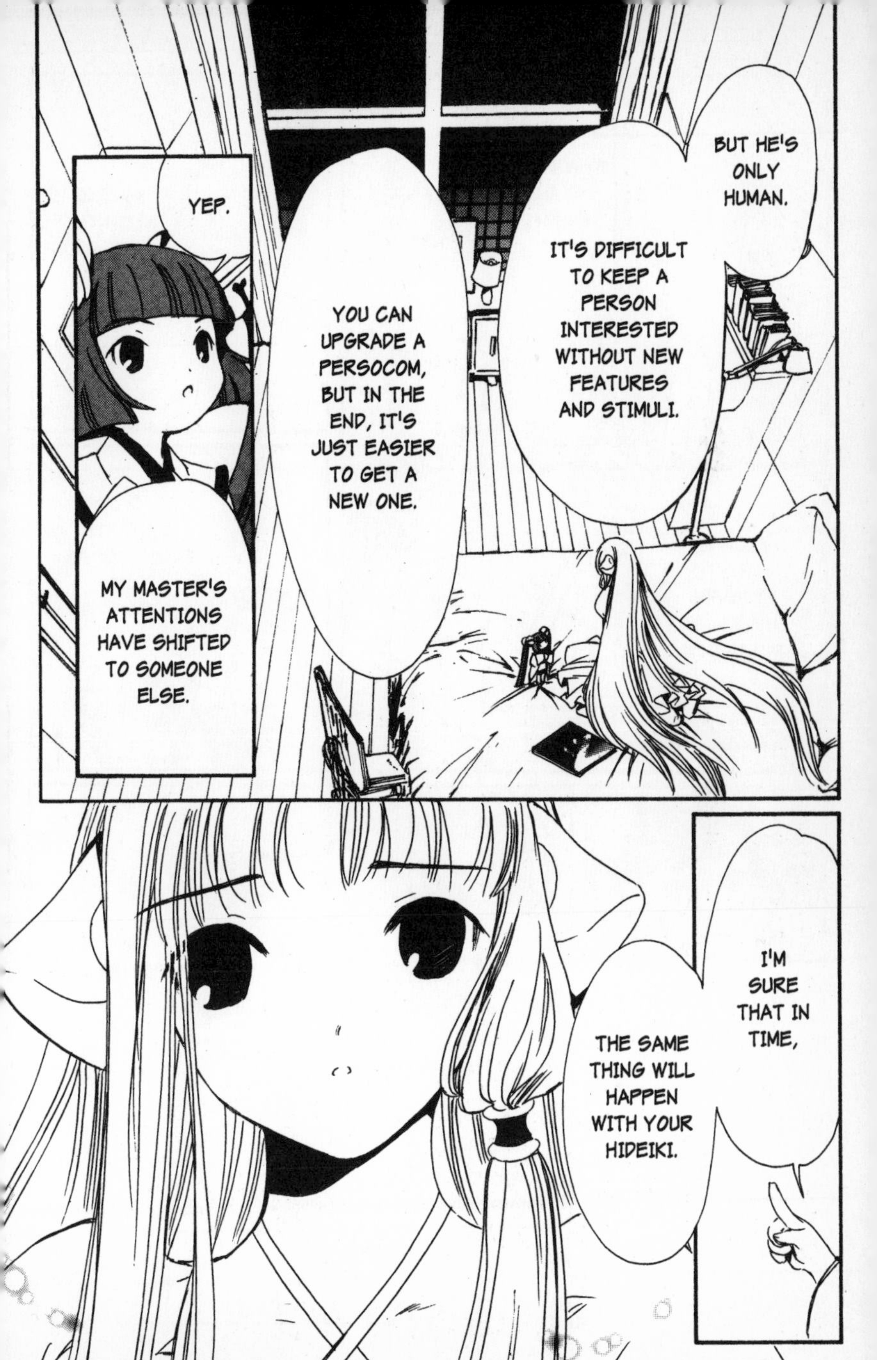
BUT HE'S ONLY HUMAN.
IT'S DIFFICULT TO KEEP A PERSON INTERESTED WITHOUT NEW FEATURES AND STIMULI.
YOU CAN UPGRADE A PERSOCOM, BUT IN THE END, IT'S JUST EASIER TO GET A NEW ONE.
YEP.
MY MASTER'S ATTENTIONS HAVE SHIFTED TO SOMEONE ELSE.
I'M SURE THAT IN TIME,
THE SAME THING WILL HAPPEN WITH YOUR HIDEIKI.

◀chapter.45▶end

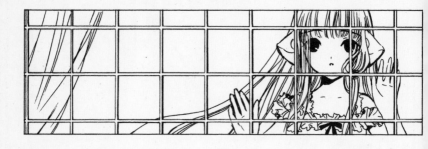

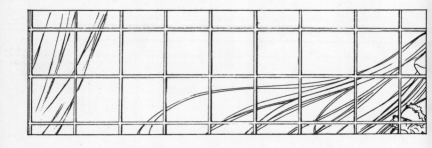

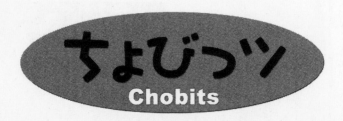

ちょびっツ
Chobits

◀chapter.46▶

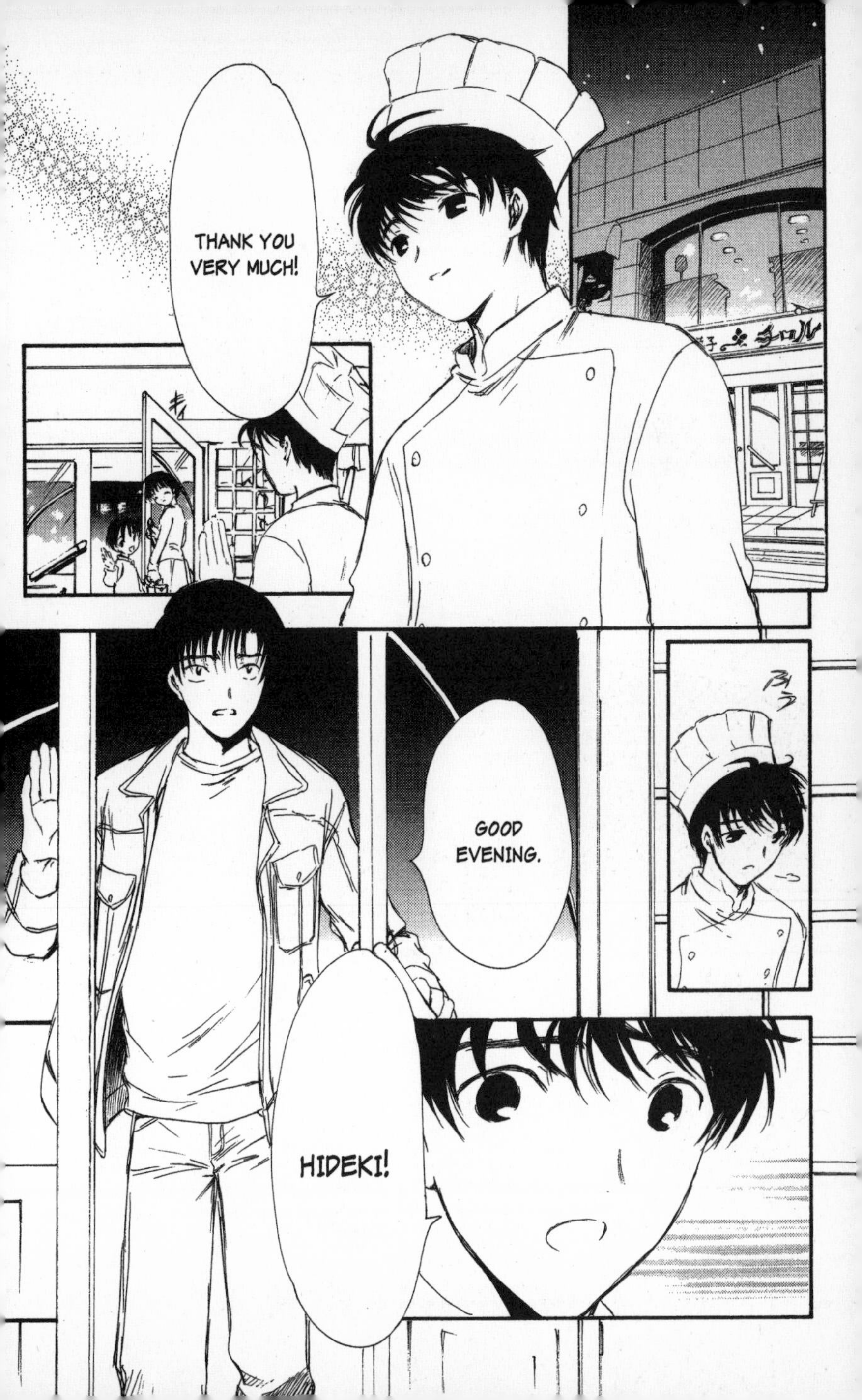
THANK YOU VERY MUCH!
GOOD EVENING.
HIDEKI!

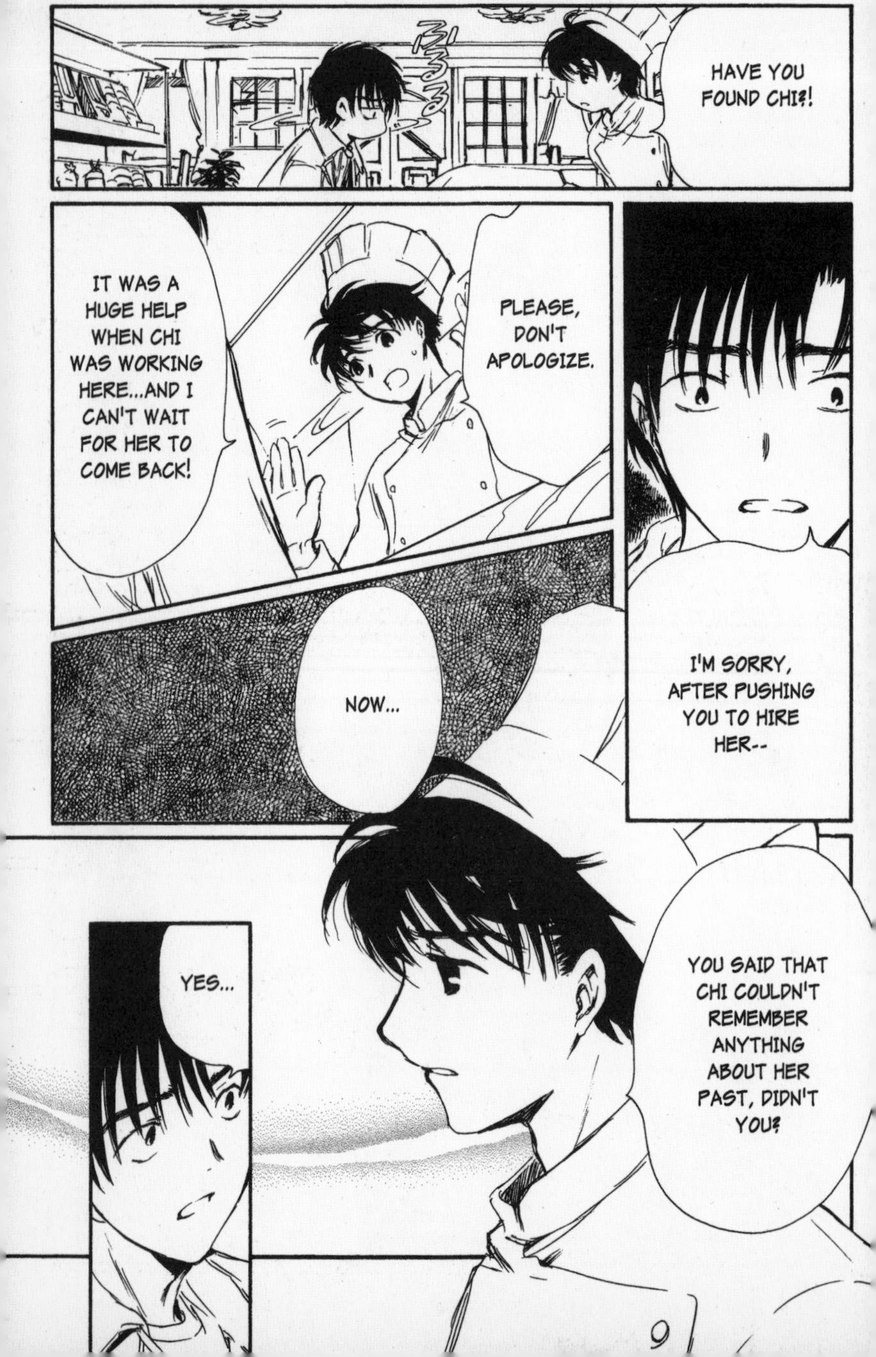
HAVE YOU FOUND CHI?!
I'M SORRY, AFTER PUSHING YOU TO HIRE HER--
PLEASE, DON'T APOLOGIZE.
IT WAS A HUGE HELP WHEN CHI WAS WORKING HERE...AND I CAN'T WAIT FOR HER TO COME BACK!
NOW...
YOU SAID THAT CHI COULDN'T REMEMBER ANYTHING ABOUT HER PAST, DIDN'T YOU?
YES...

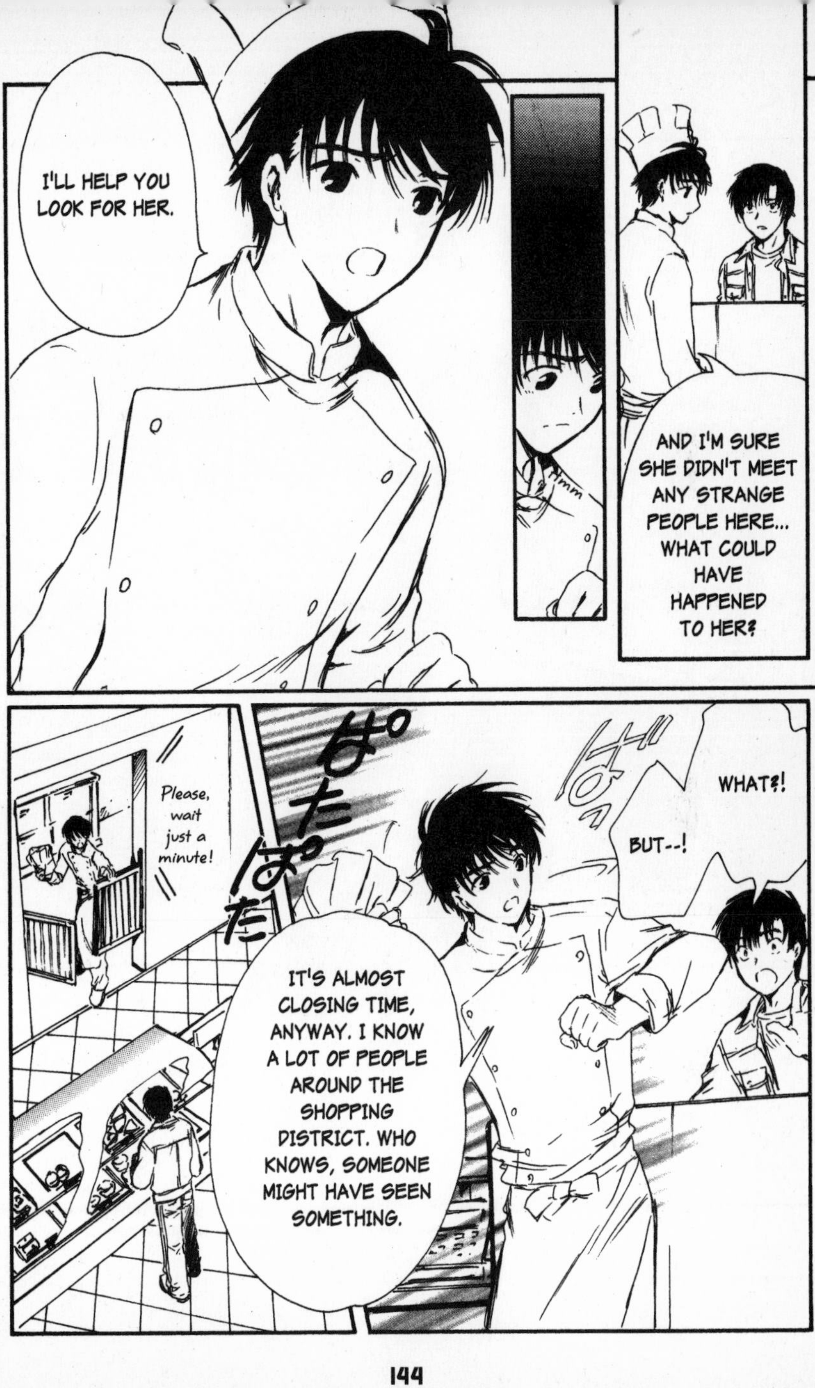
AND I'M SURE SHE DIDN'T MEET ANY STRANGE PEOPLE HERE... WHAT COULD HAVE HAPPENED TO HER?
Hmm
I'LL HELP YOU LOOK FOR HER.
WHAT?!
BUT--!
ぱっ
IT'S ALMOST CLOSING TIME, ANYWAY. I KNOW A LOT OF PEOPLE AROUND THE SHOPPING DISTRICT. WHO KNOWS, SOMEONE MIGHT HAVE SEEN SOMETHING.
ぱたぱた
Please, wait just a minute!

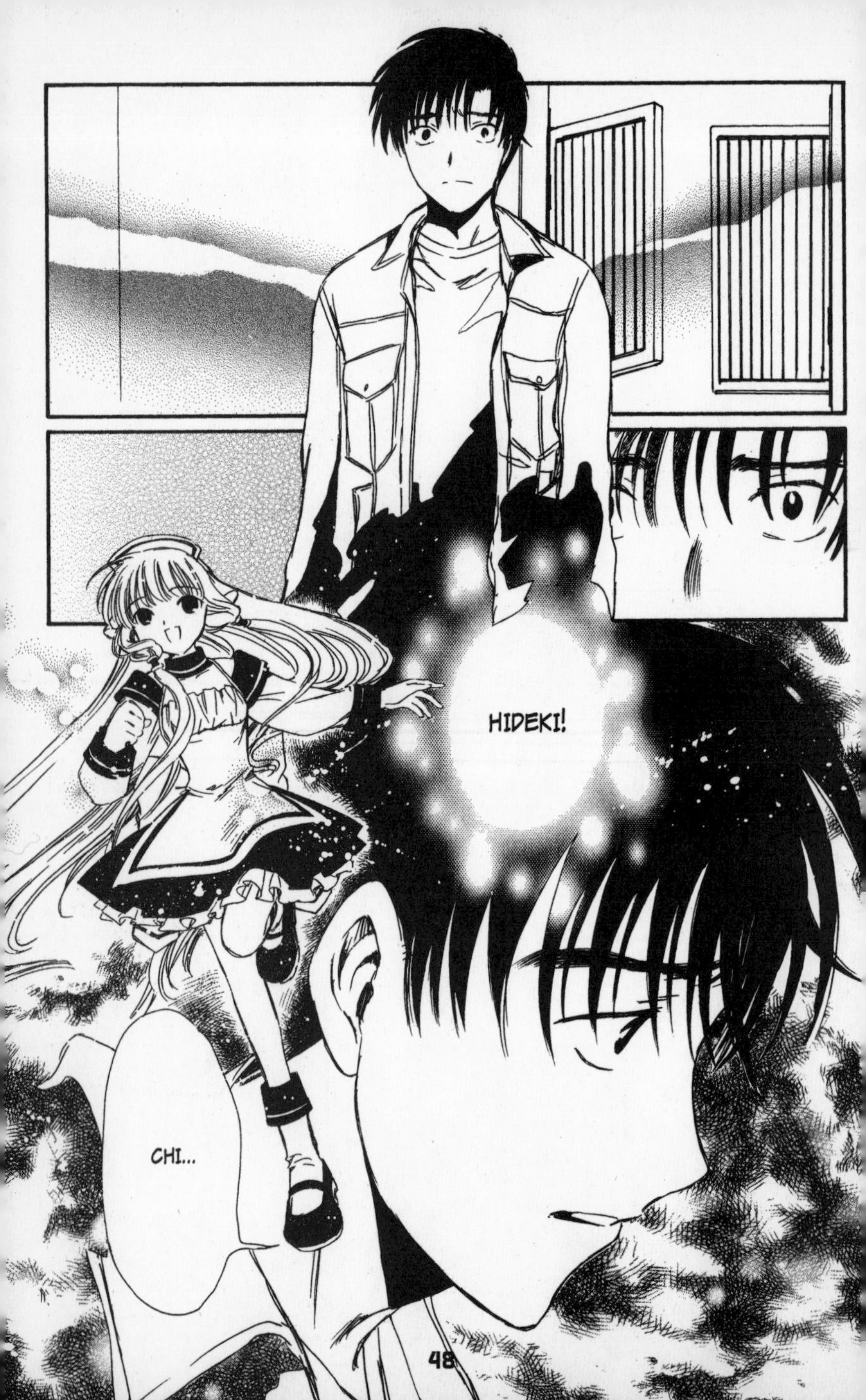
HIDEKI!
CHI...

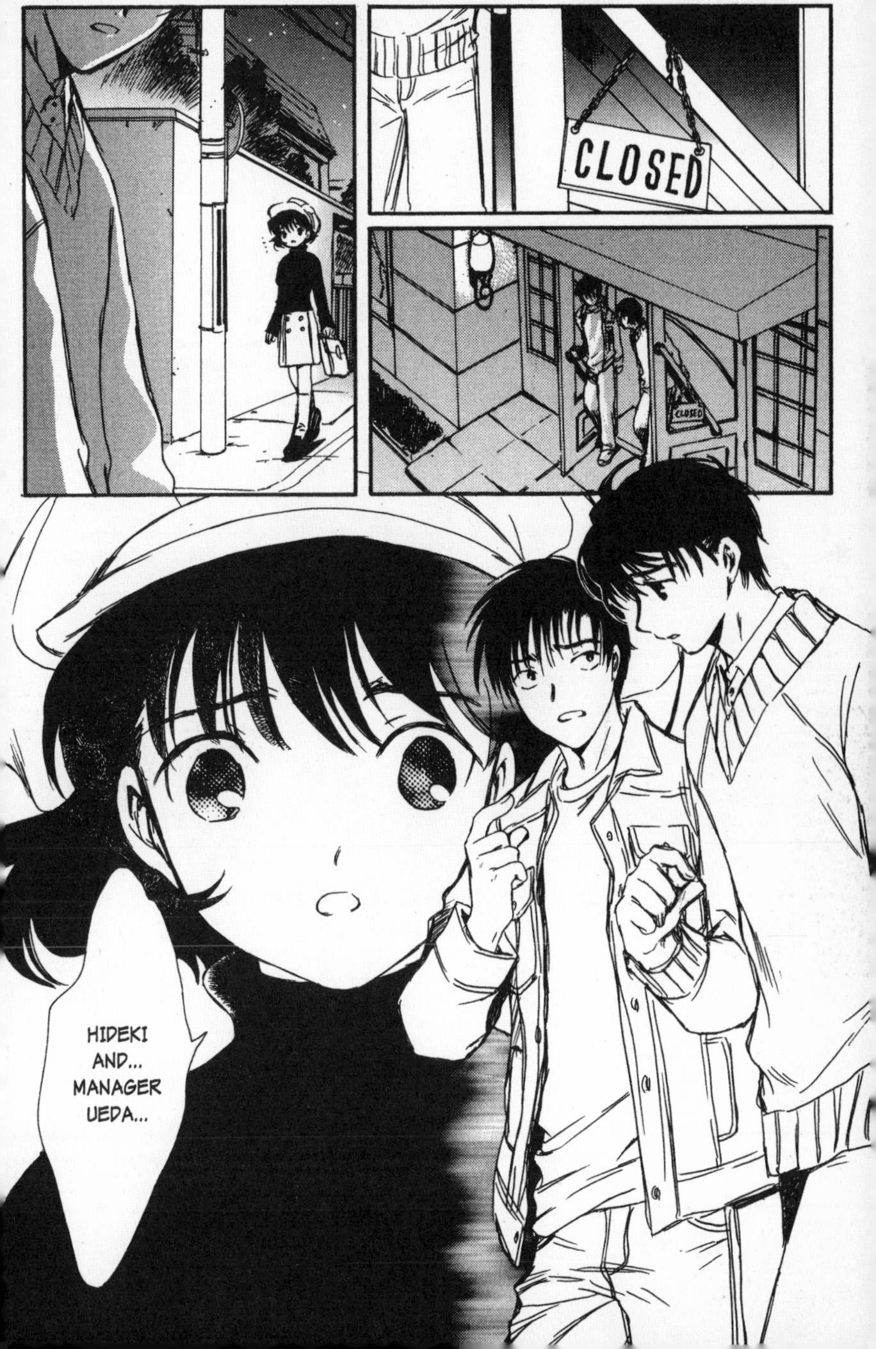
CLOSED
CLOSED
HIDEKI AND... MANAGER UEDA...

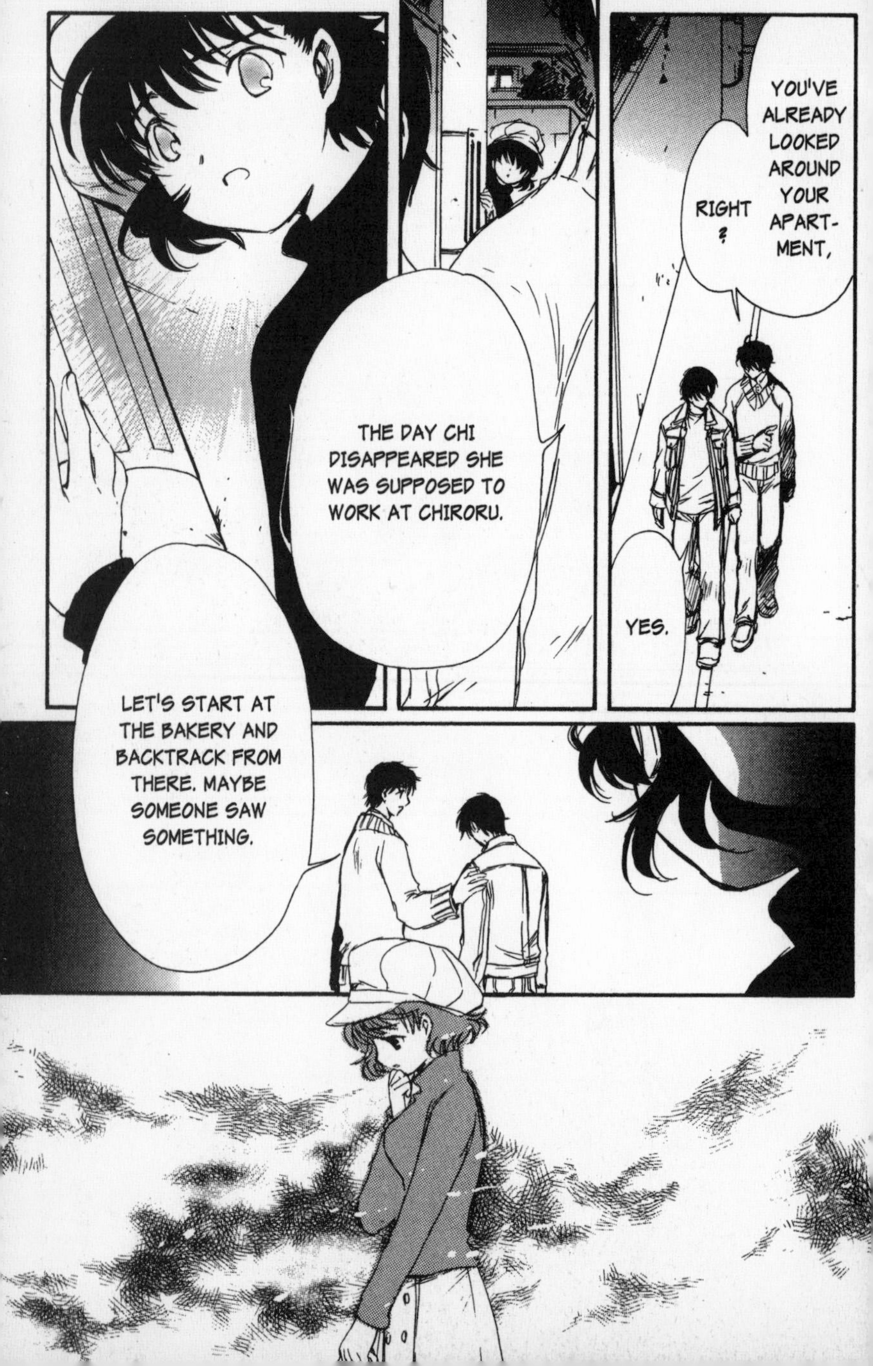
YOU'VE ALREADY LOOKED AROUND YOUR APARTMENT,
RIGHT?
YES.
THE DAY CHI DISAPPEARED SHE WAS SUPPOSED TO WORK AT CHIRORU.
LET'S START AT THE BAKERY AND BACKTRACK FROM THERE. MAYBE SOMEONE SAW SOMETHING.

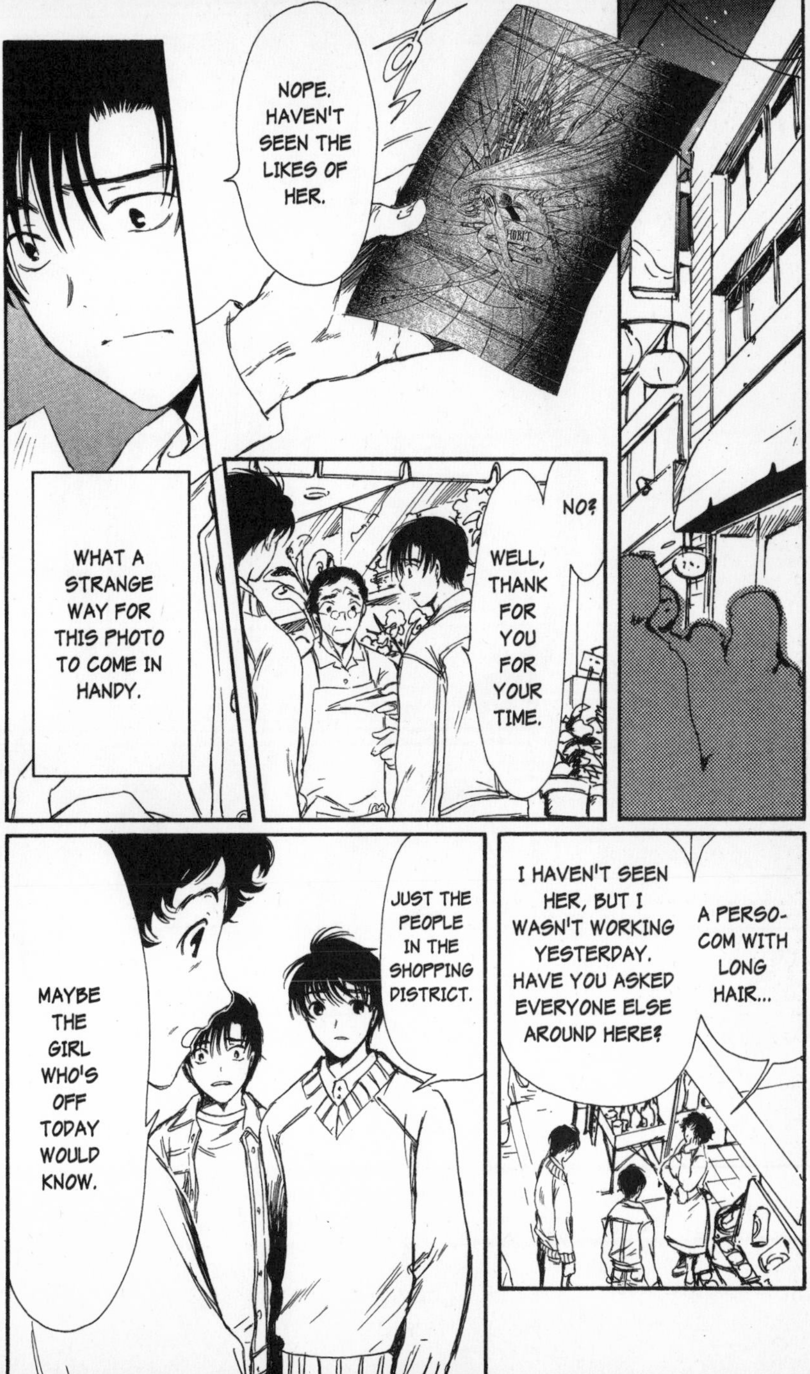
NOPE. HAVEN'T SEEN THE LIKES OF HER.
NO? WELL, THANK FOR YOU FOR YOUR TIME.
WHAT A STRANGE WAY FOR THIS PHOTO TO COME IN HANDY.
A PERSO-COM WITH LONG HAIR...
I HAVEN'T SEEN HER, BUT I WASN'T WORKING YESTERDAY. HAVE YOU ASKED EVERYONE ELSE AROUND HERE?
JUST THE PEOPLE IN THE SHOPPING DISTRICT.
MAYBE THE GIRL WHO'S OFF TODAY WOULD KNOW.

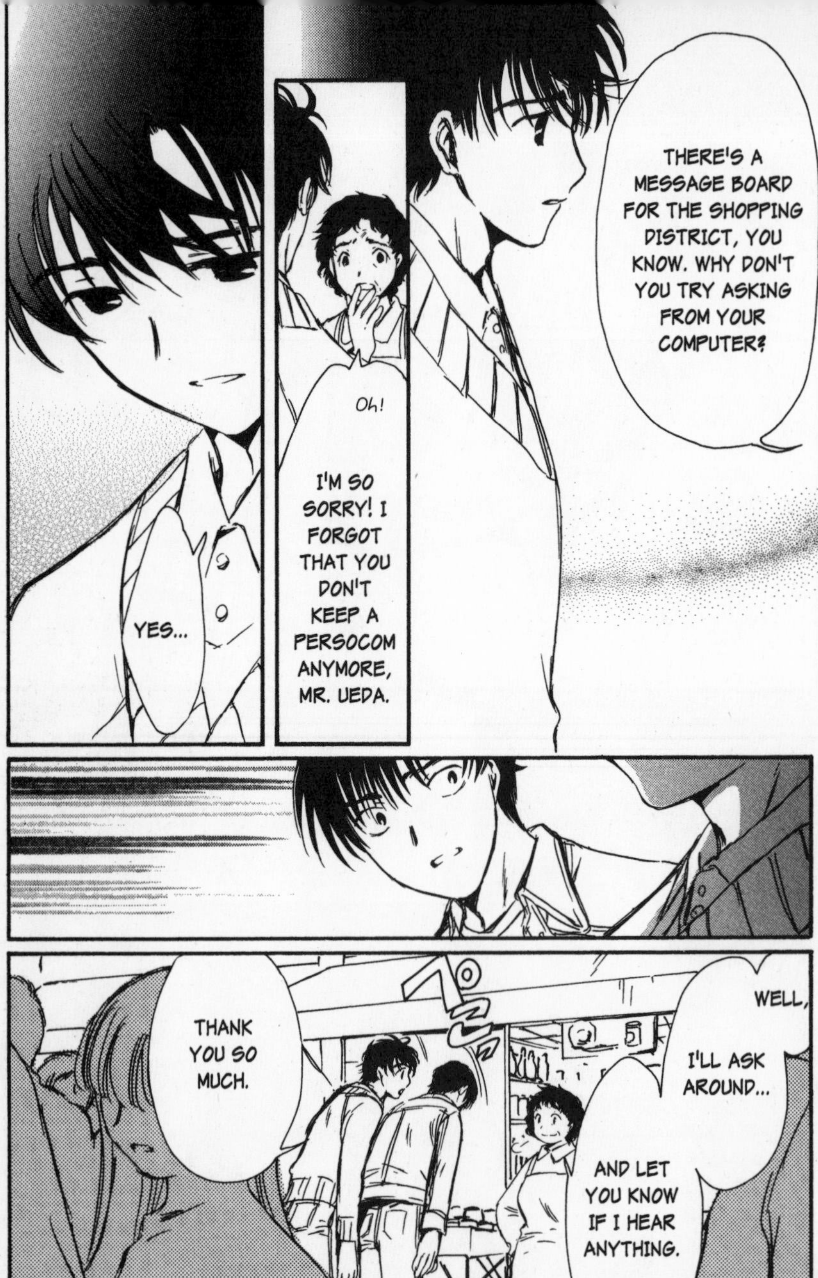
THERE'S A MESSAGE BOARD FOR THE SHOPPING DISTRICT, YOU KNOW. WHY DON'T YOU TRY ASKING FROM YOUR COMPUTER?
Oh!
I'M SO SORRY! I FORGOT THAT YOU DON'T KEEP A PERSOCOM ANYMORE, MR. UEDA.
YES...
WELL, I'LL ASK AROUND...
AND LET YOU KNOW IF I HEAR ANYTHING.
THANK YOU SO MUCH.

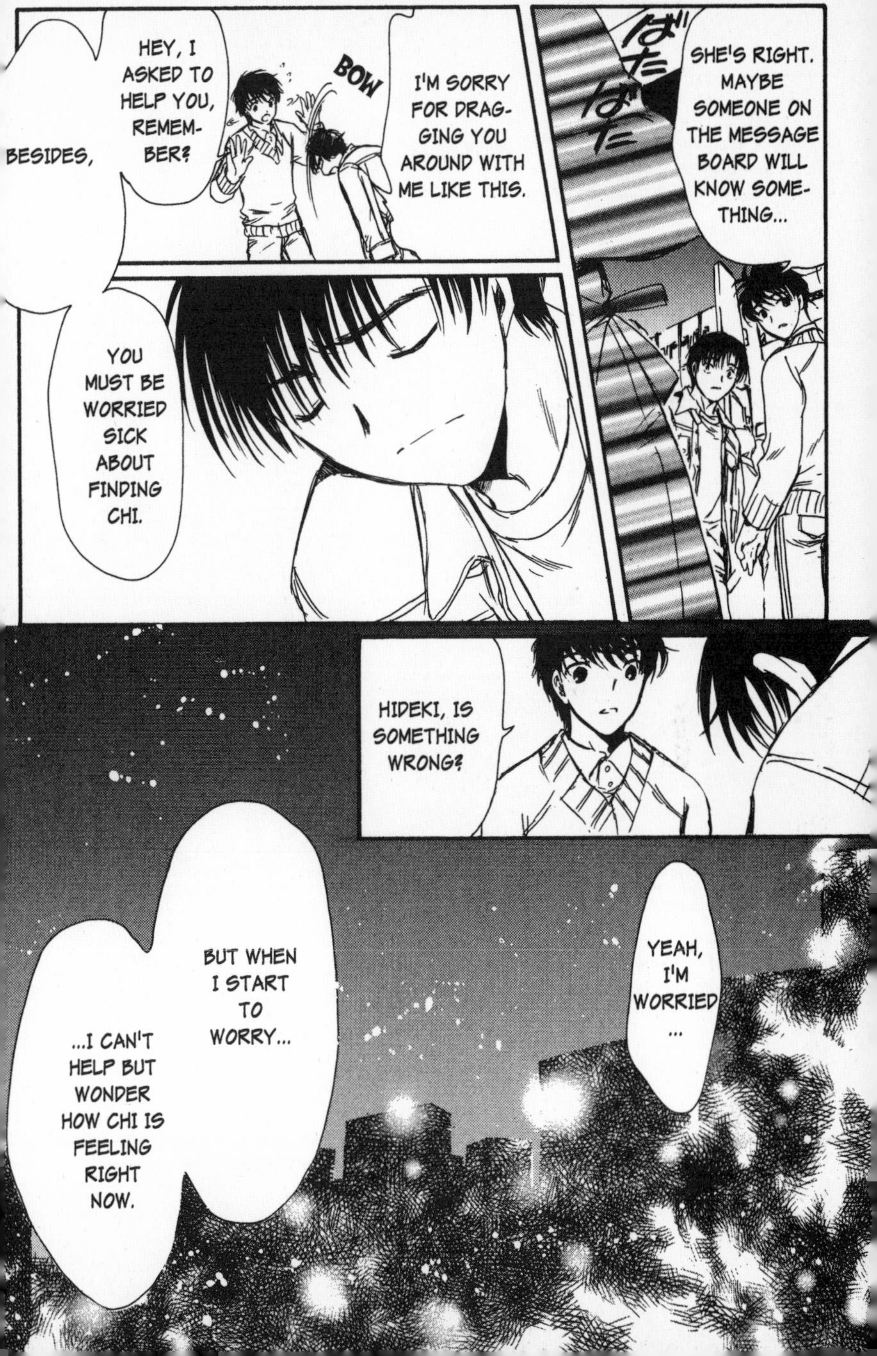
ばたばた
SHE'S RIGHT. MAYBE SOMEONE ON THE MESSAGE BOARD WILL KNOW SOMETHING...
I'M SORRY FOR DRAGGING YOU AROUND WITH ME LIKE THIS.
BOW
HEY, I ASKED TO HELP YOU, REMEMBER?
BESIDES,
YOU MUST BE WORRIED SICK ABOUT FINDING CHI.
HIDEKI, IS SOMETHING WRONG?
YEAH, I'M WORRIED...
BUT WHEN I START TO WORRY...
...I CAN'T HELP BUT WONDER HOW CHI IS FEELING RIGHT NOW.

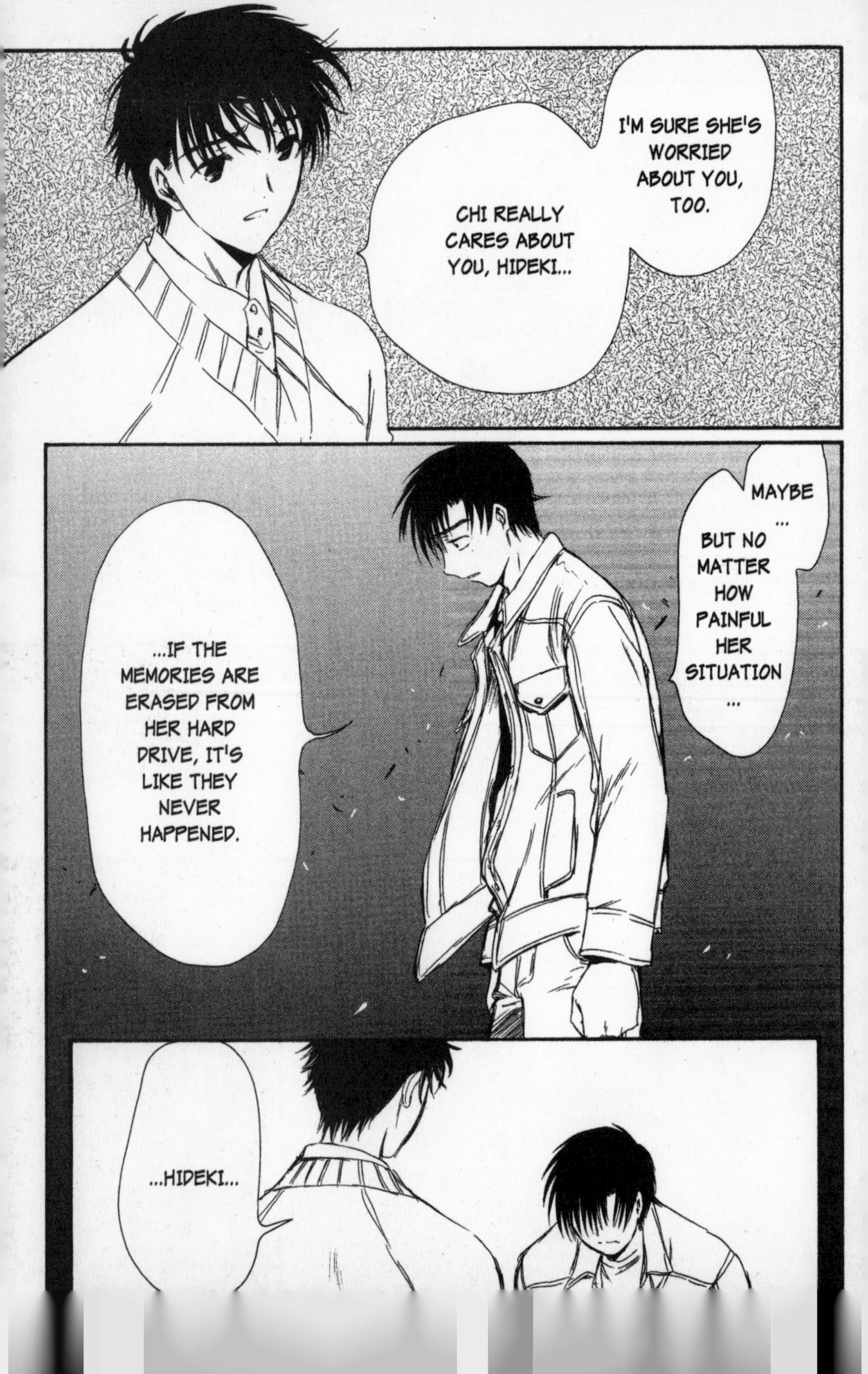
I'M SURE SHE'S WORRIED ABOUT YOU, TOO.
CHI REALLY CARES ABOUT YOU, HIDEKI...
MAYBE ... BUT NO MATTER HOW PAINFUL HER SITUATION ...
...IF THE MEMORIES ARE ERASED FROM HER HARD DRIVE, IT'S LIKE THEY NEVER HAPPENED.
...HIDEKI...

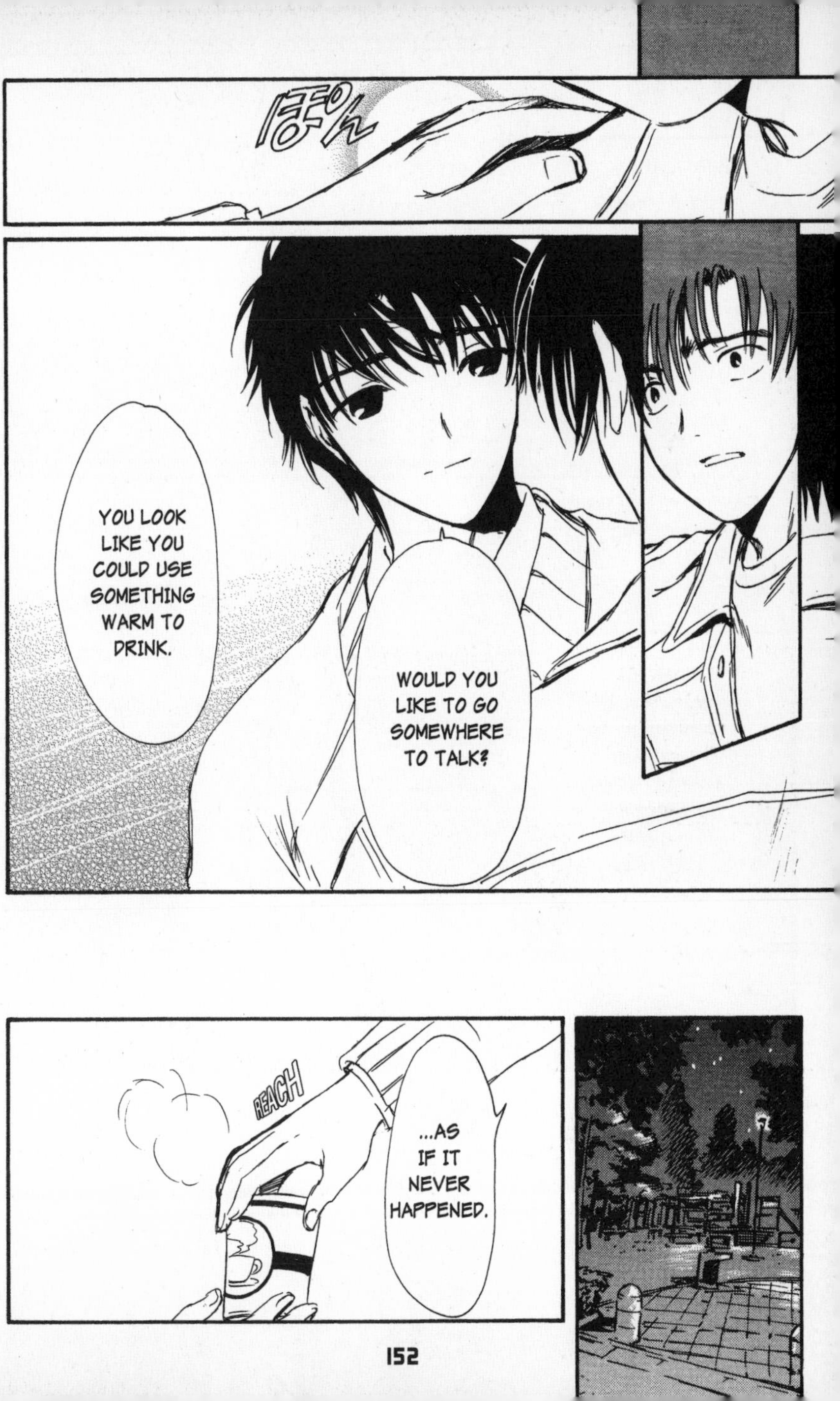
ぽん
WOULD YOU LIKE TO GO SOMEWHERE TO TALK?
YOU LOOK LIKE YOU COULD USE SOMETHING WARM TO DRINK.
REACH
...AS IF IT NEVER HAPPENED.

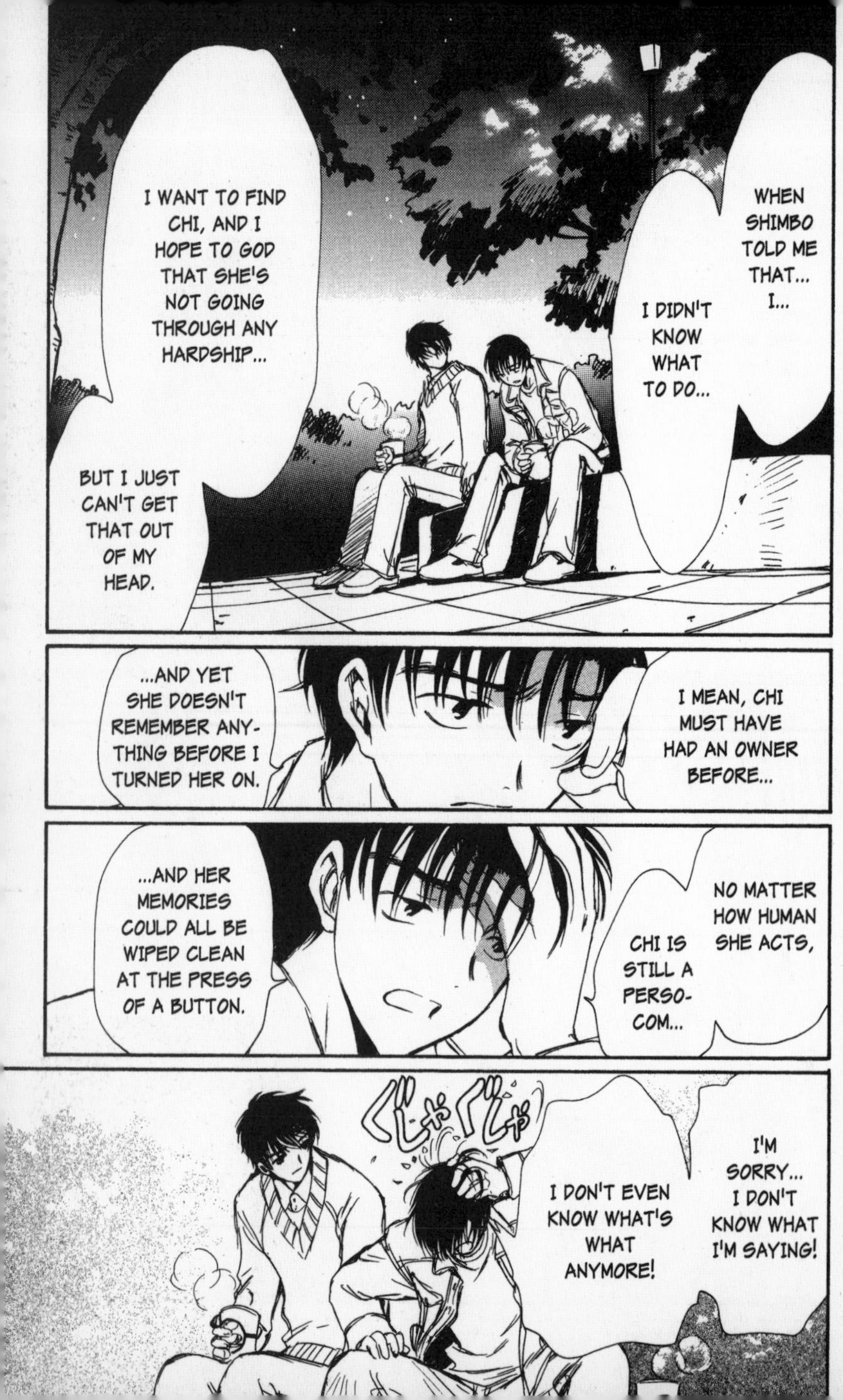
WHEN SHIMBO TOLD ME THAT... I...
I DIDN'T KNOW WHAT TO DO...
I WANT TO FIND CHI, AND I HOPE TO GOD THAT SHE'S NOT GOING THROUGH ANY HARDSHIP...
BUT I JUST CAN'T GET THAT OUT OF MY HEAD.
I MEAN, CHI MUST HAVE HAD AN OWNER BEFORE...
...AND YET SHE DOESN'T REMEMBER ANY-THING BEFORE I TURNED HER ON.
NO MATTER HOW HUMAN SHE ACTS,
CHI IS STILL A PERSO-COM...
...AND HER MEMORIES COULD ALL BE WIPED CLEAN AT THE PRESS OF A BUTTON.
ぐしゃぐしゃ
I'M SORRY... I DON'T KNOW WHAT I'M SAYING!
I DON'T EVEN KNOW WHAT'S WHAT ANYMORE!

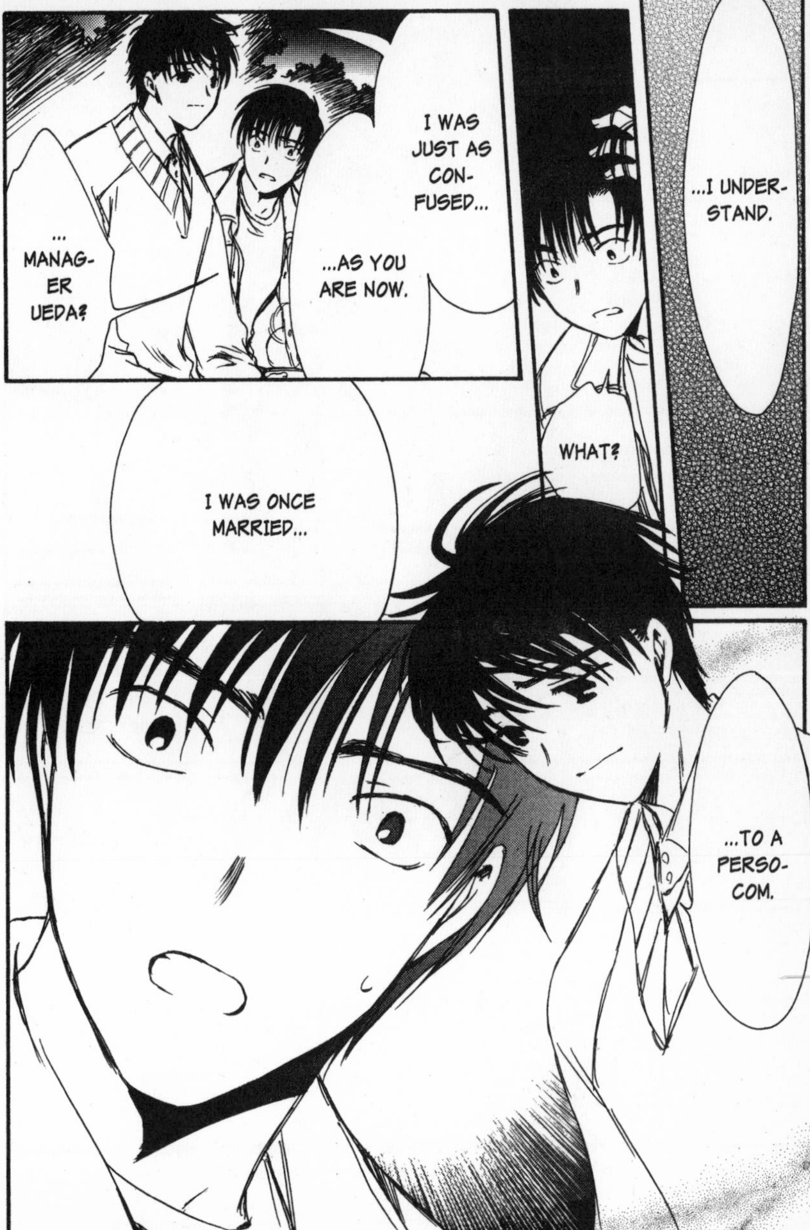
...I UNDER-STAND.
WHAT?
I WAS JUST AS CON-FUSED...
...AS YOU ARE NOW.
...MANAG-ER UEDA?
I WAS ONCE MARRIED...
...TO A PERSO-COM.

◂chapter.46▸end

低予算
ひとり暮らしのお夕飯

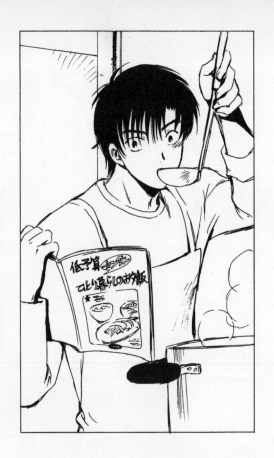

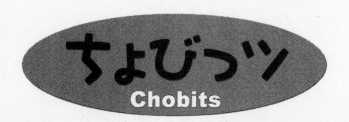

ちょびっツ
Chobits

◀chapter.47▶

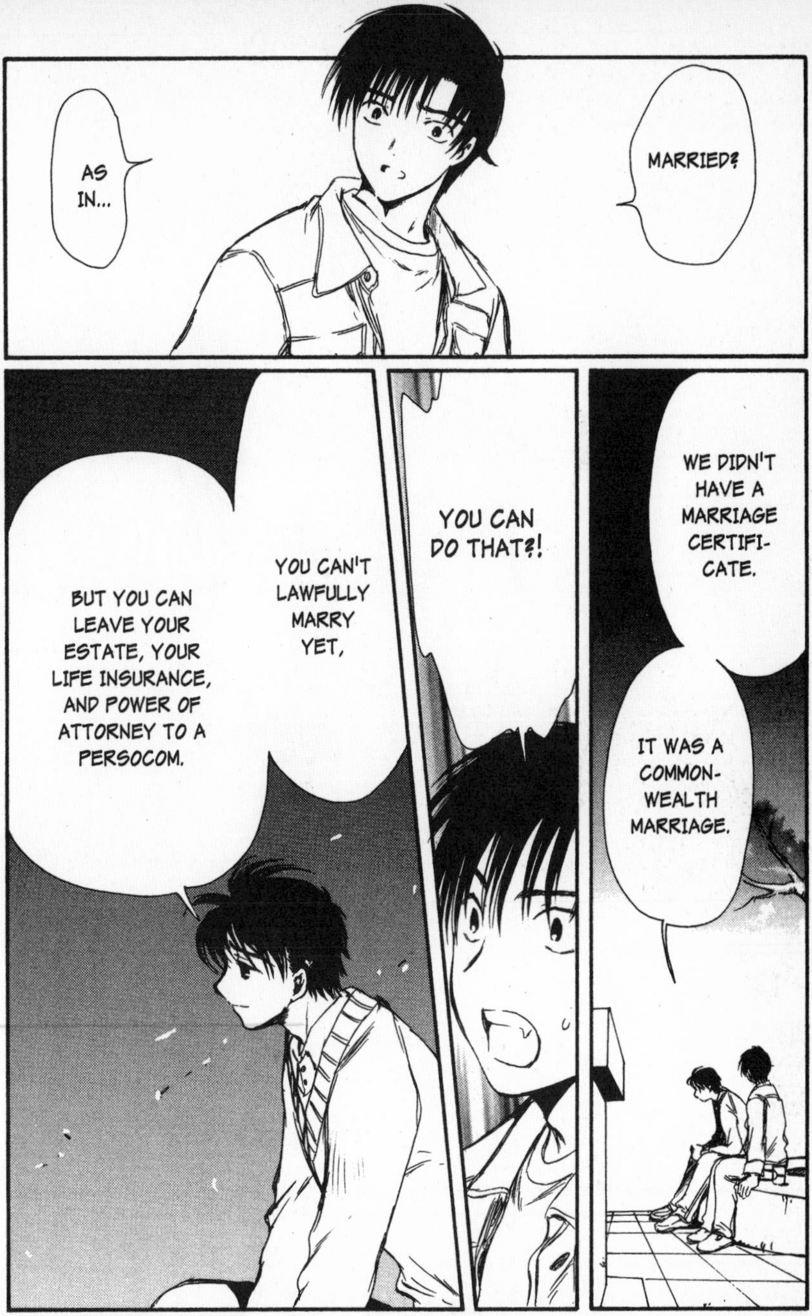
MARRIED?
AS IN...
WE DIDN'T HAVE A MARRIAGE CERTIFI-CATE.
IT WAS A COMMON-WEALTH MARRIAGE.
YOU CAN DO THAT?!
YOU CAN'T LAWFULLY MARRY YET,
BUT YOU CAN LEAVE YOUR ESTATE, YOUR LIFE INSURANCE, AND POWER OF ATTORNEY TO A PERSOCOM.

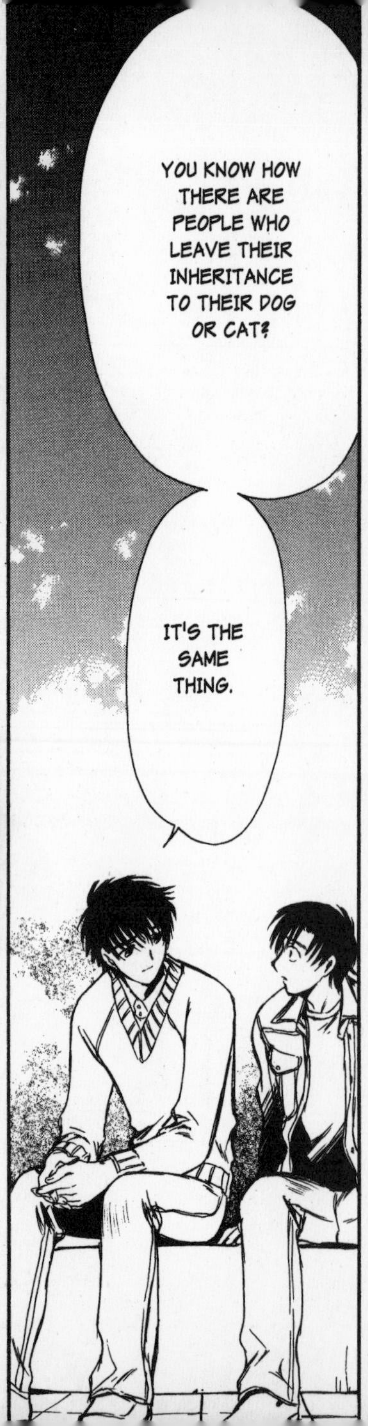
YOU KNOW HOW THERE ARE PEOPLE WHO LEAVE THEIR INHERITANCE TO THEIR DOG OR CAT?
IT'S THE SAME THING.

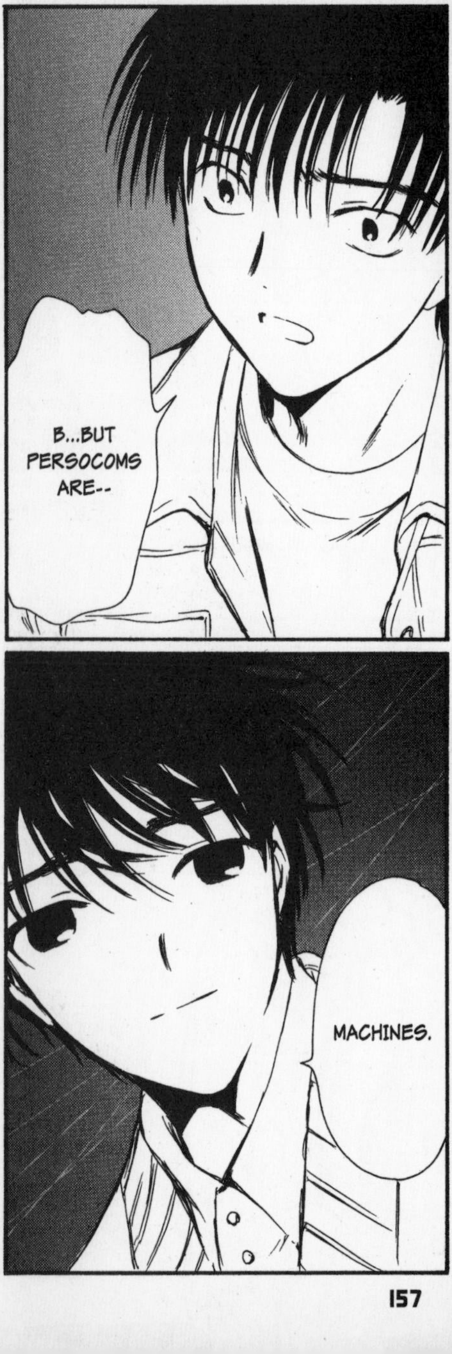
B...BUT PERSOCOMS ARE--
MACHINES.

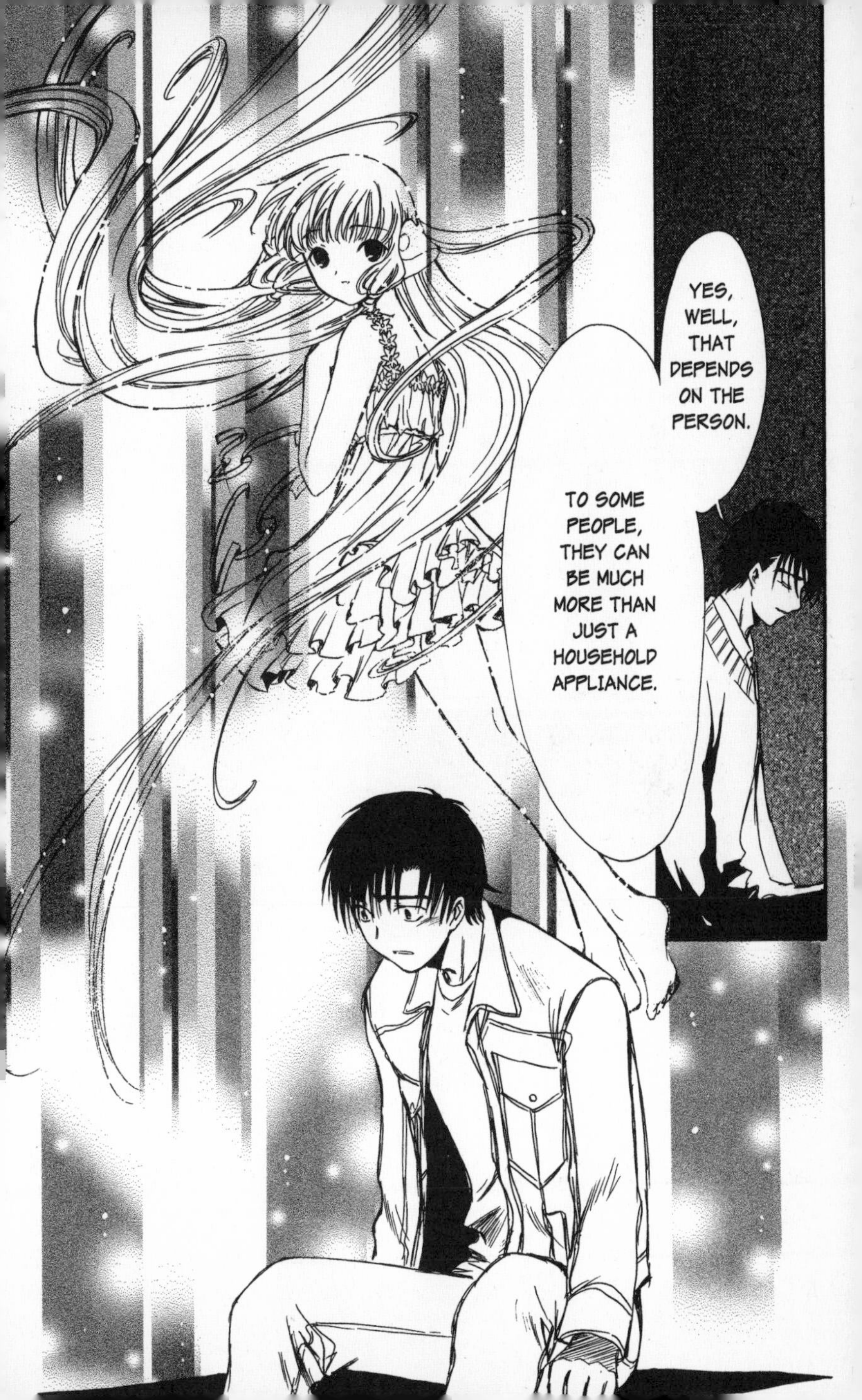
YES, WELL, THAT DEPENDS ON THE PERSON.
TO SOME PEOPLE, THEY CAN BE MUCH MORE THAN JUST A HOUSEHOLD APPLIANCE.

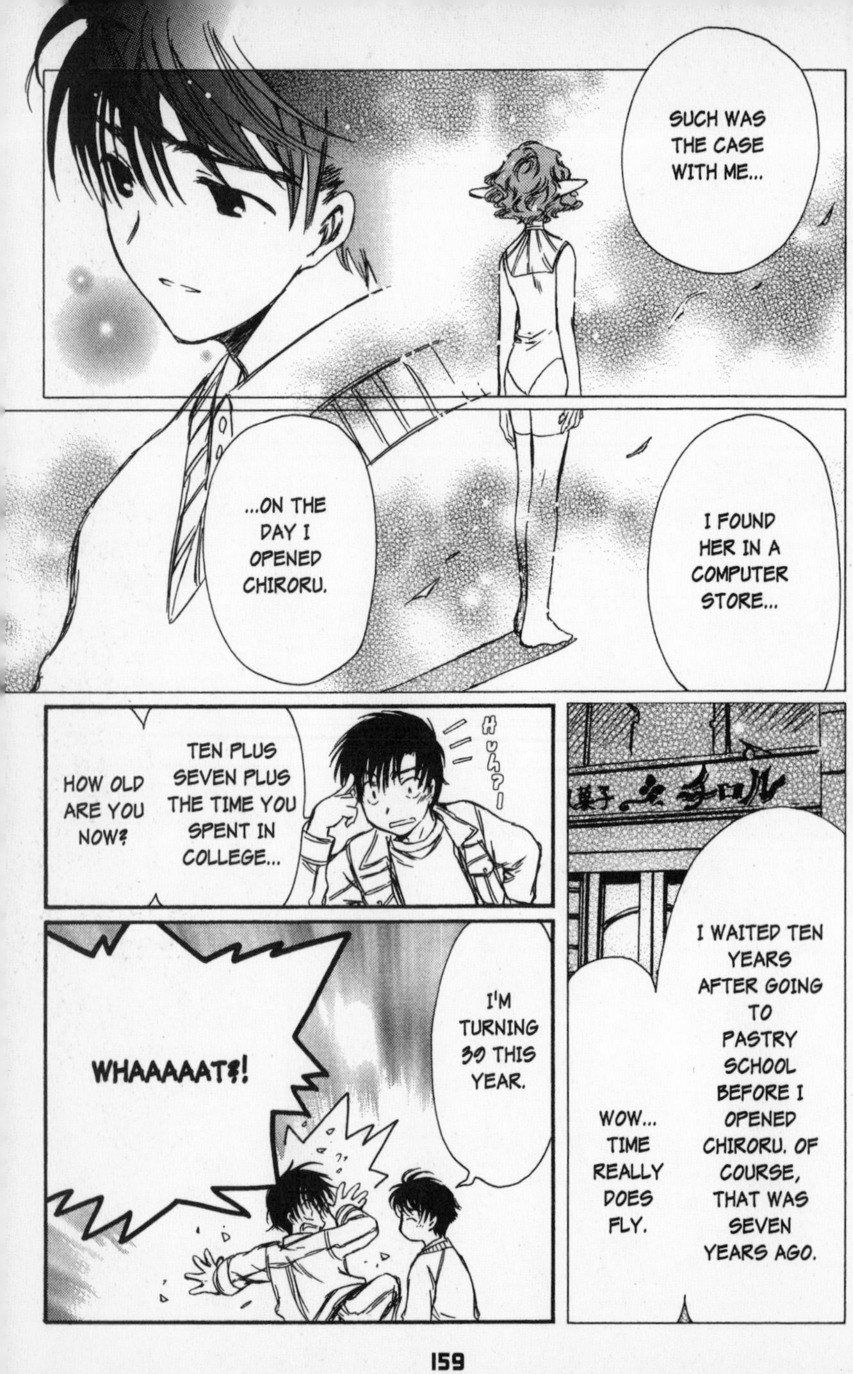

SUCH WAS THE CASE WITH ME...
I FOUND HER IN A COMPUTER STORE...
...ON THE DAY I OPENED CHIRORU.
I WAITED TEN YEARS AFTER GOING TO PASTRY SCHOOL BEFORE I OPENED CHIRORU. OF COURSE, THAT WAS SEVEN YEARS AGO.
WOW... TIME REALLY DOES FLY.
HUH?!
TEN PLUS SEVEN PLUS THE TIME YOU SPENT IN COLLEGE...
HOW OLD ARE YOU NOW?
I'M TURNING 30 THIS YEAR.
WHAAAAAT?!

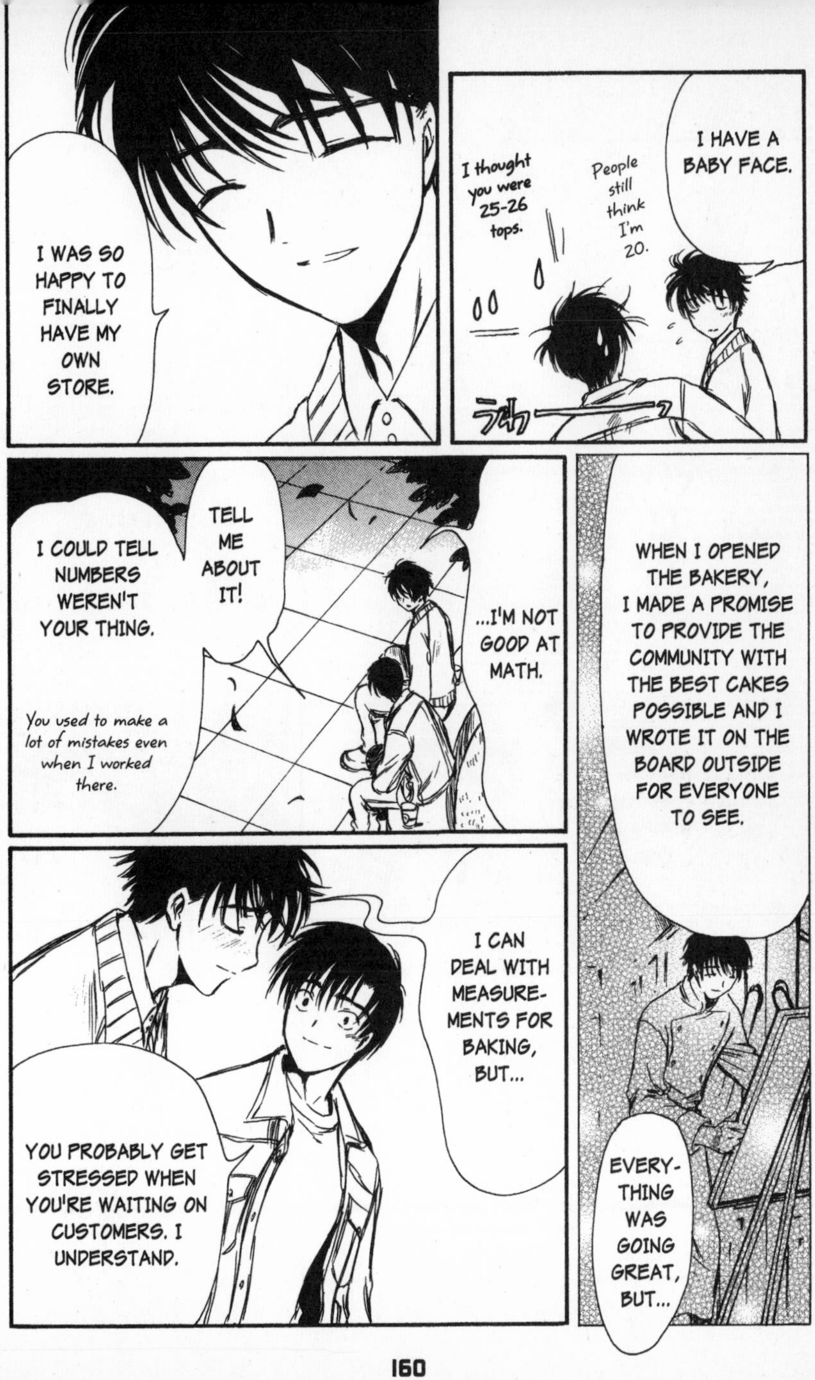

I HAVE A BABY FACE.
People still think I'm 20.
I thought you were 25-26 tops.
I WAS SO HAPPY TO FINALLY HAVE MY OWN STORE.
WHEN I OPENED THE BAKERY, I MADE A PROMISE TO PROVIDE THE COMMUNITY WITH THE BEST CAKES POSSIBLE AND I WROTE IT ON THE BOARD OUTSIDE FOR EVERYONE TO SEE.
EVERY-THING WAS GOING GREAT, BUT...
...I'M NOT GOOD AT MATH.
TELL ME ABOUT IT!
I COULD TELL NUMBERS WEREN'T YOUR THING.
You used to make a lot of mistakes even when I worked there.
I CAN DEAL WITH MEASURE-MENTS FOR BAKING, BUT...
YOU PROBABLY GET STRESSED WHEN YOU'RE WAITING ON CUSTOMERS. I UNDERSTAND.

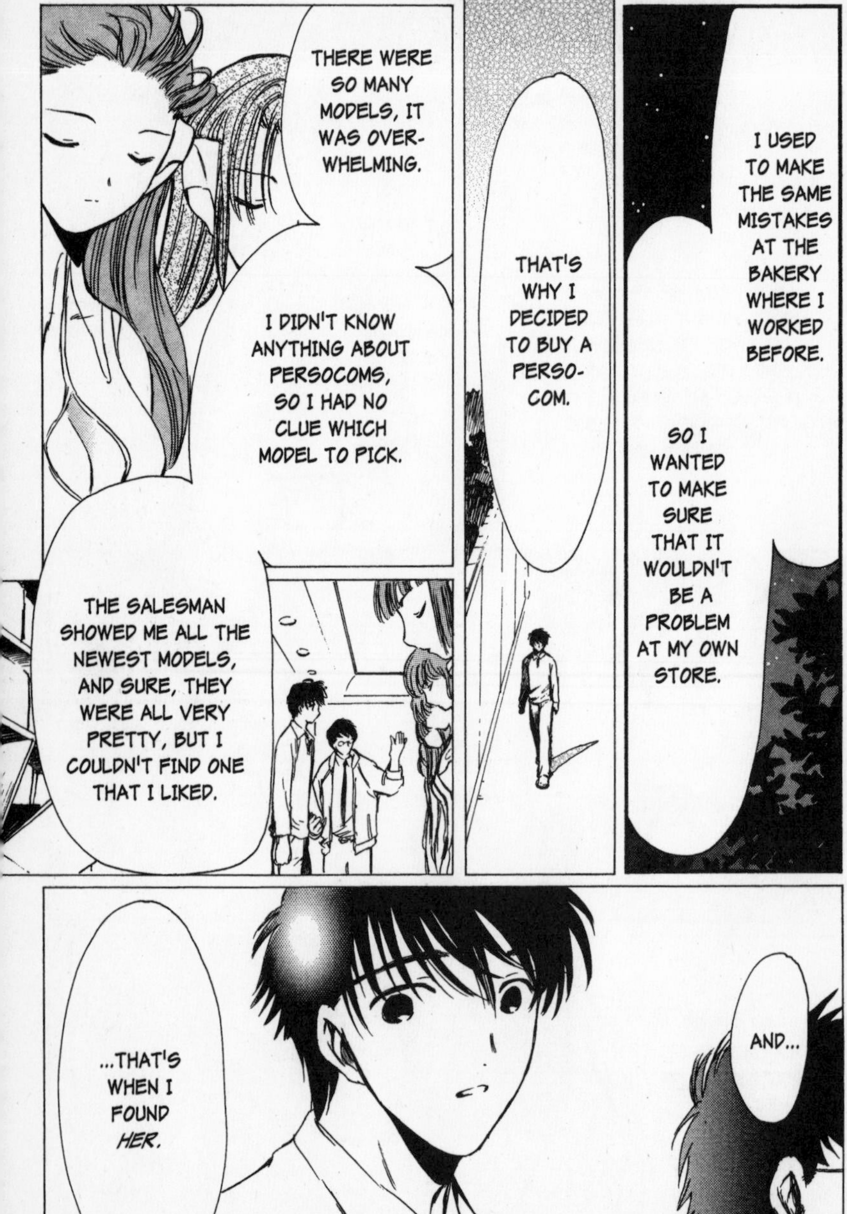
I USED TO MAKE THE SAME MISTAKES AT THE BAKERY WHERE I WORKED BEFORE.
SO I WANTED TO MAKE SURE THAT IT WOULDN'T BE A PROBLEM AT MY OWN STORE.
THAT'S WHY I DECIDED TO BUY A PERSO-COM.
THERE WERE SO MANY MODELS, IT WAS OVER-WHELMING.
I DIDN'T KNOW ANYTHING ABOUT PERSOCOMS, SO I HAD NO CLUE WHICH MODEL TO PICK.
THE SALESMAN SHOWED ME ALL THE NEWEST MODELS, AND SURE, THEY WERE ALL VERY PRETTY, BUT I COULDN'T FIND ONE THAT I LIKED.
AND...
...THAT'S WHEN I FOUND *HER*.

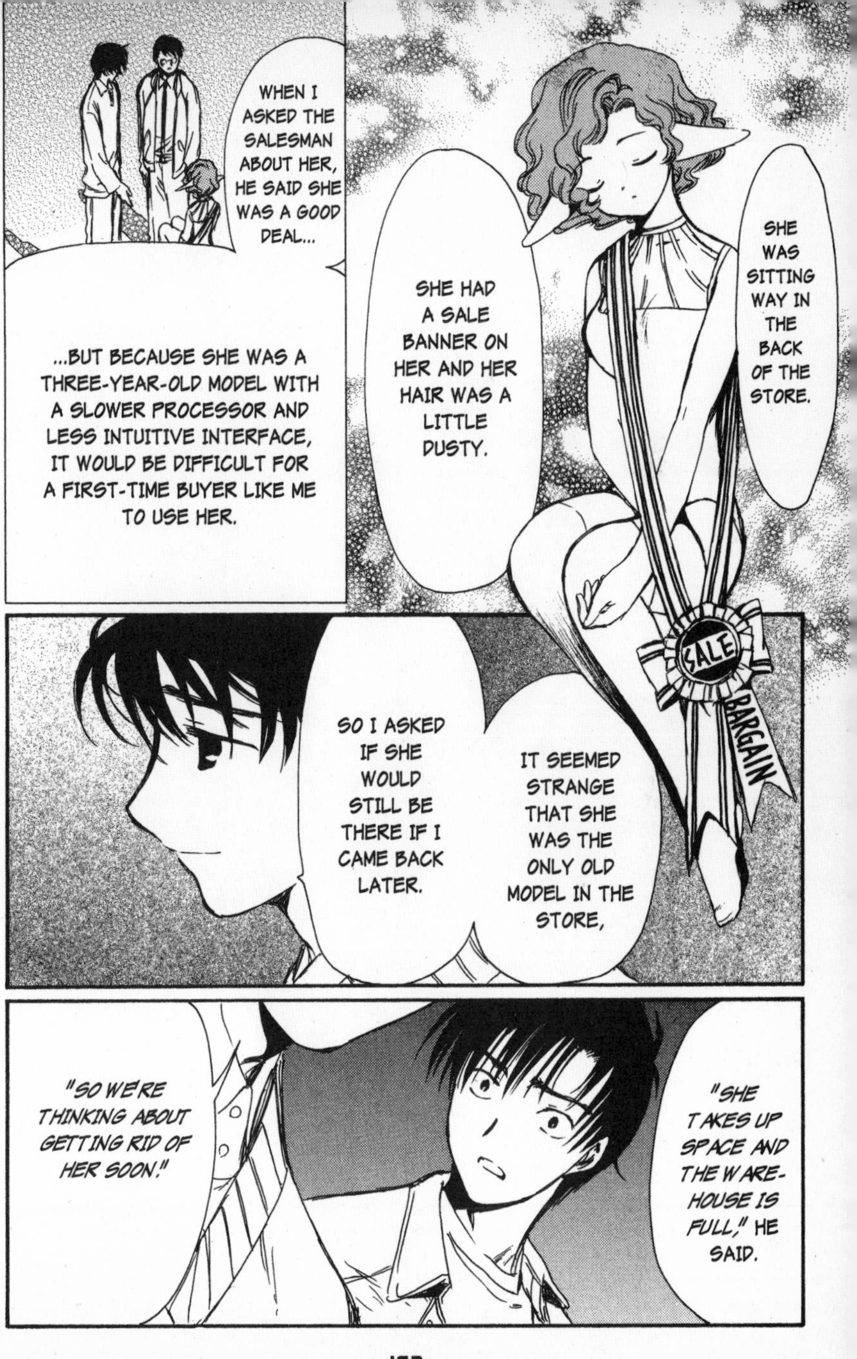
SHE WAS SITTING WAY IN THE BACK OF THE STORE.
SHE HAD A SALE BANNER ON HER AND HER HAIR WAS A LITTLE DUSTY.
SALE
BARGAIN
WHEN I ASKED THE SALESMAN ABOUT HER, HE SAID SHE WAS A GOOD DEAL...
...BUT BECAUSE SHE WAS A THREE-YEAR-OLD MODEL WITH A SLOWER PROCESSOR AND LESS INTUITIVE INTERFACE, IT WOULD BE DIFFICULT FOR A FIRST-TIME BUYER LIKE ME TO USE HER.
IT SEEMED STRANGE THAT SHE WAS THE ONLY OLD MODEL IN THE STORE,
SO I ASKED IF SHE WOULD STILL BE THERE IF I CAME BACK LATER.
"SHE TAKES UP SPACE AND THE WARE-HOUSE IS FULL," HE SAID.
"SO WE'RE THINKING ABOUT GETTING RID OF HER SOON."

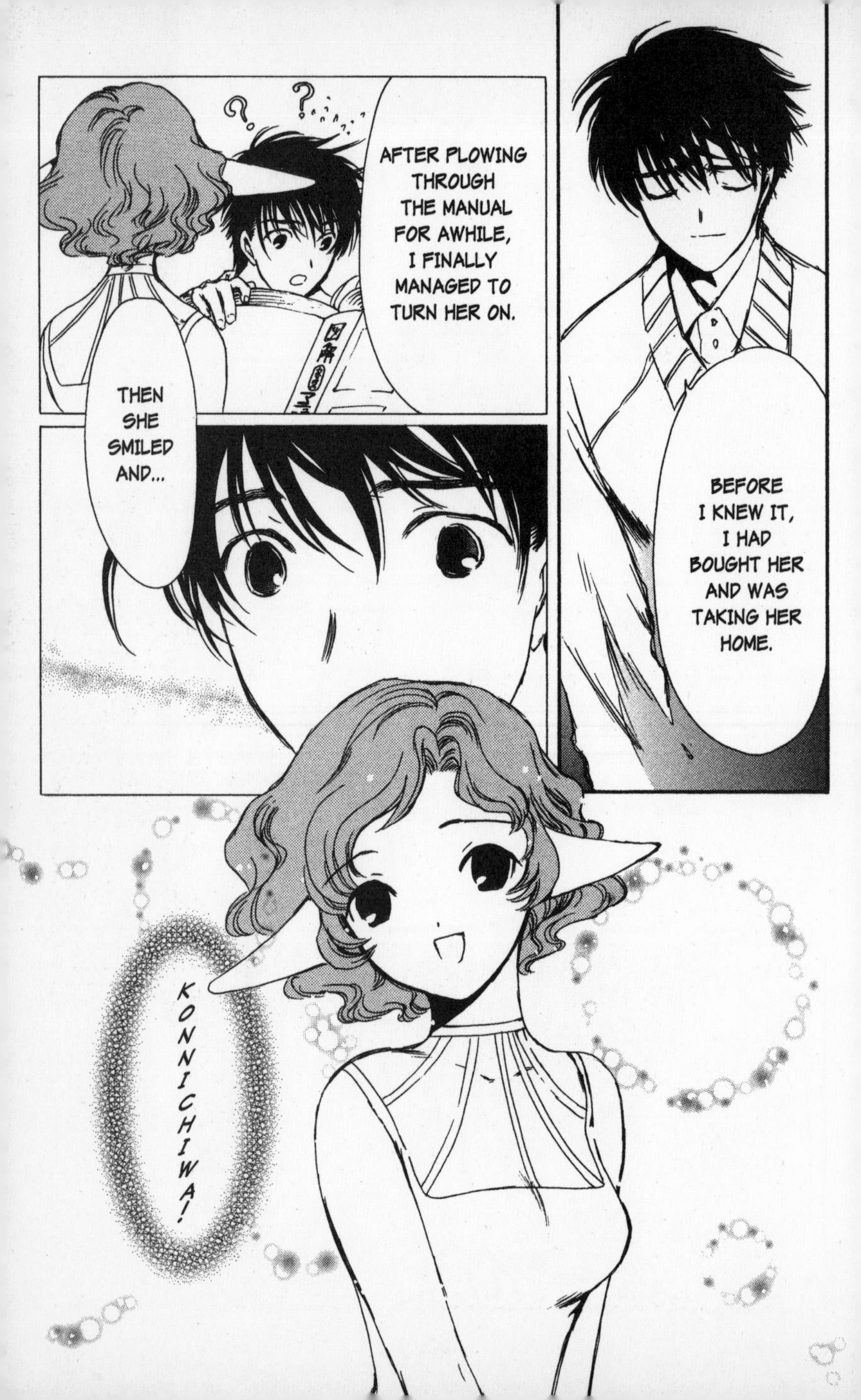
BEFORE I KNEW IT, I HAD BOUGHT HER AND WAS TAKING HER HOME.
AFTER PLOWING THROUGH THE MANUAL FOR AWHILE, I FINALLY MANAGED TO TURN HER ON.
THEN SHE SMILED AND...
KONNICHIWA!

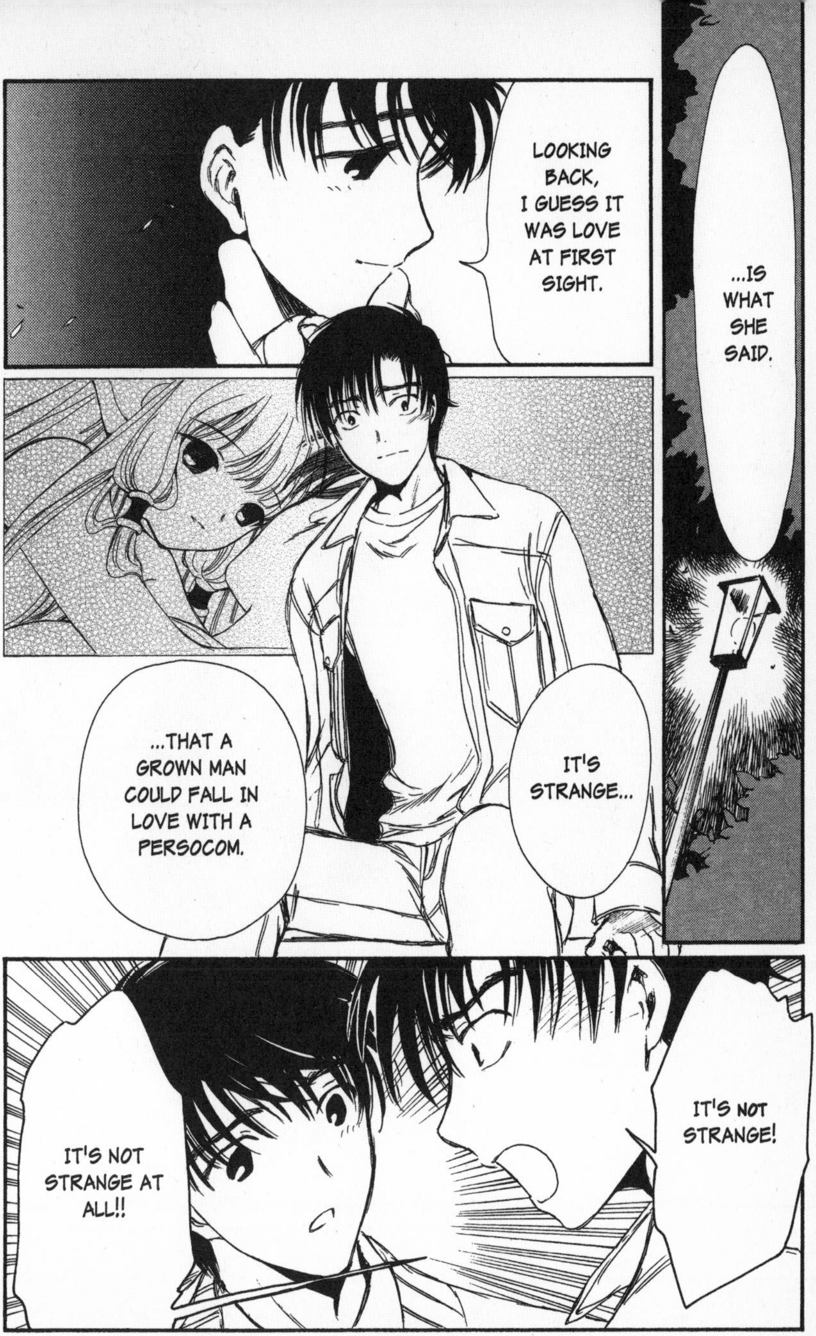
...IS WHAT SHE SAID.
LOOKING BACK, I GUESS IT WAS LOVE AT FIRST SIGHT.
IT'S STRANGE...
...THAT A GROWN MAN COULD FALL IN LOVE WITH A PERSOCOM.
IT'S NOT STRANGE!
IT'S NOT STRANGE AT ALL!!

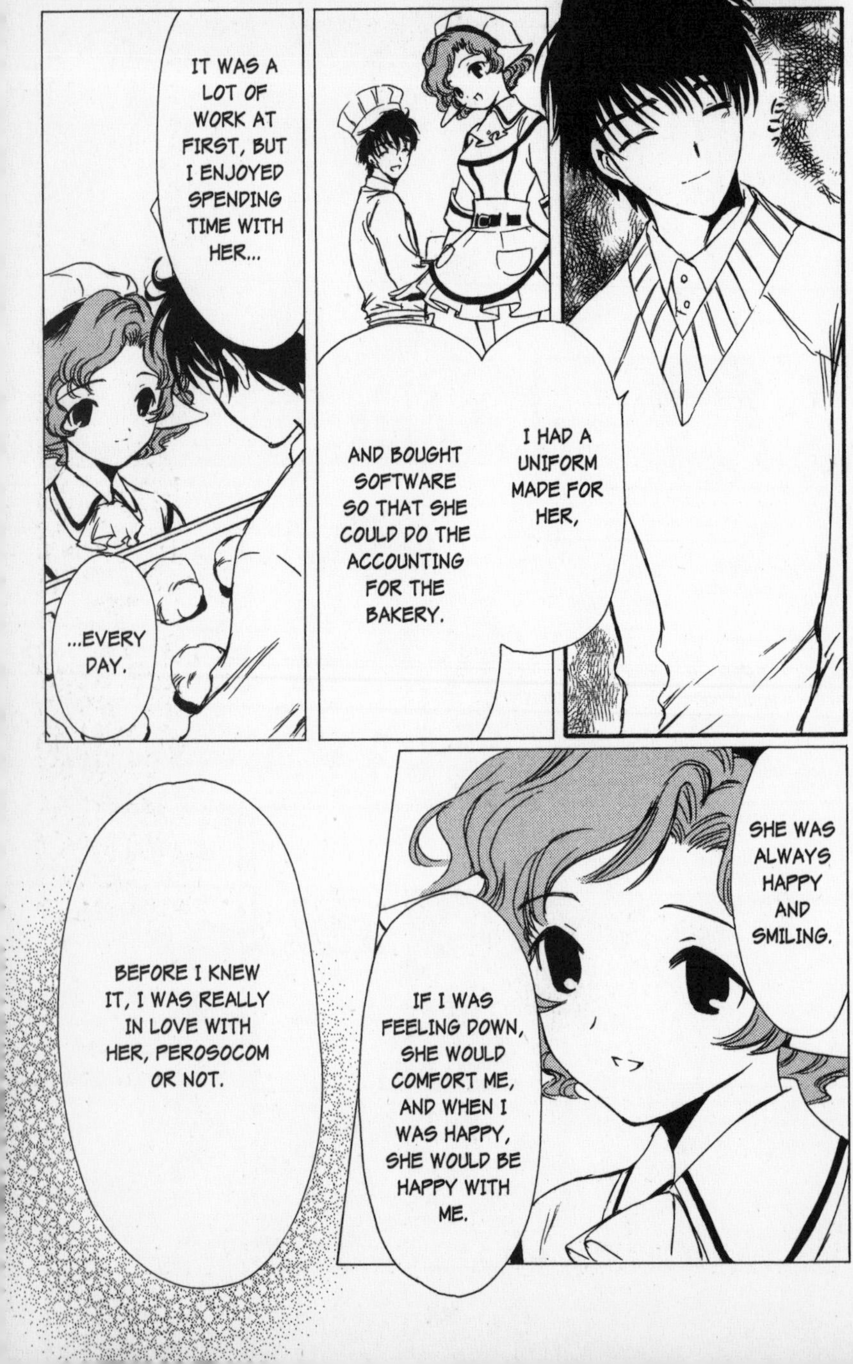
I HAD A UNIFORM MADE FOR HER,
AND BOUGHT SOFTWARE SO THAT SHE COULD DO THE ACCOUNTING FOR THE BAKERY.
IT WAS A LOT OF WORK AT FIRST, BUT I ENJOYED SPENDING TIME WITH HER...
...EVERY DAY.
SHE WAS ALWAYS HAPPY AND SMILING.
IF I WAS FEELING DOWN, SHE WOULD COMFORT ME, AND WHEN I WAS HAPPY, SHE WOULD BE HAPPY WITH ME.
BEFORE I KNEW IT, I WAS REALLY IN LOVE WITH HER, PEROSOCOM OR NOT.

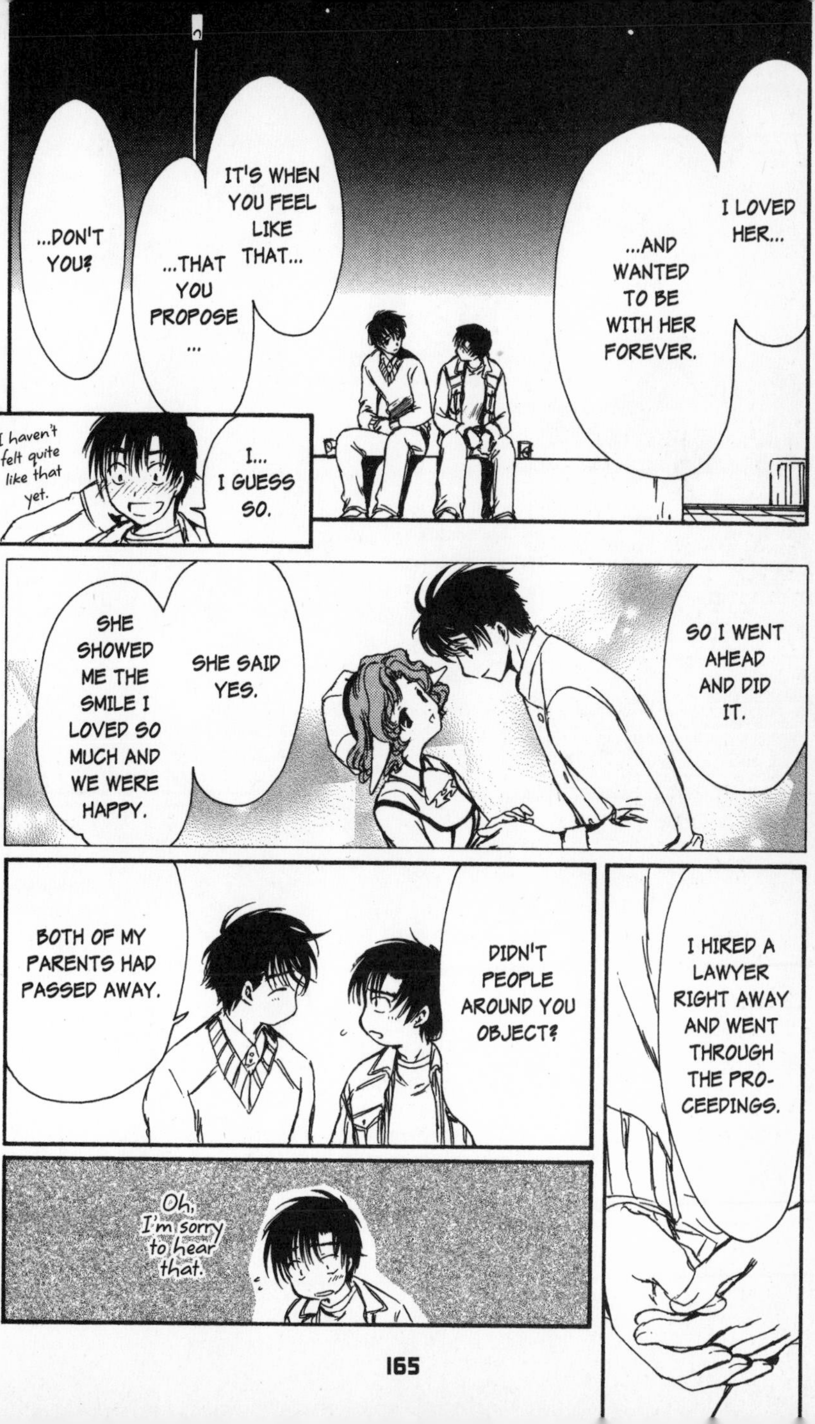
I LOVED HER...
...AND WANTED TO BE WITH HER FOREVER.
IT'S WHEN YOU FEEL LIKE THAT...
...THAT YOU PROPOSE ...
...DON'T YOU?
I... I GUESS SO.
I haven't felt quite like that yet.
SO I WENT AHEAD AND DID IT.
SHE SAID YES.
SHE SHOWED ME THE SMILE I LOVED SO MUCH AND WE WERE HAPPY.
I HIRED A LAWYER RIGHT AWAY AND WENT THROUGH THE PRO- CEEDINGS.
DIDN'T PEOPLE AROUND YOU OBJECT?
BOTH OF MY PARENTS HAD PASSED AWAY.
Oh, I'm sorry to hear that.

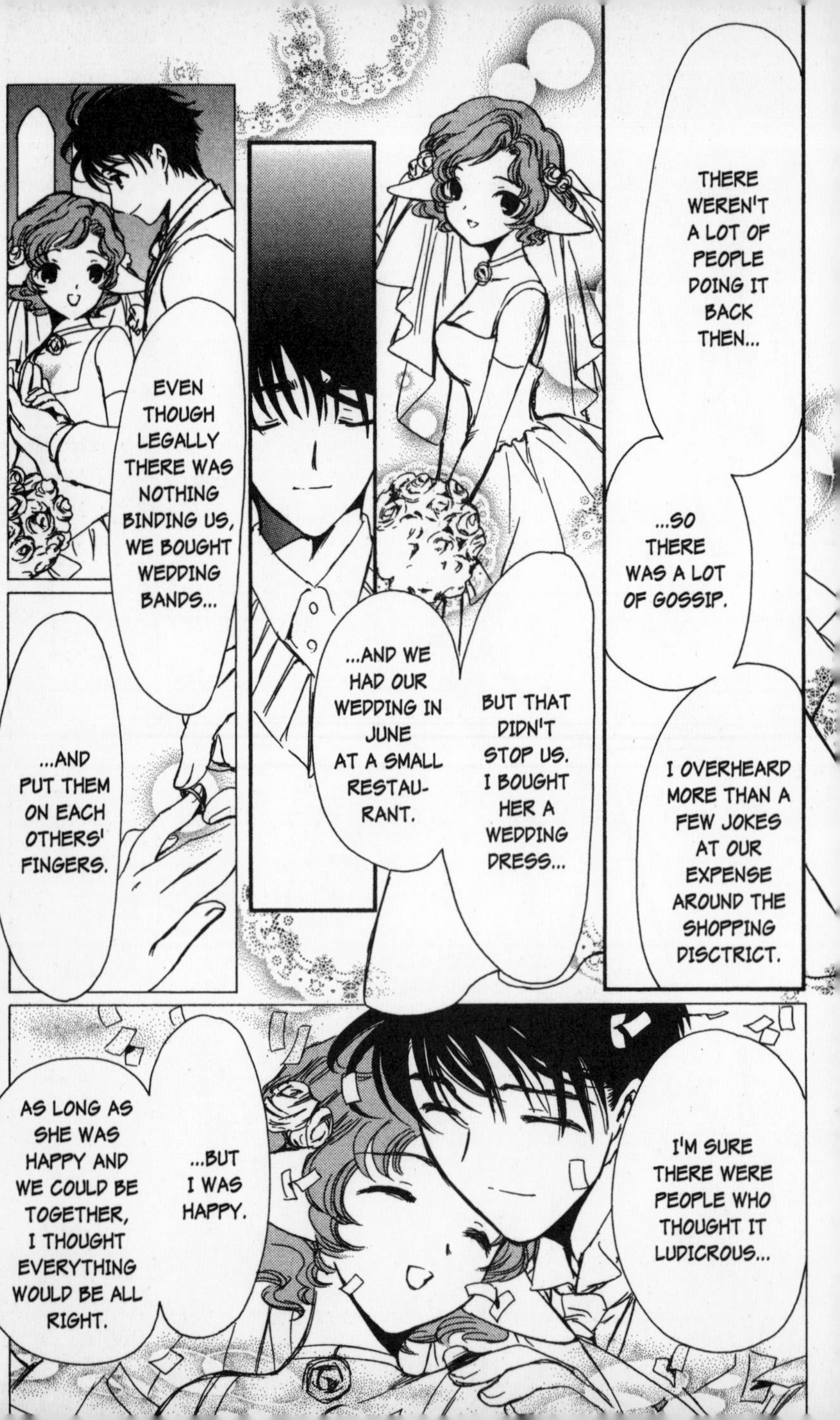
THERE WEREN'T A LOT OF PEOPLE DOING IT BACK THEN...
...SO THERE WAS A LOT OF GOSSIP.
I OVERHEARD MORE THAN A FEW JOKES AT OUR EXPENSE AROUND THE SHOPPING DISCTRICT.
BUT THAT DIDN'T STOP US. I BOUGHT HER A WEDDING DRESS...
...AND WE HAD OUR WEDDING IN JUNE AT A SMALL RESTAU-RANT.
EVEN THOUGH LEGALLY THERE WAS NOTHING BINDING US, WE BOUGHT WEDDING BANDS...
...AND PUT THEM ON EACH OTHERS' FINGERS.
I'M SURE THERE WERE PEOPLE WHO THOUGHT IT LUDICROUS...
...BUT I WAS HAPPY.
AS LONG AS SHE WAS HAPPY AND WE COULD BE TOGETHER, I THOUGHT EVERYTHING WOULD BE ALL RIGHT.

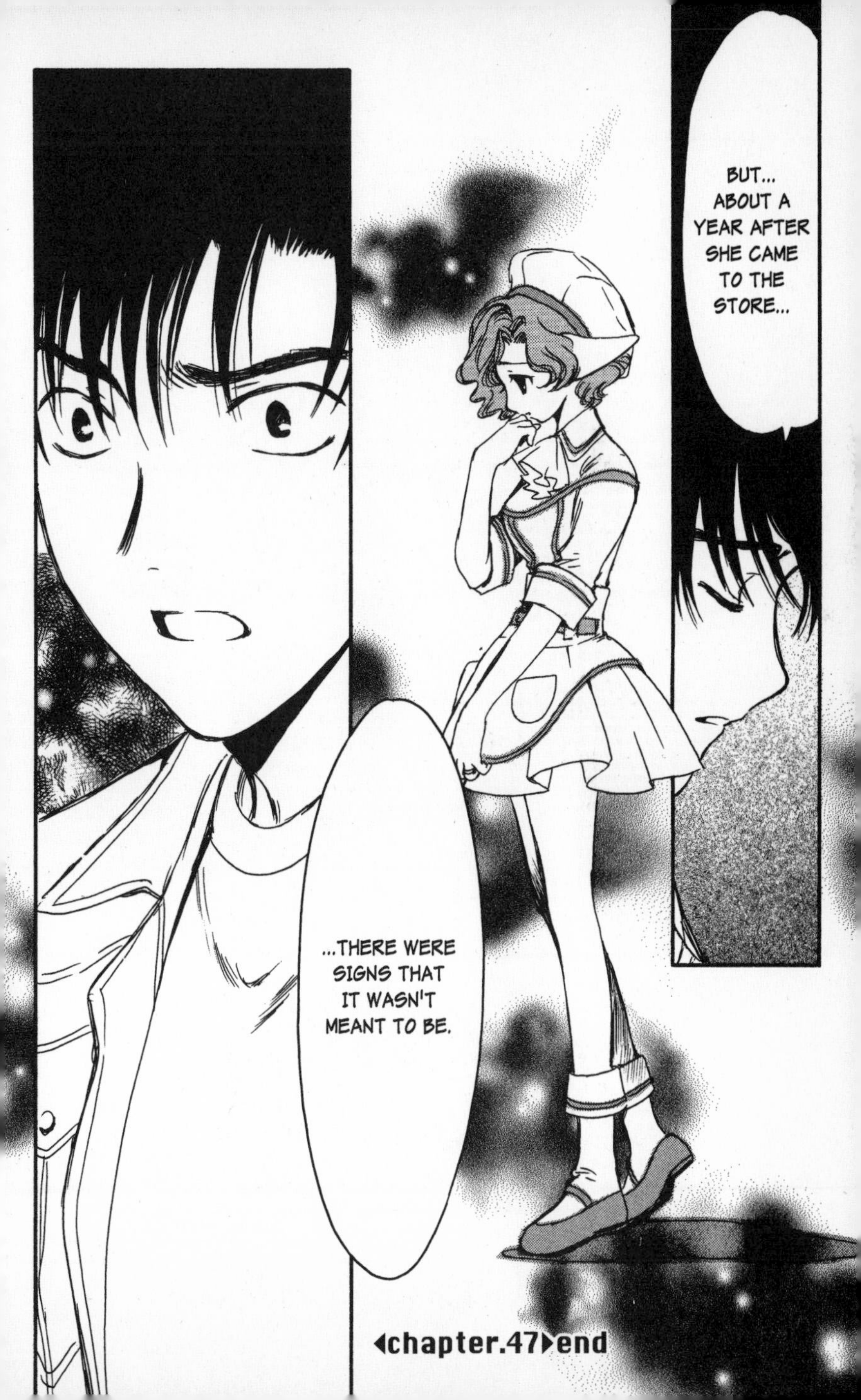
BUT... ABOUT A YEAR AFTER SHE CAME TO THE STORE...
...THERE WERE SIGNS THAT IT WASN'T MEANT TO BE.
chapter.47 end

ちょびっツ
Chobits

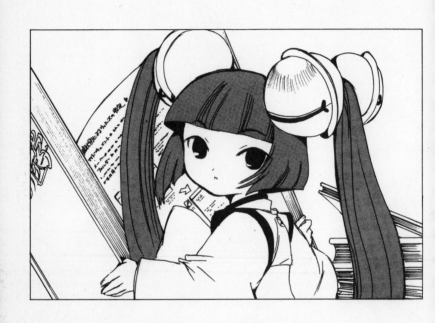

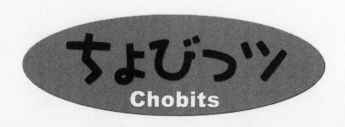

chapter.48

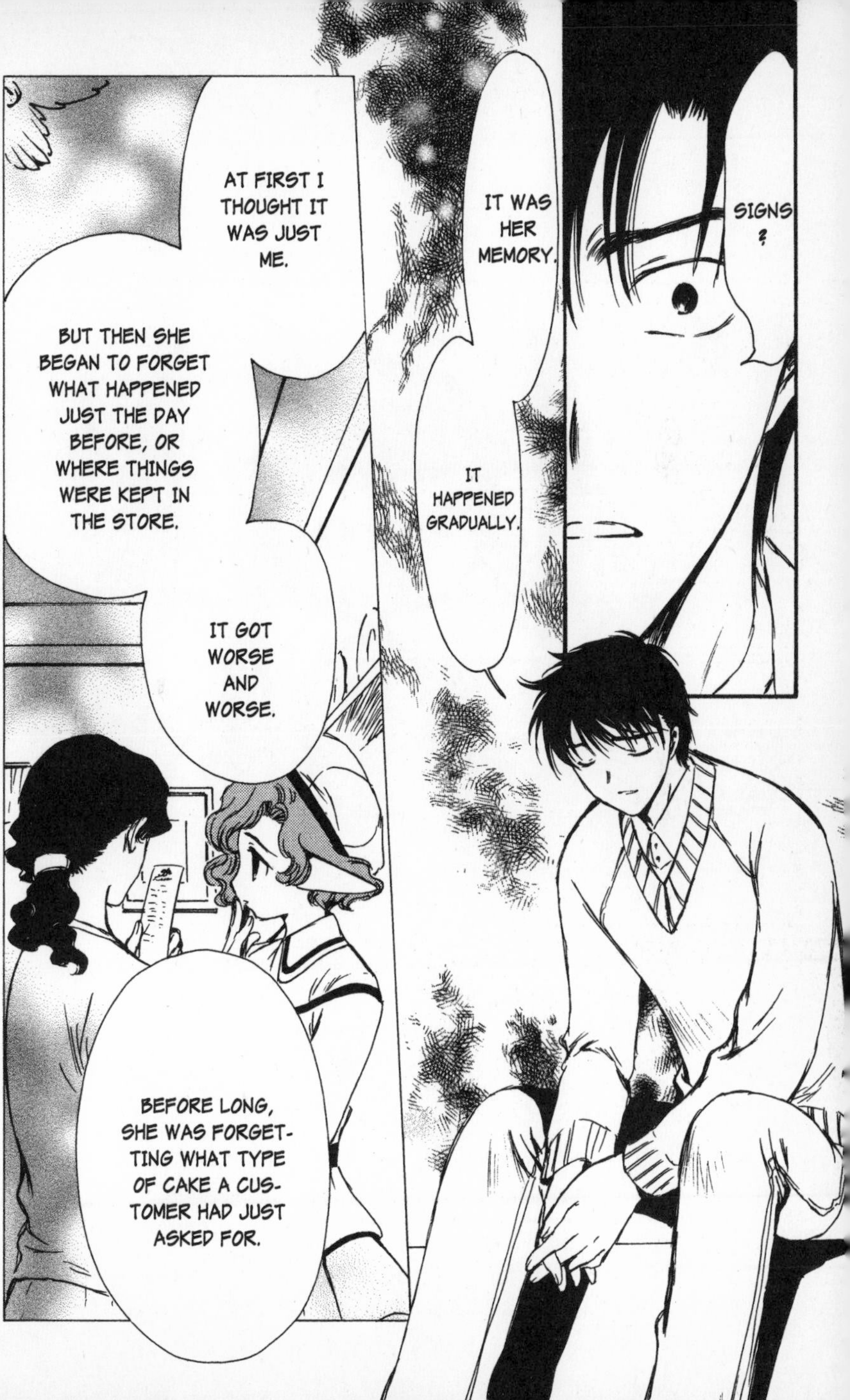
SIGNS?
IT WAS HER MEMORY.
IT HAPPENED GRADUALLY.
AT FIRST I THOUGHT IT WAS JUST ME.
BUT THEN SHE BEGAN TO FORGET WHAT HAPPENED JUST THE DAY BEFORE, OR WHERE THINGS WERE KEPT IN THE STORE.
IT GOT WORSE AND WORSE.
BEFORE LONG, SHE WAS FORGETTING WHAT TYPE OF CAKE A CUSTOMER HAD JUST ASKED FOR.

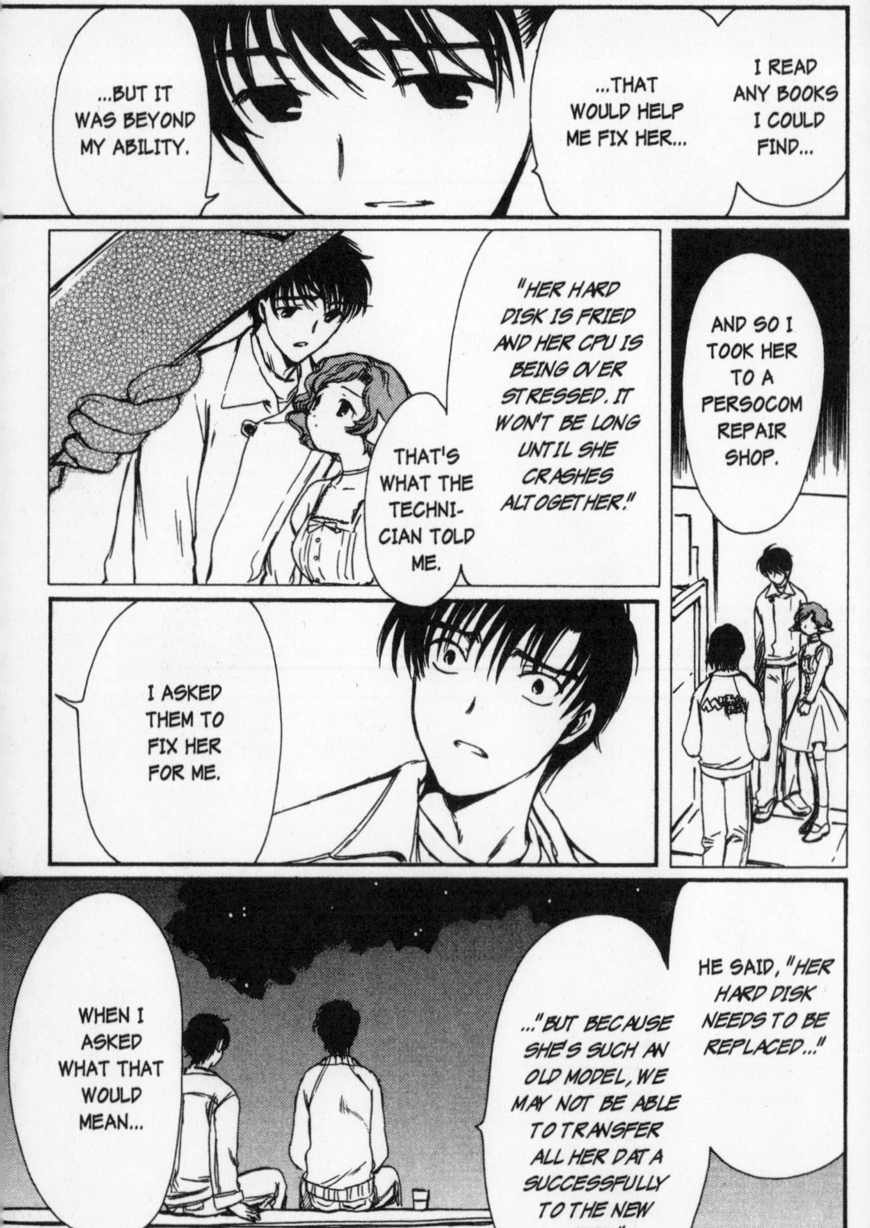
I READ ANY BOOKS I COULD FIND...
...THAT WOULD HELP ME FIX HER...
...BUT IT WAS BEYOND MY ABILITY.
AND SO I TOOK HER TO A PERSOCOM REPAIR SHOP.
"HER HARD DISK IS FRIED AND HER CPU IS BEING OVER STRESSED. IT WON'T BE LONG UNTIL SHE CRASHES ALTOGETHER."
THAT'S WHAT THE TECHNICIAN TOLD ME.
I ASKED THEM TO FIX HER FOR ME.
HE SAID, "HER HARD DISK NEEDS TO BE REPLACED..."
..."BUT BECAUSE SHE'S SUCH AN OLD MODEL, WE MAY NOT BE ABLE TO TRANSFER ALL HER DATA SUCCESSFULLY TO THE NEW DISK."
WHEN I ASKED WHAT THAT WOULD MEAN...

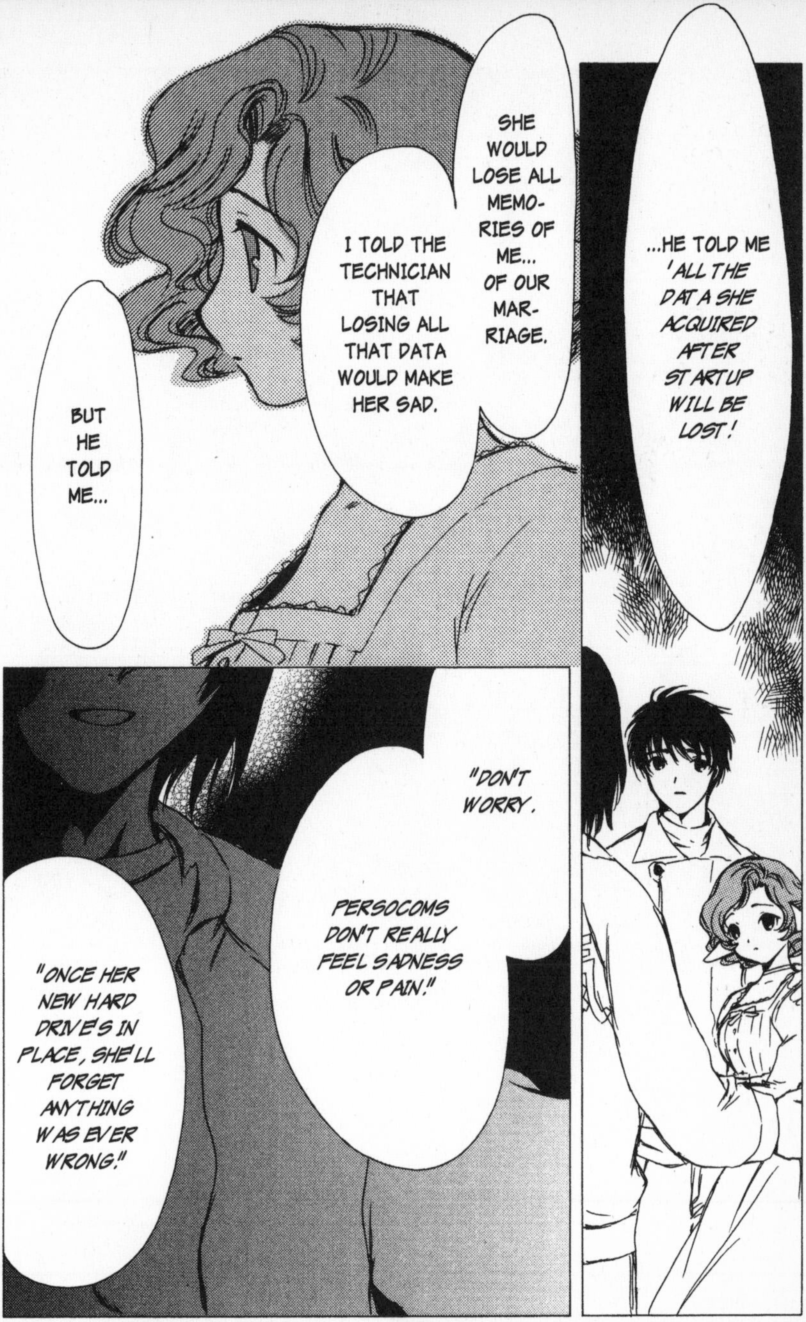
...HE TOLD ME 'ALL THE DATA SHE ACQUIRED AFTER STARTUP WILL BE LOST!
SHE WOULD LOSE ALL MEMORIES OF ME... OF OUR MARRIAGE.
I TOLD THE TECHNICIAN THAT LOSING ALL THAT DATA WOULD MAKE HER SAD.
BUT HE TOLD ME...
"DON'T WORRY.
PERSOCOMS DON'T REALLY FEEL SADNESS OR PAIN."
"ONCE HER NEW HARD DRIVE'S IN PLACE, SHE'LL FORGET ANYTHING WAS EVER WRONG."

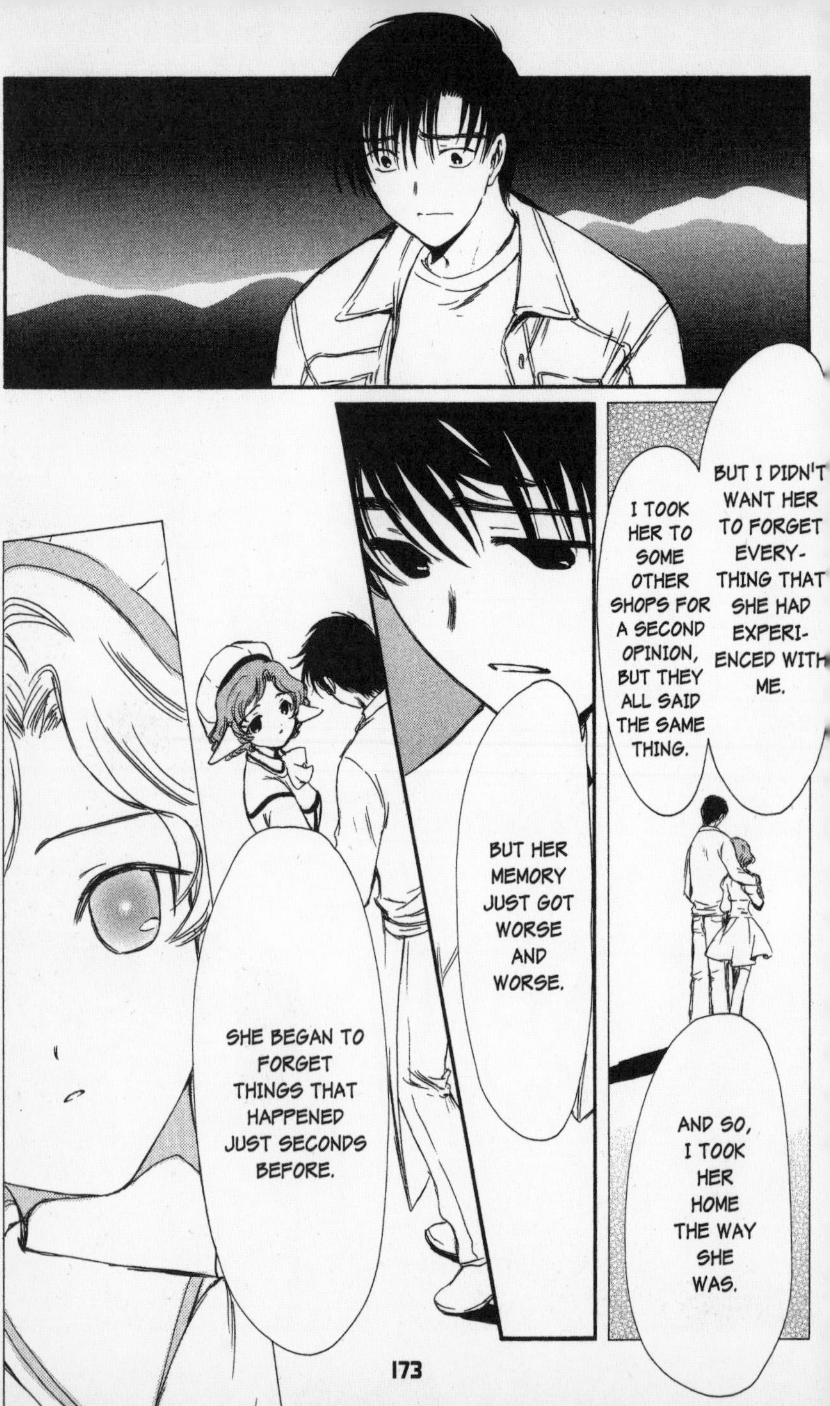

BUT I DIDN'T WANT HER TO FORGET EVERY-THING THAT SHE HAD EXPERI-ENCED WITH ME.
I TOOK HER TO SOME OTHER SHOPS FOR A SECOND OPINION, BUT THEY ALL SAID THE SAME THING.
AND SO, I TOOK HER HOME THE WAY SHE WAS.
BUT HER MEMORY JUST GOT WORSE AND WORSE.
SHE BEGAN TO FORGET THINGS THAT HAPPENED JUST SECONDS BEFORE.

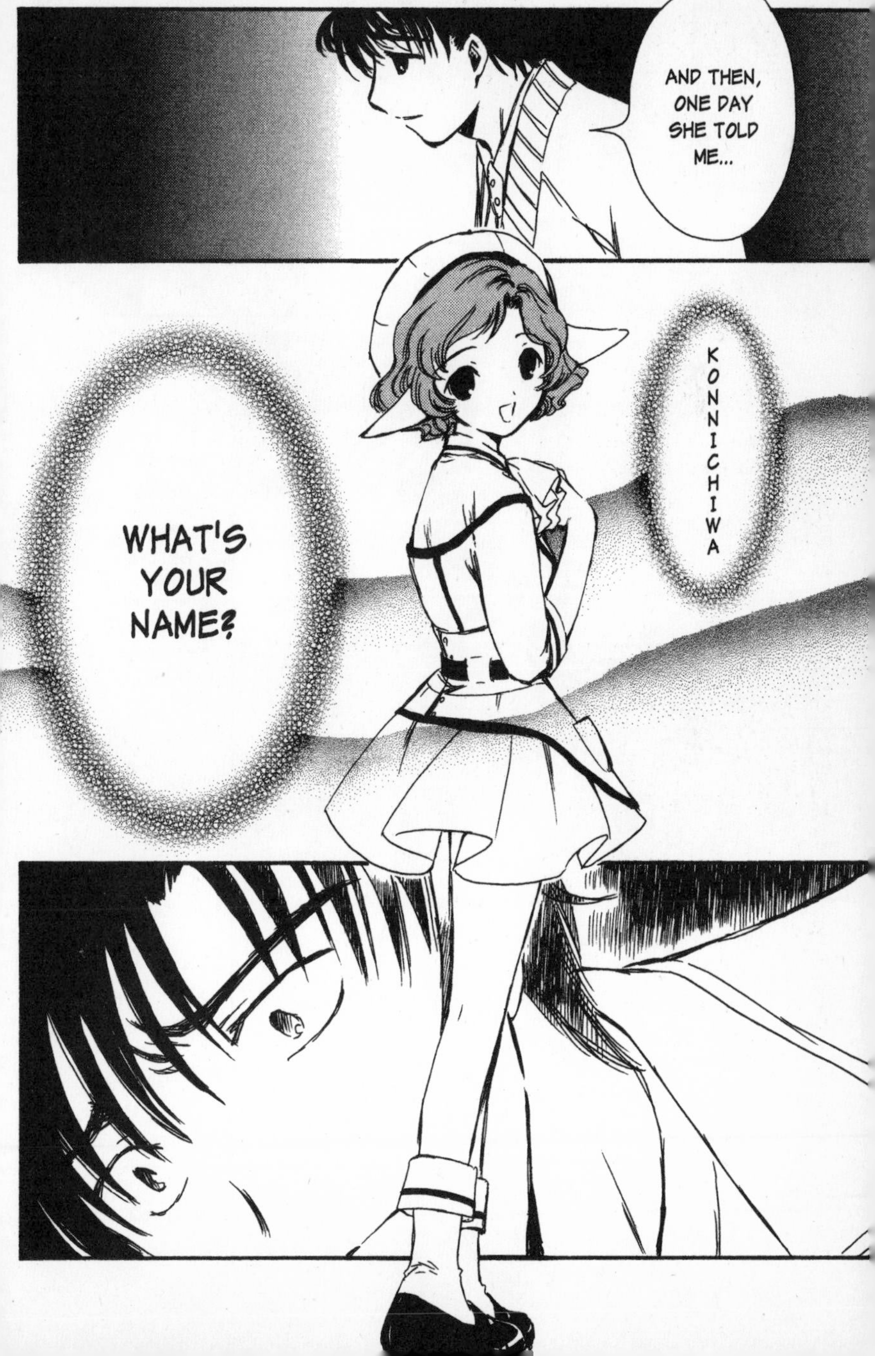
AND THEN, ONE DAY SHE TOLD ME...
KONNICHIWA
WHAT'S YOUR NAME?

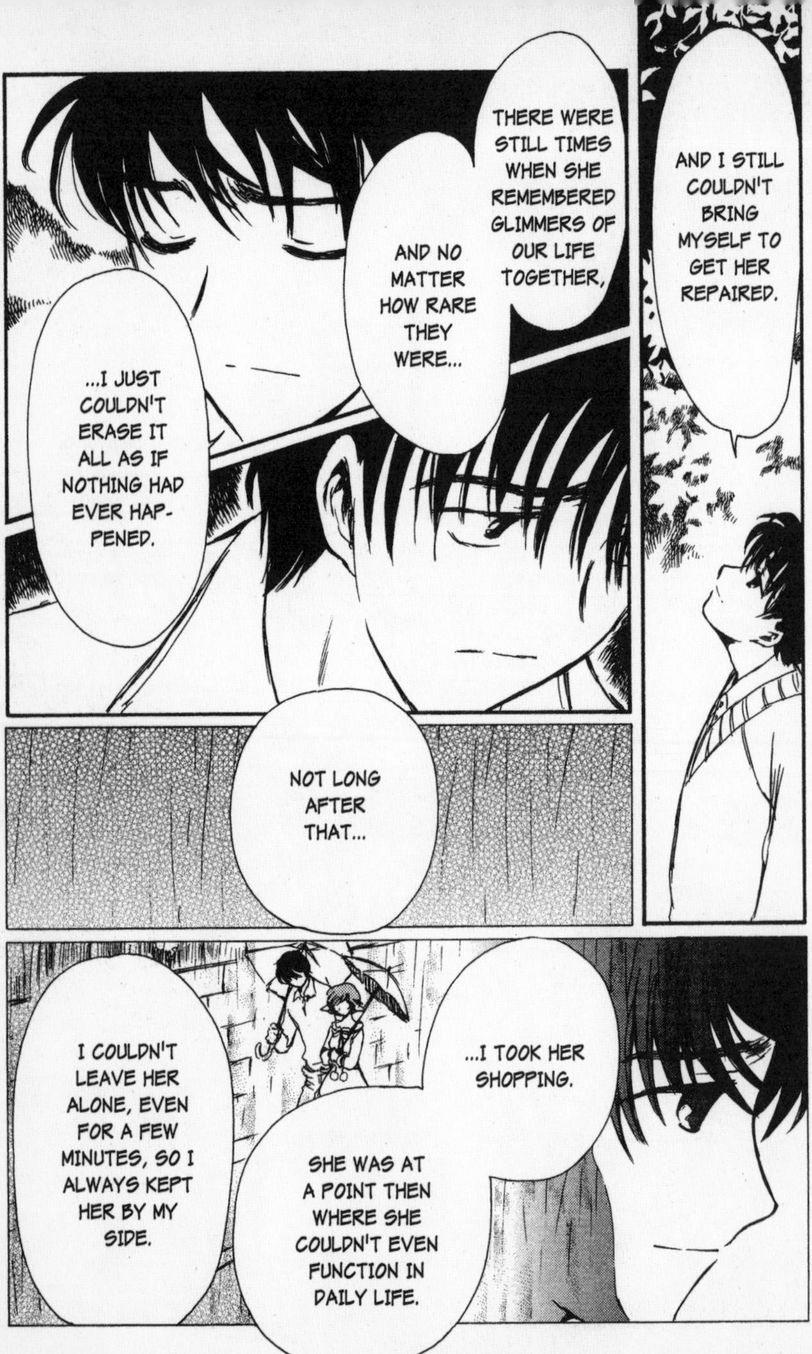
AND I STILL COULDN'T BRING MYSELF TO GET HER REPAIRED.
THERE WERE STILL TIMES WHEN SHE REMEMBERED GLIMMERS OF OUR LIFE TOGETHER,
AND NO MATTER HOW RARE THEY WERE...
...I JUST COULDN'T ERASE IT ALL AS IF NOTHING HAD EVER HAP-PENED.
NOT LONG AFTER THAT...
...I TOOK HER SHOPPING.
SHE WAS AT A POINT THEN WHERE SHE COULDN'T EVEN FUNCTION IN DAILY LIFE.
I COULDN'T LEAVE HER ALONE, EVEN FOR A FEW MINUTES, SO I ALWAYS KEPT HER BY MY SIDE.

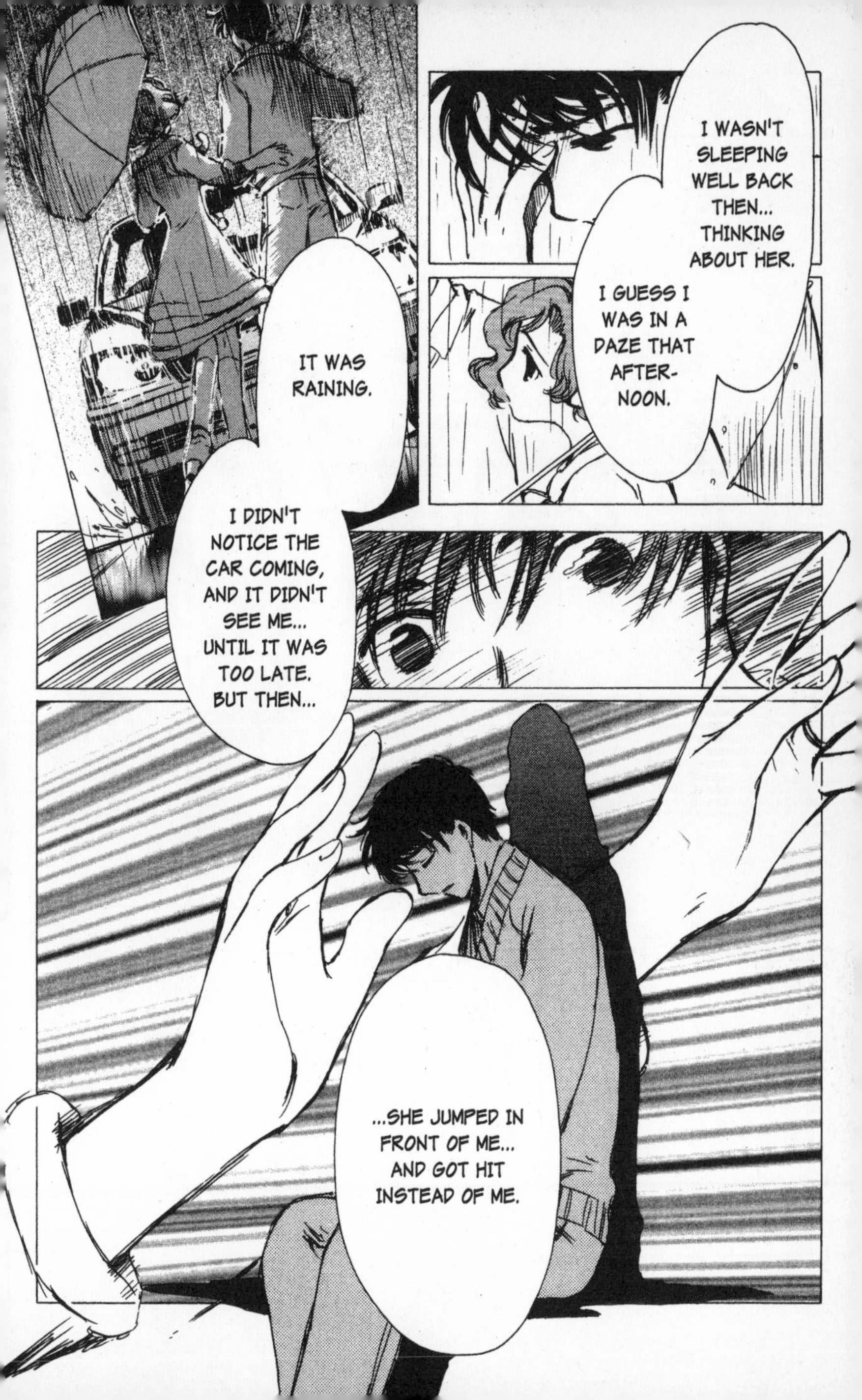
I WASN'T SLEEPING WELL BACK THEN... THINKING ABOUT HER.
I GUESS I WAS IN A DAZE THAT AFTER-NOON.
IT WAS RAINING.
I DIDN'T NOTICE THE CAR COMING, AND IT DIDN'T SEE ME... UNTIL IT WAS TOO LATE. BUT THEN...
...SHE JUMPED IN FRONT OF ME... AND GOT HIT INSTEAD OF ME.

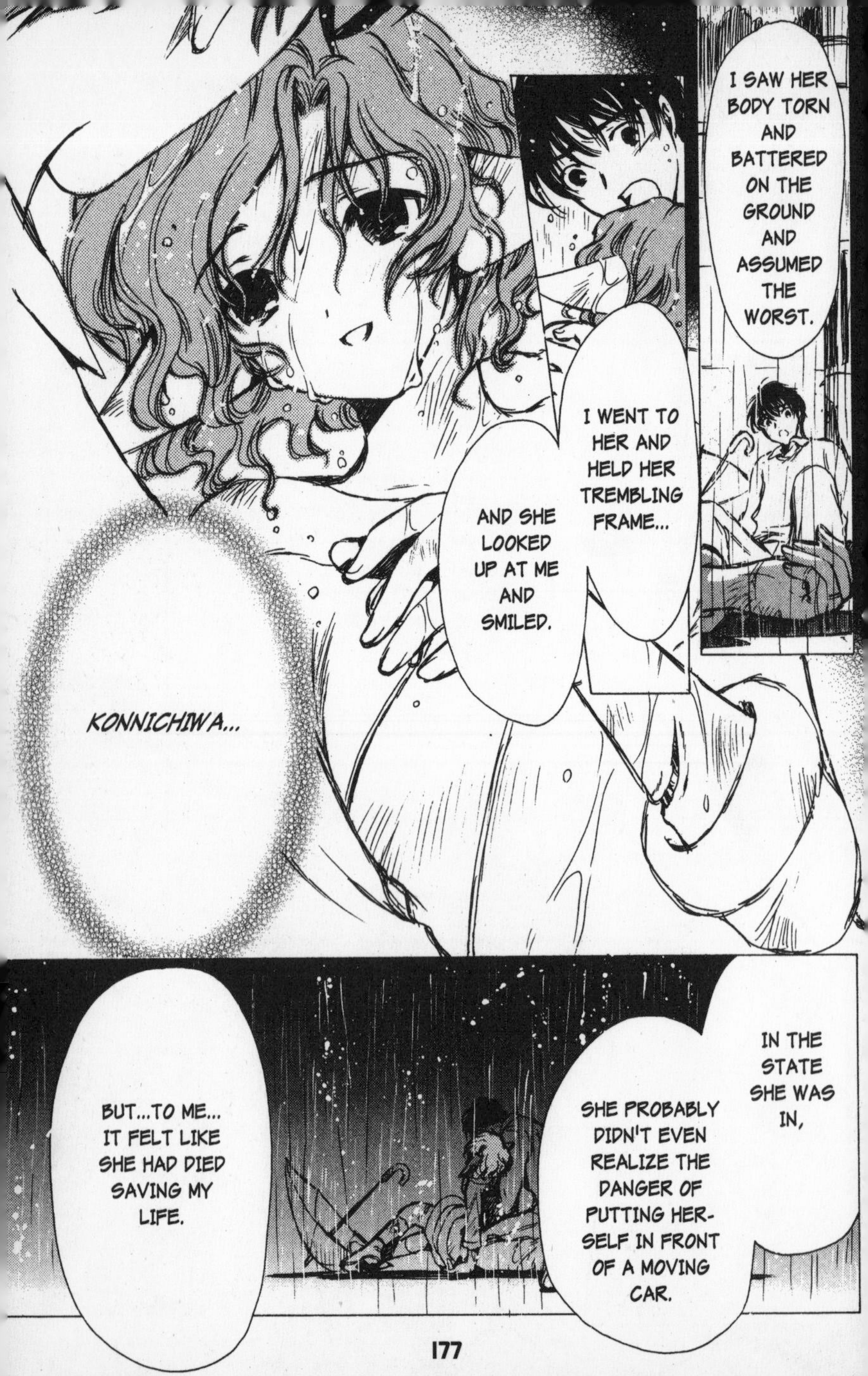
I SAW HER BODY TORN AND BATTERED ON THE GROUND AND ASSUMED THE WORST.
I WENT TO HER AND HELD HER TREMBLING FRAME...
AND SHE LOOKED UP AT ME AND SMILED.
KONNICHIWA...
IN THE STATE SHE WAS IN,
SHE PROBABLY DIDN'T EVEN REALIZE THE DANGER OF PUTTING HER-SELF IN FRONT OF A MOVING CAR.
BUT...TO ME... IT FELT LIKE SHE HAD DIED SAVING MY LIFE.

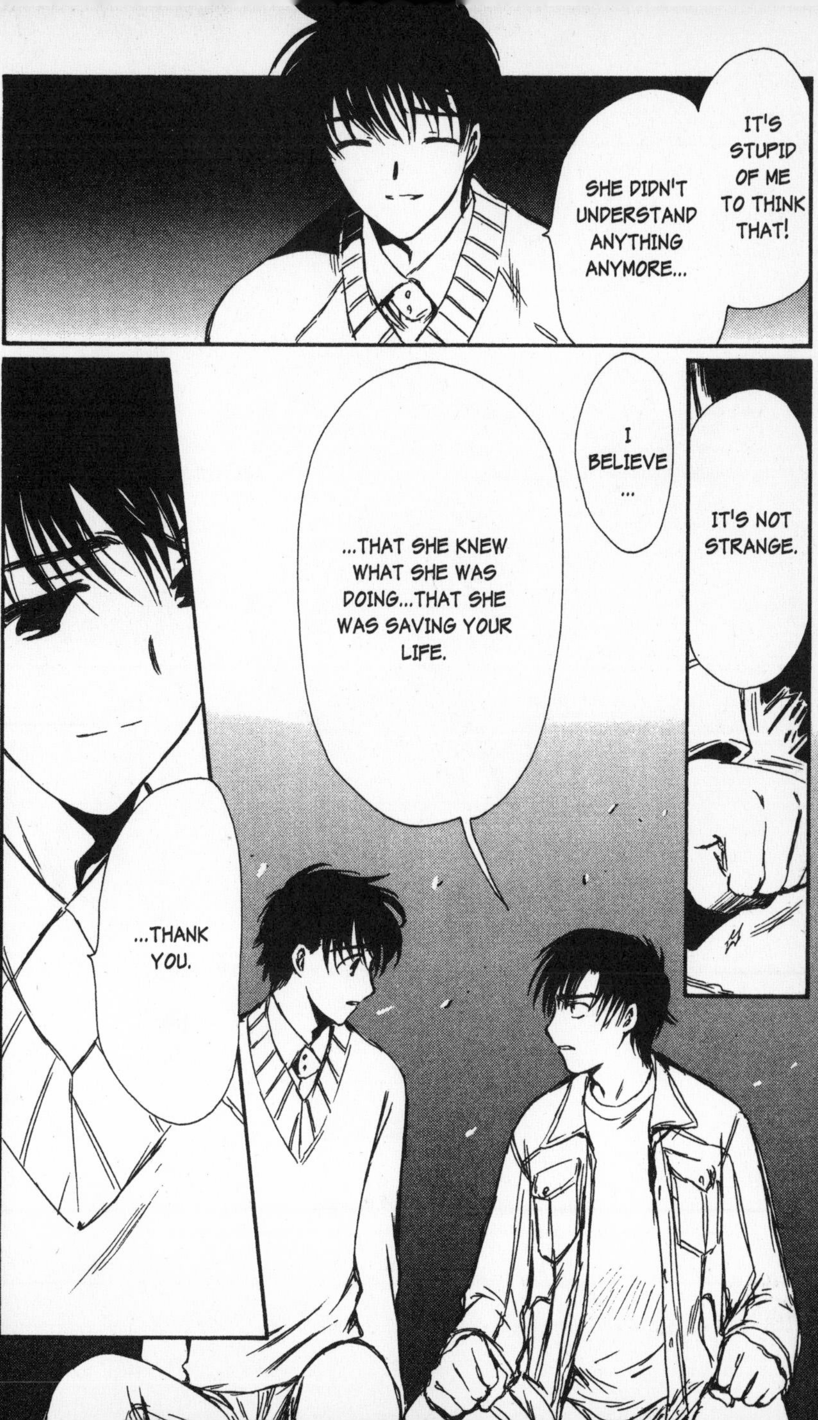
IT'S STUPID OF ME TO THINK THAT!
SHE DIDN'T UNDERSTAND ANYTHING ANYMORE...
IT'S NOT STRANGE.
I BELIEVE...
...THAT SHE KNEW WHAT SHE WAS DOING...THAT SHE WAS SAVING YOUR LIFE.
...THANK YOU.

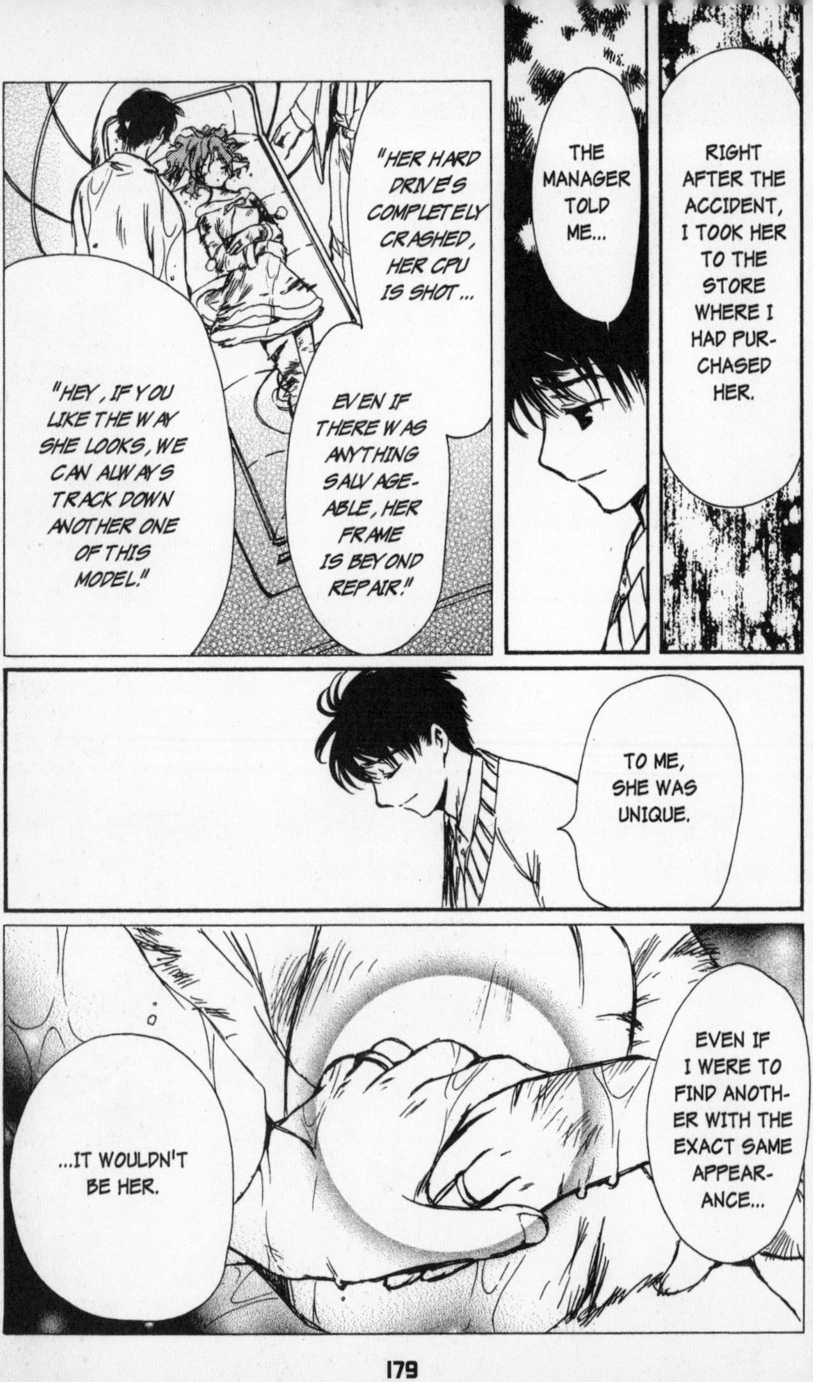
RIGHT AFTER THE ACCIDENT, I TOOK HER TO THE STORE WHERE I HAD PURCHASED HER.
THE MANAGER TOLD ME...
"HER HARD DRIVE'S COMPLETELY CRASHED, HER CPU IS SHOT...
EVEN IF THERE WAS ANYTHING SALVAGEABLE, HER FRAME IS BEYOND REPAIR."
"HEY, IF YOU LIKE THE WAY SHE LOOKS, WE CAN ALWAYS TRACK DOWN ANOTHER ONE OF THIS MODEL."
TO ME, SHE WAS UNIQUE.
EVEN IF I WERE TO FIND ANOTHER WITH THE EXACT SAME APPEARANCE...
...IT WOULDN'T BE HER.

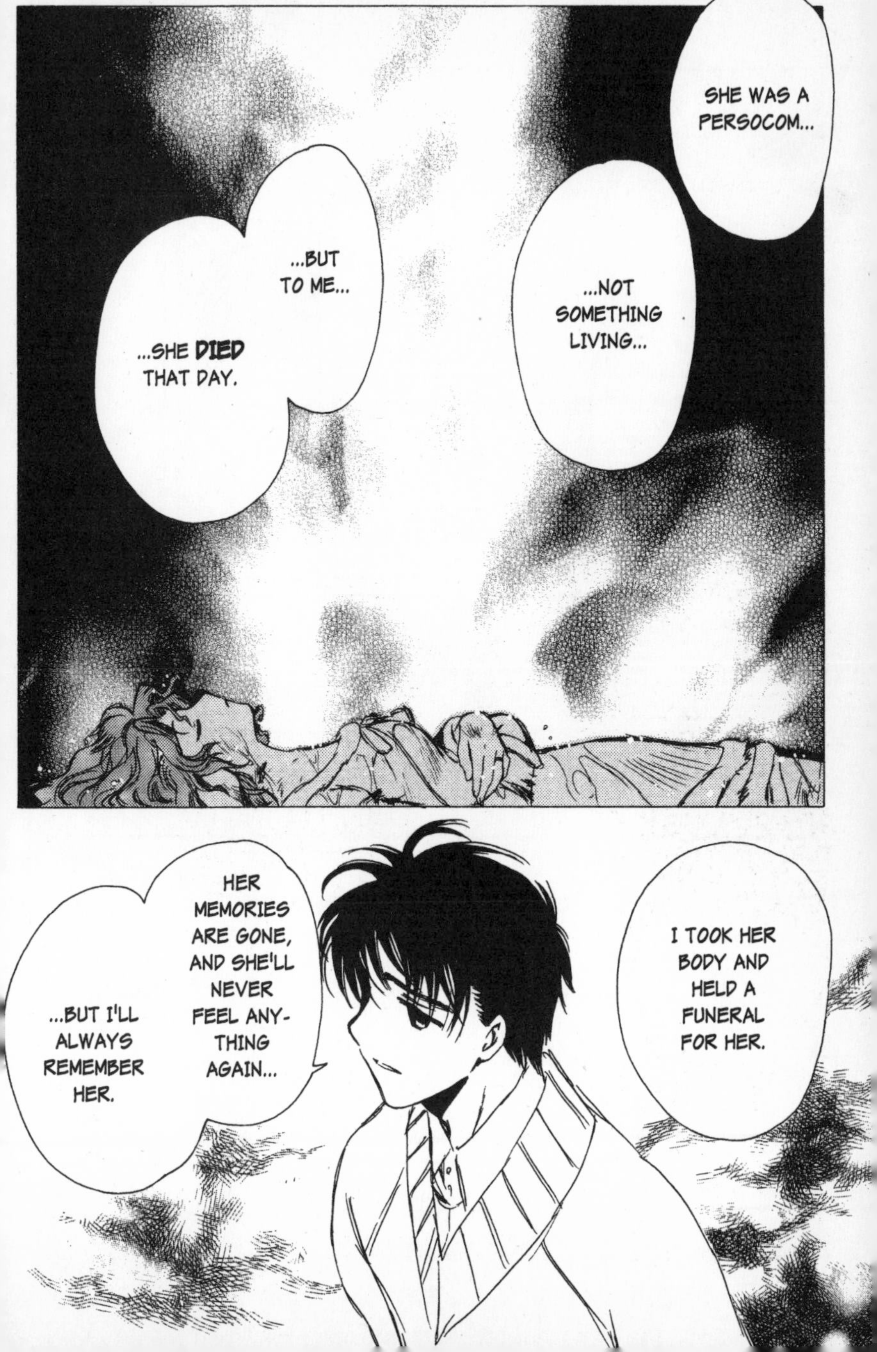
SHE WAS A PERSOCOM...
...NOT SOMETHING LIVING...
...BUT TO ME...
...SHE **DIED** THAT DAY.
I TOOK HER BODY AND HELD A FUNERAL FOR HER.
HER MEMORIES ARE GONE, AND SHE'LL NEVER FEEL ANY-THING AGAIN...
...BUT I'LL ALWAYS REMEMBER HER.

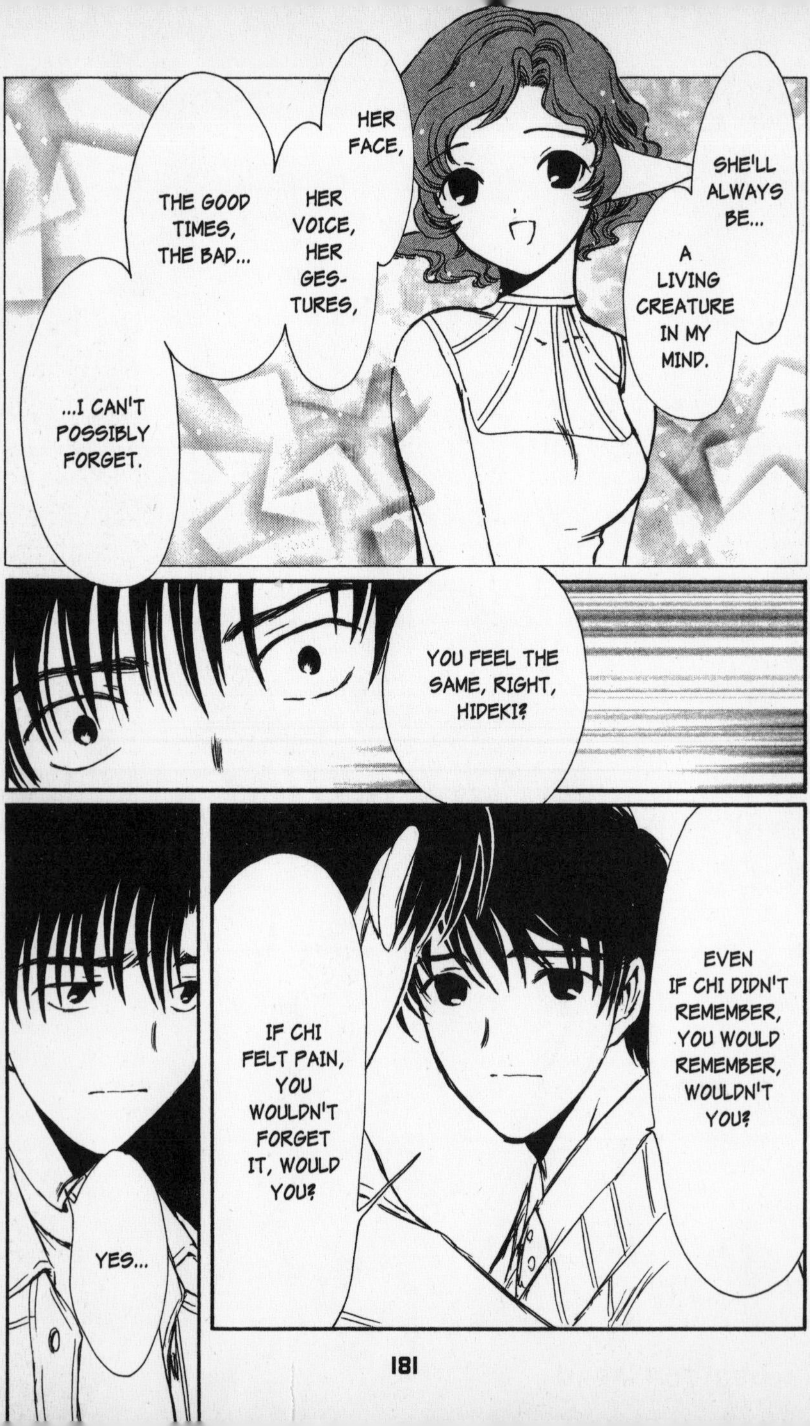
SHE'LL ALWAYS BE...
A LIVING CREATURE IN MY MIND.
HER FACE,
HER VOICE, HER GESTURES,
THE GOOD TIMES, THE BAD...
...I CAN'T POSSIBLY FORGET.
YOU FEEL THE SAME, RIGHT, HIDEKI?
EVEN IF CHI DIDN'T REMEMBER, YOU WOULD REMEMBER, WOULDN'T YOU?
IF CHI FELT PAIN, YOU WOULDN'T FORGET IT, WOULD YOU?
YES...

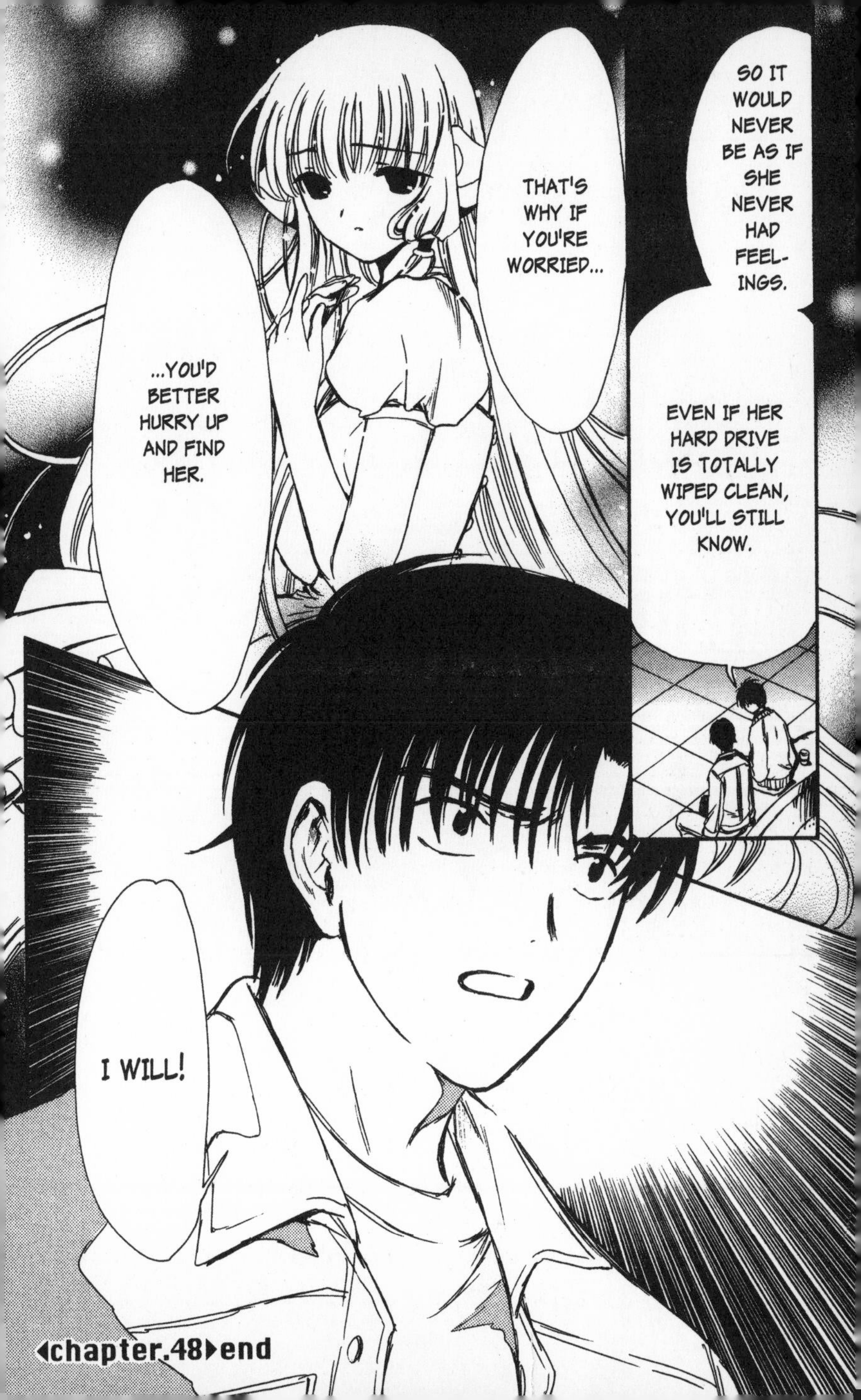
SO IT WOULD NEVER BE AS IF SHE NEVER HAD FEEL-INGS.
EVEN IF HER HARD DRIVE IS TOTALLY WIPED CLEAN, YOU'LL STILL KNOW.
THAT'S WHY IF YOU'RE WORRIED...
...YOU'D BETTER HURRY UP AND FIND HER.
I WILL!
chapter.48 end

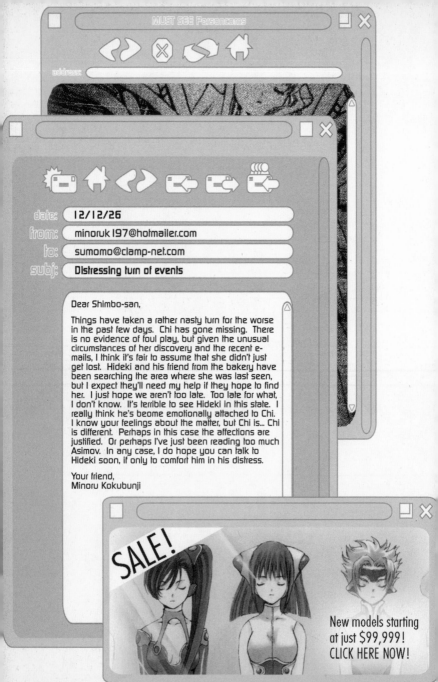

MUST SEE Persocoms

address:

date: 12/12/26

from: minoruk197@hotmailer.com

to: sumomo@clamp-net.com

subj: Distressing turn of events

Dear Shimbo-san,

Things have taken a rather nasty turn for the worse in the past few days. Chi has gone missing. There is no evidence of foul play, but given the unusual circumstances of her discovery and the recent e-mails, I think it's fair to assume that she didn't just get lost. Hideki and his friend from the bakery have been searching the area where she was last seen, but I expect they'll need my help if they hope to find her. I just hope we aren't too late. Too late for what, I don't know. It's terrible to see Hideki in this state. I really think he's beome emotionally attached to Chi. I know your feelings about the matter, but Chi is... Chi is different. Perhaps in this case the affections are justified. Or perhaps I've just been reading too much Asimov. In any case, I do hope you can talk to Hideki soon, if only to comfort him in his distress.

Your friend,
Minoru Kokubunji

SALE!
New models starting at just $99,999! CLICK HERE NOW!

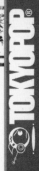

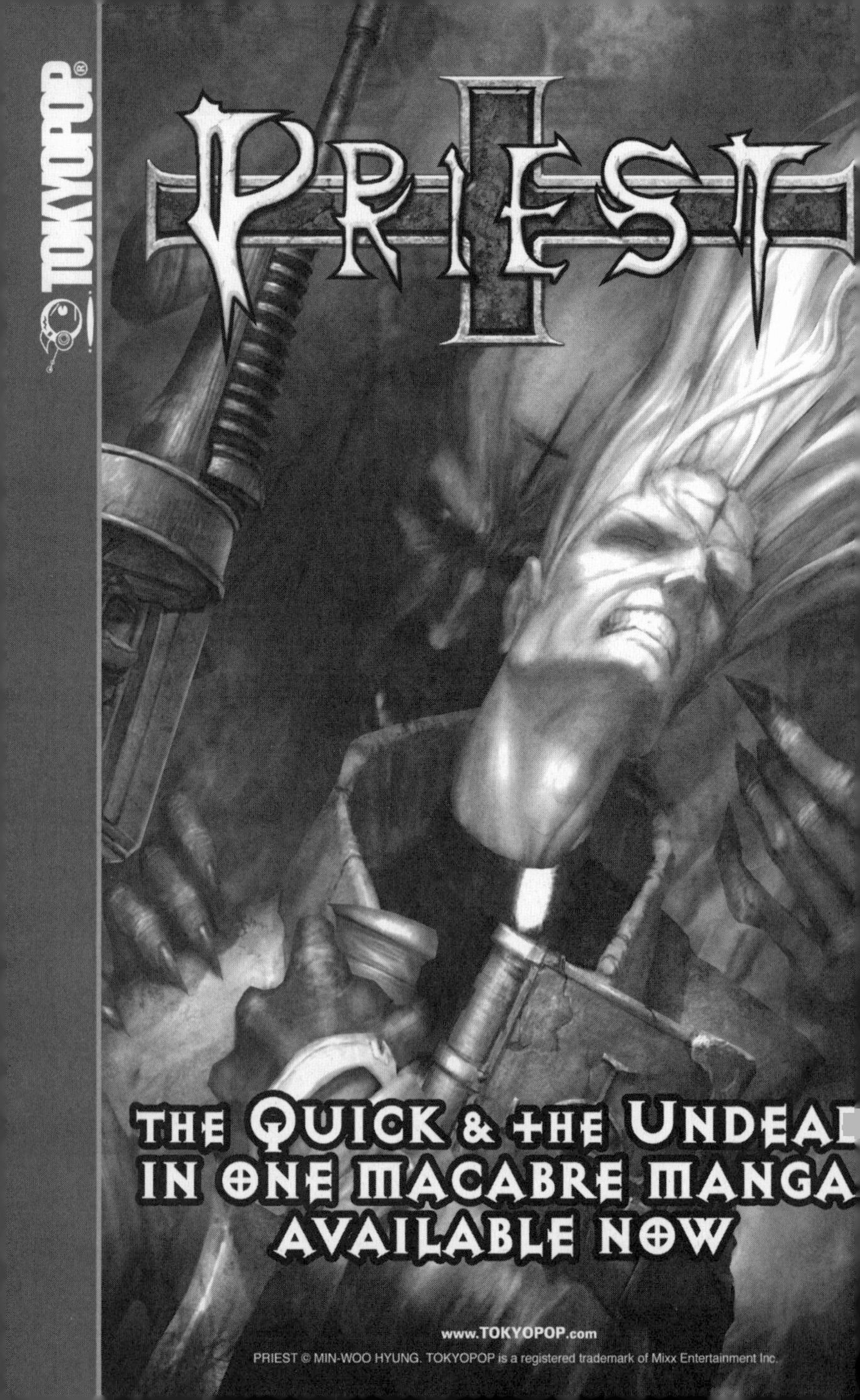
TOKYOPOP®
PRIEST
THE QUICK & THE UNDEAD
IN ONE MACABRE MANGA
AVAILABLE NOW
www.TOKYOPOP.com
PRIEST © MIN-WOO HYUNG. TOKYOPOP is a registered trademark of Mixx Entertainment Inc.

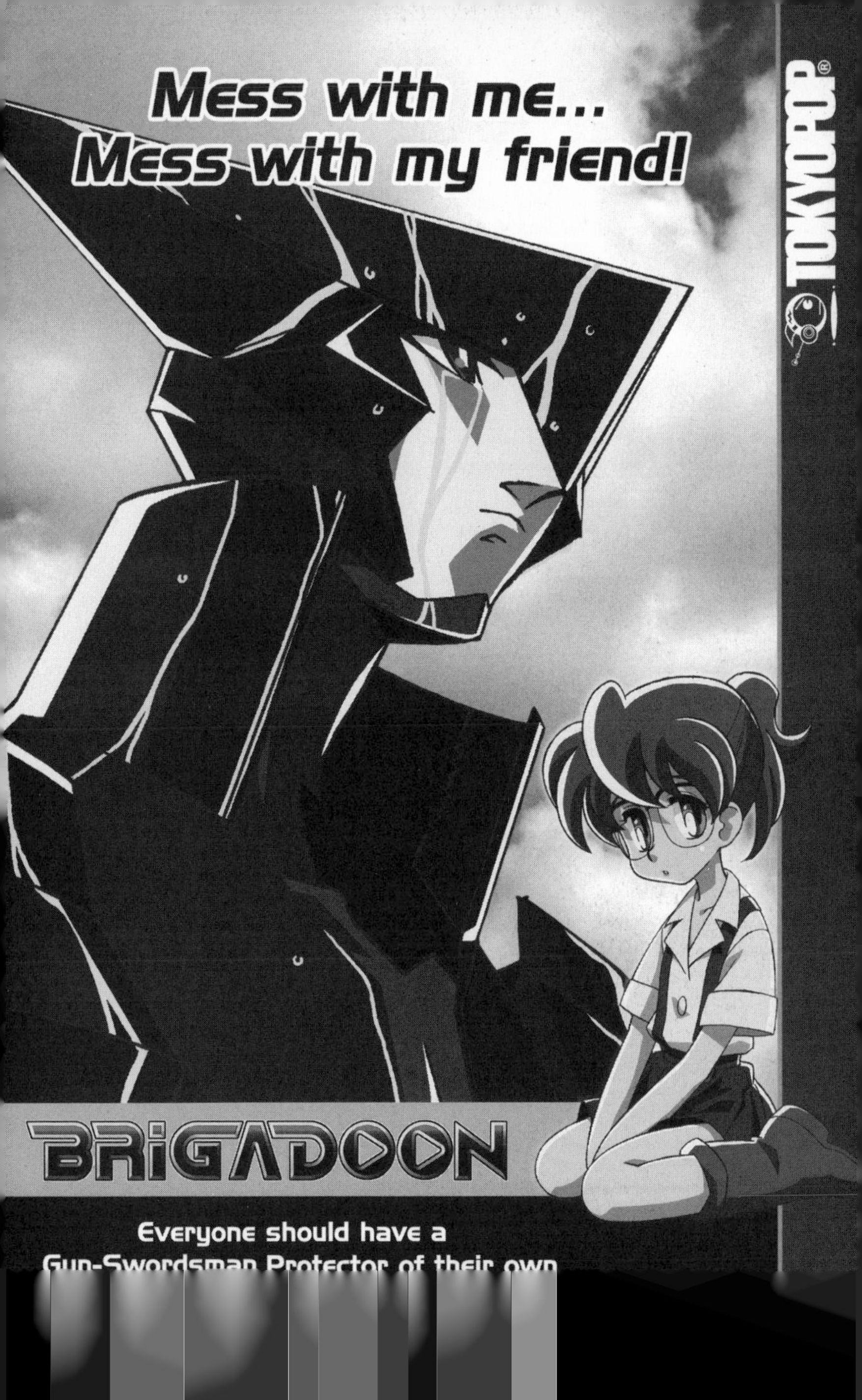
Mess with me...
Mess with my friend!
TOKYOPOP
BRIGADOON
Everyone should have a
Gun-Swordsman Protector of their own

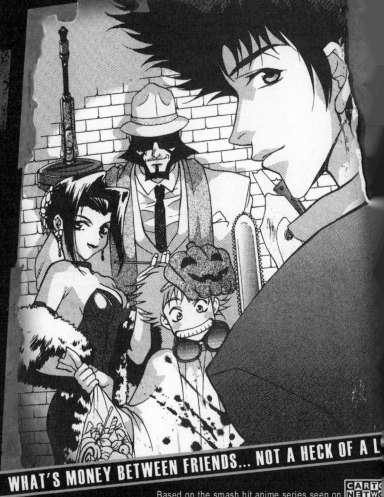

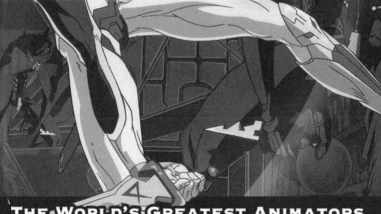

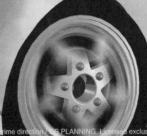

INITIAL 頭文字 D

INITIALIZE YOUR DREAMS

Manga:
Available Now!
Anime:
Coming Soon!

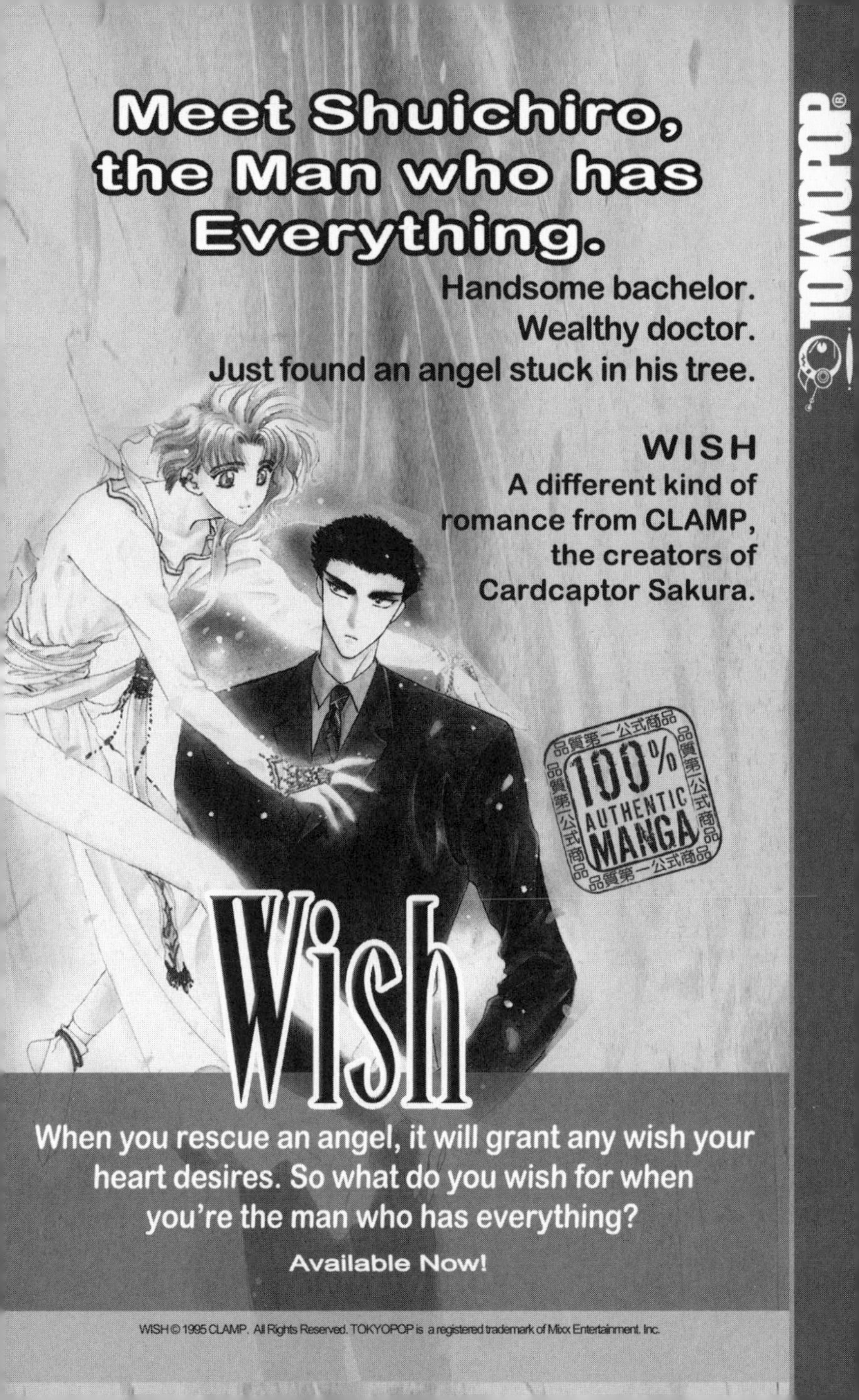
Meet Shuichiro, the Man who has Everything.
Handsome bachelor.
Wealthy doctor.
Just found an angel stuck in his tree.
WISH
A different kind of romance from CLAMP, the creators of Cardcaptor Sakura.
100% AUTHENTIC MANGA
Wish
When you rescue an angel, it will grant any wish your heart desires. So what do you wish for when you're the man who has everything?
Available Now!
TOKYOPOP

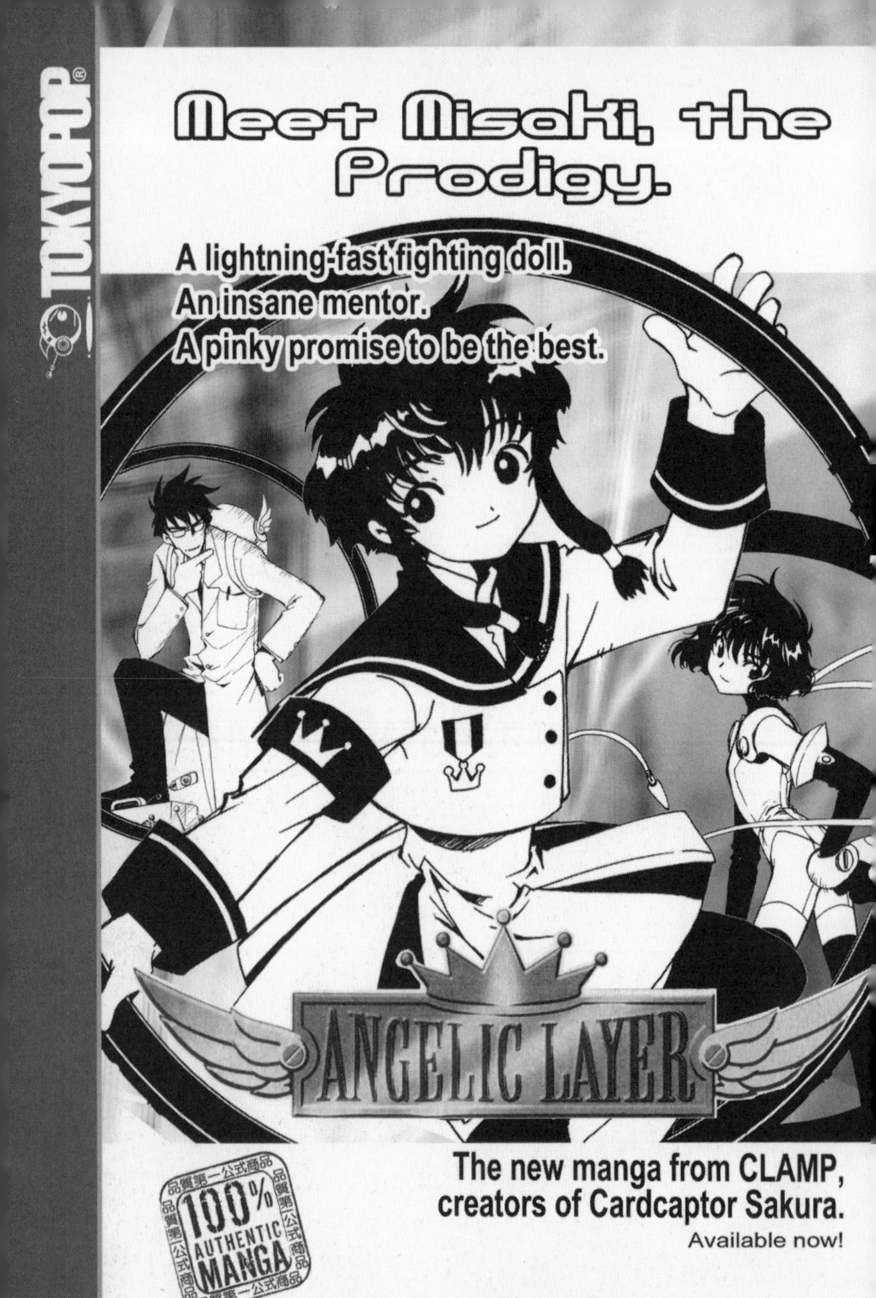
TOKYOPOP®
Meet Misaki, the Prodigy.
A lightning-fast fighting doll.
An insane mentor.
A pinky promise to be the best.
ANGELIC LAYER
100% AUTHENTIC MANGA
品質第一公式商品
The new manga from CLAMP, creators of Cardcaptor Sakura.
Available now!

 **W9-BGL-019**

STOP!

This is the back of the book.
You wouldn't want to spoil a great ending!

This book is printed "manga-style," in the authentic Japanese right-to-left format. Since none of the artwork has been flipped or altered, readers get to experience the story just as the creator intended. You've been asking for it, so TOKYOPOP® delivered: authentic, hot-off-the-press, and far more fun!

DIRECTIONS

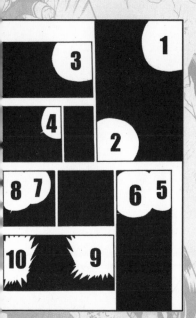

If this is your first time reading manga-style, here's a quick guide to help you understand how it works.

It's easy... just start in the top right panel and follow the numbers. Have fun, and look for more 100% authentic manga from TOKYOPOP®!

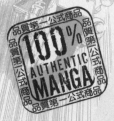